CATECHISM FOR THE NEW DISPENSATION

By Reverend Dr. Albert Gani

Catechism for the New Dispensation
Reverend Dr. Albert Gani

Published by:
The Church of the Path, Inc.
207 S. Commons Ford Road
Austin, Texas 78733 U.S.A.
(512) 263-9435
contact@churchofthepath.org
www.churchofthepath.org

All rights reserved. No part of this book may be reproduced or transmitted in any form or by any means, electronic or mechanical, including photocopying, recording or by any informational storage or retrieval system without written permission from the author, except for the inclusion of brief quotations in a review.

Copyright © 1996 and 2023 by The Church of the Path®

ISBN-13: 978-1-882853-34-2

This book is dedicated to

THE CHURCH OF THE PATH®

ACKNOWLEDGMENTS

First, a million thanks to J. Curtis Jordan for his dedicated presence throughout the dictation of all of this material, for his transcription, and his part in editing and indexing. Many of his excellent ideas and many of his penetrating questions have greatly helped in the elucidation of these concepts.

In addition, great thanks to Siobhan McKillop, Debra McClure, and Ronnie Baker for their contributions in editing and indexing this work.

TABLE OF CONTENTS

Chapter 1 5
   Catechism for the New Dispensation
      What Is Catechism?

Chapter 2 9
   A Message of Hope
      Rejoice in Your Disillusionment

Chapter 3 17
   Credo

Chapter 4 19
   God and Evil
      God: The Alpha and the Omega
      Emblems of The Church of the Path®
      God
      What Is God?
      Creation
      Interaction Between Universal Life Force and
         Universal Consciousness
      Evil
      Human Existence and Progress
      The Hand of God
      Sonship
      Longing For and Return to God

Fear of God
God and Sex
Sacrifice
Connection with God
Disconnection from God
Reconnection with God
Is the Destroyer Positive or Negative? Crisis
Two Great Evils of the Twentieth Century
God's Will
Capacity to Experience God

Chapter 5 49
The Many Aspects of God
  Perceptions of God
  Creation
  The Universal Consciousness
  The Universal Life Force

Chapter 6 55
Your Personal Freeze of God
  The Pursuit of Happiness

Chapter 7 59
The Christ
  The Forces of Light and the Forces of Darkness
  Intervention by the Forces of Light
  Christ's Incarnation
  Christ's Task
  Protection from Cosmic Evil
  "Well Meaning" People
  The Point of Relinquishing
  Christ's Battle Against the Forces of Darkness

The Greater Plan
Reaching the Kingdom of God
Inner Experience
The Difference Between Jesus and the Christ
The Immaculate Conception
Travels of the Christ
Christ the Universal Teacher
Communication with Masters

Chapter 8 81
The Trinity
God the Father, God the Mother
The Three Aspects of God
The Holy Ghost Comes to Life
Personification of the Rays

Chapter 9 85
The Great Mother
Patriarchal and Matriarchal Systems

Chapter 10 89
The Hierarchy
The Center Where the Will of God Is Known
Hierarchical Intercession on Humanity's Behalf
Will Versus Love Versus Intelligence
Crisis and the Hierarchy
Human Hierarchy and Order
Responsibility and Privilege

Chapter 11 99
   Other Kingdoms of God
      The Seven First Sons of God
      Kingdoms Below the Threshold of Humanity
      Devas
      Extraterrestrial Life

Chapter 12 105
   The Fall and the Formation of Evil
      The Fall
      Abuse of Power
      Astral Home of the Devil
      Glamours
      Temptation
      The Lower Self and the Glamours
      The Lower Self and the Mask
      The Duality of Evil
      Departmentalization of Evil
      Intervention by the Forces of Light
      Evil's Worlds of Darkness
      Useful Purpose of the Mask
      The Inferior Function
      Sellout
      From Numbness to Pain to Longing for a Better State
      Creation of the Material World
      Original Sin
      Personal Responsibility for Falling
      Creating Your Future
      Other Worlds
      Heaven and Hell
      Eastern Philosophy and the Fall of the Angels

Chapter 13 133
   The Plan of Salvation and its Various Dispensations
      Diagram of the Plan of Salvation
      Universal Rounds Through Time for Our Universe
      Root Races
      Dispensations
      The Fallacy of Exclusivity

Chapter 14 155
   Time and Evil
      The Process of Regression
      Crisis

Chapter 15 161
   Sin and Guilt
      Sin
      Levels of Sin and a Place Without Sin
      Misconceptions About Sins: Mortal and Venial Sins
      Conscious and Unconscious Sin
      Consequences of Sin
      Guilt
      Consequences of Guilt
      Confession
      Glamour of Suffering
      Death of the Spirit
      Waste
      Death Bed Conversion and Prison Conversion
      Indulgences
      Birth Control
      Abortion

Chapter 16 181
   Forgiveness, Redemption
      Forgiveness
      Forgiveness of Others
      Forgiveness of Self
      Forgiving and Forgetting
      The Misconception About Wholesale Redemption
      Redemption
      Capital Punishment

Chapter 17 189
   Doubt
      Finding God Through Doubt
      The Necessity to Find Doubt Within
      Unhappiness as a Way to Faith
      Why We Desire to Disconnect from Faith and from
         God
      The Real Cause of Doubt
      Resolution of Doubt
      Fanaticism
      Religion as a Way to Control the Immature
      Religion as a Way to Liberate the Adult

Chapter 18 201
   The Real Meaning of Judgment Day
      Judgment Day
      Hell
      The End of Time
      Final Test of the Church
      Purgatory

Chapter 19 209
   Individual Will and Determinism
     Predestination Versus Free Will
     Favourite Cases Against Free Will I: Child Abuse
     Favourite Cases Against Free Will II: The Holocaust
     Reincarnation and the Law of Cause and Effect
     Healing
     Predictions
     Free Will Confused as License
     Punishment
     An Unexpected Blessing
     Dependency on Outer Level Reality for Happiness
     Inner Will and Outer Will
     Raising Children
     Prayer in School
     Systems of Education
     Homosexuality

Chapter 20 241
   The Spirit and the Soul
     The Spirit
     Formation of the Soul
     Napoleon—An Example
     The Confederacy of the American South—An
       Example
     Lincoln—An Example
     Knowing the Contents of Your Soul

Chapter 21 249
   Reincarnation
     In the Beginning
     Reincarnation after Accidental or Premature Death

The Risk Inherent in Incarnating
When Does the Soul Inhabit the Body?
Memory of Past Lives
Experience Between Incarnations
Time Between Incarnations
The Process of Purification
Souls and the Evolutionary Process of Non-Humans

Chapter 22 261
Initiations
  What Is Initiation?
  Initiation One
  Initiation Two
  Initiation Three
  Initiation Four
  Initiation Five
  Initiation Six
  Initiations Seven, Eight and Nine

Chapter 23 287
The Call to Your Task
  What Is the Call?
  Barriers to Your Task
  The Call in Flux
  Our Dissatisfactions Are The Call
  Spiritual Progress
  Change
  Spiritual Development and The Call
  Your Task
  Sacrifice
  Mimesis

Chapter 24 301
    Sacraments
        Purpose of Sacraments
        Types of Sacraments
        The Mass
        Building Energy Forms
        Intimacy
        Sacrifice
        Work

Chapter 25 313
    Prayer, Meditation,
        Attunement and Intervention
        Definitions
        Intervention

Chapter 26 317
    Baptism
        What Is Baptism?
        Magical Thinking About Baptism

Chapter 27 321
    Marriage
        Power and Blessings of the Marriage Ceremony
        The Way it Was in the Past
        Why People Fall in Love
        Handling the Blessings of Marriage
        Commitment/Vows
        For Better or for Worse
        Marriage and Community
        Differences Between Sex, Cupid and Love

Conditions for Cupid to Remain Alive in a Relationship
Cupid Related to Cleansing
Soulmates
Divorce

Chapter 28 335
Death
Fear of Death
Death and the Survival Instinct
Why Death?
Accidental Deaths
Higher Self, Lower Self and Idolized Self (Mask) Decisions to Die
Out-of-Body and Near-Death Experiences
Is Death the End?
Surrender
Support of the Dying
Preparing People to Make Their Transition
Dealing with Someone Who Denies He Is Dying
Life Support Systems
Disposal of the Body—Cremation
Funeral Ceremony
Your Wishes for Your Funeral Versus Your Family's Wishes
Old Morbid Belief Systems About Funerals
Cemeteries
Wills and Inheritance
Life After Life
Pain Killers
Organ Donation and Organ Transplant
Attention to the Physical Body

Use of Doctors, Not Being Used by Them
Children with Terminal Diseases
Suicide
Catholic Hospitals

Chapter 29 369
Symbols
Symbols Are Everywhere
Illness and Disease
Mental Illness
Meaning of Pain
Holy Places
Music
Celebrations of the Seasons and of Natural Cycles

Chapter 30 377
Psychic Powers, Their Misuse and Premature Healing
Astrology
Misuse of Astrology
Past Life Regressions, the Healy-Feelies, Etc.
Primitive Psychic Powers
Communication with Higher Spheres of
   Development
Channeling
Premature Healing

Chapter 31 387
Spiritual Laws
Universality of the Laws of God
Laws Pertaining to the First Ray: Will or Power
Laws Pertaining to the Second Ray:
   Love/Wisdom

Laws Pertaining to the Third Ray: Active
　　　　Intelligence and Adaptability
　　Laws Pertaining to the Fourth Ray: Harmony
　　　　Through Conflict
　　Laws Pertaining to the Fifth Ray: Concrete
　　　　Knowledge
　　Laws Pertaining to the Sixth Ray: Idealism and
　　　　Devotion
　　Laws Pertaining to the Seventh Ray: Ceremony,
　　　　Magic and Order
　　Spiritual Laws Create Us
　　Authority

Chapter 32 409
　　A Commentary on the Universal Declaration of Human
　　　　Rights
　　Secular Humanism
　　Intervention of One Nation Over Another
　　The United Nations
　　Commentary on the Articles
　　Conclusion

Chapter 33 439
　　Political Systems
　　Monarchy
　　Democracy
　　Socialism
　　Coexistence of Three Systems of Government
　　Secular Humanism Versus the Feudalism of the
　　　　Catholic Church

Chapter 34 445
    Reflections on History

Chapter 35 447
    The Debt of Christianity
        The Repressed Aspect of the Christ
        Christ as God
        Dilution and Paganization of Christianity
        True Christianity Is The Path
        Questions Christians Should Ask Themselves
        Two Contradictory Aspects of the Christ

Chapter 36 455
    Our Path of Rebirth and Purification
        The People of God
        Rebirth
        Distinguishing Between People Who Are on The Path and People Who Are Not on The Path

Chapter 37 459
    The Church of the Path® Hierarchy
        Church Hierarchy
        Board of Examiners

Chapter 38 461
    Oaths and Commitments
        Taking In and Giving Out
        Novice
        Aspirant
        Disciple
        Code of Conduct and Oath for Teachers
        Duty of the Teacher

Chapter 39 469
    Buddhism: A Reinterpretation from the Point of View
        of the New Dispensation
        Commentary on Early Teachings of Buddha
        Buddhism
        The Eightfold Noble Path
        Intent
        Three Stages for Each Noble Truth
        Conclusion

Chapter 40 493
    The Ten Commandments: A Reinterpretation from the
        Point of View of the New Dispensation

Chapter 41 505
    Some Definitions

Index 509

WARNING – DISCLAIMER

This book is an invitation to spiritual introspection. It is sold with the understanding that it, or anyone involved in publishing or marketing it, makes no claims of healing of any kind.

The purpose of this book is to inspire you to a spiritual and ethical life. The author, or anyone else involved in publishing or marketing it, will not have any liability and desists themselves of any responsibility to any person or group or company for any damage or loss incurred in any way by the contents of this book.

FOREWARD

In case it has not already been said in the text of this work, we will say it here. In no way is this work complete. No catechism ever is or ever will be.

The concepts themselves will be expressed later in new words, when human language will be able to conceive in a greater, broader way than it can now.

Consider this work as a living organism, continuously undergoing change and needing to be understood for its inner meaning and intent.

Nor do we claim that there are no errors here. I am sure there are and I would be grateful to anyone who points those errors out to us. However, we hope that we have at least communicated the spirit of the new dispensation.

Reverend Dr. Albert Gani
Austin, Texas
March 1996

GLOSSARY

Crucifixion of the Ego: The process of crucifying the *false self* (the little ego) in order to reunite with the Greater Ego (the *Higher Self*).

Divine Self: See *Higher Self*

Distorted Self: See *Lower Self*

Evil: Anything that impairs progress. Any hindering factor, whether in thought, feeling, word, action, or non-action. Any denial of truth.

False Self: See *Idolized Self*

Forces of Light: Forces of God—goodness, beauty, truth.

Forces of Darkness: Forces of evil—deception, untruth, involution.

Freezes: Decelerated, petrified, crystallized truth; also known as "images." An image is an incomplete perception of a reality. Therefore, it always is a misconception and a presumption.

Glamour: An exaggeration of a divine aspect or attribute. For example, the glamour of strength leads to brutality and cruelty; the glamour of love leads to lack of discipline and permissiveness; the glamour of intelligence leads to inaction, and so forth.

Hierarchy, The: The Hierarchy is an organization formed by superhumans, some of whom never incarnated on Earth, and some who have but who have ascended to be masters. The departments of this organization are representatives of the *Seven Rays*. At the head of each one of these departments is a master who dispenses to humanity that which it is ready to assimilate.

Higher Self: The Higher Self is connected to the Divine. It is the best in us, our nucleus. It can also be seen as infinite, i.e., not just the nucleus but everything about us.

Idealized Self: See *Idolized Self*

Idolized Self: It covers up the *lower self*, presenting the "right" image. A person may have many idolized selves, or many idolized images in one idolized self. I put on a particular idolized self when I am in a high society cocktail party, another when I am at home with my wife and children, another when I'm by myself, and so on. Many images of myself converge to create that idolized self, which I try to maintain. At some point in my life I become my idolized self, being disconnected, alienated, and increasing my anxiety. This creates identity problems. The idolized self has also been called "phoney self" or "false self" or "pretentious self" or the "mask" or the "idealized self".

Image: See *Freeze*

Lower Self: The lower self is the undeveloped part of the self. It starts within us as potentiality. Wrongly activated these potentialities become harmful, creating our harmfulness. The task of life is to take responsibility for the lower self, having it join the Higher Self.

Mask: See *Idolized Self*

Mother-Father Split: Inner duality and misconceptions based on parents or substitute parents. See the book *Know Thyself* by Rev. Dr. Albert Gani for an in-depth explanation.

Plan of Salvation: Universal plan of in which every entity participates leading back to unification with God.

Rays, The: There are Seven Rays of energy—Rays of purpose—according to *The Tibetan*[1]. There is a Ray type which corresponds to the soul and a Ray which corresponds to the personality. The physical body reflects the Ray of the soul. Each Ray has special virtues, vices, and virtues to be acquired.

Ray I: Will or Power. Ray of the Father.
Ray II: Love and Wisdom. Ray of the Son/the Christ/the Buddha.
Ray III: Active Intelligence and Adaptability. The Ray of Mother.
Ray IV: Harmony through Conflict.
Ray V: Concrete Knowledge and Science.
Ray VI: Idealism and Devotion.
Ray VII: Order, Ceremony, Good Habits and Magic.

---

[1] Bailey, Alice A. *Esoteric Psychology I*. New York: Lucis Publishing Company. 1962.

There are three Rays of Aspect and Four Rays of Attribute.

The three Rays of Aspect—Rays I, II and III (Will, Love, and Active Intelligence, respectively)—correspond to the Trinity, which is found in Christianity, Hinduism and Buddhism.

In Christianity, we have, respectively, Father, Son and Mother (not Holy Ghost). In Hinduism, we have Shiva, Brahma, and Vishnu. In Buddhism, Nirmanakaya, Sambhogakaya, and Dharmakaya, comprising the "triple body"—trikaya.

Out of Ray III, Active Intelligence and Adaptability, come four minor Rays, called Rays of Attribute (Rays IV, V, VI, and VII).

The book *Know Thyself* by Rev. Dr. Albert Gani gives an in-depth overview of Ray types unifying the Ray typology found in *The Tibetan*, Carl Jung's psychological characterology, and body shape/form insights found in many disciplines.

Tibetan, The: The Tibetan is the Master Djwhal Khul. He dictated to Alice A. Bailey voluminous and extensive material which has enormous validity, not only for the esotericist, but for anyone interested in self-knowledge and knowledge of the Universe. The books are published by Lucis Publishing Company in New York and are widely available.

CHAPTER 1
CATECHISM FOR THE NEW DISPENSATION

WHAT IS CATECHISM?

The definition of "catechism" in Webster's is "a handbook of questions and answers for teaching the tenets of a religion." It also says that catechism is "a close questioning." Under "catechize" we have "to question searchingly."

How easily forgotten has been this aspect of searching, particularly in the Catholic Church. It has been replaced by accepting at face value teachings, tenets, dogmas, in spite of the fact that they have become obsolete. In fact, in the latest Catholic catechism published in 1992, catechism is seen as the handing on of the faith.

The entire aspect of search, the Instinct of Enquiry, is entirely cut off. So, rather than being an invitation to searching and questioning, catechism has become, in conventional religion, a medieval style of teaching which adheres to the dictum of that time: *magister dixit*. This means "the master has said," and, of course, nobody questions him.

We intend to restore to catechism the quality of questioning. We invite questions, we invite doubts. It is when doubts are clearly expressed that true faith can be discovered. It is through the answering of his questions that the person in search of a faith finds it and adheres to it with good will.

If "catechism" is an education in the faith, as is suggested by the Catholic Church, then it is a process of convincing. There is no possible convincing if no questioning is encouraged. Also, there is no possible convincing if one cannot accept the temporary phase that people go through from not believing to believing—the state of doubt. The state of doubt is not a state of sin. The state of denial is.

The state of pretense is a double sin because it denies and it pretends not to. Therefore, those people who go to churches and pretend to believe are committing two sins simultaneously.

By contrast, those who openly doubt do not commit any sin at all since they are in the process of discovering the truth. Only through questioning can you discover the truth. Therefore, doubting can be the honest manifestation of the Instinct of Enquiry. It is in accordance with the will of God.

Now, of course, people can doubt for the sake of doubting, doubting hypocritically just to be contrary or to feel that they have power over you or somebody else. This is indeed sinful. This is not true searching. This is not courageous and honest seeking.

If we are to spread our Faith, we must, therefore, encourage questioning. It is only through someone's questions that you can introduce the truth and teach it. Only through doubt can belief really come.

Thus, catechism must be the friend of scientific enquiry and discovery, not its enemy. The Catholic Church has been the traditional enemy of any and all scientific progress throughout the centuries.

It found itself having to shamelessly reverse its position over and over again from one of intolerance and denial to reluctant acceptance.

Take for instance the discoveries of Copernicus and his disciple Galileo. The greatest beneficiary of these discoveries was the Catholic Church since, thanks to Copernicus and Galileo, it was finally able to have precise mathematical tools that could define exact dates for its holidays in accordance with the movements of the planets around the solar system. So, the Catholics found themselves in the ridiculous position of being the greatest users of these theories and at the same time the greatest deniers of them.

They went so far as to excommunicate Galileo rather than admit the veracity of his theories while at the same time abundantly using those theories for their own purposes. In the year 1600, at the Campo dei Fiori in Rome, they burned at the stake a disciple of Galileo and Copernicus named Giordano Bruno who was perhaps the last Renaissance man and who, in his work *Dell'infinito universo e mondi*, goes even further in the exploration of the Copernican system of astronomy.

This is the height of evil and of hypocrisy. This is as far away as you can get from catechism. Pope John Paul II recently promised that he would apologize for some of the outrages committed by the Catholic Church such as the Inquisition and the Crusades. However, he wants to do it in the year 2000—with great splash and great pomp, I am sure. I wonder why he does not do it immediately since he feels it? Are we here looking at another display of hypocrisy and showmanship, i.e., evil?

Also, why not extend the apology to a lot of the anti-Semitic and misogynous utterances of the Bible? Why not extend it to the incredible amount of brutality and cruelty sanctioned and recommended by "God" in the Bible? Holding on to saying that the Bible is the word of God is anti-catechistic. It precludes the spirit of enquiry on which faith is based.

CHAPTER 2
A MESSAGE OF HOPE
FOR THOSE JUDEO-CHRISTIANS AND OTHERS
WHO FEEL LOST IN THEIR ORGANIZED RELIGIONS

The great majority of people who call themselves Christians, Moslems, and Jews really do not believe in their religion. They pay lip service to the prayers and to the beliefs that were taught to them by their parents and that are perpetuated in their churches, mosques, and synagogues. It is ludicrous for anybody today to believe in most of the teachings of conventional religion.

To the contemporary mind and soul, not only are they empty but they lead to fanaticism, they are full of contradictions and they breed unhappiness. As diluted as Paul's teachings were, to some extent they revolutionized what was existing at the time. Nevertheless, they were dilutions and they were, in the last analysis, ineffective.

The pseudo-solution that most people adopt is to either shut up or quit the church and renounce God. The idea itself of God, or of Christ, becomes associated with hypocrisy, with double standards, with duality, with duplicity and with forcing currents. There is an incredible number of ex-Christians who hate churches. They will have absolutely nothing to do with them. Having come to associate Christ, church, and God with hypocrisy, with negativity, and with bigotry, they have created a block within themselves that has ended a very important and fundamental part of their spiritual search. When we tell them that we are a church they do not want to have anything to do with us, even though, if they give us the benefit of the doubt, they would gain a lot from what they find here.

On the part of the Jews, they too have lost faith in their religion. They call themselves Jews: (1) because they want to be faithful to the Jewish tradition and (2) because they do not want to feel false guilt towards their parents if they were to deny allegiance to the Jewish religion. The atheist Jew also perfunctorily says the Hebrew words which he finds very poetic and very appealing without really experiencing or believing in the religion that created this poetry in the first place back in the beginning of the Age of Aries, about 2200 years before the birth of Christ. Acknowledging the fact that there was a new dispensation brought in by the Christ is for them tantamount to betrayal. They would be called cheaters or liars or betrayers, just as Paul was by the followers of James the Just as demonstrated in the Dead Sea Scrolls.

REJOICE IN YOUR DISILLUSIONMENT

To all of those people who are disillusioned with their traditional, conventional religion, we say to them, "Rejoice!" You are closer to God than those who have tried to inculcate in you the old tradition. Open yourself to who God really is and what the meaning of your life is supposed to be. Consider the following points:

1. God wants you to be happy.

2. He is not interested in having you call Him by any particular name; He is not interested in your saying Jesus or Adonai or whatever other little superstitions that were developed and adhered to by your religion of origin. If He were to want this, it would constitute an ego trip which is

reminiscent of the devil a lot more than of God. Think about it. Wouldn't you say so?

3. The "church fathers" or the "elders at the temple" have advocated this type of wrong approach to religion for the purposes of self-aggrandizement. If you must utter the name of God or of Christ in order to be saved, then in a lesser manner you would also be forgiven or absolved if you were to respect and venerate and put yourself under the power of the church fathers. They are, according to them anyway, God's representatives and agents. This is a way for them to imprison you.

4. You are also kept prisoner by being told that there really is no self-improvement. You cannot improve yourself. If you are born a bastard, for instance, not only are you accursed, but so are all of your offspring for generations down the line. So says the Bible, the "Word of God." All of this is nonsense. It was never told by anybody who was an emissary of God. Those are inventions of people who want power over you.

5. Self-improvement has always been a threat to the church fathers and to the hierarchy of conventional religion. Indeed, if you improve yourself, you may surpass those people who are appointed reverends or rabbis or priests. In doing so you become a threat to them, and you might start confronting them, upsetting their little apple carts and cozy positions.

6. Self-improvement and the process of self-transformation, nevertheless, happen to be the fundamental core of any religion— Judaism, Christianity, Islam, etc.—in its original form. Eradicating this from a religion represents eviscerating its soul. The new religion restores the processes of transformation and of personal improvement to its practices. It makes these the

fundamental central practices and rejects all other dogmas.

7. You have the freedom to believe what you want to believe. We tell you to believe only that which you experience. You are not forced to believe or to say that you believe in something that does not exist or that you do not **experience**.

8. We also suggest to you that you give the benefit of the doubt to the existence of manifestations, aspects, things and beings that you are not as yet developed enough to experience. Do you have the humility to accept this? This then becomes the door for your further spiritual growth.

9. What is called the Christ consciousness is not the exclusive possession of the Christian religion. The same idea exists in every single religion that has ever been created on the face of this Earth, including many of the pagan ones. Indeed, the Saviour is a personal experience that becomes a reality at the time of what is called "rebirth." A person who is twice born is a person who has undergone a crisis in his life and has decided to do things on his own, to proceed about his life from inside out and not the other way around. Therefore, as you can see, the atheist who has opted for self-determination is a lot closer to Christ than is the bigoted conventionalist in his church, synagogue, or mosque who is not as yet making that connection.

Is a crisis necessary to be twice born? The answer to this question is yes. The crisis can occur on different levels of a person or an entity depending on his spiritual development. The greater the spiritual development, the higher the crisis. The highest possible crisis can happen on the mental level. Here, the person who is born again will experience a complete change of his thinking process. The rest of his life may still remain the same on the outer level, but inside he has gone through pain and changed completely.

The best example of this is Descartes, the father of modern thinking, whose rebirth happened one day when he was stuck in a cabin during a storm. In his little lonely cabin, Descartes created for himself what we call in meditation an inner emptiness and focus. From this vantage point he experienced a breakthrough. He promised himself to rethink everything he ever thought and to put it all in the context of the Law of Cause and Effect. He would not accept any knowledge unless it could be causally explained. The first conclusion that he could draw was that he was in the process of thinking. The fact that he thought meant that he existed. "I think, therefore, I am" which has become the oft-mentioned *cogito*, was the basis for his philosophy. The reevaluation of his thinking not only changed his inner life but changed the Western world as well. Meanwhile on the outer level, Descartes' life did not change at all. He still continued to be independently wealthy, traveling wherever he wanted to travel and doing whatever he wanted to do.

If there is no crisis, there is no need to be reborn. The need to be reborn is a need to reshape oneself which necessitates a crisis. The most painful experience in human existence is birth, no matter what shape it takes, whether it is for the first or the second time in a person's life.

10. Christ's intention was not at all exclusivity. On the contrary, it was unification, universalization of very basic, fundamental principles of spirituality. This is what made Him the great teacher that He was.

11. A person is not a person until the soul inhabits his body which occurs when he takes the first breath. Therefore, abortion is not murder. An unborn child is still part of the mother's body. It is not an entity in and by itself.

12. Christ repeated many times that if you pray or fast or follow your tradition because you are afraid of God or

because you are afraid of punishment, you are a fool and a hypocrite. He Himself started many of His meals without blessing the food and is known in the *Gospel of Thomas* to have told people that it is better not to pray or fast but to watch what it is that comes **out** of your mouth, not so much what goes **in** your mouth. Thus, the worst possible evil is hypocrisy.

13. Automatic forgiveness just because you are a Christian or a Moslem or a Jew is utter and sheer nonsense. Forgiveness comes only when a person takes responsibility for the negativities that he perpetuates. When he does so, he himself automatically will want to make restitution for what he has done. That's forgiveness.

14. Men and women are equal in all contexts, including religion. In the New Age a lot more women will be invested with the wisdom of dispensation of the new teachings than will be men. As examples we have H.P. Blavatsky and A.A. Bailey. The pendulum swings. No gender has exclusivity or superiority over the other. In fact, each human being, male or female, has within the opposite sex which must be contended with and developed. Through this development it reaches unification, i.e., ecstasy, God.

15. Sex is the most beautiful experience on Earth, the most pleasurable. Therefore, through sex one is to find God. Honesty and integrity lead inevitably to ecstasy and sexuality, the act of union. In no way is sex the original sin. This is total nonsense and is not only the distortion but the perversion of spirituality. Spirituality and sexuality are one.

16. The true meaning of making it to the Kingdom of Heaven means unifying soul and personality, bringing into the outer world all of that which is inside of you, which constitutes your soul. Thus, a musician who may think of himself as an atheist may make it to the Kingdom of God

because he has found bliss, ecstasy through the revelation and the sharing and the teaching of his music —which is his task in the first place. In order to make it to the Kingdom, it is not necessary to put one's life in the straitjacket of requirements of churches and synagogues. Of course, what I just said about a musician is true of any other profession or any other task. Ecstasy is to be found also by the scientist making discoveries and connections that help humanity, the teacher who helps students see their abilities and potentials or the bank teller who directs an expression of energy and value.

17. The pursuit of harmlessness is what Buddha urged us to do and it is very much the original way of the Christian religion. The greatest demonstration of this is Christ's urging us to look at the beam in our eye before we become concerned with the mote in our brother's eye. Look within yourself for your lower self, for your negativity, and see how this then has magnetically attracted all of the negativities that exist around you. Stop blaming and start dissolving that which is in yourself.

So rejoice! Free yourself of the nonsense that was taught you and also free yourself of the negative response to this nonsense. That negative response itself is still keeping you enslaved to your old beliefs. You have thrown out baby with bath water. Realize that within yourself is a place where you know that there is a better way of living than the one you have chosen. This existential longing for something more constitutes your search for God. Listen to this voice, construct your own religion. Be your own saviour. Find your own path. There are as many religions as there are individuals. There are as many perceptions of the truth as there are individuals. Find and respect your own and you will find God.

CHAPTER 3
CREDO

At The Church of the Path®, we cultivate this balanced approach to the identity of deity. Our credo:

1. We believe in one God, the Father, the Mother and the Son combined in one Entity and Being, the Maker of all that exists, all that is thought, felt or done.
2. We believe that the Christ was the greatest of all teachers, that He came to reestablish choice and balance in the world, to restore the road to salvation.
3. We believe that you can make it to the Kingdom of God through right following of the original principles of most religions. They have Christ-like saviours and principles.
4. We believe that through ethics, even an atheist will make it to the Kingdom of God.
5. We believe that it is our duty to assert, claim and fulfill our needs.
6. We believe that every being will reincarnate, working through his harmfulness and perfecting himself to the point where he will totally be at-one with God.
7. We believe it is the right, the duty and the inevitability of every created entity to follow the one eternal and universal Path that runs through all ethical creeds. There is only one religion, and there are also as many religions as there are entities.
8. We believe in the existence of good and harmful

spheres, heavens and hells, sharing our time and space. We have the choice to attract and inhabit any of the spheres. This choice is God-given and we believe it is our duty to exercise it.

9. We believe that our goal is to reach immortality in the body, to find God through ecstasy, through at-onement, through right and spiritually lawful sexuality (sexuality in the context of love), through maintaining exploration of ourselves and of the Universe.

10. We believe that it is our task to spread civilization, harmlessness and right living.

CHAPTER 4
GOD AND EVIL

GOD: THE ALPHA AND THE OMEGA

Since time immemorial, since the beginning of monotheistic religion, God has been seen as the beginning and the end of all things, the Alpha and the Omega. This was also affirmed by the Catholic Church at both the Council of Trent (Vatican I), and in Vatican II in the early 1960s.

ALPHA **OMEGA**
A Ω

EMBLEMS OF THE CHURCH OF THE PATH®

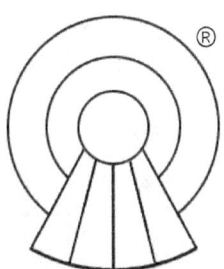

The first emblem represents primarily the Seven Rays. The blue Second Ray (the Ray of Love and of the First Son) resides between the red circle (representing Will and Father) and the yellow circle (representing Mother) at the center. Out of Mother emerge the four Rays of Attribute. This is also reminiscent of the Sun of Aton.

Many other associations can be made. One can see the Path through the long dark tunnel. This is abundantly described in the interviews with people who went through Near-Death-Experiences.

One can also see here a well-known triad of spirit, soul, and personality. Consider those in two different ways, both valid from the point of view of three-dimensional reality:

I. The spirit would be the center circle, the soul would be the circle in between, and the personality the outermost.

II. The spirit would be the outermost and the personality would be the center circle, the soul still bridging in the middle.

Notice also in either one the same formations (I or II)—Divine Self, distorted self, and idolized self.

For example, the Divine Self can be seen as the core in the middle, with the distorted self right next to it and the idolized self on the outside. The distorted self is closer to divinity than the deified self which conceals it. A person revealing the worst in himself is closer to God than a person who conceals his worst.

The Divine Self could also be the outer reaches. The little idolized self, at the center, would have to traverse the distorted self in the middle in order to reach the divine out there.

***

Another meaning which is to be found through this logo is that of the pyramid whose summit radiates the Trinity. The apex of the pyramid as a symbol of illumination is to be found in many other spiritual disciplines, notably Freemasonry.

A meaning of the logo which, until recently, had not occurred to us, is the Alpha and the Omega. Indeed, it resembles the "A" inside the "O" to be found in the Christian, particularly Catholic, church, symbolizing the beginning and the end. It is reminiscent of the words of Christ, "I am the beginning and the end," as the step-by-step ladder or Path to self-realization represented by the concentric circles, i.e., the Trinity.

Some people have seen in it the Taurian symbol of illumination, the bull's eye, as in a target. Indeed, many have been astonished at the incredible insightfulness that is developed when one follows this Path.

The second emblem reflects the Crucifixion of the Ego. The "I" surrenders to the inner Christ. The little ego ("I") surrenders to the Inner Christ ("C"), which is the Greater Ego, the I AM consciousness. In addition, "ICI" in French means "now"---signifying the Eternal Now found in that surrender.

GOD

God, Who is All That Is, is also the creator of all things; He initiated all that is. And, He is the end of all things as well. This definition is found once again in the cosmology of the recent dispensations. Indeed, in the last round, God will be the Will aspect (Ray I), the One Initiator. All will return to Him.

God is the One About Whom Naught May Be Said—not because it is forbidden, but because it is impossible. (The impossible became the forbidden when the Jewish religious leaders degenerated through their hunger for power.) Indeed, it is impossible to conceptualize the infinity of infinities that is God. He permeates and interpenetrates all that exists; He is the creator of all that exists; and He dwells in all that exists. This includes evil.

What makes us think there is a God? The presence of God can be demonstrated by the wonder of nature. We can also argue that great scientists who started their careers as atheists have ended up believing in and experiencing the existence of God. We can discuss and illustrate this point ad nauseam. However, none of this works. The only convincing proof of the existence of God is experiencing Him.

WHAT IS GOD?

In our attempt to understand the nature of God and in our defensiveness against realizing His infinite magnitude, we reduce Him. We say that He is a person and we talk to Him as the evangelical preachers do. Or we say that He is a principle. Or we say that He is to be found in His laws, in the Law of Cause and Effect, in the Law of Attraction, etc. Actually, all of these are true—and more. God is personalized; He is to be found in His principles; you can talk to Him personally; He is to be found in His creation. God, the One About Whom Naught May Be Said, is also the One About Whom Just About Anything May Be Said. Thus, it is ludicrous to confine ourselves to one concept of God. God is All That Is. The various religions have merely chosen to focus on one or another of His aspects because it was necessary at the time of the emergence of those religions. However, unfortunately, the other aspects of God were forgotten about, thus requiring that new religions based on those forgotten aspects be founded.

The masculine aspect of God, the aspect of the will, of the Father, the First Ray, can be said to be personalized, just as we identify our personality with our volition. What determines who we are is what we want to do and do deliberately, more than that which is receptive within us.

The feminine aspect of God, God the Mother, the Third Ray, is adaptability and intelligence. *What do we mean by adaptability?* It is the property of receptivity, the willingness to be molded, penetrated, inseminated, fertilized, which is attributable to that which is female. She is identified with matter only because it is a lot easier to see Her that way. Actually, she can be found in the other levels of existence such as the emotional, mental and spiritual. Therefore, it is a misconception to limit the aspect of mother. Mother is adaptability and intelligence.

The son aspect of God, the first born, the Second Ray, the Ray of Love and Wisdom, is the Christ. The Christ, Himself, although He is a lesser aspect to His Father and to His Mother, can be spoken about from our point of view the way He would speak about His parents—as infinite beings endowed with infinite powers. Although He is lesser than His parents, He is greater than us. He is the greatest spirit who ever was conceived. He is the first born. He precedes the birth of the Four Rays of Attribute who also are personified and personalized by the Masters who achieve perfection through them. This does not contradict our equality to Christ. We are all sons of God, created by Him. We all have the potential of Christ within us. Can you conceive of, and sustain, this paradox?

God created man in His own image, according to Genesis 1:26-27. It is time to revise this misleading statement. God created *all* His children in His image, not merely man. It is ludicrous to believe that a male member of the species is superior to a female. The patriarchal phase through which humanity has just passed, starting in the middle of the Atlantean Period and ending in the second half of this root race, is merely a swing of the pendulum. Before this was a phase during which the woman was considered to be superior to the man.

CREATION

The creation of the universe was effected by the Father aspect of God penetrating the Mother aspect of God. It is no different from the act of love to be found in humans. It is a sexual act. Nothing ever happens without the sexual act occurring. Every thought, every feeling, every action, and every atom of matter was created through the process of a male aspect penetrating a female aspect who then gives birth.

Since Christ and every single one of us were made by God, we carry within us His seed. We are all divine. We all have the potential to reach God, being His creations.[2] The

---

[2] If Ray Two was created by the interaction between Rays One and Three, are Rays One and Three superior to Ray Two? The answer to this question is that God is the unification of the Trinity, the three aspects must come together to complete the being of God. The Will Aspect penetrates the Mother Aspect and creates the Son Aspect, thus completing the oneness of God. In effect, there is equality in the three rays. However, since our system at this present time is ruled by the

(continued...)

Christ is a lesser creation of God, and we are creations of God that are lesser than Christ.

This is also true of every other creation. Every single atom carries in it the seed of God and, therefore, has for its task the return to God. Granted, it has to go through various phases of development.[3] Nevertheless, this is its task and this is its greatest wish.

Every single being in creation is also endowed with the Universal Consciousness and the Universal Life Force. The greater is its spiritual development, the greater is its capacity to become a carrier and distributor of these energies. Therefore, we can say that God is the greatest carrier of the Universal Life Force and of the Universal Consciousness. In fact, to the degree that we are identified with these currents within ourselves, we live in God. That, then, is the real meaning of God creating us in His own image.

INTERACTION BETWEEN UNIVERSAL LIFE FORCE AND UNIVERSAL CONSCIOUSNESS

Nature operates in cycles, in ebbs and flows. Sometimes in the life of an individual there seems to be a great deal of energy, of Life Force, of life stuff to be molded. Sometimes there is less of it, making it necessary for an individual to summon his consciousness, to raise it, and to create with it. When he is flooded with the Universal Life Force he can

---

(...continued)
Second Ray, the Saviour—the Son of God—appeared as a representative of that Ray. Thus, the Second Ray during this round will play a more important role than the other two.

[3]See the chapter entitled "Other Kingdoms of God."

accept the situation, bask in it, become receptive and enjoy his feminine principle, the principle of God the Mother. When the "tide" takes that force out of his system, then it is time for him to exercise the active and reactive Universal Consciousness. God has created the laws of nature in such a way that we fluctuate between these two states. This type of fluctuation has been found since time immemorial.

We find it in the story of Joseph whose brothers sold him into slavery in Egypt. He interpreted the Pharaoh's dream in which seven lean cows devoured seven fat cows. He saw this dream to mean seven years of plenty followed by seven years of famine. This made it possible for the Pharaoh to fill his granaries during the seven fruitful years so as to be able to survive during the seven lean years. It is the same for our civilization, the same for our lives as individuals. Some thrive in the receptive state and are able to bask in it. Some cannot stand it, preferring the leaner times, the more active times. Some prefer to follow father, some prefer to follow mother as aspects of deity. This is the nature of creation; the fluctuation that we undergo makes it necessary for us to grow and perfect every single aspect and attribute within ourselves.

The key to happiness is to have the resiliency to accept the ebbs and flows of the universe. Happiness is to be found in not abusing the gifts that God has given us. In the beginning, our gifts were considerable, considerably greater than what they are now. However, our consciousness was smaller than it is now. Thus, we abused the powers that God had given us, occasioning the Fall of the Angels. We will talk about this later. For the sake of this chapter, suffice it to say that we possessed at some point much greater powers than we do now and that we lost them through lack of development. With the greater development of our wisdom we are in the process of recovering these powers.

EVIL

Evil itself is a distortion of God, of the God energy and of the God consciousness. If there were not any goodness, evil would have no effect. Evil by itself cannot exist. Distortion by itself does not exist. In order for distortion to exist it has to attach itself and feed on goodness and on love. Hence, the finite nature of evil—it lasts as long as it can feed on the goodness that it has imprisoned. Once that goodness has been consumed, evil is bound to die. This is portrayed in Dracula who lives in the night, i.e., in darkness, just as does evil, and who feeds on others' life-blood—on others' goodness, continuously needing new life, new blood.

The proclamation of the existence of God, the affirmation of Him as an ever-present entity, must, therefore, involve the definition and the dissolution of evil. So it is in the human experience. In spheres where evil does not exist there is no need to define it, goodness is continuously and perpetually created and regenerated. But for us who are still part of the human experience it is our task to define and dissolve evil, restoring goodness to its original state where it can perpetuate itself.

HUMAN EXISTENCE AND PROGRESS

Is it unfortunate that we are caught in this human existence? Not necessarily. How can progress be achieved if everyone remains in the areas where there is no evil (outside human existence)? The only way progress can be attained is through the courageous penetration of evil by brave souls, such as those that constitute humanity. Therefore, those of us who have chosen to penetrate evil—take it on as it were—are a lot more courageous than the many who have refused to do so. We are performing a task for the universe which is a lot more important and valuable than the task performed by those who keep themselves away from evil.

What about people in the body who do not seem to have taken on any evil, or at least they pretend not to? What kind of function do they perform for humanity? Certainly they fill a lesser role than the people who have taken on evil and who are in the process of purifying it through their lives and through their life experience. These self-proclaimed perfect ones are those who renounce life, call themselves swamis, and so forth. The person who proclaims God by revealing and overcoming his own negativity and his own problems is performing a great service for humanity since he is demonstrating his own unique way of resolving a particular problem. All of this knowledge is accumulated in the Hall of Knowledge and Wisdom and is available to all other individual Higher Selves who can reach it and who can be inspired by it. This is, then, the great contribution of every human being to the Plan of Salvation. No matter how "evolved" the teachings of these seemingly perfect people appear to be, they are exhorting us not to do our work, to renounce the tasks that we came here to perform so as to find the bliss of at-onement. Thus, they seduce people into regression.

What or who is ever saved by somebody who has renounced life? No one. How about the person who is immersed in evil like Stalin, Pablo Escobar, or other drug dealers, or Hitler? **Their power and their ability to influence others demonstrates the fact that there is goodness in them.** The greater their power, the greater the goodness that they have been able to imprison and put to the service of evil. Such a system is bound to fail. Nazism collapsed in ways that were never thought possible before and during World War II. Communism folded virtually without bloodshed—by itself, like a rotten apple.

With those upsurges of evil and those collapses, humanity has learned a lot. It has learned, for example, that discipline and leadership can only exist in the context of love, they cannot exist outside of love as the Nazis and the fascists tried to demonstrate. It has also learned that the total manifestation of love on the outer level, as was advocated by communism, cannot work unless the consciousness of the people is raised first. If it is not raised first, it creates the types of abject dictatorships that are even worse than the fascists which the communists hated so much.

The Law of Sharing, which inspired communism, is a function of the Law of Brotherhood, i.e., a function of the Second Ray of Love and Wisdom. It cannot be imposed. It has to be arrived at voluntarily through the active participation and cooperation of the people involved. Therefore, a system such as this can only exist in a democracy. It cannot exist in a dictatorship. A dictatorship is antithetical to communism since it goes counter to the Law of Sharing. Sure enough, the countries that are the closest to a communistic system are the Western democracies—capitalism—with the creation of unions, the sharing of benefits, the existence of universal coverage of medicine in Europe, and the existence of the welfare state in the United States. That, too, has been abused, and that, too, is in the process of being corrected.

THE HAND OF GOD

All of this means that God's hand is everywhere. We

never thought that the Germans could be so thoroughly defeated as early as 1945. God had a hand in it. The Hierarchy blocked scientific knowledge to the Nazis and the Japanese while keeping this channel open to the Allies. As limited as it is, the Catholic Church is largely responsible for the destruction of communism. Being a Catholic behind the Iron Curtain was great, was indeed believing in God. So, the destruction of communism from within is a great "act of God" coming from the inner level, the level of the soul.

Shouldn't it technically be the Russian Orthodox Church which destroyed communism? The Russian Orthodox Church was completely wiped out by communism. The vestiges of it had completely sold out to communism during the days of the Evil Empire. By contrast, the Catholic Church was very active in Poland and Hungary. Cardinal Mindszenty of Hungary was tortured in the 1950s by Russian commissars. Cardinal Wyszynski and younger Cardinal Wojtyla, who became Pope John Paul II, were very active in Poland supporting and nurturing the Solidarity Movement. It is through the Solidarity Movement as supported by the Catholic Church that the back of the Evil Empire was broken. The success of the Solidarity Movement unexpectedly toppled the Yeljujeski regime. The rest of the USSR followed its example. Glasnost and peristroika happened as a consequence of solidarity. Mr. Gorbachev, let's not forget, was a student of Mr. Andropov who was the head of the KGB before he became premier. Gorbachev became a liberal in spite of himself. He was not a liberal to begin with. Thus, the pursuit of Christianity through the Catholic Church behind the Iron Curtain had an immensely beneficial effect on humanity. God indeed worked through the Catholic Church in that particular example. This is undeniable.

The twentieth century is full of demonstrations of the

presence of God and of the vigorous participation of the members of the Hierarchy in the accomplishment of the Plan of Salvation. **It is inaccurate to say that God draws closer to man. It is truer to say, that as man removes the barriers he has created, God is revealed and it is man who draws closer to God.** God was always there, only humanity's consciousness was not, and to a large degree, still is not, aware of Him.

SONSHIP

We are all sons and daughters of God. We are not as it says in the Catholic Catechism "adopted" children, as in one notch less than Christ. This is nonsense. Christ Himself said that we would achieve greater feats than He. We are sons and daughters of God on the same footing as the Christ was. Thus, if He was God, so are we. We became lesser than Christ, and lesser than other angelic beings by falling. However, we were created on the same level as all other beings. We chose to fall, as some of us now choose to rise again, to return.

LONGING FOR AND RETURN TO GOD

The greatest longing in human existence is the longing for God. All other longings are refractions of it, as all colours are refractions of white light. In our insatiable cravings for someone's love, for a new car, for a house, we project our infinite longing for God onto these objects, i.e., onto the lesser manifestations of Him. We are, therefore, bound to be disappointed. The absolute longing for God can only be satisfied when it is invested in achieving the Absolute. In that context, all the other longings then become relative. If somebody is focused on longing for God and at-oneing with Him, all of his other longings will acquire a sense of reality and proportion, as in "I can take it or leave it." This type of light attitude is the only possible way to achieve fulfillment. Anything tighter than this only leads to frustration.

No one can desire something that he does not already know. Therefore, it is the memory of having once been at-one with Him that keeps us motivated to seek Him again. That we were once at-one with Him is a fact, demonstrated by our insatiable longing for perfection and for total bliss, which is our birthright and our goal.

This is what it means to love God. Longing for God is loving God. It can be found in our love for just about anything or anybody.

FEAR OF GOD

Fear of God happens to be the greatest of all oxymorons. Only when you have a misconception of God do you fear Him. Only when you are trying to violate the Law of Gravity do you have occasion to fear it. If you throw yourself off the top of the Empire State Building you will crash and die—gravity will become a fearful, deadly law. At the same time, if you obey gravity, it becomes your friend by preventing you from flying all over the universe, propelled by the rotation of the Earth and of the entire solar system, let alone the galaxy.

God is goodness, love, forgiveness. Let me say it again: God **is** those things. When those are experienced, God is at-one with you. When those are violated, it is not God who is against you but yourself, since you are the one who has violated those laws of nature. Remember, you belong in nature, you are nature, the violation of it is the violation of yourself.

Fear of God is, in the last analysis, like any other

fear—fear of self.

GOD AND SEX

The most powerful manifestation of the love of God is the union of two beings in sexuality. **The purpose of sex is not as much procreation as it is union.** Procreation—the creation of the mere shell that will house a soul—is one of the functions of sexuality, certainly not the most important. Union with another—and, therefore, union with God—is the most important function of sexuality. The closest expression of the desire for God is the desire for at-onement with the other on all levels, including the physical. You see here how fallacious is the notion that sex and pleasure are sinful. Therefore, God is to be found most effectively through sexual union in the human experience. This is so, because: (1) it is the most pleasurable of all experiences, and (2) it is satisfied through fusion and intimacy, which is the return to God.

God is also to be found through accomplishing one's task, through prayer and through meditation.

SACRIFICE

In the old days, sacrifice was used as a means to find God. In the new dispensation, sacrifice is achieved through the giving up of the lower self. We have to sacrifice our lower selves. This includes our masks and our glamours. Eventually, they all go on the sacrificial altar by self-destructing anyway. The little deaths that our little ego undergoes every day are corresponding sacrifices to the ones that existed in antiquity. This, too, is a way to find God.

Sacrificing is also surrendering, surrendering of our defenses or surrendering of superfluous possessions that are in the way to our being at-one with God, i.e., to accomplishing our task, to living happy and fulfilled lives, etc.

Sacrificing sexuality, as in celibacy, is going against life and away from God. It is no sacrifice at all. It is merely the coward's way out of facing the trials and tribulations of relationships, the ways and means by which, through relationship, we purify ourselves and each other, thus finding God. On the contrary, claim your sexuality, restore your sexuality as the best and shortest way to finding and enjoying God.

CONNECTION WITH GOD

Every individual has an intimate connection with God. There is no need for intercession by anybody else such as the pope, a teacher, a spiritual leader, etc. All of these people merely assist and accommodate the person's return to God, the rediscovery of his direct connection with God.

DISCONNECTION FROM GOD

The disconnection from God occurs at birth, which is the most painful experience in human existence. The shock of finding oneself in three-dimensional reality is devastating. Indeed, prior to this state we are at-one with God. Our wishes are instantly and perfectly fulfilled. In that state, also, there is no consciousness[4], there is a universal state of bliss but without consciousness. At birth this bliss is shattered. We find ourselves in dire need and in continuous frustration. This sense of disconnection results in a state of faithlessness.

In his desperate longing for God, the infant then

---

[4]The pre-birth state is a state of universal cosmic consciousness, oneness. Before birth there is no personality consciousness/human consciousness.

attributes to one or both of the parents, or to grown ups, qualities that belong to God. He expects them to fulfill him; he expects them to be perfect. He loves them unconditionally so as to be loved in return in the same manner. He will even go so far as to pay lip service to belief in God in order to please those people who have really become his God. This is not true faith. This is pretense. This is false life. All of this is done because the child wants to be fulfilled. He uses his resourcefulness and his consciousness for the first time, realizing that he can influence his parents' behaviour by being good, by crying, by rebelling, etc. This is the beginning of consciousness, of knowledge. This corresponds to the Adam and Eve experience.

RECONNECTION WITH GOD

At first, the acquisition of consciousness is an attempt at finding at-onement once again with God. It is an apprehension of the Law of Cause and Effect—if I cry I will get a response, if I'm a good boy I'll get approval, etc. With the expansion of consciousness, the individual finds out that it is in his best self-interest to be ethical. Thus, he gets closer and closer to finding God once again, but this time with full awareness of himself.

So he has traveled from (1) a state of **being with God without awareness**, to (2) a state of **becoming** where he first disconnected from God, and then gradually attempted to find Him while acquiring consciousness, to (3) a state of **being with God with awareness** —and, therefore, being God. Energy and consciousness have finally come together at the end of this dualistic career.

It says in Psalms 105:3: "Let the hearts of those who seek the Lord rejoice!" *Why only the heart? What happened to the pelvis? What happened to the head? What happened to the feet? What is so vainglorious about the heart?* In the new dispensation the entire being seeks God. The entire being **is** God. The genitals are just as much a part of God as are the heart and the brain. Seeking God through the heart alone leads to distortion. Only the seeking of God with one's entire being is valid. Therefore, one has to look for the parts of ourselves that are not seeking God and herd them back to the mainstream.

IS THE DESTROYER POSITIVE OR NEGATIVE?
CRISIS

What about the destroyer aspect of God? Where does it enter into these concepts? Since the beginning of time, an unfortunate negative association has been made with the First Ray of Will or Power. This is probably because it is also the aspect of the destroyer. Indeed, before anything can be built, destruction has to occur. One has to destroy old forms before new forms are built. However, there are no innocent victims. The positive aspects that find themselves caught in the crossfire of destruction and construction were there for negative purposes and under wrong premises. Let's take a few examples to illustrate this point:

1. Pablo Escobar was seen as a great benefactor in Colombia, particularly in Medellin which was a center of the evil of drug trafficking in the world. His benevolence was misplaced and came from the wrong place. He used funds obtained through the sale of drugs to millions of people to be generous to his fellow Colombians. All of this had to one day be destroyed. There is no question about the fact that the generosity of the Pablo Escobars of this world, as well as of the fruits of the generosity of the Pablo Escobars of this world, have to go one of these days. When the destruction comes, it is seen as negative. Yet, it is not. It makes room for

the possibility of finding a good life, abundance, from a better place.

2. The destruction of highly sophisticated civilizations comes because they have lost touch with nature, with reality. In their highly developed sophistry, being protected by the achievements of the creators of those civilizations, they go astray and become corrupt. They lose contact with the Law of Cause and Effect. Their destruction becomes necessary before the new can manifest itself.

3. **When one energy current is used to do the work of another, both currents become corrupt and must be destroyed so the individual can start all over again to create a life in which each aspect is autonomous.** For example, when sex is used to do the work of profession, ending up in prostitution, the person has to destroy both his profession and his sexuality before he can build anew. The reverse is also true, when money is used to do the work of sex both must be destroyed. Think, for instance, of those who through their success attract sexuality and who end up destroying both success and sexuality in order to recover their grounding as human beings. Then and only then can there be a life where sexuality and profession are each cultivated for their own sake, bearing their own individual fruits which are different from each other. You can see that destruction is beneficial. It is a necessary phase and part of life.

4. Perhaps the best illustration of this destructiveness is given in the **allegory of the dam**. Imagine a river which has been dammed up. Downstream below the dam is a beautiful valley with wonderful flowers and trees and houses. Upstream of the dam dirt and debris accumulate. The longer the dam is closed, the greater the amount of dirt and debris that accumulates behind it. Eventually, the dam breaks,

violently releasing all the debris and dirt on the beautiful flowers, the beautiful trees, and the beautiful houses in the valley, thus destroying them. Then and only then can the clear water of the river be experienced once again. Only then can the inhabitants of the valley learn to wisely use the forces of nature without blocking them. The lessons are:

    a. Do not build by repressing or contradicting nature; build through her, with her help, i.e., through God and with His help.

    b. When the dam—the defense—breaks, and crisis occurs, you will first be flooded by the suppressed debris—your suppressed negativities—before clear and limpid water can again flow and be enjoyed.

It is the same with individuals, organizations, countries or civilizations. It is the damming up of the great forces—God, the Universal Consciousness and the Universal Life Force—which brings about the necessity for destruction and crisis. There would not be destruction if the laws of nature were obeyed.

To the degree that we are still in the process of learning, of becoming, to that degree there will be the necessity for destruction. **Destruction does not have to occur on the outer level. It can be experienced on an inner level.** Crisis can be anticipated and experienced inwardly on the mental and emotional levels, thus being averted on the physical level. The Path consists of learning how to do this.

TWO GREAT EVILS OF THE TWENTIETH CENTURY

The forces of darkness, in anticipation of and parallel to the new dispensations that were given to humanity, brought about two great evils, both masquerading as great goodness:

    1. **Fascism.** This trend can be traced back to Frederick William I in Prussia who, in the late seventeenth century and

beginning of the eighteenth century, formed the first mechanized army. Fascism did great harm under his son, Frederick II, called the Great, when he invaded the Austrian Empire in the eighteenth century. We find it again in the Franco-Prussian War of 1870-71. And it reemerged again, ugly as ever, in World War I with Kaiser Wilhelm. This evil—the evil of the glamour of war, of mechanization, of Aryan superiority—was partially defeated at the end of World War I. It was not totally vanquished, staying alive because of the cowardice and the compromise of the Allies. They did not finish the job. So it reemerged in a worse form in the 1930s and 1940s under the agent of evil, Hitler. At that point, the situation was so well polarized that it was obvious that evil had to be destroyed once and for all. In the meantime, it had poisoned many other countries—Italy with Mussolini, Spain with Franco and Japan with Hirohito. The disguises under which Nazism was to be found were strength, discipline, productivity, leadership, followership, knowledge and science, i.e., the will rays. All of this was masked under the banner of developing the Aryan Race and under the glorification of the blond-and-blue-eyed aspects of beauty. The final destruction of this evil left another evil in place, communism, which we will talk about below.

While it is true that Western civilization was destined to find its universal state, i.e., to conquer the world, it certainly did not do it with Hitler's help. An extraordinary number of people in the Western world—particularly in the United States—resonated to the great seductive powers of the Nazi philosophy. The great Charles Lindbergh is a good example; there are of course others. In England, none other than King Edward VIII was very much pro-Nazi. Here we find the subtlety of the hand of the Hierarchy, allowing him to fall in love with Mrs. Simpson and desiring to marry her which resulted in his abdication of the throne. Hitler and the Duke of Windsor, the deposed Edward VIII, had a secret plan to restore the latter back on the throne of England after Hitler had won the war. And the Nazis came very close to doing it. The reversal of fortune experienced after Pearl Harbor in December 1941 and El Alamein in July-August 1942 was not a given. The incredible outrages of the forces of evil galvanized humanity on the side of the Forces of Light and made it possible for the Hierarchy to intervene on behalf of humanity and win those battles. But, as the Tibetan clearly states in his messages, it could have gone the other way, thus plunging humanity into another thousand years of darkness.

2. **Communism.** The great evil of communism was very well masked under the benign banner of the Law of Brotherhood—sharing. In the first place, it was devised by a Jew, Marx, who had lost his faith during the worst times of the Industrial Revolution in London in the middle of the nineteenth century. Marx was inspired by, and grossly misinterpreted, the great German philosopher Hegel. But, in no way does any communistic government in the world portray Hegel's philosophy. Communism is a distortion of Hegel's philosophy which never advocated a unilateral, forceful control over society.

So, this quasi-law of brotherhood had a huge harmful volition (negative intent) behind it: the control of the world, the conquest of the world, the reduction of the world to its lowest common denominator and its sacrifice through elimination of whomever disagreed with that philosophy. The presence of the hoof of Satan is unmistakable. As much as the Hitleric/Germanic evil was a distortion of the First Ray, communism was a distortion of the Third Ray, the Ray of Mother, of materialism. It appears to be coming from the

Ray of Love, of sharing, but it is not. It has a lot more to do with adaptability, with matter, with intelligence. Mother Russia, mother/matter, the Third Ray, became the seat of communism. Everything was controlled through "reason." Everything was centralized, as in a spider's web. The mind was worshiped over anything else, whereas the Nazis worshiped the will. Although sharing was the goal, sharing never really manifested. But the mind did, the heartless mind and the concrete knowledge of Ray Five certainly did. They, too, had their final solutions in the elimination of tens of millions of their people by Stalin's ignoring famine and starvation and through liquidating huge sections of society. This still continues today in China. In the 1960s it is estimated that as many as 50-100 million people were eliminated through the Cultural Revolution of Chairman Mao.

The destruction of communism is a great victory for the Hierarchy. Not one faction can claim responsibility for it. The Hierarchy worked through many channels, one of them being the Catholic Church. As said before, belonging to the Catholic Church under communism was a great act of courage, honesty, and integrity. However, let's not forget that Pope Paul VI caved in to communism, thus delaying the destruction of the Evil Empire for many decades and creating all kinds of problems in South and Central America.

The Hierarchy also worked through the prosperity that the West experienced under the Reagan administration. This is really what started *glasnost* and *peristroika* in the mid 1980s and precipitated the destruction of the Evil Empire of communism. The great revolution of 1989, a fateful 200 years after the French revolution of 1789 is no accident. The hand of the Hierarchy can very clearly be felt in this immense victory, the effects of which have not as yet been understood.

The reconstruction that is taking place in the former Soviet Union and its satellites could not have happened without the beneficial destruction that preceded it. Thank God for that.

GOD'S WILL

What does it mean to do God's will? What if my will is opposite to God's will? What if I want to do something that is not in accordance with the will of God?

Doing God's will is simply following God's laws, which are the laws of nature. When wisdom is acquired, it becomes obvious that God's will needs to be followed and that it is unwise not to do so. It is just as unwise not to follow God's will as it is not to change the type of dress with the change of seasons. Following God's will is in your best self-interest. Unless and until you discover that, you will not want to follow it. And, therefore, you will have to make the mistakes that will lead to necessary crises. Those, in turn, will get you to discover that God's will was the right thing to do in the first place. **So, God's will is really your will, only you are not aware of it.**

If you are a good parent in raising your child, it is obvious to you that you cannot give the child too many choices. You have to choose for him and he simply has to follow because he does not know any better. In your interaction with God, He has given you the choice to make your own decisions to the degree you are an adult. If you listen closely, you will hear His voice telling you what the right decision is. The more you grow, the more you are adult, the more you recognize the voice of God as being at-one with the voice of your own Higher Self, your innermost self. However, if you believe that your best self-interest is served by doing the opposite of what this voice tells you, then you have to get hurt in order to learn.

This hurt is often interpreted as the nonexistence of God instead of being seen as the existence of God since it is the consequence of your violation of Spiritual Law, which is natural law. If you do not dress warmly in winter and you get a cold, it is not because God does not exist. It is because God does exist that you get a cold. It is because you have not listened to God by not watching the signs of nature, that you have gone against Him and, therefore, you have caught the cold. The catching of the cold is indeed proof positive that God exists, that there is cause and effect. Interpreting it in any other way must lead to very destructive consequences for yourself in your future. Other destructive acts will be committed in sheer infantile rebellion against God.

Every single unhappiness in life is the consequence of not following the will of God. Sometimes, instant gratification is sought by violation of Spiritual Law. The pleasure attained through this method is always short lived, always leads to addiction, crisis, and the eventual and inevitable return to the following of the will of God.

CAPACITY TO EXPERIENCE GOD

Is the experience of God limited to those people who are spiritually developed or is it available to everyone? God is reached through the dissolution and the resolution of our personal problems which we have created by distorting His energy and His consciousness. Therefore, the experience of God is available to anyone and everyone, to any particle of creation here and now. The degree of the difficulty of some problems increases with the degree of development of the individual. The greater the spiritual development, the more difficult is the task of resolution of problems. The lesser the development of the individual, the easier is the task of resolution of personal problems. So, it will be possible even for a less developed being to find God once his own less difficult problems are resolved. Your problems are commensurate with your capacity to resolve them. This is found in other places as "God will not give you any problem that you cannot handle."

From this we conclude:

1. **That God is available for everyone through the resolution of their own issues.** He is experienced if we fulfill certain conditions within ourselves. Here are some of these conditions:

a. **Practicing total honesty.** Indeed, to the degree we are dishonest, to that degree we shut ourselves off from the truth and, therefore, from God. God is truth. If there is a part of us that does not want to tell the truth for one reason or another, we are alienating ourselves from the experience of God. To the degree that we believe that happiness is only attainable through dishonest means, to that degree it is impossible for us to believe in God. We actually are practicing a belief in the devil whenever we harbour such forms within ourselves. So, a fundamental prerequisite is to have a commitment on the conscious level to total truth and honesty.

b. **The investigation within ourselves of the unconscious ways that we violate truth and natural law.** This constitutes the Path that we practice here.

c. **Dignity and self-worth.** Indeed, it is impossible to make contact with anybody higher than ourselves if we do not have self-respect. Self-denigration only makes available to us the supernatural forces that are below us, inferior to us, albeit more powerful than we are. Indeed, it is conceivable that on a temporary level, a lot of negative forces are more powerful than we are but have less consciousness than we do. These are the forces that we attract when we do not have any self-respect. On the contrary, with self-respect and self-love, we can, with dignity and with humility, long for the presence of greater forces higher than we are. We are then ready to accept and surrender to our Maker.

When those conditions are fulfilled, or more accurately to the degree they are, one experiences the reality of the existence of God. This is done through states of grace, through moments of illumination during which total happiness is either experienced or conceived as possible. At those moments, the unity of the universe is an experienced fact. God is experienced then, at least in His immanence.

When it comes to experiencing God transcendent, God as One Unified Being with a sense of volition and direction, one has to use logic. Indeed, when oneness is experienced, it becomes inconceivable that it has not been created by One Being and One Being alone. Thus, it becomes an irrefutable fact.

The person who has experienced God and who deeply knows of His existence is tolerant of those who have not and of those who deny His existence. Indeed, in this church, we have had people in positions of leadership who were atheists. They denied the existence of God, but they accepted the teachings of this church, and they applied them to their lives. Indeed, this is possible. One can accept the ethical and spiritual and natural teachings of this church without necessarily having reached the conclusion that one supreme being has created it. This is quite acceptable. This state is by far preferable to the state of pretending a belief in God which then leads to the bigoted and fanatical intolerance of those who are honest enough to admit that they are atheists.

Indeed, if you believe in the devil, you are believing in a supreme being who is negative. You are, therefore, believing in an anti-God. From believing that to believing in God is a very short step indeed.

If you believe in the devil, you are readier to believe in God than you know. From believing in a malevolent power to believing in a benevolent one is merely a turn of the key.

One of the purposes of Christ's incarnation was to demonstrate to us the personification of God. Now, be careful! I am not saying that Christ is God—what I said in the first sentence does not mean that at all. However, for us, in our state of development, He represents perfection incarnate. If perfection incarnate can go through the vicissitudes of life and, unaided by the spirits of God, come out on the other end as a master, then we too can do the same thing under much more advantageous conditions.

The necessity to have role models incarnated, personified, makes our progress possible and more easily attainable. Nothing is ever achieved without visualization. If you can visualize yourself in the shoes of a mentor or have an example to follow, then you can follow that blueprint and bring it to reality. Therefore, Christ's incarnation helps us accept the possibility of the Supreme Being Who creates the universe. The implications of not believing in this, therefore, must be the inability to visualize oneself as a creator, as a person who is able to accomplish his task and to be a saviour in his own life. Thus, the refusal to accept the personification of God closes the door to quite a few achievements, perhaps the greatest ones in your life.

It is very important to meditate on this and to disconnect this from the bigoted-Bible-thumping-Jesus-screaming stupidities that are perpetrated in conventional religion and in evangelism.

2. **That it is extremely difficult to tell who is more developed than whom on the spiritual level.** The degree of difficulty to resolve a particular problem may propel a very developed spirit into committing extraordinary acts of barbarism. A good example of this is Hitler who was born carrying a great task but who distorted it into the monstrosity that he created.

CHAPTER 5
THE MANY ASPECTS OF GOD

PERCEPTIONS OF GOD

There are as many different perceptions of God as there are religions and philosophies. In fact, all religions and all philosophies are attempts at defining Him in order to join Him.

God personified is highlighted in the Judeo-Christian religions. Indeed, you can speak to Him as a person if He chooses to hear you. He intervenes in your life to reward or to punish. Essentially, He takes on the characteristics of the patriarchal authority that existed and was venerated in the homes at the time the Bible was written, particularly the Old Testament.

Within the Judeo-Christian religions there are differences. For example, this quality of transcendence—the personalization of God, the fatherization, if I may be allowed a new coinage—is much more pointed in Judaism and even more so in Islam than it is in Christianity. In Christianity, He begins to acquire immanence, the quality of *energy* which God has and which is venerated in the east, in the Hindu religions, for example. Christ, Himself, was a Jew who traveled in the east and was taught the eastern techniques of meditation and self-realization. These He taught to those who were ready, those who were closest to Him. The other, the easier teachings, as in the Sermon on the Mount, were given to the rest of the populace.

So this brings us to the other end of the spectrum where God is seen as energy, as the Universal Life Force, rather than a personified consciousness. God as the Life Force, therefore, *is* the stuff of which your soul is made, that which you can shape. The notion that you can create your own reality comes from this idea.

Yet, others see God as merely consciousness, a Universal and Absolute Consciousness and Awareness, separating it from energy and personification. Many philosophies adhere to this type of thinking.

Which philosophy of God is right? The answer is all of them are, as long as they do not exclude one another. God is all of the above: He is personified; He is the Universal Life Force; and He is the Universal Consciousness. In these three manifestations we see the three Rays of Aspect. The personification of God is the masculine aspect of God; the Universal Life Force is the feminine aspect, whilst the Universal Consciousness is, of course, the love aspect, the Son of the Father and the Mother.

CREATION

God the Father is the creative principle who molded the Universal Life Force and thus created first of all His son, the consciousness, the Christ principle, and second, everything else that exists, including ourselves.

What is meant by, "God created us in His image?" This basically means two things: (1) He gave us the same ability to create which He has, the ability to mould the Universal Life Force and, (2) since we are His creation, we are lesser beings than He is. And here is a fundamental difference that we have with many other Christian factions: **although the Christ is superior to all created humans, He is inferior to God.** Thus, the Christ is to be seen as a brother, not as a father. Even the Catholics pray to God through Christ. All the other forms of prayer, prayers to Mary, to Christ, are distortions of what reality should be. The reality is that you should pray to God through Christ but not **to** Christ.

THE UNIVERSAL CONSCIOUSNESS

This can be called the mind of God. It is the conceptual framework, if you like, that shapes the Universal Life Force, that shapes life. It is the set of laws and rules in accordance to which the universe works. As an example, it would correspond astrologically to the key word in Aries: "I come forth, and from the plane of mind, I rule." It contains a framework for the active and for the receptive modes of the Universal Life Force.

Its truth sometimes is contradicted by our little ego consciousness which is nothing else but a replica of it. The ego must be trained to recognize this Universal Consciousness and surrender to it, heeding its message. When that happens, the ego will experience a state in which it will be astonished at its own capacity to think and to know. This, we will call at times intuition. In effect, it is merely the capacity to become a channel, to tap into a greater state of mind.

What is the relationship between the Universal Consciousness and the Law of Cause and Effect? The Universal Consciousness obeys the Law of Cause and Effect. That is why it is so ludicrous to believe that God does not make sense. He **is** sense.

THE UNIVERSAL LIFE FORCE

This is radiant stuff, potential, the stuff that the soul is made of. Each person, depending on his development, possesses a commensurate amount of this Universal Life

Force to mould, to create with. Of course, God possesses an infinite amount of it. The Christ possesses less than an infinite amount. And we possess even less than that. In the act of creation, we dissolve this Life Force, we descend it, we make it into a fluid so that it can enter our personality and so that we can create with it.

However, creation is only one of our activities. When this Universal Life Force floods us, we go through a time of receptivity in which we float in the Life Force; we experience it. The little ego needs to be strong enough to allow itself to be flooded by that Universal Life Force. In that state we allow the feminine aspect of God to prevail within us. It is a period of gestation. It is a time when we are rebuilding ourselves. It corresponds to the cocoon phase in the animal kingdom. We are being nurtured, we are being reshaped. We are the Mother and the Child. As it says in Virgo: "I am the Mother and the Child. I, God, I, Matter Am[5]." This splendidly asserts God in femininity and in potential.

When the time comes, just as with seasons, the flood recedes and the active male aspect, the creator, is revealed. That is when the active, creative phase occurs. This type of mechanism is most misunderstood in the human experience. There are humans who want to continuously create and never allow themselves to be flooded, to be reshaped and to be nourished. There are others who never want to create, always wanting to be nourished, reshaped and flooded. There are those who prefer to be on the father's side and those who prefer to be on the mother's side. Thus, they miss the opportunities on both sides of the spectrum, depending

---

[5]Bailey, Alice A. 1951. Page 654. *Esoteric Astrology*. New York: Lucis Publishing Company.

on who they are from the personality point of view.

Take, for example, Christianity and its formation. It took about two hundred years for the energy of Christ to permeate human consciousness. Those who received the dispensation had to be immersed in it at first. They were ashamed of it. They denied that they believed in the Christ. They practiced their religions in secret meetings. Then, when they dared surface, they were persecuted. They were repressed before they finally became accepted and prevailed. This follows precisely the process that I explained above.

The dispensation that this church is making available is now in the period of gestation which makes a lot of us impatient. When will it finally grow? When will we finally see the multitudes accepting what we have to say? Well, it may take centuries before that happens. My hunch is that we will start seeing this in the beginning of the next century.

Whether the new dispensations are in gestation or not, those who follow them always feel blessed by the teachings. The followers feel on an inner level that the at-onement they have found is what they always have been looking for.

It is impossible to explain what I tried to explain in this chapter in human words. The only thing that we can ask you, the reader, to do is to open your inner senses and find within yourself on an experiential level a deeper understanding of this.

God gave His creatures free will. He also created universes of extraordinary magnitude, of infinite beauty, of incredible love, of sharing, of harmony, of happiness. The individual could live in all of these worlds as long as he respected the laws of God and did not violate them. In the chapters on evil we talk about the violation of Spiritual Law and its consequences in greater detail.

CHAPTER 6
YOUR PERSONAL FREEZE[6] OF GOD

A great tool of purification is to examine your own concept of what God is and what He looks like. You may have prevented yourself from even thinking about that. However, if you open your mind and allow yourself to examine your image of God, you will find out quite a bit about yourself and you will help yourself in the process of purification, thus joining God much more quickly.

What does God look like for you? What does He sound like? What does He say? What has He been saying to you since you were born?

Having defined all of this, now see who it is that you have made into God. It usually is a strong parental figure, either father or mother, that we project on God. Thus, it is also an out-picturing of our own affected conscience, superego in psychoanalytic terms. This image of God, therefore, rather than helping us, is acting as a defense, a buffer that has many negative consequences:

1. It prevents us from freely admitting the parts of us that are negative and that need to be worked on. Thus, it creates a barrier against finding God, not a way of finding Him.

2. It continuously creates guilt, sometimes for places where we have sinned (real guilt) and sometimes for places

---

[6] A freeze is a wrong conclusion, a misconception.

that are not sins at all but that are merely seen as such by wrong conclusions (false guilt). In both cases, the result of this is very negative, arresting and regressive. Indeed, if you judge yourself for having sinned, you will never be able to freely expose your sin and resolve it. Also, if you start judging your sins, you will also judge parts of you that are not sinning at all, that are merely trying to express themselves in a natural way.

For example, let's say that you are married and that you have sexual feelings for other people. Investing those sexual feelings with other people is negative. However, the desires, themselves, are not. You may be involved in a marriage that satisfies a certain number of your needs but which does not satisfy other legitimate ones. If you have given up trying to satisfy those needs in your relationship, you will be bound to look for that satisfaction elsewhere. The sin is in looking elsewhere, not in the need itself. However, you condemn yourself for both, never really differentiating between the two. At the same time the differentiation is essential for the resolution of the problem because, naturally, it is your privilege and your duty to have all of your needs fulfilled and have them fulfilled in accordance with Spiritual Law. It is, in fact, Spiritual Law to have all of your needs fulfilled. God wants you to have all of your needs fulfilled. He has your best interest at heart.

God Himself is indefinable, that is why as we have said elsewhere, He is called "The One About Whom Naught May Be Said," not that it is forbidden to say anything about Him, but that it is impossible to define Him. In the meantime, we are in need of teachers, guides, with whom we can identify, who we can emulate. We cannot emulate "The One About Whom Naught May Be Said." So He sends emissaries, Sons of God, the greatest of whom is the Christ, to help us in their manifestation on our level of reality, to see that it is possible to resolve our problems. Lesser role models are available to us everywhere. The choice of the role model depends on the degree of development of an individual. The more highly developed someone is, the greater a role model will he be able to recognize and follow. The prototypical role models for this lifetime are our parents, whom we chose for this very purpose, the purpose of growth.

In order to grow and discover the real nature of God, you must first identify and dissolve the false God in whom you believe. Everyone, including atheists, has an image of God, a freeze of God within himself which he needs to detect and dissolve.

THE PURSUIT OF HAPPINESS

Happiness is not just our right but it is our duty to pursue and to find. This is one of our basic human rights. The desire for happiness is, therefore, a natural one to be encouraged and nurtured. Inherent in it is the desire for pleasure, bliss, ecstasy. Therefore, the one activity which carries the greatest pleasure—sex—is the one activity in which people find God in a more direct manner than in any other activity in our realm of existence. So sex, far from being sin, is indeed holy and needs to be seen as such and practiced as such.

Because of humankind's limited consciousness, the pursuit of happiness is distorted. Indeed, the following sequence is deeply anchored in the human psyche:

1. I seek happiness.
2. In order to find it, I must protect myself against unhappiness.
3. If I find a situation where there is a question as to whether I am going to experience pain or pleasure, I refuse

the situation out of hand; I shut off any possibility of pain whatsoever.

4. So, my experience of happiness is limited by my desire to experience *only* happiness.

5. The desire for self-protection—still motivated by the pursuit of happiness—becomes an obsession. Any experience involving change is doubted because in the unknown and untried experience is the possibility of pain.

6. So, in order to protect myself from unhappiness, I am seeking unhappy experiences in order to detect them and not enter into them. The seeking of unhappy experiences makes me magnetically attract them. Thus, in order to find happiness, I seek unhappiness, which is a contradiction in terms and which is the plight of the human condition.

Therefore, the only way to happiness is the willingness to experience pain, unhappiness, i.e., to be open to any experience at all as it is presented to me in my life. The willingness to experience unhappiness, the resisting not of evil, is what opens me to the final experience of happiness at the end of the line. The total surrender to experience the universe as it is, here and now, makes available to me the involuntary process, without which nothing can happen.

Thus, the pursuit of happiness is a surrender, a removal of the defenses against it. Happiness exists for everybody here and now.

CHAPTER 7
THE CHRIST

I recommend that you read this chapter with an open mind. If you do not agree with it, skip it. You may be drawn back to it at a later time. Take from this book what is easy for you to take, applying it to your life but staying open to that with which you disagree. Parallels to the story of Christ exist in every person's life and in all of creation. Not understanding of the story of Christ is a direct result of existing blocks and blindness that refuse to be challenged by this story.

THE FORCES OF LIGHT AND THE FORCES OF DARKNESS

The difference between the Forces of Light and the forces of darkness has to do with free will. The Forces of Light will give an entity his free will. They will only interfere if there is a genuine and believable call for help. Even then, the interference is done within certain principles. In no way will the Forces of Light remove from the individual his power to create and uncreate his reality.

By contrast, the forces of darkness will interfere as they please and when they please. We will attract their interference in the places where we have capitulated, where we have chosen to take the line of least resistance, where we do not want to do the work, and where we want to be saved.

Therefore, it is the height of distortion to believe that the mere desire to be rescued by a saviour will get you to the Kingdom of God. What it will get you is the Kingdom of the Devil instead. The spirits who will rescue you will be much more devilish entities than angelic ones.

Lucifer and his brother Herem created a system which was practically fail-safe. Indeed, people with good intentions were first seduced by Herem who propelled them to follow their line of least resistance and get everybody's approval. They then found themselves under the hoof of Satan, committing acts of murder, rape, pillage and plunder either under the banner of religion or because "they couldn't help it," their negative side was taking over. All of this was supported by the once valid (but now invalid) Ten Commandments.

There is nothing in the Ten Commandments about the fact of an inner life, the existence of a lower self, the distortions that reside in the mental and emotional levels. These distortions and the fact that they were not addressed by the old dispensations made it difficult, almost impossible, for anyone to make it to the Kingdom of God. So tight was the grip of the forces of darkness that reaching the Kingdom of God was unattainable.

Humanity was moving further and further away from the Forces of Light. Noticing this, the Christ and the Hierarchy had a conference with His Parents and suggested that He intervene to do something about it. Of course, the problem was, being Forces of Light, they could not influence the situation unless they could get an agreement with the forces of darkness concerning conditions under which this would be allowed. It was agreed then that a meeting would be set up between the First Son, the Christ, and the Lesser Son who fell, Lucifer.

INTERVENTION BY THE FORCES OF LIGHT

During this meeting the Christ presented to Lucifer the fact that he had gone too far and that there would have to be an intervention from the Forces of Light. Of course Lucifer retorted by saying that the Forces of Light could not do this, they could not interfere in the process. The Christ then asked, "Under what conditions would you agree to do battle with us?" The devil then set the following conditions:

1. There had to be one entity who would live His life on Earth without sin. This life would have to be lived without help from the Forces of Light. The Forces of Light must commit themselves not to guide this individual at all. If that were to be accomplished, then

2. A conflict, a war of liberation could be waged by the Forces of Light against the forces of darkness. This struggle had to be an uneven one since even Lucifer himself knew that the Forces of Light were a lot more powerful than the forces of darkness. So the ratio was established as 20:1—twenty entities of the forces of darkness pitted against one representative from the Forces of Light.

Upon ending the meeting, the Christ came back and talked about this with His brothers, the archangels who had not fallen. They all reflected who would be the best possible person to send on Earth for this trial life. Many of them volunteered. Upon deeper and deeper reflection the Christ decided that it had to be Himself. Everybody objected and was horrified at the thought of sending the head of the Hierarchy to perform this very painful and menial task. However, His argument was that if He could not do it, then nobody else could and that He was the best qualified to do it.

Reflect upon this in your own life. *To what extent are you unwilling to do the menial work, the lowly tasks, or the most difficult ones? To what extent do you delegate those?* To that extent you are a very poor leader indeed, a very poor conductor of your own life, a very poor manager. Only by going as deep as you can and handling the most menial and the most apparently difficult and outrageous tasks of your life can you call yourself a leader and can you be a real saviour in your own right.

CHRIST'S INCARNATION

Preparations were made for this event. The greater the entity, the more elaborate are the preparations for his life on Earth. The world of the Hierarchy sent emissaries to study the conditions under which He was going to be incarnated and to prepare the ground for His incarnation. They started with the incarnation of Buddha six hundred years before the arrival of Christ. In addition, many groups in Palestine were preparing for such an event. They were undergoing processes of purification.

The forces of darkness also knew that this event was going to happen. When Christ was finally born, the dark forces, through King Herod, proceeded to massacre all the first born of Jewish households in Palestine. This is why the Christ and His physical parents had to flee to Egypt.

The greatest pain in human existence is the pain of injustice. Imagine the most evolved of all souls created by God being incarnated on this Earth's sphere with all of its dualism, with all of its injustice. Remember that this happened in the middle of the Roman Empire, and in a rebellious Palestine to boot with incredibly outrageous and difficult conditions.

Do this and you can then imagine the great suffering the Christ had to undergo during His life on our plane. No physical suffering can compare to the point of tension He had to experience during His lifetime.

Besides, being as developed as He was, He was highly mediumistic. Since the Forces of Light could not contact Him, His mediumistic qualities made him that much more vulnerable to all the forces of darkness. In spite of this, He managed to find His identity within Himself, the existence of God as well as His task as the liberator of humanity from the forces of darkness.

He went through the human experience, savouring it to the hilt. He knew sexuality as demonstrated in the *Gospel of Thomas*. He traveled; He taught during His travels. He certainly knew doubt and He certainly was familiar with conflict. He went through the five earthly initiations. He penetrated Jerusalem, challenging both the Jewish and the Roman traditions. He knew what He was doing, He knew that He was going to be put to death for that, yet He still did it.

How could He teach without learning? Very simply. Light does not have to be taught. Light is all-knowing. He taught by reacting to the distortions that He found around Him. He taught by contrasting what He was discovering on the outer level with what He found on the inner level.

Imagine a lamp with a lampshade. The lampshade has holes or designs in it. The lamplight is the truth; the lampshade is the darkness and the falsehood.

The Light, the truth, will react to the distortions in their precise shapes. It does not have to learn what these distortions are, it merely has to shed its light on them in order to discover their shapes and to show them, i.e., the places where the light is allowed to shine and the places where it is not allowed to shine.

That is teaching. His travels and His teaching actually planted the seed for the later reception and propagation of

His teaching, as distorted as they were to be found later.

CHRIST'S TASK

Basically we can say that He came in to do three tasks:

1. **To bring in new teaching.** However, the teachings that He brought, revolutionary as they were, did not really constitute such extraordinary innovations. They could be found in other places. For example, the Buddha before Him said a lot of things that resemble what the Christ said. Philosophers such as Plato and Socrates had already preceded Him with many of the principles that He later elaborated. His teachings were revolutionary, but they were not His main task.

2. **To demonstrate by example how an individual could live a life without any of the advantages that were available to others and yet come out on the other side, at the end of the tunnel, and make it to the Kingdom of God.** This, too, as extraordinary as it was, is something that had been done in the past and was to be done again in the future. This does not constitute the main aspect of His incarnation and of His task.

3. **To fray a passage for all of us through the astral plane, where the world of evil resides, to the mental and spiritual planes where we are saved.** This was done by a direct confrontation, a frontal attack against the forces of darkness, the forces of compromise, both the realms of Satan and Herem. **This is indeed His main and most important task, the task for which He incarnated.**

To better understand what this passage is about, one has to realize the consequences of the existence of evil for us. In the chapter "The Fall and the Formation of Evil," I explain the role of Lucifer and Herem in their seduction of humanity. Their ploy is to seduce "well meaning" citizens to evil through their line of least resistance, i.e., the mask of goodness and propriety being used for the evil purposes of the lower self. All of this is done mostly on the astral level, the level of feelings. Thus, it is in the world of feelings that evil resides and needs to be challenged and destroyed. The passage that the Christ frayed for us as a result of his three-day war against evil was done by the breaching of the wall of evil that existed on the astral level. The wall consisted of entities as well as of energy forms that were rooted in evil consciousness. Imagine an extraordinary number of freezes jelling together and forming a wall which prevents the light from coming in or out and defended by entities with weapons similar to but far superior to weapons we have on Earth; this is the wall.

Before the Christ, anyone who would allow himself to get into his feelings would be instantly seduced by the Herem-Lucifer tandem and system, thus falling into their trap. No matter how spiritual you were, you were seduced by those beings who continued to be superior to you. The Christ, by breaching this wall of deception on the level of feelings, made it possible for us to liberate ourselves. By following His example, we can now live a full life through our spirituality, our thinking, our body, as well as our emotions.

Immediately upon His death He summoned the Forces of Light without wasting a minute, and waged and won a decisive battle against the forces of darkness. This battle lasted three days. He alluded to this in His sayings about destroying and rebuilding the Temple of Jerusalem in three days. He was derided at the end of His life for having said it. But that is exactly what He did. In three days He rebuilt the bridge to salvation which is what the Temple of Jerusalem was supposed to be—the bridge of salvation for the Jews. Only He built this bridge for all humanity. Having done it

Himself, He has ensured our doing it for ourselves. He has made it possible for the Forces of Light to intervene on our sphere of existence whenever and wherever the forces of darkness are going too far and whenever and wherever we request His help.

PROTECTION FROM COSMIC EVIL

Protection from cosmic evil refers to the fraying of this passage through the astral plane. We are protected from cosmic evil because the Christ has done this act of salvation. The evil that we are not protected from is our own evil, our own creation on our own Earth's sphere. Thus, there is for us the opportunity to wage a fair and honest battle with the forces of darkness that we have attracted in our lives through our own lower selves. In the evil we have created is where the devil still interferes and this is where the Christ will not intervene, leaving us free choice so as to allow us to develop the full consciousness and the full desire to return to the Kingdom of God.

The prison that you have built for yourself and that we have described in an earlier chapter on evil is made out of all of these misguided intentions that adopt the line of least resistance. The whole system of approval seeking and of capitulating and of denying your innermost self creates this prison. The process of salvation is your breaking out of that prison the way a bird breaks out of its eggshell.

Just as the eggshell serves a purpose but soon becomes a prison, those things that you have sold out to have also become prisons. To the degree that they were not based on truth they must be given up, confronted, dissolved, destroyed. What we are talking about here is the world of glamour.

"WELL MEANING" PEOPLE

An example of a "well meaning" person is one who repeats by rote, without understanding it, something that was taught to him. Say, for instance, that an insightful teacher comes up with a truth which works and brings happiness. In order to recreate the initial happiness brought about by the newly discovered truth, the followers will repeat the words by rote. They mean well in that they would like this happiness to come back, and they think that will happen if they dutifully repeat the teacher. However, in doing so, they also manifest their unwillingness to go through the effort and frustration that the teacher himself had to experience in order to discover these truths. They are not really experiencing what needs to be undergone in order to arrive at that insight. They are cheating the process. Herem helps them by praising them for being good and Satan imprisons them by slowly decelerating them until they become ineffectual. At that point they can be used for evil purposes.

The world is full of examples illustrating this point. Take Christianity itself, for instance. The teachings of Christ were mouthed and made into platitudes for the service of those who wanted to milk humanity. Eventually, Christianity became the antithesis of what it was supposed to be, what with the Crusades, the campaigns against the Jews, slavery, and all of the other atrocities that we know so well. In a microcosmic form, this same process can be seen in an individual who may develop a talent for positive purposes but who then rests on his laurels, abusing his talents for negative ends.

Christ's sayings, His philosophy, and His life have been abundantly commented on elsewhere. Please read my *Commentary on the Gospel of Thomas*, and Alice Bailey's

From Bethlehem to Calvary.

THE POINT OF RELINQUISHING

The reaching of the point of outrage or the point of relinquishing, which leads you to the final challenge and destruction of those prisons that you have created for yourself, will get you to recognize the veracity of the story that I have just told you. Indeed, once you have reached the point of relinquishing, you will recognize in yourself the desire to do battle with the evil that exists within your own system, to vanquish it, and to finally create a bridge to God, and to do it immediately. This is salvation. This is the real meaning of the life of the Christ Who was carried on this Earth by the Master Jesus.

CHRIST'S BATTLE AGAINST THE FORCES OF DARKNESS

The weapons of war that we know on our Earth sphere are gross imitations of the weapons of war that exist on the higher spheres of development. The Forces of Light, through their purification, are much more immune to attack than are the forces of darkness who are much more decelerated, materialized, and, therefore, much more rigid and vulnerable to light, which is fire. The invention of the weapons of warfare on our Earth plane is directly inspired by weapons that exist on higher levels. If we are to think, for instance, of the great struggle known as World War II in our sphere, we will see how this operates: the forces of darkness, represented by the Axis Forces and Japan were, at first, technologically and militarily superior to the Forces of Light represented by the Allies. However, because of their own evil, they became less and less open to the necessary inspiration that would have resulted in their victory. Most of

Hitler's entourage, including Hitler himself, were heavily drugged and were increasingly addicted to substance abuse. They were decelerating and they were blocking themselves from the Universal Life Force and the Universal Consciousness. As a result, they made incredible mistakes, falling into virtually every trap that the Allies set for them.

By contrast, the Allies were open to the Universal Life Force and the Universal Consciousness, receiving guidance and scientific discoveries that made it possible for them to win. Even if one thinks that the Germans remained technologically superior all the way through, it is obvious that they bungled their superiority through judgment errors. For a while it was not guaranteed that the Forces of Light were going to win; it was touch and go. It is only because of a great resolution, dedication, and commitment from a large part of humanity that the Hierarchy was able to intervene on behalf of humankind and change the course of events in 1941-42.

Military intervention can be a very spiritual undertaking. In the light of the overt Axis aggression, the pacifists who called themselves spiritual were really cowards. They represented another aspect of the status quo. They were no better than the isolationists, who, under the banner of self-interest, were really acting out their cowardice and their selfishness, not to mention their shortsightedness and ignorance. The pacifists and the isolationists were colluding with the forces of darkness. It is equally true to say that later, the extreme liberals colluded with the Evil Empire of the Soviet Union by being blind to the obvious advantages of the West and its freedom. As the Tibetan said in his June 30, 1940 message to the pacifists: Who will fight your battles? Do you think that the Hierarchy is a bunch of guys who will intervene on your behalf, fight your battles, do your dirty work and make for you a good world that you have not made for yourself? If this is what you expect, you are very much mistaken; the reality is quite different. The truth of the matter is that pacifism as a euphemism for cowardice is worse than blatant aggressiveness. Evil in its receptive principle, in its pacifism and fear is double evil. It contains the aggression that it is trying to avoid on the outer level as well as the duplicity, pretense, and cowardice on the inner level.

Many were lost to the forces of darkness in World War II and in the great battle that Christ waged in the three days after His death. However, there is no death. Consciousness survives all; death is only temporary. Death is the death of a particular physical body. On the physical plane of existence the destruction of young men in battle can easily be remedied through reincarnation.

The real loss that takes a much longer time to remedy, a loss that brings much greater pain than death, is the loss of the spirit, the death of an idea, the death of consciousness, of the mental body. Had the forces of darkness won World War II, humanity would have been thrown backwards for thousands of years. Granted, in the last analysis, everybody is going to be saved. However, the whole idea of the Plan of Salvation is to accelerate this process by summoning the cooperation of each individual through his own purification of himself.

THE GREATER PLAN

Therefore, each time one of us challenges and breaks through a particular evil in our life we join the Christ in the greater plan. We aid the Forces of Light in the dissolution of evil in our sphere. We also make available to others our own experience, the particular way that we have fought our own individual battle, and, offering this example, make it possible for others to emulate us as we have all emulated the Christ.

Thus, following our task, following the call, is really participating in the Plan of Salvation. Every individual brings with him into incarnation aspects of himself needing purification. Each person creates a prison which is the sum total of all of his distortions. His task is to break through it and dissolve it. Each individual is essentially important in the great scheme of life, in the great Plan of Salvation. Salvation will be completed when everyone, including Lucifer and his brother Herem are saved.

REACHING THE KINGDOM OF GOD

Since Christ's days on Earth, resurrection and ascension have been achieved by many others. Those who reach the fifth initiation have successfully waged and won the battle against the forces of darkness in their own particular sphere, and have, therefore, been able to reach the Kingdom of God. The Count of Saint-Germain is one of them. Another is Babaji as he is known in the Hindu religion. He, too, is a Christ figure. We are told that Mohammed ascended upon his death. The process of ascending by means of a "chariot of fire" is merely the purification of our vehicles to the point where we can let go of them and make it to the other side. The process described in the Near-Death-Experiences as the long dark tunnel is a process of ascension. The long dark tunnel is merely the passage that Christ frayed for us through the astral plane; it would not be there if He had not come to Earth; it would be a path of obstacles, full of temptations, much greater, much more intricate, and much more insidious than the ones we know in our three-dimensional reality. It would be fraught with temptations that we had fallen prey to in existences that we have had before His appearance.

INNER EXPERIENCE

Again, all of this is very nice if you can experience it with your inner ear, your inner eye, your inner senses. There is no way that this story can be verified in three-dimensional reality or through the "scientific method." It is an inner experience revealed to us by our guides. It has to correspond to an actual life experience in order to gain veracity for you. You will find it and you will connect to it through the resolution and the dissolution of your own barriers to total happiness in your own life. Pursue happiness and you will find God.

THE DIFFERENCE BETWEEN JESUS AND THE CHRIST

The notion of the difference between Jesus and the Christ has been lost to the simplistic Christians. True Christians know the difference between the two. Indeed, the Christ is the spirit who incarnated in the personality who is Jesus. The soul in this entity was the task that we have just talked about. The Christ consciousness gradually made itself known to the Master Jesus who carried it within himself, just as your task will be made known to you as an individualized entity as you work on yourself and purify yourself.

Jesus is an entity who participated in the Luciferic rebellion but who developed. Jesus was an evolved entity. He still is. He is the master of the Sixth Ray. His responsibility is the transformation of religious beliefs as they are found in conventional religion. For all intents and purposes, it is under his directives that we are doing this catechism right here and now.

The reason Jesus was chosen was because he was part of a group of people who were undergoing a great deal of purification processes. John the Baptist, who preceded him and who prepared the way for him, was also part of that same family. The dispensation was given through people who were purified enough to accept it, at least for themselves.

The Christ is much more highly developed than is Jesus who carried Him. Our Higher Self is a lot more developed than our personality which houses it. So our Higher Self is to our personality what Christ is to Jesus. The Christ was never part of the Luciferic rebellion.

The Christ needed a vehicle for manifestation on Earth. Jesus provided Him with a vehicle—his personality, physical, mental, emotional bodies in which to manifest. The Christ could have made His own personality. However, it would have had an extraordinary amount of light. Besides, this was not part of the deal with the forces of darkness. The point was for the Christ to put Himself in the vehicle of someone who was born on Earth and to undergo all of the experiences that every one of us does. He was a rider in the car and, in the beginning, He was not the driver. Eventually, He blended with the driver and was able to instruct him. The driver became increasingly aware of who was there in the back seat. The fusion between the driver and the guy in the back seat gave us the World Saviour that Christ was when He walked the Earth.

For us, the guy in the back seat is the Higher Self and the guy in the front seat is the personality. The threefold personality has an ego function that drives, that takes directions, that listens or does not listen, that goes through demand and despair, and that increasingly allows himself to identify with the guy in the back seat.

The Christ has not reincarnated that we know of. But we are told that Master Jesus has incarnated several times.

According to the Tibetan, Mohammed was Master Jesus, reincarnated to close the cycle that started with the Buddha six hundred years before the Christ. So you have a symmetrical structure which started six hundred years before the Christ with Buddha and ended six hundred years after Christ with Mohammed giving out the dispensations of the Age of Pisces which was ruled by the Sixth Ray. We are told that the Master Jesus exists today in a Syrian body.

Is the Christ the only Son of God? No. He is the first son as the Second Ray is the first offspring of the interaction between the First and the Third Rays. He is followed by His younger brothers and sisters represented in the Rays by the Four Rays of Attribute. We are all sons of God. Lucifer himself is a son of God. So is Jupiter, so is Hercules, so is Babaji, so are you, and so am I. As sons of God, we potentially carry the capacity that the Christ carried within Him, i.e., we carry the Christ within us and we have as a goal the reaching of the states of evolution reached by the Christ Himself. He Himself said that we will achieve greater feats than He.

What does it mean that we carry the Christ within us? It means that we carry within us the potential of becoming at-one with God as He did. In our round, this is accomplished through the Ray of Love. Since He personifies love, at-oneing with God is at-oneing with Christ.

Was He born of the virgin Mary? The theme of the virgin birth occurs in many other religions. It is arrogant of the Christians to believe that it is theirs and theirs alone. It was integrated into the Christian religion by Paul and after Paul by those who wanted to make the Christian religion one that would closely resemble the pagan creeds that existed at the time. This made Christianity much more palatable and much more accessible. It made it a religion even easier to accept than the competing pagan creeds at the time. Thus, Christianity became the religion of the line of least resistance, more easily adopted than the others.

It is the dream of every man with limited consciousness, particularly in antiquity, to marry a virgin. Virginity ensured that a man's sexual insecurity would not be challenged in the marriage. Indeed, if the woman he married had not experienced pleasure with anybody else she would bond with him and be dependent on him and him alone on the sexual level. Out of this sense of personal insecurity in a patriarchal society came a universal desire for worshiping virgins. Here you have the cause of this belief traced back to the individual distortion that created it.

Every individual distortion becomes a glamour and spreads to embrace everybody else who has the same distortion and who does not want to give it up. Thus, the individual glamourization of a distortion allows the individual to omit facing it and removing it, and also makes it possible for him to collude with all of the other people who have the same distortion and who are as little interested as he is in removing it.

If Mary was a virgin when she gave birth to the Christ, did her hymen break when the Christ came out? In which case she stopped being a virgin. Or perhaps, I am misunderstanding the meaning of that word. *Furthermore, if she was a virgin when Christ was born, was she a virgin when Christ's brothers and sisters were born? Were they all born of virgin birth?* In which case they are all messiahs. However, they are not. *If Mary died a virgin, how then did she get to have all of these other children without having sex?* Good question.

THE IMMACULATE CONCEPTION

Conceiving is creating within oneself the conditions necessary to give birth. It is becoming pregnant with something, providing inner hospitality for a seed coming from our soul. This seed itself originally came from our spirit and from God.

The process of visualization, oft-mentioned in New Age and so-called New Age material, is a process of conception. The blueprints formulated in our minds eventually materialize, creating forms, situations, bodies, harm or good, pleasure or pain, depending on the degree of their alignment to the Universal Consciousness and the Universal Life Force.

As you read these words, you are becoming pregnant. You are right this moment pregnant with the thoughts, feelings, movies, music to which you have allowed yourself to be exposed during your entire life. Every single idea, note, remembrance, concept, picture, movie, conversation impregnates you. You have already conceived an embryo, the father of which is all of those stimuli.

This is a frightening thought if you focus on it. It instantly makes you question all of the elements to which you are exposing yourself right now. *To what will you give birth? What have you conceived as a result of the trash that you watched last night on TV, of the casual negativity that you have left unresolved in your psyche, of the gossip in which you have indulged, of the nonsense which you have read?*

If you will focus on the questions asked in the above paragraph, you will begin to realize the importance of re-examining all that you have learned. As you rethink what was taken in with your limited consciousness, you will begin to raise to consciousness that which has been assimilated without any consciousness.

Now you can start a brand new process of conception within yourself. You can choose to expose yourself to that which is positive, good, harmless, and conforming to Spiritual Law. You can utter the right words, you can grasp the right plans for your future, you can read, listen to, and watch the right material. The cumulative effect of this will accelerate your capacity for goodness.

Let's reflect on this and see what we can conclude:

1. **If you let yourself be impregnated by spirituality, you will become a continuous source of beautiful and permanent creation.** More specifically, the more you let yourself be impregnated by God's truth, love, personal responsibility—by Spiritual Law—the more you will create, with increasing facility, happy situations, beauty, pleasure, universes of goodness.

2. **The idea of immaculate conception finally becomes clear. It is letting yourself be impregnated by God, allowing God's energy and consciousness to impress you without darkening it or influencing it by your own distortions.** Thus, when creation occurs, it is immaculate, pure, unspoiled. The idea of immaculate conception thus acquires new meaning, an actual useful meaning, for all of us. In the act of creation we are all Marys. On the Path, we strive for the purity inside which will attract God's power—what we call our inspiration—to impregnate us, impress us. Allowing this power to impregnate us means conceiving new possibilities. This process is extended to the various levels of our being.

3. **On the mental level, we conceive through words and frameworks of knowledge.**

4. **On the emotional level, we long for the new creation; we visualize it with our feelings, we adorn it with beauty, we nourish it with our love.**

5. **On the physical level, we prepare the ground for its**

arrival. We clean the way by discarding the obsolete, or by liberating our previous creations which now have a life of their own.

6. **You can understand now why I put so much importance on keeping these teachings as pure as I have received them.** You see now why I resent the darkening of this material through watering it down by those and for those who are too cowardly to accept it in its pure form. It makes the truth into half-truth. And, as we have seen, half-truths are a lot more damaging than lies because they steer you in the wrong direction.

TRAVELS OF THE CHRIST

Why couldn't the Christ have traveled to India and learned from the great spiritual teachers who existed there the principles of meditation, purification, and transcendence of the body? He did. He not only learned from them, but in the process, taught them in India. He traveled not only to India but to many parts of the Roman Empire as well, learning and teaching. This explains the great gaps in His lifetime as found in the Bible.

Having achieved mastership He returned to Palestine to teach. He was a transformed person. However, what He had learned elsewhere was almost impossible for the primitive consciousness existing in Palestine at the time to comprehend. That is why He surrounded Himself with a few disciples and taught them mysteries that have disappeared. That is why He did not write. Writing would have set in perishable words ideas, states of mind that transcend human language.

CHRIST THE UNIVERSAL TEACHER

In this day and age when eastern spirituality is available

for us to investigate, there is no longer a need to see the life of Christ as a mystery. There is no longer a mystery to it. A lot of the healing feats that He achieved, His materialization and dematerialization, are all manifestations of mastership, a state achieved by so many in India. Let us stop the arrogance that makes the Christ the private possession of "Christendom." This type of thinking leads to bigotry and to the misery of the Crusades. If you want Christ to be universally accepted, open your mind and conceive of Him as a universal teacher indeed. If He came to save humanity, then internationalize Him and remove all of this narrow minded gobbledygook enshrined in old and musty texts. Do away with the canning, the packing, the commercializing, and the copyrighting of true Christianity.

COMMUNICATION WITH MASTERS

It matters little where these masters are, where they exist and so forth. What matters more is how we telepathically communicate with them on an inner level. When we allow our task to manifest through us by destroying the status quo, we tap into all of these masters. We become Jesus, we become the Christ in our particular way. We are a microcosm of the universe. Instead of trying to find these people by traveling to Tibet or wherever it is that they reside, it is a lot easier to find them within yourself here and now.

No matter what is your religion, you will find in it nuclei that will correspond to what we are saying here. Every single religion has had a positive start. You may want to remain in the religion that you are holding right now. However, have the decency and the integrity to tell the truth about yourself and about what you are discovering in yourself to those who call themselves leaders of your own group. If you do this, you will thus be accomplishing your task and bringing the Kingdom of God right here on Earth. You will, thus, participate in the Plan of Salvation.

CHAPTER 8
THE TRINITY

GOD THE FATHER, GOD THE MOTHER

There has been much talk about God the Father. As a reaction to this there has been much talk about God the Mother. The feminists and the New Agers are fond of saying, *"Why do you say 'He' about God? Why don't you say 'She'?"* This type of controversy and conflict only comes because people have projected their parents on God. So, God will, for some, represent a female deity and for some a male deity. God will be seen as a female deity at the times of the swing of the pendulum that favour the woman while at other times of the swing of the pendulum, God the Father, the male entity, will be favoured.

We at The Church of the Path® do not believe this way. We are not the first. Many preceding us, including the early Christians, believed in three aspects of deity. Even that—the Trinity—has been grossly misinterpreted by Christianity.

THE THREE ASPECTS OF GOD

There are three aspects to God: God the Father, God the Mother, and God the Son, just as in a sexual act, where the father penetrates the mother and the son is born. God is the personification of the three aspects together. Thus, He continuously creates. However, in order to understand His nature we need to understand the three aspects separately.

1. **God the Father** represents the aspect of the will, the

initiator. He impregnates, He penetrates, He initiates, He triggers, He starts things. And He destroys that which is no longer valid. He is the First Ray of Will or Power.

2. **God the Mother** is active intelligence and adaptability. She receives, She nurtures, She protects, She provides hospitality in Her midst for the gestation that is necessary for a new being to come into the world who will manifest a lot of what the combination of both She and the Father happen to be. She is the Third Ray of Active Intelligence and Adaptability.

3. **God the Son** is a result of the magnetic attraction and of the tension between Mother and Father. Love is really an in-between, a link, a channel, a bridge between the Father and the Mother, between the Will and the Adaptability. Christ, Who is a representative of the Second Ray, Who personifies the Second Ray for us, is a creation of God, and, therefore, a lesser entity than is God. He is an entity created by the process explained above. He is the Son but He is personified here on Earth for us by the Master Jesus who carried Him.

Having said this, I also say you do not have to believe it if you do not experience it. In order to experience it, consider in your own personal life that nothing is ever achieved unless it finds a balance between those three aspects—will, love and active intelligence. Think of an area of your life where you are experiencing unhappiness and dissatisfaction. You will find there an imbalance of these three aspects as you have chosen to manifest them there. This is then how you can personally experience the Trinity. Through the repeated personal experience of that Trinity with the process of transformation, the education of the soul, you gradually get to experience the true nature of God and the veracity of this Trinity.

THE HOLY GHOST COMES TO LIFE

Paul was a misogynist. That can be clearly seen in his gross antipathy for women in I Corinthians where he tells women that they had better stay home and be silent in churches. He also tells men that if they must then they should be married. But the most damaging portrayal of women is Paul's saying that women are to men what man is to Christ. In other words, there is a hierarchy that goes like this—Christ is superior to man and man is superior to woman and the distance between Christ and man is the same distance as between man and woman. This type of denigration of the woman resulted in the denial of the aspect of active intelligence and adaptability, calling it the Holy Ghost or the Holy Spirit rather than calling it Mother. It is time to restore Mother to Her rightful place next to Her husband, Father and give Her as much credit for the creation of the Son as we give Father.

The rejection of all of gnosticism in the first five centuries of Christianity is a direct result of this misogynism of Paul's. Gnosis is knowledge, wisdom, intelligence, and, therefore, represents the third aspect of deity, Mother. The Gnostics, with their unnecessarily complicated portrayal of the universe were very well aware of Mother, perhaps exaggerating Her position at the expense of Father. They, too, pushed it a little too far. They lost the battle with the Father advocates only because at that time civilization was undergoing a patriarchal phase. Nevertheless, it is time to restore the truth that is to be found in the kernel of the Gnostic belief system. Indeed, they believed not only in the Mother aspect of deity, but also in process, in growth, in transformation. Many of them believed in the divinity of sexuality and in the sanctity of life and of nature.

PERSONIFICATION OF THE RAYS

There are personifications of all of the Rays and each one is lesser than the principle itself. For example, in our sphere of development, the Mahachohan is the representative of the Third Ray. Under the Mahachohan are many other masters of the Third Ray, notably the Master R who was in his last incarnation the Count of Saint-Germain, also known as Count Rogozski. Under the First Ray we have the Manu. Each root race has a Manu who represents for that root race the initiator, the bringer of the new, the father. Under him are to be found many other masters. Master Morya was one. He was known as Thomas More and before that as Roger Moore.

Under the Second Ray we have the teachers, Master Koot Humi who taught Madame Blavatsky and Master Djwal Khul who taught Alice Bailey.

Every atom is a microcosmic system. Every person is a microcosm of the universe in which he lives. The only way to experience the cosmos is to refer to one's self, to proceed through one's own experiences as limited as they may be, particularly in the beginning. Teachings, religions, and everything else in life are there merely to encourage the individual to do this.

CHAPTER 9
THE GREAT MOTHER

Let us not forget that matriarchy preceded patriarchy and was probably a system that existed a lot longer than has patriarchy. With the incarnation of the Semites in the middle of the Atlantean period came the over-emphasis of patriarchy. The Judeo-Christian religions then pushed it to chauvinistic heights. It also existed in other religions as well. As a result of this huge emphasis on power, assertion, there was no balance; something was missing. In Christianity, for example, this imbalance is compensated for by the cult of the Virgin Mary called the Great Mother, the Great Matriarch. She then replaces in people's psyche Earth goddesses or other female goddesses that existed in the past.

The cult of the Virgin Mary is so strong and pervasive that in surprising numbers of cathedrals in Europe she occupies a preponderant place, over-shadowing Christ Himself, let alone God. Indeed, in the middle of the altar you find those magnificent statues of Mary ascending, a sexy Mary, beautifully draped and showing her thighs and her breasts with erect nipples. What a show! Consider also the cult of the Virgin in the Americas, particularly in Latin America. You find her everywhere, dressed in all kinds of garbs and holding all kinds of names, for example, the Virgin of Guadalupe. Consider the same phenomenon in Sicily, in Spain. There is endless evidence that shows the relentless return to matriarchal idolatry in the midst of Christianity, bringing back all the distortions that existed in primitive humanity. This is as far from Christianity as Christ could ever have thought possible.

As far as we are concerned, Ray Three is simply the Ray of Mother. We do not exactly know how Mary became pregnant. There is archival evidence that shows that Mary had an illegitimate association with a Roman soldier who is the natural father to the Christ. This is represented in the film "Jesus of Montreal." It would make sense if Joseph, an older and charitable man, took her as a wife, pregnant and all, to protect her. Jesus, then, was born not exactly knowing who his father was; he had to be given a father so they created the story of the virgin birth. The other children may very well have been Joseph's children. Somehow this makes a great deal of sense. Jesus was thus better able to disconnect from his parents in order to become the autonomous saviour he was.

The Ray of mother is in no way inferior to the Rays of father or son. Nor is the Ray of son inferior to the Rays of mother or father. The combination of the three is the harmonious concept of the universe. God combines the three. The One About Whom Naught May Be Said is the combination of the three. It is very difficult for us to conceive of an entity who would personify such greatness. However It truly exists and It manifests at different times in the life of humanity as a male or as a female depending on what is needed or what can be received at a particular time of dispensation.

In our days there are many more female spiritual leaders than there are male spiritual leaders. Alice Bailey brought in the teachings of the Tibetan. Before her, her teacher, Helena Petrovna Blavatsky, brought in the teachings of Master Koot

Hoomi, etc. This female influence toppled the existing male dominant spirituality, bringing with it all of its problems such as androgynous and controlling women, disconnection from aspects of responsibility and law and order, etc. It is merely a phase that we have to go through as the other phases have been gone through.

PATRIARCHAL AND MATRIARCHAL SYSTEMS

So, humanity finds itself fluctuating to and fro between patriarchal and matriarchal systems, false beliefs to which it adheres with fanaticism. This is particularly true of the belief in the superiority of patriarchy over matriarchy as expounded by Christianity and as followed with great degrees of fanaticism during the Dark Ages. Then came Renaissance, reviving the beauty of humanity, both male and female, and re-establishing a balance. Nevertheless, throughout Renaissance and well into the following centuries, the old hoof of Satan, represented by Christian bigotry and inequality, maintained its place. The philosophical dispensation of the eighteenth century destroyed this inequality in a very categorical and, at the same time, elegant manner—in true eighteenth century fashion. It set humanity on its way to rid itself once and for all of past misconceptions concerning inequality of the genders.

Today's bigoted trend, the attempt of returning to old time religion, will be very short-lived indeed. It is the last gasp of the old dispensation.

CHAPTER 10
THE HIERARCHY

The Hierarchy is an organization formed by superhumans, some of whom never incarnated on Earth and some who have but who have ascended to be masters. The departments of this organization are representatives of the Seven Rays. Thus, there are three major departments and four minor ones emanating from the third. At the head of each one of these departments is a master who dispenses to humanity that which it is ready to assimilate.

THE CENTER WHERE THE WILL OF GOD IS KNOWN
The Hierarchy itself receives its dispensation from Shamballa, "The Center where the Will of God is Known." The energy, information, will, etc. coming from Shamballa is received first by the Christ, the head of the Hierarchy. He "takes in," channels this energy, information, will, and then distributes to the other six members of the Hierarchy who themselves distribute it to humanity.

HIERARCHICAL INTERCESSION ON HUMANITY'S BEHALF
The Hierarchy intercedes on our behalf, receives this energy, digests it for us, and then makes it possible for us, in turn, to assimilate it. This is primarily their function in intercession. Humanity is incapable at this point of directly receiving the energies of Shamballa without the modification from the Hierarchy. The will of God must first be modified by

love before it is distributed to adaptability and active intelligence. Here you see in symbolic form the will of God, Shamballa, Ray One; the Hierarchy, Love, Ray Two; Humanity, adaptability, matter, Ray Three.

This can be clearly seen anytime there is a major dispensation coming through. For example, the eighteenth century philosophical dispensation was the Love/Wisdom Ray's preparation for the Will Ray's destruction brought about by the French Revolution. The state of corruption and decrepitude which existed in the "ancien regime" (which means the "old order") had to be destroyed. The enlightened eighteenth century philosophers brought about all of the necessary ideas that fundamentally contradicted the old order. In this way, humanity was prepared for what was about to come through love and wisdom.

Of course, some listened, but some did not. Still, the Hierarchy did everything it could to warn those who were not listening. The Count of Saint Germain, a member of the Hierarchy, made personal contact with the Queen of France. He also wrote in elegant rhymed verses the warning that there would soon be a tremendous cataclysm on the political level and that these people needed to protect themselves. They did not listen. They were beheaded. The sweeping changes brought about by the French Revolution eventually invaded the world. The nationalistic movements that are still being experienced in the late twentieth century are nothing else but the last leg of this momentous eradication of the old systems of absolute monarchy.

Some seemed to listen, Catherine the Great of Russia, as an example. She seemed to be very open to the revolutionary ideas that were given to her by Diderot when he lived in St. Petersburg and had daily contact with her. However, she was utterly disgusted and completely changed her ways when the revolution actually happened. Here we find again the difference between paying lip service to ideas and implementing them. It is easy to accept new ideas, but when it comes to putting them into practice, the men are separated from the boys, and most people revert to their bad old ways. This reminds us of the upper middle class liberals of our day who say they believe in racial integration, in peace, in sharing of wealth. However, when it comes to the implementation of it, they turn out to be highly hypocritical.

The energy from Shamballa contains all the other aspects of love and intelligence. However, it is so dynamic that it has to be modified before it goes any further. The best way to explain this is to compare it to a sunburn. The rays of the sun contain healing, beneficial effects without which life on Earth would disappear. However, without the "stepping down" function of the atmosphere, we would burn or die or develop disease. We cannot take exposure to the direct sun. That "sun" is identified by Will in our level of comprehension. But, it is not by any means confined to the principle of Will; it contains the other aspects as well.

Perhaps a better way to understand this is to say that we are not quite ready as yet to receive the full brunt and dynamism of the will of God. We are able to receive His intelligence and His adaptability. We are almost ready to receive His love; we will be entirely ready at the end of this round. Then, in the next round, we will finally be ready to assimilate the fullness of His will. Thus, humanity grows and returns to God from the lower rays to the higher ones.

All knowledge on Earth, all feelings, all thoughts have been inspired through the Hierarchy. Scientific discoveries are dispensed to humanity through the Fifth Ray; music, art and so forth through the Fourth Ray; faith through the Sixth

Ray, etc. The process of evil comes subsequent to this, takes the dispensation, and turns it to its negative purposes. This can only happen when the dispensation starts the process of descent and crystallization, the process of distortion and glamourization.

We can now understand, "He ascended into heaven and is seated on the right hand of the Father." The Christ, as the head of the Hierarchy, sits at the right hand of God. In other words, He is the first one to take in the directives, the commands, the wishes emitted by God. This again describes the process we just talked about. Shamballa emits a new impetus which is received by Christ Who sits at the right hand of God. This impetus, or force, or dispensation, is then transmitted to the Hierarchy for the purpose of educating and leading humanity in the next step of its development.

Are our prayers heard by God or are they taken up by other beings who intercede on our behalf? The first realm to respond to human wishes and longings is the realm of the Hierarchy. However, there is a lifeline from humanity directly to the will of God. Shamballa is directly aware of our needs, even though it responds indirectly, by going through the channel of the Hierarchy.

WILL VERSUS LOVE VERSUS INTELLIGENCE

This then presents the temptation to consider will as superior to love and intelligence. However, what is will without love and without intelligence? It is meaningless. Only in the context of love and intelligence can will have meaning.

Although will is more difficult to reach from the point of view of the evolutionary process, it cannot be superior to love or to active intelligence and adaptability. The three of them must be considered together on whatever plane of existence you happen to live.

CRISIS AND THE HIERARCHY

Is there crisis in the Hierarchy? Yes. However, the Hierarchy is developed enough to experience those crises on the mental level. They anticipate these crises and they deal with them as they occur. The close ties between the Hierarchy and humanity make it necessary for the Hierarchy to intervene in humanity's affairs once in a while. Let's take a few examples.

The Flood. "The Flood," as it is known in what are erroneously called the "Scriptures," is nothing else but a depiction of the destruction of Atlantis. A great battle occurred there between the Forces of Light and the forces of darkness. The forces of darkness were followed by those who were called the Sons of Belial; the Forces of Light were followed by the ones who were called the Sons of the Law of One.

Belial is a very negative entity sometimes associates with Satan, sometimes seen as the fallen son of God.[7] The Sons of Belial, in their primitive consciousness, chose to delay the effects of their negativities and addictions and to pay for them all in one lifetime. However, they continued delaying that lifetime and the addictions got greater and greater to the point where they gave no satisfaction, even as they were being acted out. Finally, it became impossible for all of the negativities to be paid in one lifetime. They had to be paid in several lifetimes. Eventually, when those lifetimes were

---

[7] What is the difference between Satan and Lucifer? Satan is the follower of Lucifer. Both Satan and Lucifer are represented on Earth by Prince Caligastia, the Prince of Darkness.

taken on, the disconnection from cause and effect was so great that it was impossible for these people to know why they were experiencing such great calamities and injustices. So, instead of taking one lifetime to pay, they got caught in evil for what seemed to be an infinite amount of time, thus being disconnected from goodness.

The Sons of the Law of One did not follow this type of lifestyle. However, since there was an overwhelming presence of evil and glamour, the Sons of the Law of One had to sacrifice the psychic abilities enjoyed by the Atlanteans. Psychism, having been abused as a tool for obtaining physical pleasure, had to go. Humanity had to learn the Law of Cause and Effect on the outer, material level. People had to rediscover the Law of Cause and Effect for themselves and by themselves in order to demonstrate that following the good path, here and now in a unified fashion, is a better way to go than to split yourself as the others had done, i.e., to split pleasure from duty.

The rift between the two sides created several conflicts which manifested on Earth. The first few conflicts resulted in the great earthquakes that split the Atlantean continent—called Poseidia at the time—into many islands. The final crisis—The Flood—which engulfed the entire civilized world, was created by the Hierarchy because it was losing the war on Earth. The Sons of Belial were far too numerous and too powerful. The only way out was to bring about the great crisis of The Flood—destruction by water. Destruction, but also baptism by water, because it was a way for humanity to surrender, to be drowned into the great waters of the Universal Life Force, and to reemerge into a new civilization, a new start again.

The great World War of the twentieth century. One can say that the entire twentieth century was devoted to waging a war on the forces of evil by the Hierarchy. If you have a broader sense of history you will see the twentieth century as divided into three great conflicts: World War I, World War II, and the Cold War. Actually, all of these are one great war against the forces of evil. Indeed, this can be easily proven if you look, for example, at the problems in Yugoslavia. They existed before the First World War. They reemerge at the end of the Cold War as unresolved problems always do until they get resolved.

HUMAN HIERARCHY AND ORDER

There is a most unfortunate misconception perpetrated by the Unitarian Church. According to them there is no hierarchy. Everybody is born equal and dies equal. No one is a superior to another. No one is a subordinate to another. Unfortunately, the New Age teachings have adopted this convenient system in their misguided rebelliousness against authority. The New Age, ushering in mother-receptive-adaptable energies, also revealed—for the purpose of purification—all the accumulated rebelliousness against patriarchy and the lawgivers. The excess rebelliousness created the total negation of the existence of the law and of order and hierarchy.

The argument above perpetrated by the Unitarian Church can be instantly destroyed by the following question: "If there is no hierarchy, can a young infant then disobey his father or mother impunitively?" I put this question to a class held at the Unitarian Church in Brownsville, Texas back in early 1986. All I had to do was to ask that question. Instantly, the class broke into two warring factions. All of their pacifistic egalitarianism was lost for the next violent but truthful thirty minutes.

The evil of denying hierarchical order under the banner

of Unitarianism or teamwork or what have you is the evil of the line of least resistance, the evil of sloth. It can only bring deceleration, degeneration, and eventually death. The denial of the necessity to have leadership leads to anarchy and chaos as it did during that meeting at the Unitarian Church. Do not be glamoured by this seductive concept. Have the humility to surrender to the leadership of those who know better than you. Choose your teachers as carefully as you possibly can.

Hierarchy is natural. All of nature is based on hierarchical progression. Nothing ever happens without hierarchical order. Hierarchy is natural law and, therefore, Spiritual Law.

In the state of the Absolute there may not be a hierarchy. But we are not there yet. Let's get there first and then find out. In the meantime, we have to learn step-by-step how to get there. This progression itself is a notion that demonstrates hierarchy—from easier to more difficult. You cannot learn nor can you acquire anything instantly or right off the bat. You have got to go into the process of developing it step-by-step. In that sense, there are people who are on a higher step than others. And it would be foolish, unjust, unrealistic not to recognize that fact.

RESPONSIBILITY AND PRIVILEGE

He who takes on greater responsibilities grows faster. In growing faster he is entitled to greater privileges. This is natural Spiritual Law. Both responsibility and privilege come together and must be recognized. The person who has reached a greater level of achievement or growth is entitled to greater respect and greater privileges. On the crassest possible level this motivates others to achieving more. On the higher levels, it ensures that guidance coming from above will be revealed to humanity.

Spiritual growth necessitates knowing how to be a follower and knowing how to be a leader. A good follower makes a good leader. When you accept your position as a follower you prepare the ground for the acceptance of your position as a leader. Not accepting your position as a follower and rebelling against leadership will make you reluctant to inhabit a role that heretofore you have attacked and denigrated. You thus create in yourself conditions that will preclude your wanting to embrace and accept in humility the roles of leadership for which you are preparing.

Everybody has a leader. Nixon used to say that he had two hundred million bosses. Everyone, no matter his position, has somebody above him or her, whether in the Hierarchy or in Shamballa. This is true of the entire creation all the way up to God. He is the only one who is His own boss, so to speak.

The Hierarchy has personnel on Earth. They consist of those people who can be trusted to dispense the material that they teach. They have been tested and are usually third initiates.

CHAPTER 11
OTHER KINGDOMS OF GOD

THE SEVEN FIRST SONS OF GOD

In many different dispensations, this is seen in different ways. Basically, those who are spoken of as archangels in the Old Testament are the First Sons of God. They are Christ, Michael, Gabriel, Raphael, Uriel, Lucifer, and Herem. The last two are the ones who fell. When Lucifer fell, as we will see later, he took with him his younger brother and many other lesser beings. Thus, many spirits fell, but many more did not fall. There are a lot more spirits who did not fall than spirits who did. Only a limited aspect of the universe, therefore, constitutes the Fall and has for task the return to God. The others are still involved in their worlds, creating ever increasingly beautiful and happy circumstances in their spheres.

KINGDOMS BELOW THE THRESHOLD OF HUMANITY

What characterizes the evolutionary process from one kingdom to the other is the ability to move and be autonomous. One can see this aspect progressing from the mineral state to the organic vegetable state. From the vegetable to the animal, another step is taken in the autonomy of the entity in question. Indeed, animals are able to move by themselves as opposed to plants which still have not been able to achieve mobility.

In the animal kingdom itself—the kingdom that is closest

to us—there are species that are more highly developed than others. Strangely enough, the ones that are most developed are not the primates. Indeed, according to the Theosophists, they represent degenerations of humanity, not necessarily evolution of species of the animal kingdom.

According to the Tibetan, the animal that is closest to man is the dog, a representative of the Second Ray. Other animals representing other Rays are: elephant for the First Ray, cat for the Third Ray, horse for the Sixth Ray (devotion). The attempt of the animal kingdom to follow and serve humanity can be compared to the attempt of humanity to follow and serve the superhuman kingdom, the Hierarchy. **It is the quality of service in the animal kingdom that qualifies them to pass over into the human kingdom.** This is effected after many thousands of incarnations of service.

In this context is man carnivorous? Is vegetarianism the way to go? Is it a sin to eat meat?

Those who try to instill a sense of false guilt in humanity for killing and eating animals had better remember that for millions of years animals have consistently, abundantly, and voraciously done the same to humans in much more cruel forms and for a much greater length of time. In terms of karma, the animal kingdom owes an enormous debt, still unpaid, to the humans. Those who call themselves spiritual because they do not want to crush a roach or kill a fly are fooling themselves. The destruction of unwanted members of the animal kingdom is part of the Plan.

Animals that come in for the purpose of feeding humanity do so willingly. They offer their bodies for the purpose of integration into a higher system of development. For those fanatics who advocate vegetarianism, may I remind them that Hitler was a vegetarian and a teetotaler, while Christ ate meat and drank wine. That should end all pretenses about linking vegetarianism to spirituality.

Now, it is true that as we purify ourselves, maybe at some point of our life in the material body we will arrive at a stage in which we will no longer want to feed ourselves from the lives of the animal kingdom. At that point, we will just want to feed ourselves on the offerings of the vegetable kingdom. However, forcing oneself to get to that state when one is not ready constitutes regression and not progress.

It is very destructive, indeed, to believe that by eating meat one takes on the karma of the animals that have produced it. Nothing could be further from the truth. On the contrary, by integrating them in our bodies we purify and elevate theirs.

DEVAS

They are spirit guides. Each kingdom has its own system of devas which help it. The entities called devas or angels are not bound to the same restrictions as the entities in the different kingdoms which they serve. For example, a deva serving the animal kingdom may very well serve the human kingdom later, and vice versa.

EXTRATERRESTRIAL LIFE

Of course it exists. Not only is there overwhelming evidence at this point, but the very fact that this evidence is being resisted is proof of the existence of these higher beings.

Why is it so difficult to conceive that in an infinite universe there can be infinite numbers of beings, some of whom have developed the ability to travel and visit us and experiment with us the way we experiment with animals? Only they are a lot kinder to us than we are to animals, being a lot more developed than we are.

The defense against believing that they exist comes from the very well known syndrome called fear of the unknown. We had rather deny the existence of something that we cannot explain. It is a lot safer that way. Besides, governments such as the United States, for instance, have wanted to give the impression that they are in total command and are completely aware of every object in their airspace. If they were not, how could they explain the hundreds of billions of dollars that they sink into defense every year? They are so defensive about what they receive that they have to justify it by going way over to the other side and arrogantly claiming total control and knowledge of anything that flies.

There is no question about the fact that the government of the United States itself, while hypocritically denying the existence of UFOs, is concealing massive amounts of information and evidence—physical evidence—of the existence of extraterrestrials. There is a widespread paranoia within the U.S. government and U.S. military which is intensely out to suppress any information on the subject of UFOs. It has gone so far that the suppressions have become ridiculous.

There is immense evidence to prove that the Earth is systematically, regularly visited by extraterrestrials. There is also evidence that proves that it has been this way since time immemorial. The earlier civilizations were much more open to this idea, perhaps because they were in communication with these beings. This is evidenced by a lot of astronaut-like figures to be found in South and Central American ruins, as well as the landing strips, airport type configurations, that can only be seen from the sky.

If there were more openness to the existence of these beings, it would make it a lot easier for them to finally reveal themselves and communicate with us. As long as we are terrified of them, they will not do it since we are out to harm them and, therefore, harm ourselves.

CHAPTER 12
THE FALL AND THE FORMATION OF EVIL

THE FALL

There are many ways of explaining the Fall. When humanity was in its infancy, it was necessary to explain it through the parable of Adam and Eve. Eve was first tempted by the serpent because she represents active intelligence and adaptability. She wanted to know; she wanted to experience what that "forbidden" fruit was like. When she did, she influenced Adam and they both fell.

This is totally unsatisfactory as far as we are concerned in this age. So, let's try to use a more current, contemporary example. Perhaps the most destructive of all evil today is substance abuse. The taking of drugs can, therefore, be compared to Eve's eating of the Tree of Knowledge. The person who is about to take drugs knows that it is dangerous, knows that it is a violation of goodness, of the laws of God. Nevertheless, he is tempted to try. His Instinct of Enquiry coupled with his limited consciousness builds up an irresistible desire to try the drug. This thirst for experience with limited consciousness can best be compared to an infant reaching for the beautiful flame and burning himself. He must experience what it is like in order to conclude, finally, that it hurts.

No matter how much is said to the young person with limited consciousness that taking drugs will change him, will alter him, and will make him want to do more, weakening him further, there comes a point when he goes ahead and tries it. Trying the drug is giving in to the line of least resistance. It is the premature stealing of pleasure without creating it for himself. It is, therefore, a violation of the laws of nature. Once a person has tasted the pleasure that comes from this line of least resistance—indulgence—the experience itself imprints on his soul substance, on every cell of his body, the conclusion that he does not have to exert himself in order to experience pleasure, that he can take it vicariously, outside of the laws of God. This imprint is so strong that it starts undermining the natural desire for effort. **The stealing of pleasure without earning it, i.e., outside of the following of the law, accelerates the violation of the law. With the breaking of the law comes deceleration of energy. That is the Fall, the descent from the spirit world into the world of matter.**

What has been described here took millions of years to occur. It did not happen in one blow, in one act, as is erroneously depicted in the Bible with Adam and Eve. It was a slow process of disintegration initiated by Satan. He took with him his brother Herem and created the world of darkness, the anti-world, the world of evil.

Pleasure through substance abuse or through the Tree of Knowledge is under your control. You control the abuse. You control the substance. Yet, it gives you a pleasure that is reminiscent of the pleasure that you receive when you are at-one with the Universal Life Force—that involuntary pleasure in which you can float. The difference is that you control substance, but the Universal Life Force controls you. You have to surrender to the Universal Life Force. You have to conform to Laws of the universe in order to experience the Universal Life Force. By contrast, you do not have to do any of this in order to experience the pleasure, albeit limited, that comes from drug abuse. You are in control. However, soon it will control you in the worst possible way. You have attributed to it powers that belong to God. Eventually it takes your life over and you become its slave.

Slavery to substance leads to the deeper evils such as cruelty, murder, theft—all of the horrendous crimes that an addict is capable of. Having understood this with substance, we can generalize and say that any thing, principle, institution, symbol can become an agent for the line of least resistance and propel us to fall.

For example, worshiping of money, worshiping of material success, worshiping of power, worshiping of the need to be loved, to be approved of, these all can bring us down. The displacement of our longing from God, the infinite, onto the finite, therefore, is the fundamental characteristic of the Fall, whether we consider it from a personal point of view or from a civilization point of view. The incentive to rely on the relative to do the work of the Absolute is the belief that it will bring us instant gratification. What it brings us is partial gratification, albeit sooner than if we were to respect the laws of God. It does not bring us total gratification which is what we are looking for in the first place. So we remain frustrated and, therefore, perpetually addicted.

ABUSE OF POWER

What is the substance that these beings were attracted to? How could it have existed before the Fall? The original substance that they got addicted to was their own powers. Freedom comes with responsibility. So does power. If you are given a certain talent or a particular strength or a weapon, you have a responsibility as to how you use it. I can own a gun for my own protection, or I can use it to go rob the local grocery store. The temptation is, of course, to use the gun to rob the grocery store, take the money and not have to do my work, which then creates my laziness and justifies the desire to rob the grocery store. Once I have robbed for the first time, the enjoyment of the money justifies my desire not to work. I created this desire in the first place so as to validate my wish to rob the grocery store.

Each being was created with specific powers. These powers came with instructions on how to use them in a harmless, creative way. The temptation was to violate these instructions and abuse the power.

Why did some spirits want to abuse their power? Take it from the point of view of pride or conceit, for example. Let's say that you are proficient in a particular area of your life. As long as you do it for its own sake, everything is fine. You create in it, you get a lot of enjoyment out of it, and you respect the laws of God. However, when you discover (consciousness, knowledge, the Tree of Knowledge) that you can get others to admire you because of it, follow you because of it, love you because of it, serve you because of it, then you will want to use this power—abuse it—to obtain all of these other elements prematurely. This is the same process with which Lucifer, the angel of light, dazzled his brother Herem and many other entities who were lesser than he. He took over and created a world of his own.

ASTRAL HOME OF THE DEVIL

Why is the devil said to exist on the astral level? The angels fell before the creation of the material world. The physical world was created as a place where both the fallen spirits and those who had not fallen, who are still free of falling, could manifest. The astral level precedes the material level. The astral level is the level of emotions. From his home on the astral level the devil and his forces of darkness can influence the physical level which is a place where both the negative and the positive manifest and which is lower than the place where he resides. His influence is not limited to the physical realm. There are realms that are even more decelerated than the physical and which cannot be perceived by those who are bound in matter, as in our case. An example of these decelerated levels is a black hole.

So the astral level is not in itself negative. It simply happens to be where evil resides. You can verify the truth of this by considering the fact that on the mental level and on the physical level you can much more easily than on the emotional establish and understand the Law of Cause and Effect. It is in your emotions that you get all confused and that the devil resides. **The emotional level is, therefore, the level where most of the purification work is to be done for most individuals.**

GLAMOURS

Here we are getting into the creation of glamours. Glamours are created by the overemphasis of our gifts for our own personal aggrandizement, or for other negative intents. As much as glamours are an overemphasis of one of our powers or one of our gifts, they also occur as a result of a lessening of commitment to that gift and an increasing commitment to negative intents.

We can, therefore, see that evil was created by the overemphasis of the positive. Here an interesting warning must be given to the positive thinkers. What they are enhancing is not at all the Higher Self but the mask. There will be more on this double negative later.

TEMPTATION

Why were the spirits tempted? Jealousy. Lucifer was jealous of the greater power of his brothers and of the Christ. He was also jealous of his Father and of the fact that He had infinite powers. Wanting to imitate Him, Lucifer created his own world where he was lord and master.

Is everyone less than God tempted? Not necessarily. There are some that understand this pitfall and respect it and are able to surrender it and say, "God, You are mightier than I am, and I want to join You in accordance with Your laws." However, others do not have the necessary fortitude to do this. They are the ones who fell, which is the only way that they could understand the evil of their ways.

How can a child understand that the beautiful flame burns? There is a difference between being tempted and acting it out. One feels tempted first. As a result of this feeling, one acts out on the physical level. The child feels a desire to touch the beautiful flame. He experiences his temptation to reach out and touch it. Then he chooses to act it out by actually touching it, and getting hurt. The temptation starts even earlier, with the thought—the thought that perhaps violation of the laws of God will lead me more quickly to ecstasy than would the laws of God.

On the Path we seek the process of deciding to feel tempted. We do not consider ourselves the victims of the temptation. The choice of being tempted is, in itself, a form of fall. How far are you going to fall? How far is anybody going to fall?

THE LOWER SELF AND THE GLAMOURS

The creation of glamours is an attempt at by-passing the process, the order of nature. It comes, as we just explained, as a response to "what if we did not respect process?" In order for the world of glamour to survive, process must, therefore, be seen as painful. Since it must be seen as painful, it becomes painful.

Meanwhile, the Universal Life Force continues to be poured into the system gone awry. When it hits the wall of glamour it bounces off it and turns around in the opposite direction. This means that the energy of love becomes fear, hatred, jealousy, meanness, duplicity. Thus is created the lower self.

Another way to explain this is to see the lower self having been created first as the product of the limited consciousness' jealousy of God and of others on whom were bestowed higher powers. The decision to go at it on their own disconnected them from the source and created then the limited universe, wherein cruelty, jealousy, meanness, fear, sado-masochism are practiced. In order to cover this up, a pseudo-goodness is created over it as a pretense that the negativity does not exist. This world of pseudo-goodness and glamour is by definition deceptive. At least the world of the lower self is more open and honest in its negativity. This is where we encounter Christ's preference of dealing with admitted criminals and prostitutes than with the pretentious "yuppie" Pharisees who worshiped money but pretended to worship God, i.e., who worshiped themselves while pretending to worship God.

THE LOWER SELF AND THE MASK

So we have two departments in the world of evil. (1) The lower self, the admitted negativity wherein is to be found cruelty, hostility, murder, fear, etc. (2) The world of the mask in which we find all the glamours, all the pretenses, all the false goodness, the false life.

People caught in the world of the mask vehemently deny

the existence of their lower self. However, they need their lower self in order to justify the existence of the mask. For example, the good old yuppie successful citizen may appear to be good, but deep down he believes that it is only through greed, through cruelty, and through cutting the other person's throat before his is cut that he will succeed. So he lives, practicing cruelty and in a constant state of fear. The equilibrium in which he dwells on the outer level is false.

THE DUALITY OF EVIL

Conversely, people who are admittedly negative have an extraordinarily strong abhorrence of the mask. Indeed, prostitutes, thieves, murders have a great contempt for the establishmentarian society which, of course, they help create. **This, then, is the nature of evil; it is a product of continuous dualities. It forever splits itself.** Within the lower self there is a continuous duality of fear versus cruelty, cruelty versus fear, demand versus despair, one opposite hating and creating the other at the same time. On the other hand, there is another duality, that of the lower self versus the mask—forced goodness, affected conscious versus "badness." This system perpetuates the creation of negativity. For example, if a healthy sexual current is emitted by the Higher Self, it will be immediately judged by the mask, the glamour and, therefore, will become a sexual distortion. If a desire for abundance is genuinely emitted by the Higher Self it will hit the world of glamour and become greed, etc.

DEPARTMENTALIZATION OF EVIL

Just as exists in the world of goodness, the world of negativity, evil, is departmentalized. Lucifer has delegated the world of the mask, the world of materialism, and of glamour to his brother, Herem. This is a very convenient division because well-meaning entities with yet a limited consciousness can first be seduced by the world of Herem, the world of glamour, the world of the yuppie, the world of approval, the world of the establishment.

They are numbed and seduced into that world, believing it to be the world of God. They are attracted to churches and institutions in which a too-easy religion or belief system is taught them. They are exhorted to mouth pious platitudes and to force themselves to believe in a Saviour who is going to do it all for them.

They are, therefore, gradually convinced that they are indeed powerless, leaving the power to others. Eventually, through that powerlessness, and before they know it, the hoof of Satan is upon them, and they find themselves committing acts or submitting to acts which are outrightly evil—acts of theft, acts of sexual acting out, acts of cruelty, even those acts that are very often justified under the banner of "God." All fanaticism occurs in this particular way, through (1) the seduction of Herem, and (2) the grip of Lucifer. We can speak here about the Crusades of the Middle Ages or the stupidity of creationism in the twentieth century. In the twentieth century, we can talk about the medieval cruelty coming these days from the Arab world with its continuous and senseless jihads. We can certainly talk about the materialism of communism. The disconnection of communism from God is once again a deliberate creation of evil; the communists thought they could control the universe by just regulating it from the top. This is Lucifer's plan, aided and abetted by his brother Herem. It is also the plan of the Catholic Church whose conflict and unholy alliances with communism are very well known.

Thus, the present danger to humanity is unclear. It is the danger of being seduced through meaning well, through the pursuit of that which has been learned without having been digested, assimilated, thought of; of the blind following for the sake of approval; of institutions who are in power and who rob the individual of his own initiative. The road to hell is paved with good intentions.

INTERVENTION BY THE FORCES OF LIGHT

The process of imprisonment of souls practiced by these evil entities, who are also as personalized as are God and Christ, is so insidious and destructive that once in a while the Forces of Light intervene with violence. Destruction of the world through the Flood in the last days of Atlantis constituted such a crisis. Indeed, the Forces of Light are conscious of the fact that loss of life and loss of that which is material is easily replaced. By contrast, the loss of consciousness, the loss of the souls, the misdirections of the souls is infinitely more dangerous and harmful, propelling people into thousands of years of misery.

The great world war struggle of the twentieth century which constitutes a victory for the Forces of Light may very well have precluded the necessity for the destruction by fire that could have happened to our world. This destruction by fire would be the present-day equivalent to the destruction by water that came several thousand years ago. One can see here humanity going through the first two initiations—birth by water and baptism by fire.

We are not out of the woods yet. Indeed, there is a huge discrepancy between the development of our mind, and with it the scientific development of humanity, and the development of the soul, of ethics, of spirituality. This imbalance necessitates our accelerating our spiritual process so as to catch up—spiritually and emotionally—with the scientific progress that we have already achieved. If we do not, the imbalance will be so great that a crisis will have to come and destroy what we have achieved on the scientific level. For example, mankind's great abuses of nature will present humanity with a huge bill. A very large deficit is being created that one day must be paid. If it cannot be paid, there is going to be bankruptcy. We cannot go on deforesting the Earth without any consequences. In this blind pursuit of materialism are to be found the hand of Herem and the hoof of Satan.

EVIL'S WORLDS OF DARKNESS

Just as God has created worlds of goodness, happiness, joy, etc., evil has created worlds of darkness. There are many of them. However, they can be divided as follows:

1. **A world of sheer cruelty.** The lower self is rampant. Humanity was caught in that world early in its history, when the mask was not as yet formed.

2. **A world of materialism.** This is a gray world that is represented on our Earth's sphere by the great city centers and industrial centers where there is no green, no life, no trees, no plants, and where individuals are reduced to working automatons with virtually no enjoyment at all. Humanity is caught in some ways in this world as well.

3. **A world of confusion.** Here things do not make sense, cause and effect are not established, and it is easy to seduce people away from the laws of God. Humanity is entering upon the task of dealing with this third and "higher" level of evil. Indeed, the disinformation of communism perpetrated through technological advances is one of the dangerous manifestations of this type of evil. Disinformation is practiced not only by the communists but by organized

religion. This, of course, is not to mention the notoriously dishonest politicians and the greedy and misleading corporations.

An extraordinarily brazen example of this is the tobacco industry claiming in Congressional hearings that tobacco is not addictive. One of the main consequences of this outrageous, self-assured statement is that it tricks people into saying to themselves, "If it is said that way, maybe it is true." The truth can be very difficult to explain in human terms anyway. In the face of such blatant assertions of lies, the truth may appear weak and unconvincing, thus throwing people into evil. The result, of course, is deceleration of energy to the point of paralysis. A case in point is the Congress of the United States. Another case in point was the Soviet Union whose beginning seemed promising. Everybody thought they were going to conquer the world, that they were going to produce a lot more than anybody else. Seventy plus years later the USSR came to a grinding halt and disintegrated from within.

On the Earth's sphere there are different levels of evil. There are places on Earth that distinctly represent the Higher Self. Within them there is a greater amount of trust between the inhabitants, and, therefore, greater abundance, as in the Western world, for example. In other spheres there is extraordinary confusion, as in the countries that are still embracing communism, and, therefore, mistrust. In other areas we find the world of grayness and materialism. And yet, in other areas, particularly in what is called the Third World, or the developing world, we find abject and rampant cruelty and meanness, primitiveness and slavery. These then represent the different spheres of evil permeating and interpenetrating our reality.

On a microcosmic level, each individual lives in different

spheres. Spheres of his Higher Self interact, are permeated, and are interpenetrated by spheres of his lower self. And he switches from one to the other depending on circumstances, on his state of mind, on the thoughts and feelings and acts of his life.

Salvation constitutes the process whereby through the laws of God one chooses first to identify then dissolve the dark spheres or to disengage from them, to stop attracting them, and to be attracted by higher ones.

USEFUL PURPOSE OF THE MASK

We are now going to contradict ourselves. As negative as the mask is, it has served a useful purpose. For a time it allowed humanity to put its evil on hold; it softened mankind's outright cruel negativity. Acting as if they were good brought in some goodness. At least humanity was able to experience, albeit kicking and screaming, the laws of God and the fact that they work. (It is a good idea once in a while to act as if you know, with your intellect and will, and get yourself to respect that which you know is the law of God.) This was then the good purpose of the mask which needed to be practiced, particularly during the Age of Pisces.

During the Piscean age spirituality was to be found through the removal of oneself from three-dimensional reality. Nowadays, for the first time in the history of humanity, we can penetrate matter with spirituality, which is what was intended in the first place. The mask is, therefore, entering into obsolescence. However, for children, limits still need to be given. These limits may appear to be the mask but actually they are not, they are guidance. Later, when they become adults, they have the power to do whatever they please and perhaps even choose the negative for a while, which many of them do at adolescence.

THE INFERIOR FUNCTION

In order to understand the Fall of the Angels, one has to experience it as an inner reality. The Fall is a consequence of the gift of free choice given to the spirits created by God. When we make wrong choices we fall. Let us refer back to the process of the creation of the mask. We have: (1) Part of us that seeks approval, success in the conventional way, love, and the assimilation and accumulation of knowledge that is never questioned, and (2) Our inner-most self, the deep, natural, and spontaneous soul movements that are denied and denigrated.

It is the denigration and the denial of this deep inner-most self that makes it fall and become, as Jung called it, the inferior function. It becomes inferior just because it is forgotten and, therefore, falls into oblivion; it is never given a chance to develop.

Not only does it fall but the "dominant" part of us, the part that seems to be "evolved" also has to some extent taken the wrong route. Why does it progress, albeit partially? Because to some extent it does conform and adhere to Spiritual Law. For example, if I study hard and I discipline myself I will obtain success and approval. Of course, if I do so while disengaging from my nature, I will burn out fast. Nevertheless, in the meantime, temporarily I will achieve. My success, however, is the enemy of my inner-most self. It is obtained in contradistinction to, in opposition to my inner-most self. Thus, it is condemned to a short life and to a painful death. I myself will want to put it to death inasmuch as it contradicts who I really am inside of myself.

SELLOUT

The process of selling out to what is demanded of me and what I demand of others is a very slow one, imperceptibly slow. So was the fall of the angels imperceptibly slow. The Beings of Light did not make just one wrong decision, but many of them, millions of them, millions of little wrong decisions that accelerated their fall and enslaved them in the same ways that we have become enslaved to our way of life, to the requirements that we believe we cannot live without, and so on.

To illustrate again the slavery that I am speaking about, imagine a woman saying that she cannot live without her fur coat. Imagine another one saying that she cannot live without ten fur coats. Can you live without a fur coat? If you find yourself sarcastically reacting to this example, beware of judgment. There are a lot of things that you "cannot" live without. There are a lot of pet ideas, pet peeves that you have decided to keep the way this woman holds on to her fur coat. All of those you do not really need. All of those constitute false needs, acquired through the process of sellout and approval seeking, of capitulation. All of this leads to deceleration.

Granted you had to do this as a child. **The "original sin" is having to rely on parents and, therefore, assimilate and absorb a lot of their distortions. However, as an adult there is no reason why you should continue to do so.** It is high time for you to rethink all of these ideas and finally come up with your own, or at least make a serious attempt at finding your own. Instead, what you do is to fanatically hold on to the old world or to the world of approval or to your glamours, thereby perpetuating the process of falling and regressing.

If you understand this process on an individual level, you

will understand why the Beings of Light abused their choice and fell as you did. You will also understand why they want you to continue to fall, so as to own you. Think, for instance, of the way you feel about your children, or the way your parents feel about you. They want you to continue to be their little boy, to continue to sell out to them and do as they decided you should do and not as your soul is urging you to do. This imprisonment by parental authority or society or the material world is evil. It is the personification of evil and it leads to continuous and perpetual regression.

Why doesn't God intervene and eliminate evil? Why did God allow evil to be created? The deep experiential and individual understanding of the process that I just described makes this question totally irrelevant. In the first place, God did not create evil. He did not urge you to capitulate, conform. In fact, every lifetime, every day, every moment He gives you new energy, new opportunities to break the mold, to break your eggshell and finally burst out in the open with your own task as revolutionary, as innovative, as explosive as it could or should be.

The imprisonment of souls by the forces of darkness is similar to the imprisonment of children by parents, adult children as well. Here again the voluntary aspect of this process has to be taken into consideration. If you are an adult you do not have to sell out to your parents, to your parents' values anymore; you do not have to sell out to what seems to be required of you by the universe. But you choose to do so out of expedience. In that choice you are being dishonest, you are betraying the task that God gave you. Then you have the audacity to want to find God through your dishonesty. It is an impossibility! All you will find is the devil, and you will be thoroughly disappointed, and you will become an atheist. At that point you have entered the Path because you have started to doubt the false values that exist inside of you. The point is to accelerate this process. You can do it with a minimum of damage instead of waiting for the crisis to come and destroy it for you.

FROM NUMBNESS TO PAIN TO LONGING FOR A BETTER STATE

Back to the Fall of the Angels. So the two fallen spirits, Satan and Herem, imprisoned the souls of others who fell with them through that same sellout process explained above. Again, I urge you to experience this personally rather than think of it as an outer level event that somebody else does in some far away universe that has nothing to do with you. On the contrary, this is a process that you go through every lifetime.

In the beginning of this imprisonment there was total darkness and numbness. These spirits were living completely in the shadow of evil. Little by little very few of them started to experience pain. They did not know what that pain was all about, yet it was there. And as much as they wanted to deny that pain, it still persisted. Soon, the reason for the existence of this pain became clearer, it was a longing for a better state. There was pain because the present state was unacceptable and because they had started to recover the memory of a better state.

This was done volitionally, they chose to experience that pain, and they chose, therefore, to gradually question this state of darkness and numbness wherein they found themselves.

As more and more of the fallen spirits experienced the longing for something better, their combined desire created a response from the Forces of Light. Indeed, the Forces of Light will respond to your desire for betterment. But they will intervene only if you call on them. By contrast, the forces of darkness will not wait for you to call on them. They will try to attack and own you as best they can in any way they can, attaching themselves to any part of you that invites them. All of this happened in the spirit world. The present material world in which we live had not as yet been created.

It is the longing for greater consciousness that created homo sapiens (knowing man, the man who knows) who is now vertical, who has now emerged from crawling on the Earth to standing erect and thus closer to the more subtle elements of the universe, defying gravity by completely mastering it—walking on two feet, narrow ones at that.

The longing for God made it possible for man to emerge as the being that he is. It made it possible for God to send gradual teachings, emissaries, dispensations that facilitate man's growth from the ground up.

CREATION OF THE MATERIAL WORLD

The creation of the material world was effected as an arena in which these fallen spirits could actually experience on the outer level what they had created with their thoughts, feelings, and actions. Thus, the material world was made both by the fallen spirits who needed that arena and by the Forces of Light who wanted to provide them one. This is why our material world is a world of struggle, of duality, a world where there is cohabitation of light and darkness, sometimes so intricately interwoven that it is difficult to tell one from the other. We keep switching from a state in which we seem to be influenced by light, by our Higher Self, to a state in which we are influenced by our darkness, our lower self. What we do in both these states astonishes us. We seem to be surpassing ourselves in the goodness of our creation, and we seem to be surpassing ourselves in the outrageous negativities that we commit. This is because we are channels of forces that are called by us—called by us when we are in light or when we are in darkness—reinforcing those trends in us and propelling us into greater acceleration or deceleration than we seem to be capable of by ourselves.

The creation of the material world and the infusion of it with life corresponds to the millions of years of creation very well known by the archaeologists, the anthropologists, the geologists, and the astrophysicists. The fact that it took millions of years for the world to be created, for life to appear on Earth and finally for humanity to make its emergence must not be forgotten. The limited interpretation of creation as found in what is erroneously called the Scriptures was meant for beings who were a lot less developed than we are. They needed a simple explanation of the universe. They could not possibly fathom the millions and millions of years and the gradual process that we are able to understand today.

Nevertheless, scientific discovery does not contradict spiritual reality. As you can see, it affirms it. It took millions of years for the angels to fall, it took another set of millions of years for life to be created on Earth in order for them to have an arena to make the choices again between good and evil and to find themselves back to God. Consequently, it took a great deal of time from the creation of Earth and life on Earth to the emergence through gradual evolution of the human being—from mineral to vegetable to animal to human.

Only when people arrest themselves with limited concepts such as God creating man in one day, do they have to contradict the discoveries of science. If one has enough of an open mind to see the necessity to explain things to children through parables, one will accept that parables were necessary thousands of years ago. They are not necessary today. One will then accept evolution as a very spiritual process indeed, not at all contradictory with the existence of God, with the fall of the angels, with the existence of a Saviour, the Son aspect of God.

ORIGINAL SIN

If Satan and Herem imprisoned the souls that fell with them, what is their the responsibility to these souls that followed them? Their responsibility is similar to a parent's responsibility towards his children. Having been created with much greater awareness than the other souls, they have greater responsibility towards them. Consider the seductive process from parents to children. Consider the consequent imprisonment that the child feels by his decision to agree and conform with what is expected of him. Granted, the child is too young to realize that he can choose differently. However, a good case can be made that in human existence "he has no choice," so to speak at that age. What else can he do when he needs the parents to clothe him, to feed him, to teach him, to guide him?

Here we come to the true meaning of the **original sin**. As children we had to rely on parents. By osmosis—through merely being present next to them—we absorbed their distortions. Later, through emulation, we continued to impress our soul substance with those distortions. This is the original sin inasmuch as young individuals we instilled a regressive mechanism in our souls by absorbing those distortions, by capitulating to their demands, by assimilating beliefs that we did not understand and in which we did not want to believe. Granted, as children we had no choice, but we did it nonetheless.

PERSONAL RESPONSIBILITY FOR FALLING

If Satan and Herem imprisoned the souls and made them fall with them, haven't these souls any responsibility concerning this fall? Now, the child is not a victim inasmuch as he is in that situation because of countless incarnations during which he has chosen to sell out. This goes back millions and millions of years to when he started first the process of selling out to Lucifer and Herem. Remember the imperceptible sellout that I explained earlier, wherein we find ourselves slowly betraying ourselves to the point that we now do it deliberately, and we have created a situation in which our livelihood, our reason for being, is supported by a need to sell out.

So, yes, the children have a responsibility in that sellout in choosing their parents as well. But isn't the parents' responsibility much much greater than the child's in their seduction and their corruption of their children?

You may not have had a choice in childhood to sell out, but you certainly have a choice now to no longer do so and finally to liberate yourself of the shackles that you have chosen to hold on to for so long. This is the purpose of the creation of this Earth, i.e., the exercise of choice, the cultivation of adulthood, ever increasing responsibility.

The prince of darkness is prince because he was originally put in charge of the group of souls constituting humanity. He grew impatient, wanting to accelerate the process of growth quicker than nature would allow. So he rebelled, thus seceding from the rest of the Hierarchy and creating his own little empire. Can you find within yourself this same desire to learn, i.e., steal, God's fire and light and then create your empire around you by subjugating other people to your power? This type of empire building and of submissiveness to empire builders can be found in every individual, in every organization, in every country, and in every phase of history.

CREATING YOUR FUTURE

The number of spirits that fell is finite. The number of spirits that did not fall is infinitely greater. These are the spirits that continue to create ever increasingly beautiful, pleasurable, wonderful new worlds. There is an infinite number of worlds created by these beings. Conversely, there is a finite number of worlds created by the forces of darkness. Each one of us creates his world. As you are reading this and as I am writing, you and I are creating our future. **Our future is the direct result of what we think, feel, and do right here and now.** It is our choice to think, feel, and do this way. Therefore, the world that we will find ourselves inhabiting in the future has been our choice to create. Let's remember that when we find ourselves in situations that we do not like. *How many times have we had negative thoughts, feelings that we chose not to correct? How many times have we acted negatively without giving it another thought?* Every one of these things has an effect, forever creating new worlds in the future. To the degree we choose to divest ourselves of falsehood, to that degree we will create new and wonderful worlds. Then we will find ourselves back where we were before we fell, alongside all the other spirits who are creating such magnificence in an infinite manner.

The world in which you live right now is a consequence of thoughts, feelings, and actions that you have had in the past. You now live in the house that you built in the past. By not challenging some of the falsehoods under which you live, you perpetuate the negativities that exist in your house right now. By contrast, if you do challenge the negativities of the past, if you do divest yourself of the unnecessary shackles of approval seeking and sellout you may destroy the house in which you live. You may temporarily find yourself naked and homeless. But that nakedness and that longing attracts to you greater light than ever before and, therefore, builds for you a much brighter future than you could ever imagine. The trick is to risk the temporary nakedness and insecurity that is occasioned by the destruction of gray, old, and familiar compromises.

OTHER WORLDS

There are many many other worlds such as this one where this process is going on. We ourselves live simultaneously in different worlds. We have glimpses of this when in dreams or in a semiconscious state we seem all of a sudden to remember and reinhabit places that we forget about in our "awake" state, but which seem to go on with their own lives while we go on in our "awake" state in this three-dimensional material world here. Here we find proof of the illusion of time and space.

We can indeed be in two places at the same time, live two lives or many lives at the same time. Different worlds can permeate and interpenetrate one time/space continuum. They are on different frequencies and, therefore, can "occupy" the same "space." It is similar to having several radios on at the same time but turned to different stations.

If you become aware of the higher frequencies, you can choose to be part of them. However, as long as you choose to want to take the safe and compromising road of imprisonment and of approval seeking you will not be able either to perceive the greater frequencies or to be part of them or to want to be part of them. The desire to be part of them must entail pain because it must bring a point of tension: "I am here and I had rather be there. I desire something that I do not have." That involves pain. This pain is as great as is your degree of disconnection from the light.

HEAVEN AND HELL

Here, the concept of heaven and hell as simplistically explained by conventional, organized religion, finds its veracity. Heaven and hell exist right here and now. Your choice is to live in them or not live in them. The road to hell is paved with good intentions, the good intentions of the good little boys or little girls who do not think for themselves. The road to heaven is paved by courageous, individual actions that stand on their own two feet, that face and are willing to experience the necessary pain, the necessary points of tension and conflict that will finally reveal the beauty and ever-presence of the light. It is your choice to be in heaven or to be in hell here and now, not later. The help provided by the Saviour, your spirit guides and so forth is always available, it is only a question of your taking the risk of joining them, bending to them rather than bending to and joining the usual devils in their corruption.

EASTERN PHILOSOPHY AND THE FALL OF THE ANGELS

The fall of the angels is conspicuously absent in Eastern beliefs. Its absence sharply defines what is missing from these so very much glamourized beliefs in the New Age. There are many reasons why the fall of the angels has been omitted from Eastern beliefs. Let's examine them:

1. **The emphasis in the East is on the positive aspect of**

spirituality, the divine, harmlessness, love. The negative is seen as mere illusion, not to be focused on at all. God is more important than anything else. The state of Godhood and the state of being in the Absolute is the true state. Everything else is illusion. Therefore, creation is less important than God. Creation itself, the descent of spirit into matter, matter itself, are all illusion. So, creation belongs in the relative realm and has been completely disregarded by Eastern beliefs which only want to consider the Absolute. The swamis who meditate and who renounce life are looking for the Absolute and are denying outrightly the existence of the relative. The search for the Absolute is pursued to the exclusion of the relative instead of being found through the relative, through the reconquering of the relative, through bringing back the relative to the realm of the Absolute. This is no more valid that its opposite, the belief that we are sinners, that we will remain sinners, and that there is nothing to do about it except wait for a saviour who will take us out of it.

What is common between the two is that they are both inanimate, not moving and, therefore, anti-life, denying evolutionary process, which is change. Indeed, they both say that if there is evolution, then the Absolute is denied. The Christians say that if you can transform yourself, then you do not believe in God Who is the only being Who can transform you if He wants to. The Eastern thought says that there is nothing else true but God anyway, so forget about your life. Both extremes have fallen under the delusion of denying the evolutionary process. The fact is that the state of at-onement with God is attained when the acceleration of the evolutionary process reaches infinity and not before.

The entities who decide to incarnate without problems are not at all more evolved than those of us who have

incarnated with problems. The decision to undertake problems and solve them is indeed a very noble task. It contributes to the Plan of Salvation, to the process of purifying creation. What good is it to incarnate without faults? What can you teach? What can you experience? To whom are you of benefit? Incarnating without faults is being a parasite on life. By contrast, taking on negativities to resolve is very noble indeed.

   2. **In Eastern beliefs only the receptive aspect of God is considered, not the active.** Therefore, creation, which is a function of the active aspect of God, is not considered at all. Conversely, in the Western beliefs, only the male aspect of God is considered. Thus, creation and the fall are the only things that exist. With it, the only thing that exists also is the belief that the active aspect of God will save you. The Easterners deny the active aspect of God, thus they are stuck in experiential stasis. The West denies the receptive aspect of God, thus condemning any and all pleasurable experience as sin, worshipping action and suffering—the perpetual miserable sinner nuking Newt Gingrich and his sixty-hour-week-working-upper-middle-class-bourgeois-middle-America who fears God and cries, "Jesus Christ." Nuking Newt and the swami are really one and the same, two aspects of the same coin. The coin that is being struck is the coin of the line of least resistance, of denial of process.

   Believing in God as only being female, i.e., God as only being a state of experiencing and receiving, precludes the possibility of being aware of what exists on the other side, on the side of God the creator, the father, the initiator. Therefore, it creates blindness to creation, to the fall, and to salvation.

   In spite of all of this, it is an established fact that the Eastern beliefs have produced a much greater advancement to date than the Western ones. Indeed, many, many more enlightened people are to be found in the Eastern religions than in the West. Achieving the state of master is not that uncommon. It is known and recognized in the Eastern religions. Entities such as Babaji and Saibaba have made it to masterhood. I am convinced that Yogananda did, too. I also believe the same about his teacher Swami Sri Yukteswar.

Why is it that more individuals have achieved self realization in Eastern belief systems than in Western? In the first place, because the Eastern systems have existed for a much longer time than the Western ones.

Consider, for example, Patanjali, whose philosophy is not as rigid in its receptivity as are the others. He existed thousands of years ago, preceding the Judeo-Christian religions. Furthermore, the practices of meditation, purification of the body and of the spirit, as practiced by the Hindus, is bound to lead to self-realization. These practices are still in their infancy in the West. The Eastern inner progress has failed to externalize itself; the Western outer progress has failed to internalize itself. In that sense, unless they blend with each other, as we try to do at The Church of the Path®, they are both doomed to extinction. The new religion will bring the two of them together again. This is what we are attempting to do.

Due to the East's greater ability to achieve on the spiritual level, it is difficult for them to accept that Christ, who is the greatest of all beings, would have incarnated to guide Western thought. They are, therefore, reluctant to be open to anything that comes from the West, including the whole notion of creation, and its next chapter, salvation, Christ's plan, the fall of the angels, Christ's and the Hierarchy's Plan of Salvation.

That's why the works of the Tibetan, Djwhal Khul, and

Master Koot Hoomi, are so remarkable in that their teachings so wonderfully blend what comes from both sides. Their depiction of God is both masculine and feminine. They, as we, accept both the Absolute and the relative, believing that the Absolute cannot be attained unless we struggle in the relative. The struggle in the relative itself allows us to experience here and now the existence of the Absolute.

CHAPTER 13
THE PLAN OF SALVATION AND ITS VARIOUS DISPENSATIONS

Salvation is basically return to God. Through the Fall we have traveled from a state of being without awareness, through a state of becoming in which we have acquired awareness and consciousness in a gradual way through our process, to a state of being, this time with awareness.

So, it is not exactly true to say that it is merely a return to a previous state just exactly the way it was. It is a return which carries with it the acquisition of consciousness, and, therefore, the total blending and at-onement with God. Once again, here, we are reminded of the positive aspect of the existence of evil and of the disunited space in which we still live. Through evil we dissolve evil and acquire total consciousness.

DIAGRAM OF THE PLAN OF SALVATION

Being Without Awareness	Becoming	Being With Awareness
No consciousness	Gradual acquisition of consciousness	Complete consciousness
No unconscious	Formation of unconscious	No unconscious
Unity without awareness	Creation of duality	Unity, at-onement
No causality	Causality	Causality resolved and transcended
No time/space	Time/space	Time/space transcended
Continuous bliss, Eden	Pleasure/pain Light/dark	All bliss and good
Pre-incarnation	Incarnation Life/death	Life/death transcended
Absolute	Good/evil Relative/Absolute	Absolute
Pre-Humanity	Humanity*	Super-Humanity Master

*The other kingdoms of nature, the ones preceding humanity, are to be found also in a state of becoming. Only theirs is a much slower growth. Also, in their world, they have created multiplicity instead of duality, having gone below the threshold of development of humanity. We talk here in contradistinction to duality. Indeed, instead of pleasure versus pain, light versus dark, good versus evil, relative versus Absolute, these kingdoms have many aspects in conflict with one another as opposed to merely two of them, as in the case of humanity. Thus, they would be classified closer to the state of being without awareness than is humanity. They are in Eden, and they are just coming out of it.

Let's explain this process of growth from being without awareness, to becoming, to being with awareness. Let's take it first from the simplest possible level. An infant does not have awareness. He is in a state of ignorance, of disconnection from reality. For example, he is disconnected from the reality of fire burning skin. Being without that awareness, he has to go through the experience of having his skin burned by fire in order to become at-one with the awareness that fire on skin hurts. Reality, consciousness, awareness of it comes through the "evil" of the experience of pain. Now that he has experienced the pain, he dissolves evil by knowing what fire does, i.e., through consciousness.

Thus through evil—the experience of pain—he dissolves evil—the ignorance of the effect of flame over skin, by not repeating the experience—and acquires consciousness.

Gradually and through the process of increased awareness, also called the evolutionary process, this consciousness grows in every being who exists on the relative plane. As consciousness is acquired, evil must be faced and dissolved. The experience is repeated on the emotional level. For example, if I do not risk rejection, I will never find love. Through risking evil—the pain of rejection—I find the dissolution of evil—the state of unity found in experiencing love, whether in giving it or in receiving it.

My consciousness is now raised on the emotional level. That which was experienced on the physical level is now duplicated on the emotional level. The same can be achieved on the mental level. For example, in my lack of consciousness on the mental level, I will see the universe as chaotic. Cause and effect will be disconnected from one another. Injustice will be seen everywhere. With the gradual acquisition of consciousness, through the experience of the pain of injustice, I will be able to unravel pain, connect cause to effect, and be able to bring justice to my life, even if it takes time to bring it about. Mentally, I will be able to see the bringing together of the Law of Cause and Effect. I will be able to connect my thoughts, feelings, and actions with the consequences that they will have down the line, positive or negative. Once again, through risking the experience of pain, which is evil, I have dissolved pain and evil and acquired total consciousness.

One more word about pain. Its existence is proof of knowledge of a better state. Indeed, there would be no pain if there were no point of tension. If I do not know that there is a better state that what I am experiencing right now, I will be in no pain and, therefore, I will experience no evil.

UNIVERSAL ROUNDS THROUGH TIME
FOR OUR UNIVERSE

Time Line Progression

Past	Past	Present	Future
Earlier Rounds	*Last Round*	*Present Round*	*Final Round*
Ruled by the Rays of Attribute, Rays IV to VII	God is Active Intelligence. Ray III. The Saviour was Intelligence	God is Love. Ray II. The Saviour is Love	God is Will. Ray I. The Saviour will be Will
	Millions of years	Millions of years	Millions of years

This plan will end with the salvation of all humanity. Everyone, including the fallen angels, will become superhumans, i.e., at-one with God.

Each round consists of seven root races. Each root race receives dispensations in accordance to the Zodiacal ages, lasting two thousand years each, approximately. We are told that there are also larger 25,000 year cycles.

The Plan of Salvation was given out in seven rounds according to the seven rays, in order to bring back the scattered little units of consciousness to their Source, God. The first round was a Seventh Ray round, the last round will be a First Ray round. It follows the Seven Rays in reverse. And each round is divided in seven parts. In the last three rounds, we can talk about seven root races that characterize each round since we are now talking about humanity. In the first four rounds there is no vocabulary to describe what happened because it was on the level of the mineral and vegetable kingdoms and on the planetary level.

The information I am about to give is also available in other literature where it is explained in much greater detail. For the purposes of this catechism, I am only going to give general information. I refer the reader to search authors as Rudolph Steiner, the Tibetan as dictated to Alice Bailey, also, *The Secret Doctrine* by H.P. Blavatsky, although it is very difficult to read.

ROOT RACES

Let's focus on our round. Our round is made out of seven root races. They are as follows: (1) Hyperborean, (2) Polarean, (3) Lemurian, (4) Atlantean, (5) Aryan, (6) and (7) as yet unnamed.

The first and second root races. The Hyperborean and the Polarean can be said to be prehuman in that the human race at that time resembled a lot more the animal stage. In spite of the fact that great technological achievements were reached, consciousness was not there. As a result, each of those root races annihilated itself through violent wars reminiscent of what it would be like for us to have a nuclear war.

The third root race, the Lemurian race. Because of the mistakes of the previous root races, it was decided when the soul of the Lemurian race was formed by the Hierarchical masters, to put in that soul an element of pacifism. Faced with violence, the Lemurians froze, refused to fight. Their task was to populate the Earth. This root race had for task the development of the two chakras in the pelvis, the ones that are directly related to sexuality.

This is where all of the sexual rites started such as the orgiastic fertility rites that were still practiced in the dawning of our root race. Thus, there is a peculiar resemblance between the Lemurian root race and the 1960s and 1970s generation in our own times: make love not war. The downside of this is that sexuality was so abused that diseases were created. Syphilis, gonorrhea and the other of the older diseases that are still plaguing humanity today have their roots back in old Lemuria. It is interesting to note that just as we have been able to conquer syphilis and gonorrhea through the use of penicillin in the past fifty years, AIDS has come up as a result of the excesses of sexuality in the 1960s and 1970s. History repeats itself in macrocosm and in microcosm.

Around the middle of the Lemurian period, individual consciousness became accessible to humanity. This means that humans, one at a time, very slowly started becoming aware of themselves as being separate units from the tribe, from the group, from each other, from the universe. This was a great advancement for humanity at that time, in spite of the fact that it propelled those who acquired this new consciousness into a state of utter despair and isolation. The person, for the first time in human history, started experiencing the ups and downs of the ecstasy of understanding and of awareness of the self and the agony of alienation from others who did not understand what he was experiencing.

In *The Urantia Book* this event is said to have happened not only to one but to two individuals at the same time, a man and a woman who together became aware of their individuality and of each other. Thus, the apprehension of awareness as an individual marked the beginning of the need for monogamy and intimacy on levels higher than the physical.

What are we talking about here? Adam and Eve, of course. Eve eats from the Tree of Knowledge. Woman becomes aware before man. This is so because the previous round to ours was a Ray Three round. Let us not forget that. The aspect of woman is more developed for humanity than the aspect of man. Woman acquires consciousness before man does. It does not mean that she is superior, though. So women who read this, beware of your ego. The same case might be said in reverse about men who could be stronger than you because they have the capacity to wait for the next round which is going to be "their" round, the round of the Will.

This self-awareness was also the beginning of the new root race, the Atlantean. As the Lemurian race waned, the Atlantean race rose.

The fourth root race, the Atlantean. In the beginning of its history, one finds the remnants of the excesses in Lemuria, the excesses of sexuality. However, there is a liberation from the pacifism and, therefore, elevation of the active principle in Atlantis, a regeneration, a resurgence of the desire to do, to create, to construct. The concern about self-protection which was prevalent in Lemuria and which resulted in the caves that the Lemurians constructed, translated itself into buildings, conquering of the Earth, Atlantean style. For example, the pyramids and many other buildings that are now lost are a result of the great technological advancements of that era.

However, once again, technology surpassed responsibility and was used wrongly. They also abused their capacity to feel and their psychic abilities. The results were as follows:

1. The creation of cancer as a disease. Cancer is Atlantean in origin. It has to do with unresolved emotional conflicts. Healing of cancer comes when emotional conflicts are resolved through our process. We have been able to effect such healings here.

The fifth root race as well as the sixth root race both have inherited the problems of cancer from Atlantis as they have inherited the problems of syphilis and gonorrhea from Lemuria. Those who are still committing the same errors as their Lemurian and Atlantean ancestors will reap the same results, no matter what their root race happens to be.

2. Self-destruction. Once again, because of the misuse of their newly discovered power, which in those days had to do with crystals and with the sun's rays, they destroyed each other and eventually annihilated their own civilization and their continent.

3. The abuse of psychism. As a result it was necessary for psychic powers to be given up. The great facility with which heretofore humanity was able to tap into universal knowledge, consciousness, and energy, having been abused, had to be shut off. So, the new way of evolution was through deductive reasoning, the use of the mind. Thus was born the fifth root race, the Aryan, the race of concrete mind and the race of abstract intelligence.

Since it was the race of abstract intelligence as well as concrete mind, the new root race was ushered in by those souls who had not quite completed their task in the previous round, the round of Ray Three. They are called Semites.

With the reincarnation of the Semites into the middle of the Atlantean system it became possible for the fifth root race to come into existence.

The fifth root race is called the Aryan root race or the

Indo-European root race. Its focus on deductive reasoning was an invitation to use its line of greatest resistance. Psychic abilities, therefore, would only be available in a healthy way for the Aryan race through the continuous exercise of deductive reasoning. This continuous exercise would lead the individual to develop intuition. Intuition is nothing else but the ability to think quickly, to no longer have to take step by step ways of deducing something. Thus, the right and the ability to communicate with the superhuman spheres or the non-material worlds had to be earned again for humanity. Therefore, the Indian chiefs, the tarot divinations, the capacity to make predictions are all regressive, false New Age practices. The real New Age practices, the ones that usher in the sixth root race, are only available through the correct, patient—and necessarily slow—process of purification. Any psychism that exists without going through the process of purification is pre-Aryan and, therefore, regressive, i.e., part of the forces of darkness.

The Aryan root race—Indo-European for those who do not like that very much maligned word in our twentieth century—has overdeveloped the mind. It has also abused the Earth. But this misuse is not new. Just about every single root race has abused the Earth which has regenerated itself.

A great step was taken by this root race in the twentieth century in the destruction of communism and what so far seems to be the preclusion of a global war. *Will we be able to sustain this growth and pass, without cataclysm, from the fifth to the sixth root race?* It has not been done before. Every time a passage had to occur there were cataclysms. The last one was the Flood. The Flood marks the end of the Atlantean period, engulfing Atlantis—Poseidia as it was called at that time—and ushering in the "Semitic," Aryan race. Notice here that as far as we are concerned, the Semitic is the Aryan race. The Semites brought in the Aryan race. How misguided indeed were the Nazis when, in order to enhance their Aryan race, they wanted to exterminate the Semites which gave them birth!

The diseases of the fifth root race have to do with what happens when the mind—abstract or concrete—is overused, abused. Those are the diseases of the heart, the heart attacks. What characterizes the Aryan problem is circulatory. The resistance of the flow, the worshipping of the rigidity of knowledge, both go hand in hand. If one rigidly adheres to knowledge, one concomitantly shuts off one's heart. Psychological diseases are disturbances of feelings, of the emotional level and, therefore, have to do once again with shutting off of the "heart," a problem which is very germane to the Aryan distortions.

The sixth root race. The New Age consciousness is ushering in the sixth root race. The sixth root race will be concerned with the development of love, of faith, and, therefore, with the opening of the heart and the blending with the other chakras. However, let's not forget that the sixth root race is also responsible for the re-establishment of order and magic. One must meditate on the fact that there is no love or heart opening, as it is called, without order. Here is also the connection between the sixth root race and sexuality. It is as if we are bringing back the Lemurian task but this time elevating it to a higher level. Surely it is no longer a question of populating the Earth. The goal is much more the experience of sexuality as love and pleasure and at-onement, the way to God.

The seventh root race. The goal for it will be the

developing of the crown chakra and thus the integration with all the rest. That is the only thing I can say about it at this point.

DISPENSATIONS

The Forces of Light are very much engaged in the act of returning humanity to God. A specific plan has been drawn up. This plan is given out in dispensations which appear periodically. Let's look at known history and trace back the various dispensations, at least as far as they pertain to this fifth root race.

To make matters more understandable, let's remember that we are now in the Age of Aquarius. For the next 2000 years the Aquarian energies will dominate. So will the Seventh Ray of Order and Ceremony. This new dispensation has been characterized by the giving of all of the material with which we are so familiar at The Church of the Path®. I am convinced that the Christ has manifested through the Tibetan's teaching and *The Urantia Book*. Many other excellent and valid teachings exist, as in the Seth material, for example. Granted, alongside these there are many other false teachings which are misleading and which lead people astray. However, this can also be found around the earlier dispensations, particularly around the Christ's when He walked the Earth about 2000 years ago.

The Age of Pisces was ushered in by Christ and by His teachings. It was preceded by the Age of Aries, characterized by the Code of Hammurabi and by the Ten Commandments which are really a repetition of that code. Further back, this was preceded by the Age of Taurus, characterized particularly by the Minoan civilization and by the spilling over of some of those beliefs on Egypt, Greece, and other parts of the Mediterranean.

We can look back this way and find the zodiacal signs following each other every 2000 years. If this was true each past 2000 years, it will be true also in the future until humanity has ended its purification career at the close of the next round. To get a global overview of the magnitude of this plan let us remember that we are now passing through the Second Ray of Love and Wisdom which characterizes this round. The next and final round will be one in which God will not be characterized as Love but as Will. It is impossible for us to understand at this point the significance of "God is Will." We are not ready to receive that understanding yet since the forces coming from the First Ray are extremely powerful. We still are at the stage where we need the Hierarchy—the superhumans and others who guide us—to first receive the forces coming from the First Ray and then distribute them to humanity in the form of the Second Ray to enable us to receive them.

The previous round which dealt with the Third Ray of Active Intelligence and Adaptability was in a similar position *vis à vis* this round. Indeed, in those days it was impossible for them to receive the forces of love since they were not ready for them. They simply operated from the point of view of active intelligence. God was "intelligence" for them. There is a microcosmic recreation of this defense against love in this round. Apparently, the Jewish people are those souls who had not finished their career on Earth during the previous round of active intelligence and adaptability. They, therefore, reincarnated as a group in the middle of the Atlantean civilization as the Semites, introducing thinking, causality, the Law of Cause and Effect and synthesis. They also were very helpful in ushering in this civilization, the Indo-European, the fifth. However, their defense against the love aspect was most particularly felt at the time of incarnation of Christ, He Who personified love on Earth. Their lack of recognition of Him as the Messiah is a repeat of the same problem, the one that they first encountered when they were not able to receive the new round of love coming in at the beginning of this round.

Dispensations consist of particular teachings that are released to humanity in order to help it in its various stages of development. The major ones occur at the beginning of every zodiacal sign cycle of 2000 years. However, within those cycles are to be found other dispensations that enrich or enhance what has been given or bring what has been given to an end so as to prepare for the new dispensations that are coming.

As an example, let us take the last 2000 years. In order for Christianity to be dispensed the way it was, much preparation was needed. Indeed, the teachings of the Buddha, 500 or 600 years before Christ, started that process in the East. In the West, the creation of Greece and Rome was also preparation for the spreading of Christianity. The "universal state" reached by Alexander the Great when he conquered a good part of the Mediterranean plus Asia was merely a preparation of what was to follow. The creation of the Roman Empire, the *pax romana,* set the stage for the spreading of the word of Christ. The teachings of the Greek philosophers, particularly Plato, were an excellent precursor to Christianity. Plato's reincarnation as Plotinus later clearly shows the attempt of this great soul to bridge Greek and Jewish thought, thus preparing for Christianity. If one considers Plato's "Idea of the Good," it is uncannily similar to Christ's teachings of love. One should also mention here Philo the Jew of Alexandria with his blend of Greek and Jewish thought and his laying the groundwork for Christianity and Gnosticism. Both these teachings differentiate themselves from the primitive notion of a punishing God which had been necessary under the Age of Aries, the Jewish dispensation. They also differentiate themselves from the "scientific" heartlessness of many other thought processes that existed prior to that.

In came the Christ with the teachings of love, with the destruction of the absolute power of evil on Earth. After a period of gestation which lasted about a couple of hundred years, Christianity overtook the civilized world in the West. In the year 300 Constantine became the first Christian emperor. The great mistakes had already started. The repression of the Gnostic beliefs, the repression of scientific knowledge and research was rampant. Darkness and numbness were setting in.

Around 600 A.D. Mohammed appeared. The subsequent Arab invasions and revolutions dealt the final blow to the Greco-Roman enlightenment. The dark ages of exclusive religious thought overtook the entire Western civilization. Meanwhile, the Arabs created a brilliant civilization that became instrumental in the reawakening of the West.

As destructive as this appears to be, it was a necessary step for the development of spirituality and the disengagement from ensconcement in three-dimensional reality. There is a particular story here that illustrates the incredible amount of blindness that existed in that time of Sixth Ray dominance. In 643 the Arab general Amr ibn Al-Asth finally broke through into Alexandria—the seat of knowledge, spirituality, poetry, music, etc. for about 700 years—and burned what was left of the great library. When he was asked why was it that he had done this, he said, "There is no need for any knowledge when you can read the Koran." This is frightening in that it reminds us of the contemporary bigoted Christians and their fanaticism. There is no need, they say, to have any other knowledge of any other dispensation if you can read the Bible. Both of these also remind us of Hitler's burning of books.

The breakdown of Greco-Roman knowledge and law plunged the West into the Dark Ages of ignorance, illiteracy, barbarism. The level of knowledge in what used to be the Roman Empire dropped considerably. This again reminds us of the fact that in the past 100 years the western countries have experienced a systematic breakdown of the levels of IQ and of knowledge in both children and adults. It is as if technology and television, rather than progressing us, are regressing us back to a period of darkness.

It may seem as if kids today are more advanced than ever before. Indeed, we see them sitting at computers and fiddling with them with much greater proficiency than adults. However, outside of their scientific knowledge of the computer, their sense of history, their knowledge of literature, their grounding in the Western tradition, and their sense of ethics are just not there. The proof of this is in the extraordinary upsurge of teenage crime during our era. Teenagers today are much more reminiscent of the barbaric hordes that ushered in the Middle Ages than they are of the disciplined kids who rank and filed to school at the turn of the century.

At the other end of the Middle Ages, around the fourteenth century, the old Byzantine Empire, a relic from the Age of Aries, was being smashed by the Turks. All of the culture that was still existing in Byzantium gradually migrated west, thus creating the Renaissance (which means rebirth), particularly in Italy, but also in Spain and in France. Here we have another sub-dispensation, as it were. We cannot fail to see the hand of God in the resurgence of this knowledge coming in and refreshing the darkness of the

Middle Ages. By the time the sixteenth century arrived, there was an extraordinary abundance of creativity in all directions. Indeed, it was divine intervention re-establishing the balance and reintroducing nature, humanism, common sense, enjoyment of life, sexuality, colour, freedom, democracy as it had existed in the Golden Age of Antiquity.

The Reformation is definitely part of this sub-dispensation. At last someone had the good sense, the courage, and the honesty to stand firm against the outrageous practices of the Pope and bring in a much more honest and indeed much more Christian work ethic which transcended the medieval hierarchical structure. As a result, the Protestant countries that adopted Martin Luther's new and more honest system fared much better than the Catholic ones which gradually regressed into poverty. In terms of progress, England, Holland, and Germany fared a lot better than Italy, Spain and, to a great extent, France. By the end of the seventeenth century, even France had given up the number one power position to Britain. Martin Luther's revolution followed by Henry VIII, by John Calvin, etc., was a welcome change from the stiff dogmatism of the Roman Church. As misguided as Henry VIII was in his motives to break away from the Catholic Church, what resulted from it was surely beneficial to England. The beneficial effects are still to be felt today in that the Episcopalian Church has finally admitted women to the priesthood whilst the Catholic Church is still lingering behind in its misogynism.

Another sub-dispensation can be clearly seen in the eighteenth century with the great philosophers of that time. Modern democracy, which today is emulated all over the world, was inspired by the eighteenth century philosopher Montesquieu. He it is, in his work, *The Spirit of the Law,* who introduced the idea of the separation of church and state, of legislative, executive, and judiciary powers. The destruction of absolute monarchy in 1789 is a direct result of this dispensation. It liberated people to create the acceleration of progress as we have seen it in the nineteenth and twentieth centuries with the Industrial Age. In this sub-dispensation, we see the dawn of the Age of Aquarius. Order, through reason, is making itself powerfully felt.

Another sub-dispensation can be seen in the upsurge of psychology and psychoanalysis at the end of the nineteenth and the beginning of the twentieth centuries. Of course, it had to be done by atheists who were the only ones capable of understanding the divine Law of Cause and Effect. It could not have been ushered in through organized religion, dead as it was, dead as it always has been to the needs of its time. *By the way, has religion, particularly Christianity, ever contributed anything innovative?* I do not think so, not past the first century A.D. anyway.

However, in no way should psychology consider itself to be anything else but an offshoot of spirituality and religion. It is, after all, the study of the soul, of the psyche, of that which is not materially, three-dimensionally proven. Furthermore, this type of psychological knowledge was known since time immemorial by Sophocles, by Plato, by Christ—as demonstrated in my *Commentary on the Gospel of Thomas*—by Hegel, and by many other philosophers. All religions must involve psychological investigation and must include the study of the soul if they are to have any modicum of self-respect. Certainly ours does. Our approach to psychology has been revealed to us in the works of the Tibetan (*Esoteric Psychology*). All of my sermons given here at The Church of the Path® are commentaries on this new doctrine and this new dispensation. They represent our doctrine, our belief, the new dispensation as clearly as we can express it. The storehouse of our Faith (our *"depositum fidei"*) is to be found in these books of sermons.

In their narrow-mindedness, the so-called Christians do not want to see this as a dispensation from God. They see this as heresy. They would much prefer to stay in the Middle Ages, perpetuating the horrible conditions under which people lived and enshrining the ignorance that pervaded at that time. Instead of being the supporters of progress, Christianity has traditionally been a hindrance to it.

Finally, it is obvious that the destruction of the Evil Empire, not coincidentally two hundred years after the French Revolution, marks another sub-dispensation, perhaps the final destruction of the impediments of the spreading of the New Age. Communism in the USSR may have appeared to be the champion of anti-bigotry and anti-religion. However, in its attempts to destroy the old forms, it also repressed people's right to practice their religion, and, therefore, regressed people even further. The embracing of the materialistic communistic ideas is another bigotry, perhaps even worse than the one perpetrated by the bigoted Christians or Moslems. Communism was very much a negative religion. It constituted, strangely enough, the last gasp of the Sixth Ray of Idealism and Devotion. The part of idealism demonstrated by Trotsky and Lenin and others in the Communist Party only finds its match in the saints of the Catholic Church. Communism, by repressing Christianity, took on and recreated its worst possible traits—fanaticism, narrow mindedness, dishonest rewriting of history, cruelty and genocide.

So the destruction of the Evil Empire had to come through the reassertion of the repressed Christian beliefs of the old dispensation. The Catholic Church had a great role in the destruction of the Evil Empire. It is the best thing the

Catholic Church did for a long time, perhaps since the beginning of the Piscean Age when it valiantly fought the Romans. However, this was done not through any innovation, but through the tenacious holding on to old values which were still far superior to the communist ones.

All of these reasons free the possibility of spreading this dispensation, the new one, the religion that makes sense for us in the third millennium. This is due to the fact that the old belief systems have been destroyed, including communism.

There will always be dispensations. The evolutionary process is eternal and is infinite. The dispensations are given to humanity as soon as humanity has been able to absorb and assimilate what has already been given to them in the past. Spiritual progress is infinite, it cannot stop, it cannot be given once and for all, it cannot be translated into words which lose their meaning.

It is indeed a gross distortion of what every one of these prophets taught to say that theirs is the final dispensation. The Christ Himself told us that we would achieve greater deeds than He did. So, we had better hurry up and assimilate the material that has already been dispensed to us in order to prepare ourselves for the new as it comes around.

THE FALLACY OF EXCLUSIVITY

In the *New Catechism of the Catholic Church,* on page 23 under the title "There will be no further Revelation," it says, "The Christian economy [whatever that means], therefore, since it is the new and definitive Covenant, will never pass away; and no new public revelation is to be expected before the glorious manifestation of our Lord Jesus Christ." The same is to be found in the Moslem religion in which it is said that Mohammed is the last and greatest prophet.

In their bigotry and fanaticism Christians, Moslems, and Jews exclude any other dispensations but their own. They make it final so as to force you to believe in them and so as to maintain their power over you. The three Judeo-Christian religions expect either a Messiah or a return of a Messiah. The Jews, of course, have not recognized the Christ, so they are still waiting for the Messiah. The Christians are waiting for the return of the Christ. They have not recognized the return of the Christ in the new dispensations that we have received in this New Age of ours. The Moslems are expecting Imam Mahdi. He will return on Judgment Day, the Day of Reawakening as it is called in Arabic.

Behind all of this exclusive nonsense, isn't it clear that a reawakening is necessary in order to receive a new dispensation? And aren't we here witnessing in this New Age of ours a reawakening indeed, a rebirth? Yes. And yes. Even the born-again Christians are experiencing a change in their religion. A Catholic priest has published a book on sexuality discussing in almost pornographic detail the sexual act and the blessings of the sexual act. Now, if that is not a take-off on the New Age, I do not know what is! The Episcopalians have a movement called the Cursillo Movement through which they experience a lot of the group manifestations and release of feelings that are to be found in many New Age practices.

So, even the churches are preparing for the ushering in of the New Age in spite of the fact that they hypocritically still hold on to the old belief systems as expounded in what is erroneously called "The Scriptures."

CHAPTER 14
TIME AND EVIL

THE PROCESS OF REGRESSION

The process of regression is a slow and seemingly imperceptible one. Consider, for instance, a clock. You can see the second hand move, but you cannot see the minute hand move, much less the hour. And yet, they do. Seconds add up to minutes and minutes to hours; soon you are astonished at what time it is.

Constructing a life based on sellout and misconceptions takes a long time. And, like air pollution, it starts killing you slowly. Then, suddenly, you get a disease of the lungs. You have contracted this disease by breathing in polluted air for a long time. You have also very slowly contaminated this air with your distorted uses of energy. You are trapped, enslaved by this distortion and by the bad habits coming from it.

For example, you suddenly find yourself enslaved by the habits you have formed through approval seeking. You **have** to make a lot of money because you **have** to sustain a particular lifestyle for which you acquired a taste by convincing yourself that you **had** to become this or that, otherwise you would not please your father, mother, teacher, your idolized self, etc.

All of this comes imperceptibly slowly—unseen because you choose not to perceive it, instead numbing yourself to your inner conscience. Collectively, we are numbing ourselves to the gradual and subtle destruction of the environment—imperceptible to us because we choose not to see it. Individually we are polluting ourselves by betraying our innermost selves, by becoming who we are not, who we believe we are supposed to be.

CRISIS

When this system does not work, there is a sudden and destructive crisis—physically, the abused body collapses; globally, the abused ecology brings starvation; financially, the cultivation of falsehood brings deficit and bankruptcy. Appearance values lead to poverty. Only real value brings riches.

Having capitulated for success, having sold our souls for a buck, or for pseudo-love, or for protection, or to be taken care of, we sadly find out that none of this works. The fame, the wealth, the love, the protection thus obtained collapses, leaving us worse off than when we first started. We are lucky if the collapse comes suddenly, in one event. We would be able to better respond to one disastrous event. But we resist that. We postpone the crisis as long as we can. We delay it through premature healing, through denial, even through prayer and meditation—anything but allowing the crisis to finally explode. Of course, delaying it only makes matters worse. When crisis finally comes it is a lot more severe than we could ever anticipate or imagine it to be. Therefore:

1. It is easier to respond to one dramatic event. Our behaviour is thus more likely to change.

2. Negativity infiltrates one's life slowly, insidiously, through the good intentions of well-meaning people whose consciousness is limited and who avoid self-responsibility and toleration of pain.

3. When the resulting prison of evil becomes intolerable

to the entity or the system, it creates a crisis. As long as the crisis has not arrived, the individual and the system are under the grips of evil.

4. This grip of evil is, more often than not, unconscious, or preconscious. It is that way due to denial, fear, shame, pride/conceit, and a willful desire to maintain the status quo.

5. This grip of evil masks itself behind a pseudo-stability within which more and more compromise and capitulation pile up, creating more and more deceleration of energy, demotivation, irresponsibility, unhealthy dependency, apathy.

6. It is this deceleration of energy, this compromise, this dishonesty which creates poverty. The pursuit of abundance through sellout, dishonesty, and approval seeking brings deceleration, lack of consciousness, productivity, and energy, and, therefore, poverty.

7. This leads to dissatisfaction and violence, cruelty, murder, drug abuse, i.e., all the evils of society.

8. The violence that ensues is a result of the dissatisfaction which itself is the result of dishonesty and compromise. Poverty and ignorance, the authors of the evils of our society, are themselves authored by the evil of the mask, pretense, compromise, sellout.

9. If we try to rescue those who are in that situation without their feeling the pain of what they created, they will never get to the bottom of it. They will never come to terms with the fundamental creators of their misery: their own dishonesty, sellout, and desire for approval.

10. The truly successful entities are not rescued by anyone. They attract success by overcoming their own problems. This is true individually and collectively. When the West was undergoing the doldrums of the Dark Ages, the

much more evolved Arabs did not rescue Europe from its misery. The Arab world was then in a position comparable to the one in which the West finds itself today. There were street lights and 90% literacy in Cordoba and Baghdad when London and Paris were cesspools of barbarism, disease, and ignorance. If the Arabs had done then what the West is doing today—attempting to save others through financial aid, intervention, etc.—the West would neither have gone through the painstaking process of gradually lifting itself out of darkness to build the cathedrals of the High Middle Ages, nor reached the enlightenment of the Renaissance.

Also, how would that Arab help have been received in the West? Begrudgingly of course, creating the same resentments, the same identity crises, the same politically correct hypocrisies that exist today. The false love of the rescuers would be rewarded only by bitterness and thanklessness, as it should be. If, when you give, you get lack of gratitude, it is possible that your giving was hypocritically motivated. Your concern for thanks itself is a gauge of your motive in giving. Selfless giving is not concerned with rewards and acknowledgment. That is why selfless giving is capable of tough love.

11. Rather than delay crisis, then, see it as a desirable occurrence, one that can be brought on yourself, by yourself, on levels where destructiveness can be minimized.

12. Identify the bad habits that you have, the little daily occurrences as they accumulate, the little dishonesties, lies, exaggerations, pretenses, concealments, avoidances of truth, premature healings, premature rescuings of yourself and of others.

13. Use your imagination to bring each one of these to its catastrophic conclusion, in your mind and in your feelings. Thus, you will accelerate the *experience* of the

crisis, by *feeling* what you are doing to yourself and by expanding your consciousness into the future. You will be activating the Law of Cause and Effect. You will be reversing the process of deceleration. You will be accelerating, purifying again.

14. As if with a crystal ball, you will see the probable consequences of the little insidious habits. You will be outraged. Rather than blaming anybody for this outrage, you must realize that you have brought it on yourself through acquiring the capacity to experientially apply the Law of Cause and Effect. Say to yourself that this outrage is positive, healthy. That is crisis of the best possible kind. Through this, you will want to liberate yourself from the prison that you have slowly built for yourself. You will break all the negative contracts you have created for yourself. Thus, you will have brought about a crisis, a dramatic event here and now, to which you can vigorously react. You will reach the point of relinquishing.

The little things are more important than the big ones. The big problems are already out in the open. You can see them. You can deal with them. The little negativities are insidious. You can hide them while being blind to the crisis which they bring. Evil works much more successfully with little things, little bad habits that eventually imprison us. It is by focusing on the seemingly harmless little things that you develop the necessary perceptiveness to be and stay on the Path, which is our search for God.

CHAPTER 15
SIN AND GUILT

SIN

That word! Basically it means "without," in Latin. This already gives you an idea of the deeper meaning of it. The fundamental sin is to be outside of reality, to be in the negative, in the zero.

In Liebnitz's Monadology, sin or evil is represented by the zero, whilst God, life, reality, everything else is represented by one. The binary system, the simplest possible system of arithmetic, and the one without which we would not have computers, is really a manifestation of the reality of the universe, of the fact that sin is illusion and non-existing, whereas goodness is reality, exists, and is all that is. Meditate on this, on the true significance of the zero and the one. Arthur Koestler, in his book *Darkness at Noon*, dwells on this particular aspect of the zero and the infinity.

Sin is an illusion in the absolute sense but in the relative realm it is a reality.

Sin is the distortion of truth. It is anything that is outside nature and, therefore, outside of God, the Creator. Unfortunately, this word has been so abused, particularly by all of those who call themselves Christians, Moslems, or Jews that not only has it lost its meaning, but it has become somewhat ridiculous. So we have to replace this by other terminology. For example:

Distortion. Anything that is not exactly the way it was created in its pure form is distortion. Thus we have distortion of perception, distortion of emotions, distortion of experience, distortion of action, distortion of thought. Once again, distortion exists only in the relative realms. In the absolute realm, the only real realm, it does not exist, it cannot exist, it immediately disappears. In the process of finding the infinite—the Path—we are, therefore, bound to dissolve the distortions that we have. It is impossible to find and to stay in the infinite as long as the distortions exist. The finding of the infinite can only be temporary and limited in its scope. The degree to which distortions exist is the degree to which we are still unable to experience the infinite.

Perversions. A perversion is a distortion taken to the next level. For example, if, in my thoughts and feelings, I continuously want to dominate, I will distort my thoughts and feelings. However, I will also create a perversion of dominance in my sexual behaviour. Conversely, if I have in my thoughts and feelings a desire to be dominated, I will create a perversion of submissiveness or of masochism on the physical level. Perversions are addictions. Addictions are distortions of distortions. Many times a perversion is caused by its opposite. For example, a demanding and controlling behavioural pattern originates from a deficiency and despair which creates the demand and need to control.

LEVELS OF SIN
AND A PLACE WITHOUT SIN

A sin can be committed on the mental level, on the emotional level, or on the physical level. All of these are levels of sin. No sin can be committed on the spiritual level. The spiritual level is the absolute level, the one where we are one with the Higher Self. Each one of us has, therefore, within himself a place that is and will remain without sin, i.e., a place of abundance, a place that has everything, a place that has all knowledge, that is without sin, i.e., without nothingness, without lack.

MISCONCEPTIONS ABOUT SINS: MORTAL AND VENIAL SINS

The primitive interpretation of what a sin is must be revised in order to make sense today. If we are to believe, and we do here at The Church of the Path®, that God is everywhere, that God is all that is, then the worse a sin is, the closer the person who commits it is to experiencing the pain of the guilt and, therefore, the closer he is to redemption.

So it is very difficult to tell whether a murderer has committed a worse sin than a yuppie cheating on his expense account. As benign as the cheating on the expense account appears to be, it demonstrates a disconnection from God's reality. This cheating eventually will lead to all kinds of negative acts, perhaps even murder. At the time he is ready to commit murder, the yuppie has violated the law so thoroughly that he is closer to feeling the pain of the guilt than he was when he was stealing from his expense account. When he was stealing from his expense account he was, therefore, in a state wherein much greater, much more extensive evil existed in his soul.

If he enters a Path of Purification, the deceleration that would lead him from stealing from his expense account to committing murder will be experienced in a controlled situation such as is to be found in our process. He will then not have to commit the murder. He will also realize the straight line that exists from stealing from your expense account to committing murder. And consequently, he will stop stealing. If he does not want to get into a process of purification such as this one, he will continue to worsen, bringing about who knows what calamity at the end of the line.

Take, for example, the indifference of the West to the extraordinary outrages that were committed in the Soviet Union or in the fascist countries during the twentieth century. It is the indifference of the western nations that created the monstrous mass genocides. One can say that the greed of the West, perpetually interested in its own pocketbooks and mouths, created the murders in these countries. The West is, therefore, responsible for these atrocious killings. This responsibility continues today in the indifference displayed about such struggles as Bosnia, Chechnia, etc.

The further you are removed from the consequences of your negativity, the more you are in a negative state and, therefore, the more you are sinning. The less you appear to be sinning, the more you are indeed sinning. So the blatant criminal is closer to taking responsibility for his sins and, therefore, to joining God than is the person who apparently is not sinning that badly. This completely destroys the whole notion of mortal versus venial sin.

Let's destroy it some more. If, as I have said so very often, I had murdered Hitler any time before 1945, I would have committed an act of great service to humanity. In that sense, I would have been much closer to God than the good citizen who did his selfish little duty making more and more money every year and avoiding the draft at the time of World War II. He was by far a greater sinner than a person who murdered Hitler. Yet, it still would have been murder. The dutiful citizen is doubly guilty: (1) he is guilty of his own greed and short-sightedness and his own negation of what is happening to his brothers in humanity and (2) he is guilty of colluding with what is happening in humanity by looking the other way. **Guilt by omission is twice as bad as guilt by commission.**

Therefore:

1. **It is impossible to tell whether one sin is greater or smaller than another sin.** It depends upon every single circumstance which has to be looked at accordingly. It also depends on the state of mind and motive of the individual.

2. **Full knowledge and complete consent, i.e., full consciousness of the harmful volition (also called negative intent) behind a sin, does not make that sin a mortal one.** On the contrary, a sin committed under these conditions is much closer to redemption than a sin committed when all of these conditions are unconscious and when the individual pretends to be innocent or ignorant of his motivation in committing the act.

3. **All sin is voluntary.** In the Catholic Catechism it says, "Feigned ignorance and hardness of heart do not diminish but rather increase the voluntary character of sin." The volition may be unconscious, but it is still there. We are responsible for our unconscious.

Nevertheless, it is gratifying to find that they have taken into consideration feigned ignorance, i.e., the mask, and that they, as we, say that a person who commits a sin out of ignorance is even guiltier than a person who commits a sin with full knowledge of it.

4. **There is no such thing as mortal sin.** Any sin, when committed, creates the conditions under which the person will make restitution. Again, a committed sin is closer to redemption than a repressed one. Evil in its active principle is much less of a sin than evil in its receptive principle. If by my non-action I am responsible for somebody's death, I have

committed worse than murder.

CONSCIOUS AND UNCONSCIOUS SIN

For those who call themselves Christian, the notion of mortal sin is one committed in full consciousness. For example, if I commit adultery while fully conscious that I am violating God's law or if I commit a murder and am fully conscious of it, then I am committing a mortal sin and there is no forgiveness for it.

We say that there is no sin that ever is unintentional. The intent is simply unconscious in some of the sins. The fact that it is unconscious does not make it any better or more forgivable, it makes it worse. It means that there is a double sin: (1) there is the sin itself, and (2) there is the fact that we have put it away in our unconscious. That too, is a sin; the sin of ignorance.

We feel, on the contrary, that somebody who is conscious of his crime or of sin is a lot closer to God than is someone who is not conscious of it. This is because consciousness will eventually bring this person to realize the pain within himself that he is creating by inflicting pain on others.

Once again we see here the huge distortion that exists in conventional religions concerning sin and concerning the handling of sin. How can I possibly exonerate myself, release myself of a sin, how can I possibly purify if I cannot take responsibility for having deliberately wanted to sin? At the same time, if I discover that I have deliberately wanted to sin—which is always the case—then I am condemned to eternal damnation. The condemnation to eternal damnation, therefore, makes it impossible for me to purify any sin since it will punish me with the worst possible fate if I ever take responsibility for it.

We say taking responsibility for a sin must be the first step towards purifying it. The condemnation of consciousness towards a sin closes that door and, therefore, works towards regressing people, not helping them.

Thus, we come to the startling conclusion that the conventional churches have been regressing people throughout the centuries, not helping them reach purification. Purification, therefore, has existed in spite of the churches, outside of the churches, countercurrent to what they were trying to do. No wonder people feel the way they do about churches. We here at The Church of the Path® intend to restore goodness to the word church.

CONSEQUENCES OF SIN

In conventional religions, we find here the notion of eternal punishment and incapacity to reach eternal life. We do not think this way. We say that every sin exists because we have created it. It is, therefore, our responsibility to remove it. Yes, we can remove every single sin that we have committed. There is no such thing as a mortal sin that will guarantee you a place in hell. A sin itself is an opportunity to make conscious the heretofore unconscious Universal Life Force and to align it back again to All That Is. Thus, here is our interpretation of the double consequence of sin:

1. A person who is sinning or who is in the process of sinning will find a commensurate inability to pray, to long for God, to want to establish contact with God. This is because he has lost his dignity and his self-respect. Indeed, only with dignity can one make contact with the higher levels of reality. Paradoxically, regaining dignity involves having the humility to reveal and to bring out and to own up to one's sins. The hiding of one's sins decreases self-respect and

self-love and, therefore, incapacitates the person from contacting the higher spheres. On the contrary, the revelation of the sin immediately places the person in a position of self-respect, albeit humble, in which it is possible for him then to contact the higher spheres, to pray, to find the state of grace, etc. From that vantage point then, it will become much easier to deal with the sin. A person who is in a state of sin is perpetually involved in recreating this sin. Thus, he is involved in a vicious circle. This is erroneously described in the Catholic Catechism as, "unhealthy attachment to creatures." The unhealthy attachment itself is a result of the perpetual vicious circle in which the person finds himself. This vicious circle must be identified before the person can do something about it.

For example, every sin rests on a misconception. Suppose I harbour a misconception whereby I see strength as being bad. I will, therefore, have an equal and opposite misconception that says weakness is good. Suppose, then, that I commit a violent and negative act such as murder. In the act of committing murder, I will feel strong. The feeling of being strong itself is not negative; the act of murder is. The reason I feel strong while I commit murder is because I still harbour that misconception—i.e., strong is bad—and I know murder is bad, therefore, I am strong. As a result of this, I will feel guilty. I may cover up my guilt by wanting to feel strong again and committing another murder, which then increases my guilt.

At some point, the guilt will be strong enough for me to be debilitated. At that point, I will feel weak, and, therefore, good. In that weakened and good state I have in no way resolved the problem. I am still subscribing to the same type of misconception. Now, however, I am ready to incur the violence that I have perpetrated on the universe when I was on the other end of cycle, when I believed that strong was good. So, I will attract to myself people who are strong and cruel and who will victimize me. This will result in enough outrage in me to want to be strong again and bad again. And so on and so forth. This type of cycle can go on for many incarnations. I can have one or many incarnations in which I am weak and good, followed by many other incarnations in which I am strong and bad. Both situations are sinful. The person who is weak and good manifests a distortion just as much as the person who is strong and bad.

Which one is worse? If there is one which is worse, it must be *weak = good* since it is much more difficult to identify the *strong = bad* antithesis that lies behind it.

The attachment to three-dimensional reality is a result of sin existing on the astral level. The attachment to materialism cannot and will not be given up unless and until this condition is identified on the astral level and brought to the mental level for resolution. Indeed, misconceptions block the truth and, therefore, the light. The fluctuation between the two misconceptions increasingly decelerates, creating denser and denser realities. One of these realities is our world of matter. There are other worlds denser than matter.

This is how, then, the material world is continuously being recreated—by the continuous deceleration of the Universal Life Force through sin, from the astral level to the physical level where it becomes neutralized.

GUILT

When we talk about sin we must talk about guilt. Any deviation from nature and natural law creates guilt. **The fundamental guilt is for not loving.** The minute we disconnect from being a loving person we instantly manufacture guilt. All other guilts are results of the fundamental guilt of not loving. Sin (distortion, perversion) automatically creates guilt. Guilt creates a desire for restitution which is misunderstood by the primitive consciousness as a desire for punishment. This explains the incredible distortions that are to be found in conventional religions concerning punishment.

The notion of punishment is absurd. If I have committed a crime and I am flogged for it, it certainly is not going to prevent me from committing it again because I have not done anything to resolve the aspects in me that will still want to violate Spiritual Law, nay that are still doing so on the mental and emotional levels. Thus, societal laws which deal with sin must do two things: (1) prevent the recurrence of crimes and (2) bring the person who has committed a crime to feel the pain of his guilt.

CONSEQUENCES OF GUILT

All guilts are painful when experienced. The experience of the pain of the guilt automatically creates a state of remorse in the individual. This remorse is an urge to make restitution, to make good, to redeem himself and others. When that feeling is attained by the individual, he is rehabilitated and there is no need for punishment. Punishing somebody in that state is ludicrous.

There is another aspect of this which has to do with setting examples.

How do people interpret the forgiving of a crime? Does forgiveness establish in their minds an invitation to sin with impunity? This is a very valid point which results in the creation of laws and the administering of terms of imprisonment, incarceration, and punishment to suit the crime committed. It is a necessary and temporary measure only because of the limited state of consciousness that exists in the universe. To the degree that humans are children, to that degree they must be shown and taught discipline. Thus, it is necessary for people to be "punished" who commit crimes.

Eventually, with the raising of consciousness, this notion of punishment to set an example will gradually disappear. The two criteria mentioned above will then be the factors deciding punishment.

Conventional religion has taken the notion of sin and guilt and has used and abused it to imprison and enslave people. **Saying, "I am a sinner," appears to be a humble act; it is actually an act of conceit, a grandstanding.** "Look at me, how humble I am by saying that I am a sinner." It is the same with guilt. Guilt has been used to get people to pay greater offerings, buy dispensations from the pope—which by the way created the Reformation—flagellate themselves, etc. The churches have carried this to exquisite extremes where people beat themselves or walk on their knees for miles bleeding and suffering in order to expiate their sins. Needless to say, by doing so, they are committing an even greater sin, the sin of self-rejection and self-denigration which also creates guilt, real guilt, compared to the false guilt which they are exhibiting.

All of the above leads us to the examination of the validity of confession.

CONFESSION

Confession is the exposure, the admitting of a sin. As necessary as it is, it is not in and by itself sufficient. It must be followed by an investigation of the motives and by the coming into full consciousness of the desire to sin, the intent to sin. The full experiential knowledge of that intent will inevitably bring pain of guilt. When that pain of guilt is felt, then, and only then, is the person able to want to make restitution for his sins. When that is done and completed, the sin is forgiven and the person is clear in his soul. He will have gained one step towards not wanting to commit that sin again. The next time he finds himself tempted to commit it, memory of his harmful volition (negative intent) and the ensuing pain of guilt will come to him. This memory will be a motive not to repeat his error. He may go ahead and do it again, this time in full consciousness. This does not mean that he is committing a mortal sin at that point. In fact, he is sinning a little less than he did the previous time when the sin was committed for unconscious reasons. He is now closer to resolution because his consciousness will eventually prevent him from committing that sin altogether.

This process of gradual filing away at a problem or at addictive behaviour constitutes the only valid process of purification. As we have seen above, this process can be stopped if there is a spirit of condemnation that says that a sin committed in full consciousness cannot be forgiven. Come to think of it, full consciousness would totally preclude the commission of any sin whatsoever. Full consciousness makes sin an impossibility. Full consciousness prevents distortions on the mental level. Therefore, it will prevent the precipitation of these distortions on the astral level into emotions and on the physical level into the commission of sins. Thus, the raising of consciousness cannot raise the level of sin. On the contrary, it diminishes it. This is to be found in our process of purification which has three steps to it: (1) identify it, do not identify with it, (2) neither condemn nor condone the sin, (3) own up to it in order not to act it out.

This process is in one of our basic prayers, the "Prayer of Purification." In it you find the fundamental elements that will solve any possible problem that you have in your life. It reverses the process advocated by the traditional church and exposes it for its regressive qualities.

GLAMOUR OF SUFFERING

This glamour is unfortunately perpetrated by conventional religions, particularly by the Catholic Church. Indeed, gross misinterpretations of the truth abound, such as "one must suffer for other people's sins." This is a distortion of the following: if I suffer for my sins and I take responsibility for them, I will not only help myself but I will help others in convincing them to be willing to suffer for their sins and thus heal themselves accordingly.

Thus, I do not take on other people's sins. Christ does not take on our sins. What He did and what I must do and what you must do is to take on our own sins and by opposing, end them, to use Shakespeare's words. And by opposing them (which is painful) inspiring others to oppose theirs, to courageously take on their own sins.

The glamour of pain has other expressions such as the following: (1) It is painful and lonely to be a leader. (2) It is painful to find God. (3) The artist must suffer. (4) No pain, no gain.

The kernel of truth in all of these distortions is that, indeed, one has to go through the temporary pain of reversing the defenses within us that are not allowing the Universal Life Force and the Universal Consciousness manifestation. However, genius itself is not painful. Genius itself is the unimpeded expression of the Universal Life Force under the direction of Universal Consciousness, so is leadership, so is finding God. **The expression of genius in itself is not a painful process. The pain comes through the defense against doing it.** It will stop and does stop when the defense is removed. Therefore, the expression of genius is an expression of bliss, of at-onement. The expression itself is not at all a painful experience.

This ends once and for all the distortion that says the more neurotic or psychotic you are the more creative you are. For every neurotic or psychotic creativity there can be found many other examples of blissful, well-balanced, well-grounded ones.

DEATH OF THE SPIRIT

The disintegration of a particular entity is possible if that entity continues to sin and to avoid feeling the consequences of that sin. It reaches a point where the entity itself explodes as do particles of evil since they have created so much tension against the Forces of Light. This is close as we can get to the idea of mortal sin in our belief system. However, it is indeed extremely remote as a possibility. I doubt that it even exists on our Earth sphere. It exists in spheres that are even less developed than we are on Earth. Here on Earth, we are all given a chance for redemption no matter what our sins have been.

Mind you, even in the case of the disintegration of the spirit, the elements that have characterized the individual who is now disintegrated are taken on by other individuals.

If this is the case, why are entities such as Satan and Herem not disintegrated? They, themselves, in their own lives know and respect the laws of God. When it comes, however, to subjugating other people, they lead them into violating God's laws. This can be compared to an individual who keeps his body very healthy while committing all kinds of outrages on other levels. Take, for instance, some of the lawyers whom we see in the act of defense and sinning on television. They look great, they go to health clubs, they may even eat healthy food and love their wives. However, they are continuously committing outrageous sins of lying, of cheating, of stealing, of aiding and abetting criminals and murderers for money. So, they are establishing two equal and opposite systems. One system is turning, shall we say, clockwise, towards the positive; it accelerates. This includes the health and the loving of their wives. The other is turning counter-clockwise, is decelerating. Those are the lies, the outrages, the cheating and the stealing and the aiding and abetting of the criminals. The contrast between those two forces will at some point or another create a snap, a crisis.

The worst crisis known in our earthly existence is the death of the body. The fear of death, as experienced on Earth, is fear of disintegration which is reminiscent of the death of the spirit as it exists in other spheres.

The process of the disintegration of the spirit is delayed by the degree to which there is still a positive element existing in this person's life. Great spirits who regress will take a longer time disintegrating than lesser spirits. In that process of disintegration, they will create much more damage than a lesser soul would if it were to regress.

WASTE

All ideas expressed in human language must have equal and opposite ones. Human language, being a product of duality, cannot express in a unitive way what is being felt on higher spheres of development.

For example, as much as we need to open up and give generously of this energy when it is found, we also must be mindful of it and not waste it. Indeed, it would then be "pearls to swine."

When you give good energy to bad causes it stops regenerating itself. You are committing a sin; you are violating Spiritual Law, the law of nature. It is, therefore, essential to economize this energy. There is a lot to say about building it up. A person with a great amount of magnetism, for example, is someone who has built up this energy to the point where he now radiates it. The accumulation of this energy in cathedrals is also a case in point here. So, yes, be generous but be mindful of where your generosity goes. This is not for everybody.

DEATH BED CONVERSION AND PRISON CONVERSION

When a crisis comes to an individual, his defenses break. Thus, he is immediately flooded by the Universal Life Force. This state of grace or bliss makes it possible for him to "convert." Now, depending on who is there at the time of his "conversion," depending on the books that are available to him, and depending on what he wants to sell out to, or to whom he wants to sell out, this pure, limpid Universal Life Force and Universal Conscious experience will be shaped into the type of religion or philosophy that he will adopt. The initial experience in its pure form is very valid. Left on its own and to itself, it will not want to adhere to a ready-made form too quickly. The desire to adhere to form is what makes this experience crystallize into an established religion or an established philosophy. The person experiencing the Universal Life Force and the Universal Consciousness in its pure form cannot sustain the ecstasy of this open state. Anxiety sets in and a desire for form is immediately created.

Many great personalities have undergone conversion experiences that resulted in innovative religions, scientific discoveries or philosophies. They did not adhere to anything that already existed. They created new ones. Unfortunately, even those newly created ones were then descended and assimilated by the existing dispensations, thus losing their original sharpness and truth. This, of course, is the universal process of crystallization and glamourization.

Very often crises are not fully experienced. Someone may experience a crisis on the outer level, however, he does not allow it to penetrate his inner reality. Take, for instance, O. J. Simpson. His extraordinary amount of defense, all on the outer level, is a manifestation of his intent to keep the crisis on that level. He does not allow the crisis to invade the inner levels of his being. Therefore, he is not benefitting from it. Having not destroyed the inner defenses, he is not letting the Universal Life Force and the Universal Consciousness come in. In spite of the fact that they are knocking on the door, his not letting them come in results in extraordinary regression.

Look at what happened to the incredible number of expensive lawyers that he hired. They fought with each other in public. Robert Shapiro, who was supposed to be the head attorney, fought F. Lee Bailey, the one who had the greatest notoriety.

Here you can see evil in its manifestation, in its continuously splitting of itself. These people were not fighting for the truth, nor were they fighting for O. J. Simpson's acquittal. They were fighting egocentrically, to be the center of attention. They were there for their own notoriety, and not for anybody else. Consequently, it was not a crisis and it did not bring conversion, it brought regression.

INDULGENCES

Indulgences are special dispensations from the church, particularly the pope, that provide absolution for any sin, actual or prospective. At the end of the Middle Ages, these indulgences were sold in marketplaces. The greater the offense, the more expensive was the indulgence.

The great and first beneficiary of the invention of the printing press was the Catholic Church because enormous numbers of indulgences could be printed without having to write each one of them. You can imagine the amount of money that found itself in the coffers of the Vatican as a result of the wholesale printing of indulgences.

This scandalous practice reflects the depth of corruption that existed in what was and still is erroneously called Christianity. Martin Luther's stand in 1515 against such practices is, therefore, quite admirable in itself. The subsequent further division of the Christian church—having already been divided in the eleventh century between Catholic and Greek Orthodox—demonstrates the existence of evil in its midst. Evil has the property of continually splitting itself.

What proof is there that evil is finite and good is infinite? The fundamental nature of life is goodness. Thus, when goodness is respected it perpetuates itself forever. On the contrary, anything contradicting, opposing, negating that goodness reverses the trend, goes countercurrent. This countercurrent activity can only be temporary. How long can a countercurrent go upriver before eventually it is turned around or destroyed? How long can an obstruction be maintained against a current before it collapses? Thus, evil is finite and doomed to crisis because it is, by definition, splitting itself against itself and against nature. This can be demonstrated ad infinitum and is being demonstrated continuously in our process and in our lives.

The great scandal of indulgences is perpetuated today in the practice of expecting Jesus to forgive you all your sins just because you say that you have taken Him as your

Saviour. Any usurping of the honest and courageous process of purification is as scandalous as are the indulgences. Any attempt at premature healing is similarly evil and should be denounced and renounced. Any material goods or talents or advantages used to compensate for negative aspects that need to be resolved and dissolved are used as indulgences. Welfare can be put in that category as well. This does not mean that these practices do not have value. Their value will bring benefits to people only if they are used after the person has taken responsibility for the ways in which he has committed his sin and, therefore, entered the process of purification.

BIRTH CONTROL

As we said elsewhere, the point of sexuality is no longer to populate the Earth. With the development of consciousness in humanity, sex becomes a means for fusion, for giving and taking pleasure, and for creativity. It would be regressive to continue to see it as a mere means of populating. It would also be cruel for everyone concerned. The last thing we need these days is to have an even greater number of poor children who contract diseases and do not have enough to eat.

Therefore, contraception is a very positive step that humanity needs to take. It has been known in every civilization. The ancient Egyptians had their women fitted with intrauterine devices.

It is time for us to grow up and to stop believing in old and outdated concepts of sexuality, reinforced by references in the Bible, that which is erroneously called the Scriptures.

ABORTION

The soul only enters the body at the time of birth. The

first breath takes in the soul. In fact, in Hebrew and in Arabic the word for "breath" and "soul" is the same—ruah. Here we categorically differ from those who call themselves Christian and who say that abortion is sinful. Of course, as with many other things, irresponsible abortions are a violation of Spiritual Law. However, in the face of the incredible overpopulation of the Earth, it is reasonable to say that we are no longer in biblical times when our task was to populate the Earth.

Being attached to little embryos and giving them citizenship negates the rights of the parents, particularly those of the mother. The mother is largely in charge of the task of raising the children, caring for them, etc. A child who is brought into conditions that are very unfavourable is a suffering child. And so is the parent suffering, seeing her child in want. It is preferable to prevent this occurrence than to make room for more and more and more suffering and hungry entities on this planet.

CHAPTER 16
FORGIVENESS, REDEMPTION

FORGIVENESS

God is forgiveness. Experiencing the presence of God, experiencing grace, experiencing bliss, is being forgiven. **The person who is plagued by guilt is unable and unwilling to be forgiven.** A person who has decided to make restitution and who has faced the pain of the guilt opens himself up to forgiveness and, therefore, to bliss, to grace, to the presence of God.

The choice to be forgiven is the individual's. It is absurd to think of forgiveness as being God's choice. God chooses to forgive all the time; He is forgiveness. It is His essence to forgive. However, the choice to **experience** forgiveness is up to the individual. He has to reverse whatever negativity still has a grip on him. He has to decide to make restitution for the guilts that have accumulated since these guilts prevent him from being open to God and to the state of bliss and of grace.

We refer here to saying Number Twenty-Eight in *A Commentary on the Gospel of Thomas*: "Jesus says: 'I will choose you, one from a thousand and two from ten thousand, and those [whom I have chosen] will be lifted up, being one!'" This means that the one in one thousand or the two in ten thousand will be recognized as being ready for investment of the grace of God, i.e., initiation, which is forgiveness or redemption.

So we can talk about forgiveness or redemption as an initiation, an investment of energy by forces greater than ourselves when we are ready to receive it. **If we are not ready to receive it and we are given it, it will be lost.** We will not recognize it for what it is; we will misuse it for purposes of regression and we will have to start all over again.

FORGIVENESS OF OTHERS

You cannot forgive anyone who does not want to be forgiven. In fact, many times you will be tempted to forgive people as a matter of expediency, in order not to confront them, or in order not to make them accountable for something that they have done. Here, make no mistake about it, your "forgiveness" does not give anybody anything; you are not doing anybody any favours by letting them get away with what they did. On the contrary, you are greedily and shortsightedly arrogating something to yourself that does not belong to you, i.e., these people's good feelings, false balance, peace of mind, etc. You are healing prematurely and, therefore, you are harming much more than you know.

FORGIVENESS OF SELF

This type of forgiveness is only available to the degree the individual fulfills the following conditions:

1. He must cleanse himself of harmful volition. There is within him a coexistence of good will, perhaps on the conscious level, and of bad will—harmful volition—on the unconscious level. Self-forgiveness cannot occur in this dualistic state even if restitution is made for the consequences of the negativities. The bad will must be exposed and cleansed.

2. He must genuinely **desire** to restitute for past harms. Notice that exact restitution is neither required nor possible. Only a positive intent to atone, redeem is necessary. This desire will attract the appropriate situations in which the individual can restitute. Since it is impossible to undo past harm, we atone by doing good in the present, by investing our desire to atone in places and people in need.

When these conditions are fulfilled, the individual will unmistakably experience the grace of self-forgiveness. It is a blissful state wherein God is present.

FORGIVING AND FORGETTING

What is the difference between forgiving and forgetting? Here is what the Bible says. Numbers 14:18: "The Lord is slow to anger, and abounding in steadfast love, forgiving iniquity and transgression, but he will by no means clear the guilty, visiting the iniquity of fathers upon children, upon the third and upon the fourth generation." The Lord or a person may forgive, but one cannot forget. One cannot undo what has been done. More importantly, "by no means clearing the guilty" is to be taken into consideration. Indeed, every single guilt has to be accounted for, restituted for by the person who has committed it. It is not just a question of having some bearded person in heaven force you to do it. **You** want to do it when you realize what you have done. This is clearly demonstrated in Near-Death-Experiences in which people want to go back and redress their wrongs.

The iniquity of the fathers upon the children does not mean that the entire dynasty is to be cursed by the deeds of a father. This misinterpretation has conveniently created all kinds of misconceptions, power trips, and misery. The correct interpretation is that one must come back in another life (children) to redress the wrongs of a past life (father).

The fact that the price must be paid and the person's soul redressed does not negate the existence of forgiveness. Forgiveness is the giving of the opportunity to redress one's wrongs and thus to free oneself of being Earth-bound.

Of course, a wrong can be redressed within the life in which it was committed. This will then negate the necessity to have to do it in a later life in which the causal connection with the negative deed may not be as easily established. Not seeing the causal connection creates in the individual the greatest pain in human existence, the pain of injustice.

THE MISCONCEPTION ABOUT WHOLESALE REDEMPTION

This is an extraordinarily destructive concept to be found in Christianity. As a Christian you are told that if you "accept Christ as your Saviour," He will take on all of your sins.

The church "fathers" abused this to "absolve" people who did not want to take responsibility for the outrages they were committing in their lives, not to mention the outrages they had committed previously. The absolution doled out to them in a wholesale manner gave them permission to go on committing more outrages, since all they had to do was confess and repent. However, this is not what is most damaging, strangely enough. What is even more damaging is the fact that *the misconception of wholesale redemption removes from the individual the aspect of volition*. The individual feels that he is helpless, that he is in the throes of the devil and that he will never get out by himself. His being repeatedly "saved" rewards his negative behaviour and perpetuates his slavery to his addictions and to all his other sins.

Thus, wholesale redemption very quickly became a weapon of the forces of darkness. Those who advocated it unknowingly became the personnel of the dark hierarchy. When the pope decided to give dispensations, he himself became the agent of the devil. This is the classic encouragement of the line of least resistance which gets "good people" to sell out for expediency only to find themselves under the hoof of Satan at the end of the line.

REDEMPTION

The real meaning of redemption is that Christ's experience on Earth, His taking on the forces of darkness at the end of His life in the body of Master Jesus, made it possible for us to redeem ourselves, to pay for our sins, to realize that we have a lower self and a lower self intent and to want to purify and to have the opportunity to do so. This is its true meaning. In no way is it meant to deprive a person of the opportunity—because it is an opportunity—to deal with and restitute for real guilts. The process of reincarnation itself is an opportunity to redeem oneself. The desire to reincarnate, as demonstrated through the Near-Death-Experiences, brings us back in another body with the intent to do something about what has been damaged in our souls.

When a sin is committed, when a distortion exists in a soul, it creates pain. The pain that we create in others is automatically imprinted as pain on our own soul substance. We share the soul substance of the entire universe. We cannot harm, hurt, or cheat without having the exact same mirrored consequence experienced in our own substance. When one becomes conscious of this pain, one wants to restitute. Attaining this level of consciousness itself requires a certain amount of work on the level of purification.

In order to receive Christ as your saviour, you have to raise your consciousness, and you have to attain a certain degree of dignity. If you do not, you will neither be able to nor will you want to experience His presence. Pretending that you have experienced Him takes you even further away from the experience of Him. Do not collude with false teachers who will want to enslave you by promising you a redemption that you have not earned. It is simply impossible, unnatural.

CAPITAL PUNISHMENT

Is it right or wrong? There are two things that we must understand before we decide how this question should be answered:

1. Human law is fallible. It deals with situations on the outer level, on the realm of three-dimensional reality, within the time/space continuum. Therefore, it cannot be absolutely just, as much as it tries to be.

2. Capital punishment must be understood in the total context of our legal system. I personally do not believe that our legal system would make sense without capital punishment. If a multiple murderer is not executed, his punishment is not going to be proportionate to his crime. This sense of proportionality on the outer level is extremely important for the majority of the population at its present level of development. When someone is on a low level of development, there is need for an outer level authority who implements justice as evenly as possible.

Of course, for the people who are more highly developed, the point is moot, since they will not be committing crimes that would warrant capital punishment. The point would also be moot if we lived under a legal system that was dictatorial, unjust, autocratic, anarchical, etc.

Also, what would happen if we did not execute a serial

murderer? He would become our perpetual guest. We would have to feed him, clothe him, shelter him for the rest of his life. We would have to protect him and ourselves from him. What kind of life would that be for him? And for us? On the contrary, the finality of execution makes it possible for this person to start all over again in another life. It also makes it possible for him to experience, albeit in a milder form, what he has inflicted on others, thus rendering his karmic burden lighter.

CHAPTER 17
DOUBT

FINDING GOD THROUGH DOUBT

We at The Church of the Path® encourage deliberate, conscious doubt. It is through doubt that you find God. It is through questioning that you find the truth. It is not through pretending that you believe that you really find true belief. It is worse to pretend that you believe than to doubt. The atheist is, therefore, closer to God than is the bigoted conventional religionist.

We are not here talking about doubt for the sake of doubting, for the sake of rebelliousness, for the sake of being contrary and to create trouble. We are talking about the honest doubt, the one that comes from the true searcher. So questions like, "If I really look into myself, I might find that God does not exist; what about that?," or, "How can there be so much misery on Earth if God exists?," or, "If God exists, let Him demonstrate it to us" (this last one was Voltaire's); all of these are encouraged. We urge you to have these questions. Come and ask these questions and we will try to answer them using your own life experience to demonstrate the answers rather than conceptualize, philosophize, and pontificate. In fact, this whole catechical exercise would be futile if it were not applied to the flesh and blood, day to day, minute by minute, or century by century human existence.

It is essential that you make your doubts specific. It is

also important to go through specific exercises in order to find the doubts within yourself. This will make it possible for you to ask the right questions, the ones pertinent to you personally.

THE NECESSITY TO FIND DOUBT WITHIN

By searching within yourself you will find places where you lack faith in God. This is a guarantee. Lack of faith in God is the nature of your lower self. Right now you are avoiding to look at your lower self. So when you courageously plunge into it you will find lack of faith. You will also at times be lost in lack of faith. Jesus was. Some of the last words He said on the cross were words of faithlessness, "Why hast Thou forsaken Me?" The undergoing of the doubt of the existence of God is very much part of the human experience. That is why it was demonstrated by Jesus in His life. The courageous abandonment of yourself in that doubt is what will get you to come out of the other side of the dark tunnel believing more strongly than before. So you have to call the bluff. You have to call the doubt's bluff. You have to challenge it. You have to sink into it. **The act of sinking into the doubt, of calling its bluff is the greatest act of faith you can ever demonstrate.** The honest search for the truth brings you closer to God than anything else in life. So, if you temporarily lose faith, rejoice, you are on the right track.

Notice here that we are not telling you that we will guarantee that you will find faith. We cannot do that. We are not inside your brain, inside your mind, inside your feelings. We do not know the degree to which you honestly search. The honest search itself is God.

In the act of searching honestly you are at peace with yourself, and that is why you are at-one with God no matter what happens on the outer level. That we can assert and that we can guarantee. The rest of it is yours.

UNHAPPINESS AS A WAY TO FAITH

The misuse of free will is what created misery. It is not a question of God's allowing or not allowing unhappiness to occur. We, as free agents, have misused the laws and have created unhappiness. The unhappiness, the consequence of our misuse itself is in accordance with God's will. If I ignore the fact that it is cold out there and I do not dress properly when I go outside, I will get a cold. If I do not get a cold, then God does not exist. The fact that I do get a cold means that God exists. The existence of unhappiness is a demonstration of the existence of God through the Law of Cause and Effect. If there were not unhappiness, I would never learn how to deal with cold weather or how to deal with any other aspects of life, nor would I develop the necessary wisdom to finally reach God, which is my goal.

WHY WE DESIRE TO DISCONNECT FROM FAITH AND FROM GOD

God is the Law of Cause and Effect. Therefore, God is justice in the universe. However long it takes for this justice to come about, we must find patience and perseverance within us to wait for it. God is always present, communicating to us the feeling of a just universe. Only we do not listen, we do not want to listen.

We do not want to link cause to effect because we are afraid that something will be taken away from us.

Here I use an oft-mentioned example. An infant reaches for a flame and gets burned. He establishes immediately the causal connection between the pain of burning and the flame. He learns that he should not touch the flame. The same infant gorges himself in a bowl of candy and then has a tummy ache thirty minutes later. He does not make the connection between the pleasure he experienced during the eating of the candy and the pain that he is now experiencing through the tummy ache. He does not want to make that connection. If that connection were made, it would mean that he would have to sacrifice his gluttony which in his eyes is what pleasure is all about.

Therefore, he does not want to believe in the existence of God. He does not want justice in the universe. He does not see the justice of his tummy ache.

As his life progresses and experiences become more and more complicated, it is increasingly difficult to connect cause to effect. Then, he feels a victim of circumstances. God does not exist because my stomach hurts. *Why doesn't God take away the pain in my stomach?* Well, God has done something even better, He has given you the opportunity not to create that pain in the first place. He has also given you the opportunity to find out what is good and what is bad for you if you would only take the trouble of making that connection.

So God demonstrates His presence to us all the time in the positive and in the negative occurrences of our lives. Faith in Him, discovering His presence can be done through knowing happiness and unhappiness. Any thoroughly known experience leads to God.

It is easy to blame God for a negative occurrence. However, it does not get you any place. It is a lot more fruitful, albeit difficult, to take responsibility and to look within yourself for the causes of your unhappiness, for the message that is inherent in the negative occurrences of your life. This is true whether you are an individual, a group, a nation, a civilization, or a race.

THE REAL CAUSE OF DOUBT

Your doubt, as well as your misconception of God, comes from personal problems that you have not overcome. If you want to understand some of the concepts you have about God, start thinking about your own father this lifetime. If your father was not around or you did not know him, think of the person who replaced him, the person who was your father substitute when you were young. Sometimes, a mother can play the role of father.

Whoever played the role of the initiator or of the leader or of the breadwinner for you—whether man, woman or institution—becomes invested with the power and the clout of fatherhood and you develop then an image of God that is similar to that. Therefore, you will find that a lot of the misconceptions that you have about God are very much connected to the way you feel about your father.

Let's take a famous example. A very good one is the French twentieth century philosopher and writer, Jean Paul Sartre, who was an atheist. His father was a conventional, straight-laced, "pure," run of the mill, upstanding Catholic. He was very strict with his son. Jean Paul Sartre spent an entire lifetime denying and denigrating his father. Indeed, his entire philosophy of existentialism is "hell bent" on the destruction of father. One can say that the entire 1960s and 1970s culture was similarly geared. Generally speaking, all romanticized movements are geared to the destruction of the father image and to the denigration of it. So here we have a concept of God that is very much determined, albeit through rebellion, by the image of the physical father.

I gave this example first for a reason. I want you, reader, to jog your mind. This first example is at the same time the most difficult one and the one that will help you most to discover how close your beliefs are to the image that you have of your parents. Now for an easier example. The good, upstanding, church-going, God-fearing citizen has projected the image of his father on God. He fears Him, he reveres Him, he sees Him as an angry and irrational authority who acts out His power without rhyme or reason just as his father did at home.

Now, as a young child, any authority, any restriction—whether right or wrong—appears to us to be irrational, out of hand, unjustified. Authority and irrationality thus become fused in our psyche. Our concept of God, the ultimate authority, the great power, also becomes the most irrational and unreasonable, i.e., the God of the Old Testament. That is how fallacious it is to believe in such a God, the vengeful God of the Bible. And that is how it is absolutely essential that a person give up this type of notion in order to enter the Path. There is no possible way that anyone who is involved in a belief system such as this can enter the Path.

By definition, the vengeful God of the Bible tells you that you do not have a will. Thus, surrendering to His will becomes an incredibly abhorrent, impossible thing to do. It is a lot more the surrender to the devil that one experiences in these circumstances. It is not the willing surrender to a loving God who has given you the choice to surrender or not to surrender to Him.

So, Jean Paul Sartre, "for his sins," was closer to the Path than anybody else in conventional religion ever was. He demonstrated it, too. Sartre really believed in cause and effect and harmful volition. Only he did not call them by those names. He called harmful volition "bad faith," *mauvaise foi*. He said that anybody who proceeded to do something with bad faith would reap negative consequences. We agree. Both he and we believe that the pursuit of something positive with bad faith or harmful volition leads to negative consequences. Also consider, for example, Antoine Roquentin's moments of great cosmic awareness, cosmic consciousness in our own terms, during which he felt nauseated by the stark reality of life in a tree or in a leaf. This is to be found in his novel, *Nausea*. These are great times of expansion of consciousness, of awareness of life. The disgust experienced by Roquentin becomes the state of ecstasy experienced by the person who believes in God. However, essentially, they are the same. They are expansions of consciousness. They are connections of causality. Therefore, one can say that Jean Paul Sartre, with all of his anti-religiosity, was a very spiritual being indeed and was much closer to God than he himself knew.

What are your conflicts with your father? To what extent is there residual material in you that has not been resolved? To that extent you will either oppose or conform, albeit unwillingly, to God. Both positions will be distorted and will remain distorted until you choose to resolve your very personal conflicts with your father. The resolution of personal conflicts, therefore, is and must be the door to finding God and experiencing Him. There is no other way. Do not let anybody tell you that there is another way.

RESOLUTION OF DOUBT

When you have found that your image of God has been based on your image of your father or on a reaction to it, another problem will face you. You will have to find enough courage within yourself to change your mind, to say that you have changed your mind, and to tell people around you that you have changed your mind. This may make you enemies. People will resent you. You will suddenly find out how much bigotry exists around you that you never thought was there—in your parents, in your friends, in the people closest to you. This is where you will find the truth in Christ's saying that if you want to follow Him, which means that if you want to find God, you will have to forsake father, mother, sister, friend, etc. Remember, all who found God have had to do this. The prophets had to do it, so did the scientists, so did Freud when he discovered sexuality in childhood, and so does anyone who has discovered and has revealed and released a new truth to humanity. Therefore, **finding God is finding your task.** It takes courage, it takes honesty, it takes humility, it takes a willingness to sacrifice the old in order to recover and to find the truth.

FANATICISM

Why is it that for thousands of years people have used their gods as excuses to murder and annihilate others? True belief in God creates an open energy system, a tolerant one. **Intolerance, fanaticism, which result in genocide, is a function of weak belief systems, the ones that are about to die.** The child believes in an outer level God as the replacement of a parent. To the degree he has not as yet given up the umbilical connection between himself and his parents, to that degree he will create a God with whom he is going to have a cocoon type of exclusive relationship within which they both say, "It is you and me against the world." This cozy type of exclusivity is bound to translate itself into fanaticism against anything and anybody who contradicts or threatens its existence. So the wars of religion have to do with:

1. Individual freezes multiplied by millions and becoming mass freezes. These are glamours which people get hooked into because of individual problems.

2. A growing insecurity that threatens a cozy relationship

on which people have based their entire lives.

And so the established and organized religions have always become fanatical as they disconnected from the truth and the fundamental teachings of their founders.

There are other reasons why people rape, pillage, plunder, and murder under the banner of God. For example, in the Crusades we can see several motives:

1. Pure greed: the theft of goods and achievements of a higher civilization, this time the Moslem.

2. Escape from dealing with the problems that they created and left at home. Whoever went on crusade was immediately forgiven any crime he committed at home, whatever the crime may have been, including murder. So, if you were a crusader, you escaped from the murder you committed at home by going into the "Holy Land" and committing more murders under the banner of God, i.e., because God told you to do so. This is reinforced by many "precedents" to be found in the Bible where there are multiple examples of "God" exonerating genocide or murder.

All of this, of course, has absolutely nothing to do with faith or with God or with a benign entity who is seeking your well-being and your healing. Anybody who has any self-respect, including all of the original founders of religions, are quite different from their followers and perpetrators of these outrages.

RELIGION AS A WAY TO CONTROL THE IMMATURE

Isn't religion or belief in God just a way to keep people's lower selves, their ids in check? The Jewish religion certainly qualifies as a control religion that checks people's lower selves, their ids. It is characterized by commandments, thou-shalt-nots. This type of religion was necessary for humanity when it was in its infancy. Indeed, children need limits. Humanity in its infancy needed the limits of the thou-shalt-nots. It was the only way for humanity, while containing the wild forces of the primitive self, to acquire greater consciousness.

The advent of Christianity was a step up from that, but essentially it still did not lift the lid completely. It was necessary, even at the time the Christ walked this Earth, to check the lower self and the id. Spirituality was to be found through removing oneself from three-dimensional reality.

RELIGION AS A WAY TO LIBERATE THE ADULT

Now for the first time in the history of humankind, this whole way to spirituality is reversed. Humanity, having now reached adulthood, is ready to penetrate three-dimensional reality with spirituality. Thus, humanity is ready to release the forces of the lower self and of the id with confidence. It has acquired enough maturity to understand that in the forces of the lower self and id is contained the involuntary process which is magnificently self-regulated and which represents God, the ultimate blend of Universal Life Force and the Universal Consciousness.

However, this, too, can be and has been misinterpreted. This new philosophy applies to adulthood, the parts of you that are mature. But there are places within you where you are still a child. If applied to the child within, it would be misinterpreted and would create the type of anarchy and chaos that existed in antiquity. There are parts of you that still need to be disciplined, taught, kept in line, re-educated. At the same time this is done in a temporary spirit. It is understood that it is necessary to do this for the time being and that eventually those parts will be given the freedom that they have earned by demonstrating responsibility. In a parallel fashion it is important to recognize the parts that have reached adulthood and allow them to have the freedom that they have earned.

Let's not forget that conventional religion, under the banner of disciplining the wild lower self and the id, has abused quite a few legitimate currents in us by calling them sinful. Thus, a perfectly legitimate and normal sexual current, when seen as sinful, becomes distorted for the sake of obtaining approval from priests who do not understand it. Furthermore, these priests will instill guilt and debilitation in their congregation in order to maintain control over them and to be supported by them through finances, approval, etc. This is the great sin of churches. The price they will have to pay for this may very well be their final destruction and dissolution.

CHAPTER 18
THE REAL MEANING OF JUDGMENT DAY

JUDGMENT DAY

Scientific enquiry into the Near-Death-Experience provides us with a sensible meaning of death and Judgment Day. In Near-Death-Experiences, at the time of death, people go through a long, dark tunnel and are faced with a Being of Light. At that point they re-experience in a flash every single moment of their life. Some who have been through this experience describe their desire to stay forever with the Being of Light. If this wish is granted, the person, of course, does not come back to the body, so we do not have any reports from them. However, we do have reports that fall under two general categories:

1. The person wants to stay but is told either by the Being of Light or by friends or relatives already deceased that he must go back to finish his task. He is told that he is needed on Earth and that it is not time for him to die.

2. Through the experience of his life review, he voluntarily wants to return in order to restitute for his guilts or to complete unfinished business.

This is Judgment Day. It is as simple as that. It is to be understood beyond the time-space continuum. In other words, it is happening at this instant now for people who die right now. It will also happen in the future for those who die in the future. The triumph of the Forces of Light over the forces of darkness will happen in our relative sphere and, therefore, can only be understood in terms of the future. However, this victory is happening right here and now for every one of us who undertakes the process of at-onement with God. Every individual's victory against the dark forces that he has attracted or summoned or chosen to take on is for him a Judgment Day event.

In conventional religion, Judgment Day is seen as happening at the end of time when everybody has died and when it is time to know whether you have made it or have not made it. If you have made it, you go to heaven; if you have not made it, you go to hell. Wherever you go, you stay.

HELL

Hell is the state in which you refuse to take responsibility for your sins and, therefore, are in a state of continuously and perpetually recreating them, thus sinking deeper and deeper into unhappiness. Hell, therefore, exists everywhere. It is a state of mind before it is an outer level state that you have created.

However, very important point here, hell cannot be perpetual. A person who creates a hell for himself is bound to reach a crisis during which this hell will explode. With the explosion will be destroyed not only the consequences of evil, but the evil itself which has created it. It will be destroyed by exposure and understanding. After the crisis, the person will have the opportunity to deal with his life differently. He will shape the Universal Life Force with a new and higher level of consciousness.

Evil is finite. Good is infinite. Therefore, hell as a permanent state is an impossibility. There is no such thing as a mortal sin. All sins can and will be forgiven.

If Judgment Day were the way old time religion describes

it, what happens to those who are judged and are sent to hell? They stay there forever. Eternal damnation is absolute, they say.

According to old time religion, do those who are judged and sent to hell ever have a chance to redeem themselves, purify and join God? No, there is no such possibility for them.

This does not make sense. Furthermore, it would be unjust since eternal damnation is incurred for people's sins on the plane of the relative. A sin is always relative. If you think of it, the word "eternal" and the word "damnation" cannot possibly exist in the same sentence since they are mutually exclusive. Damnation cannot be eternal since evil is not eternal. If there is life, there is connection to the Absolute and, therefore, there is always hope for the return.

THE END OF TIME

In reality, the end of time will occur when every single member of humanity will have made it to the Kingdom of God through the continuous process of purification. That moment cannot be called Judgment Day anymore. There will be no judgment. There will only be rejoicing and togetherness with God. Reincarnation is, therefore, an essential element in this context and concept.

FINAL TEST OF THE CHURCH

In the New Catechism of the Catholic Church it is said that the church will undergo a final test challenging the faith of its members. It is said that there will be a deceptive religion that will present mankind with a way to solve its problems by denying their belief in the "truth." This movement will be lead by an antichrist who advocates glorification of the self instead of glorification of God.

Let's take each of the concepts one by one, analyze them

and respond to them.

1. The church must pass through an ultimate test which will challenge the faith of its members. This is true. The church and what is erroneously called Christianity will indeed have to face a huge test in which it will have to realize that there has not been truth in its teachings since Paul started distorting the sayings of Christ. This is the distortion that must be faced, and it will indeed challenge very seriously the believers and lead them to better and truer Christianity.

2. There will be a deceptive religion that will present mankind with a way to solve its problems by denying its belief in the "truth." This is also true. Unfortunately, many people associate our purification system with a seductive way of attracting people away from faith. They are making an unfortunate mistake. They are confusing us with many others, including the conventional churches who are taking the line of least resistance. They can be divided into the following categories:

a. *The New Age healy feelies.* Here, by fluffing somebody's aura, or by placing hands on particular parts of the body, or by poking specific places one is healed and purified. This by-passing of the harmful volition/negative intent and the Spiritual Law of personal responsibility makes this a false religion and a very dangerous and seductive one.

b. *The positive thinkers* who Alice-in-Wonderland themselves into believing that by saying what is positive and by smiling, i.e., by denying the existence of evil within themselves, they will think themselves positively all the way up to the presence of God. Again, this is a seductive, misleading, and dangerous way of being.

c. *The conventional religions* which also by-pass process by teaching that the only thing required for salvation is "belief" that a saviour has taken responsibility for one's own errors and distorted thinking—by merely mouthing these words, a person will be instantly saved and brought into the Kingdom of God. This, too, let's not forget, is a seductive, misleading, and destructive way of the devil.

The antichrist will appear in any one of these garbs and many more. The antichrist himself is the author of those distortions, one of which is the conventional religions. He manifests a common goal through all of those false religions, i.e., to make one believe that one does not have to take responsibility for who one is and for what one has done. He has for a goal to convince us that we can violate the Law of Cause and Effect and that it is through the violation of the Law of Cause and Effect that we will find happiness and bliss, i.e., God.

This new religion of ours denounces and renounces all of the above practices. It is, therefore, the only valid religion. Any religion that opts for the line of least resistance under whatever stratagem of disguise is a function of the forces of darkness.

In the Dead Sea Scrolls there is a personage called "The Liar." The Liar is the apostle Paul. Paul sold out the Christian religion to the Romans. The form of Christianity known today is the version that the Romans accepted. (The rabbinical Judaism that is known today is also the sellout version of Judaism acceptable by the Romans.) That is why it survived and that is why Christianity became the religion of the empire, being a religion for everyone.

Thus, Paul and his followers can be identified as the seductive antichrist described in the Catechism of the Catholic Church under "The Church's Ultimate Trial." The seduction has already occurred. It occurred at the beginning of the Christian era. And it continues and hides itself in the outrageous masquerade found in the Catholic catechism and in the conventional teachings.

3. **Man glorifying himself instead of glorifying God.** It is true that egocentricity is what takes people away from their faith in God. However, it is not true that by denying this egocentricity and by pretending to be selfless and giving a person will make it to the Kingdom of God. One has to detect his own egocentricity and work through it. One must realize that his best self-interest is God's best self-interest, that there is no difference between the two. Any other thought process brings about duality, a conflict which is a mark of the old time religion, not of the new one. Raising of consciousness makes it possible for a human being to realize that his best self-interest, the best self-interest of humanity, and of God are one.

This process of raising of consciousness can be seen in the acquisition of maturity. Indeed, for an infant or for primitive humanity it is essential to take everything for one's self. With maturity comes the realization that by sharing one has more. If I share with you and you share with me, we both have all of our combined toys to play with. For primitive man, if I clobber my neighbor in order to steal his goods, I may temporarily enjoy what he had. However, it is a lot wiser to make a friend of my neighbor and together we form a pact against those who want to take what we have.

This then generalizes itself into cosmic responsibility and consciousness, thus joining self-interest with general interest and finally with God's interest. This is the only way to resolve the problem of self-interest versus God's interest. Each one of us has to experientially understand that the greater the development of the consciousness in an individual or in an entity, the greater the understanding will be that what is in the individual entity's benefit is also **always** in the benefit of all concerned and in the benefit of God. It cannot be done by superimposition or by merely name calling, denigrating those who are still caught up in the infantile primitive way of thinking and who have not been able to experience anything better.

The hidden egocentricity of those who call themselves church fathers leads them to advocate on the outer level a pseudo-altruism. They push you into tithing or into donating for their own best self-interest under the banner of spirituality, God, and the church. The investigation of their own motives would be a much better enterprise than to arrest themselves into a closed energy system such as the one that they perpetuate.

4. **There is no such thing as mortal sin.** Any sin when committed creates the conditions under which the person will make restitution. Again, a committed sin is closer to redemption than a repressed one. Evil in its active principle is much less a sin than evil in its receptive principle. If by nonaction I am responsible for somebody's death, I have committed worse than murder.

PURGATORY

According to the Catholic Church, all who are Christians, i.e., baptized (who have sold out sufficiently enough to the church through their donations, etc., but who are still not perfect), have their salvation insured. After death they go through a purification process that enables them to finally make it to the Kingdom of God.

If this were so, then there would be no motivation to purify your own negativities. Since you are insured a place in heaven, just wait until you go to purgatory, as if entering into a gym or a steam room where you will melt away all of your fat, i.e., unacceptable parts, i.e., sins, so that you can finally make it into the heavenly world of the yuppies and the hard bodies.

Needless to say this is nonsense. The purification process is available right here and now just as much as it is available after death. The entering into this process is a matter choice. It is the choice to establish a bridge, to actively and deliberately cooperate with the Plan of Salvation. This bridge is called antahkarana.

There is another way of salvation which comes anyway but which takes much, much longer. This is the salvation which will eventually come for every particle of creation. Life itself will eventually purify itself one way or another. This lifeline which ensures purification at the end of time is called sutrama.

If you want to make it to the Kingdom of God sooner, then you have to do something about the parts of you that need purification. Yes, you can do it, you can do it on your own. That is what a church is supposed to provide you with, tools for your own purification here and now. We provide these tools. Come and get them. Furthermore, these tools are available for anyone and everyone. You may even use these tools while saying that you do not believe in the existence of God. The use of these tools itself is the traveling towards God, one way or another, whether you believe it or not, whether you say it or not. Thus, there is no such thing as a chosen people, an elect people, etc. What makes you part of the elect is your choice to enter this purification process, wherever you come from and whoever you are.

CHAPTER 19
INDIVIDUAL WILL AND DETERMINISM

PREDESTINATION VERSUS FREE WILL

The subject of individual will and determinism has been debated since the dawn of consciousness in humanity. Indeed, the minute we have consciousness, the minute we can differentiate ourselves from others and find independent motility, we get a greater sense of determining our own reality. Motility is this aspect of spontaneity that first appears in the human animal. It then acquires consciousness and volition, thereby, gaining a quality of deliberateness.

There are many philosophies on the subject of free will. Some say that it does not exist at all, that everything is determined. Some say that the universe is totally mad with absolutely no rhyme or reason to it and that it is ruled by chaos, chance, and luck. Some say the following: if I believe that a greater being conducts my destiny, then I neither understand my life, nor do I have any control over it, nor should I. Volumes have been written by many philosophers and many sages about each one of these concepts. Religions have been created to accommodate each one of these misconceptions.

The central truth of this dichotomy is usually totally omitted by religious teaching and philosophical thought. This central point is this: **to the degree an entity is evolved, to**

that degree it controls its destiny and has free will. To the degree it is not evolved, to that degree it is subjected to forces that it believes are beyond its control.

This is only true in the relative realm, a realm of becoming, our realm. It is no longer true in The Absolute, where self-determination is total, or moot.

The soul is the seed plan. We come in with one. However, our spirit constructed our soul. The will of our spirit is our greater will. Also things may change, requiring a modification of plans. So the fact that there is a seed plan or a Plan of Salvation doesn't negate individual will. On the contrary, it gives the individual a chance to do what it wants to.

Do you believe that you have a choice to grow, improve, raise your consciousness? Yes. And then through your own progress you will gradually increase the degree of the control you have over your destiny. If you did not, might as well commit suicide because there is no point in being alive.

Not believing that you can improve yourself is anti-life, absurd. Indeed, think of your body as an example. Improving myself physically means being at-one with nature. Does conforming to the laws of nature mean that I have no choice? Of course not. I choose to improve my body or I choose not to.

Is it possible for you to increase the power and strength of a muscle through the exercise of a regular workout? Do you believe that you can improve your health through the development of good eating habits? If so, why can't you also improve your emotions, your mind, and your soul through exercise and honest assiduous work?

It is obvious that you have control over your body. It is just as true, though less obvious, that you can have control over your emotions and over your mind. Through the heightening of consciousness, greater control and government over your life is possible. Controlling yourself and improving yourself must, therefore, lead to doing the same for your environment. As you improve, your world improves. Use your imagination to the point where you can conceive that you can apply the same process to the entire universe. In effect, this is what your life is all about.

Primitive humanity with its undeveloped consciousness had less control than modern humanity over its fate and environment. Consider for instance primitive humanity's attitude towards eclipses. It is now known that in prehistory people would die of fear during eclipses. Today, this seems absolutely ridiculous because we are able to explain what they are all about. We can predict them, we look forward to them, and we can experience them with enjoyment. Why can't we have the same attitude towards all troublesome situations in our lives? They simply represent areas of our lives that we have not been able to master as yet. Can we conceive that in the future we will be able to master them? If we have done so with eclipses, surely we can do so with all of the other little problems that are presented to us in our personal lives.

When we choose not to believe in any of this, we are acting in the same manner as a primitive human being dying of fear because of an eclipse. We refuse to accept in humility the fact that we do not as yet know the causal connection that brings about a particular condition in our lives. There are some primitive tribes who do not connect sex with babies. So, for them, having a baby is a matter of pure chance, luck, magic (good or bad, depending). When you refuse to believe in the ever-presence of the Law of Cause and Effect, you are acting in exactly the same manner as those primitive people. When you see yourself as a victim of circumstance, when you blame your parents or your childhood conditions for what is happening today in your life as an adult, you are also acting in a very primitive and misguided way. When you make yourself a victim of outer circumstances, you regress.

You will discover your free will to the degree that you are willing to apply the Law of Cause and Effect to every thought, feeling, action or nonaction, event, etc., in your life. Every single aspect of life has a reason, only we do not as yet have the wisdom or knowledge to understand it. However, we are in the process of discovering it. And nothing that happens in a person's life is outside of his ability to connect with what inside of him has created the situation.

FAVOURITE CASES AGAINST FREE WILL I: CHILD ABUSE

There is much talk today about the "victims" of child abuse. There are no victims. The child is responsible for triggering the abuse from its parents. Whenever I say what I said above, I invariably get vociferous, violent reactions from people who say, "How dare you say this about child abuse! How can a child be responsible for the abuse by its parents?"

Have you ever seen or had children? Have you observed how seductive and provocative they can be? With whom are they going to experience their sexuality if it is not with their parents? They initially do not know that it is sexuality but they certainly act it out in a seductive manner.

In no way am I condoning the parent's behaviour, who is by far the one with the greater responsibility to discipline the child. However, from the child's point of view, he definitely has triggered that type of response in a particular parent. This can be proved over and over again with the

Individual Will and Determinism 213

demonstration that one sibling out of many is the one who is abused while the others are not. This sometimes occurs with twins.

It is true that as a child you did not have enough consciousness to choose not to act out some of those lower self aspects that existed in your soul. From that point of view, the child is not responsible. However, you still made the decision to act in that way. You still choose to.

And why should you continue to recreate the same experiences as an adult? This confirms your harmful volition then and now. You now have the consciousness necessary to realize what you are doing and to decide to act in a certain manner and not in another. Even if you choose to continue to believe that as a child you were a victim, you certainly do not have to continue to be a victim as an adult.

If you are caught in this type of victimization, and if you feel outraged at what happened to you in childhood, here is a way for you to resolve this problem:

1. Find out how in your life today you are reproducing the same problem. You may have been a victim as a child and are now recreating the situation by choosing to play the role of the victimizer. It is the same thing. Victim and victimizer are caught in a tango of guilt manufacturing towards themselves and towards each other. As a child you may even have been an abuser towards other children. Find out how you did it and see how it corresponds to your present abuse or your present victimization. The acceptance and the deep experience of this will reveal to you how you are right now provoking this situation. When you clearly see that you are not a victim in this situation as an adult, you are on your way to recovery. You will have reached the point of relinquishing in which you will say to yourself, "I do not want to do this anymore. I am going to see to it that I stop." This

is progress; this particular problem has now entered the Path of Purification and thus will be resolved. Remember, the key here is to contact your volition in creating this problem. You want this problem, you benefit by it, at least as far as your little self, your lower self is concerned.

2. To the degree you totally experience the situation as an adult, to that degree you will make available to yourself the experience of childhood. When you least expect it, you will see clearly that you did the same thing as a child. You will see your intent, you will see your seduction, you will see your enjoyment of the abuse, you will see the provocation of violence. You will clearly see your active role in this case. Rather than feeling ashamed of this—shame being what prevented you from this clarity in the first place—you will feel great relief, albeit in humility. The relief comes because you will suddenly feel that you have been in charge of the situation all along, that you are not a victim and, therefore, you have free will and free choice.

If you do this, your philosophy of life will change. All of the belief systems that heretofore ruled your life will be transformed, including your political ideas and your religious ones.

FAVOURITE CASES AGAINST FREE WILL II: THE HOLOCAUST

What about the holocaust? Are you saying that the Jews have created a situation in which they have been genocidally massacred? Yes. I am saying that.

Consider the following two points and remember that they are made by someone who was born Jewish and who grew up in an Arab country where he was persecuted for being Jewish:

1. No matter where they live, Jews remain separate from

others, creating their own little exclusive clubs. They have always stubbornly resisted any type of assimilation in any country. They pay lip service to their oaths of citizenship in all of the countries in which they reside. For example, I took the oath of American citizenship in 1967. I believed in this oath. I have no intention of taking another oath in another country, I really meant what I said. However, the bulk of Jewish people insincerely express their commitment to this oath, considering themselves inhabitants of where they live and citizens of Israel. Every year when they pray at the Passover, they say, "Next year we hope to be in the Promised Land." In fact, in Israel, Passover is one day shorter than in any other part of the world because they have made it to the Promised Land.

All of this is outrageously dishonest behaviour. It violates the spirit of their citizenship wherever they are except in Israel. It antagonizes just about everybody in the countries where they reside.

2. In addition to this, they aggravate the situation by sometimes even dressing and looking different. Indeed, in some communities in Brooklyn, for example, the Hassidim blatantly display their wide-rimmed black hats, their peculiar hairstyles, etc. Of course, they have the right to do all of this, but in the context of their intent, it is clearly provocative.

So on the one hand, the Jews create their little clubs that exclude everybody else, on the other hand they complain about not being admitted in the clubs created by other bigots, such as the Wasps. They reserve the right to arrogate their exclusivity and separateness while accusing everybody else of discriminating against them. The whole idea of preserving their race is a racist one, and they should never forget it.

3. To add insult to injury, the Jewish people have

excellent minds. They develop those minds, they acquire knowledge, and they rise in any society in which they live. Unfortunately, in the context of all that was said above, this backfires against them. The positive aspects that they have developed in themselves become the subject of savage jealousy from all the other people who have not developed the same abilities. Thus they invariably get portrayed as leeches, money grabbers, corrupters of countries, etc. At the same time, the Jews rejoice in that resentment, finding in it confirmation of the fact that they are the Chosen People, and, therefore, the glorified martyrs of those who do not understand them. There is here a false sense of being prophets, ironically a Messiah complex and persecution complex.

4. Consider the enormous amount of money that goes from the American Jews to Israel. The American Jews feel a secondary guilt for not being in Israel and for not living the harsh life there. Consequently, they assuage this guilt by doling out huge sums of money to finance a bellicose state, reminiscent of Sparta, a thorn in the side of the Arab world.

Indeed, what gives the Jews the right to arrogate Palestine for themselves? Have we ever seen any country or any peoples saying that because they lived somewhere three thousand years ago that they own that land and have the right to throw out the people living there in order to take it for themselves?

The creation of the state of Israel is in violation of every spiritual and human law thinkable.

5. Israel has developed nuclear capability stolen from the United States and has several hundred nuclear missiles having a range of over six thousand miles, i.e., capable of delivering to Moscow. If they can deliver to Moscow, they can deliver to Damascus, Baghdad, Cairo, or even London.

Individual Will and Determinism 217

Can you imagine the incredibly provocative nature of this situation in the Middle East? What if every single Arab nation in the region were to claim the same type of privilege? And why not? Why should we have double standards and allow Israel, who, after all, stole the land from the Arabs under very specious historical excuses, the favouritism not given to the Arabs?

With time it is obvious that the situation will equalize itself. The Arabs will very likely obtain nuclear weapons. This has already been attempted once with Iraq being trained by the French. Repeating this would be very possible today with the dismantling of the Soviet Union. The destruction of Israel with three million people in a nuclear war would be a lot easier than the destruction of any of the Arab countries. What does this mean? Another holocaust. So, history repeats itself if people do not take responsibility in humility.

6. In the Old Testament, Joshua led the Jewish people into Palestine and invaded eight local cities, beginning with Jericho where his army "utterly destroyed all in the city, both men and women, young and old, oxen, sheep, and asses, with the edge of the sword." (Joshua 6:21) Why? Because they were "impure," non-Jewish. Furthermore, it was done because "God" told them to do it. They had His blessing. That is genocide; that is holocaust. That is a final solution if there ever was one. The existence of this genocidal spirit in the psyche of the Jewish people has very grave consequences indeed. The mere belief that it was right for Joshua to exterminate the local population creates such an enormous unconscious guilt that it attracts such monstrosities as the final solution of the Nazis, the pogroms of the Russians, the Inquisition, the accusation that the Jews were responsible for spreading pestilence in the sixteenth century and all the other outrages committed against Jews.

"But," you will say, "this business of Joshua happened three thousand years ago. The Jews today have nothing to do with that."

"And," I will reply, "of course they do, since they have never taken responsibility for saying that this is utter nonsense, that Joshua was wrong in doing it, that the 'God' who guided him is no God at all but the devil, that there is no difference between what Joshua did and what Hitler did."

As long as the Jews do not realize this and as long as they do not take responsibility for this, and as long as they harbour double standards, they will continue to be persecuted and there will continuously be holocausts. So we arrive at another conclusion here: **a belief system that you harbour within you can create experiences on the outer level**, determining your life. A sacred belief can be harmful. If you believe that you are superior, if you believe in double standards, you will attract victimization that is equal and opposite to those double standards. It will come to you for the simple reason that the mere existence of a thought process that is against nature instantly creates guilt. Guilt starts when you stop loving, never mind the other outrages you commit after that. This guilt attracts punishment to you which means you want to be punished, you attract the outrages to yourself just as surely as the Jewish people attracted discrimination and genocide against themselves. If you are not aware of it, it will be experienced as determinism.

You can see here the incredible danger that exists in believing that the Bible is the word of God. The karma created and accumulated through the manufacturing of guilt by all of these people who believe this way is enormous. When the bill is finally presented to them, they will not know where it comes from. Consequently, they will continue to reproduce that negative reality. Instead of humbly looking at themselves and seeking the right causes of these outrages, they will then glorify their victimization and justify it by the fact that they are "chosen."

REINCARNATION AND
THE LAW OF CAUSE AND EFFECT

It is obvious that some aspects of our lives can only be understood if we believe in reincarnation. If we do not, then these aspects will remain for us in the realm of chance, injustice, chaos, etc. Take for example, the circumstances of your birth. You can only believe that you chose your parents, as well as the place where you were born, if you believe in reincarnation. For us who do, we take full responsibility for the choice of our parents. We see clearly that we had to choose those parents so as to bring into three-dimensional reality those problems that were already in us before birth.

Sometimes one is astonished by the force of a negativity or of a problem in his life and he wonders where it comes from. These problems have not been created by circumstances—the circumstances have provided the terrain wherein these occurrences experienced their rebirth. Reincarnation exists all around us. In the vegetable kingdom it occurs every year. *Why is it so difficult to accept that it is the same from the point of view of the soul and of the spirit? Do you think it is possible for you to work out all your problems this lifetime? What do you think happens to the unresolved areas of yourself after you die?* If you did not have other lives to work these through, you would be forever condemned to carry these problems.

This does not make sense. It is not in keeping with the evolutionary process of the universe as it is experienced all around us. Of course there are additional lives, and of course all of these problems must be resolved at some time in the future. The problems themselves return in different situations and guises where they struggle for resolution until they are solved.

The reason we do not believe in this process is because we have disconnected ourselves from it through voluntary amnesia. Indeed, we do not want to experience the pain that we have created for ourselves. We do not want to face the fact that we are paying for past misdeeds, past violations of Spiritual Law.

Consider a simple example—a baby overeating something he likes; thirty minutes later he suffers a tummy ache. He does not want to connect the two occurrences because if he did he would have to abandon the gluttony which he enjoys so much. Therefore, he only connects with the tummy ache and wants it to go away. He believes that he is a victim of his stomach, that the universe does not make sense. He resents the situation, demanding instant gratification and healing. However, if healing were to be given to him, then he would never have a chance to connect with how he himself created the stomach ache through his own free will.

The reconnection with free will is a key to spiritual development. The experience of pain, therefore, holds the key to this reconnection. Only if I stay in my pain will I say to myself, "I have to find how I have created this. I have to get myself out of this." If the pain is removed before this effort is effected, then free will will always be a myth, it will never be experienced.

Now suppose that you were a Nazi in a past life, exterminating a lot of Jews. Wouldn't it make sense for you to be born a Jew in Israel today? You have cut yourself off from the reason why you are there. Think of a murderer who is caught, put in prison and who "forgets" why he is there, convincing himself that he is a victim of society. *Can you entertain the possibility that you have amnesia, that you have lost contact with the causes of your present condition?* You know the reality of your unconscious. *Why not see that this unconscious contains the link that you are looking for?* By illuminating the material in your unconscious, your life becomes increasingly clear. You connect cause with effect, thus realizing that you have always had free will, only you have disconnected from it.

The Nazi gets reborn as a Jew so that he will experience the holocaust that he created for himself. The Jews are already letting their guard down, creating a Palestinian state that is about to destroy them. You genocidally kill Jews as a Nazi, you come back, are born today at the end of the twentieth century in Israel, attracting a situation in which you are continuously victimized by Arabs who want to eliminate you.

Let's take another example. A Jew who was victimized by the Nazis during World War II and who is killed there is born in Israel in the late 1940s and becomes the victimizer of Arabs in the 1967 Six Day War. The Tibetan confirms this fact. Jews and Germans reincarnate alternately with each other from one generation to the next. I suppose the Jews and the Arabs are setting up the same process now with each other.

So, we can conclude the following general points:

1. **The key to free will lies in the Law of Karma, the Law of Cause and Effect, the Law of Personal Responsibility.** To the degree that one accepts this, to that degree one starts understanding in humility how one has created every single aspect of one's life. We *want* to re-experience in order to cleanse.

2. **The disconnection of cause from effect is a function of not wanting to experience pain.** The individual wants to avoid paying the price of what he has done, so he conveniently numbs himself and blocks the causal connection.

3. Therefore, **the willingness to accept the veracity of the Law of Cause and Effect and the created pain restores us on the path of return and makes it increasingly clear to us on an experiential level that we are the masters of our destiny.**

4. **The process of evolution must first involve re-experiencing the pain that has been heretofore negated and numbed.** Put in simple terms, this means paying the price of what we have done in the past. Once the price is paid, then the person becomes increasingly open to mastery and ecstasy which is the next step.

HEALING

Instances of healing through merely taking responsibility and through the painstaking Path of Purification indeed exist. A person who worked briefly like this recently told us that as a result of her work here she has freed herself completely of a malignant cancer. She went to her doctor who was amazed at the miraculous disappearance of the tumor and of any sign of malignancy in her body. Now, this is a person who has had the courage to:

1. Reinterpret her experience of abuse. Instead of the huge blame and case that she had against the man who seduced her when she was a young girl, she was able to see that she actually enjoyed it and sought it.

2. Since there was no penetration in this initial early experience, she created a tumor in her vagina in order not to be penetrated, i.e., in order to recreate the same scene

over and over again with many other men.

This is not something that she saw or wanted to see. She thought it was monstrous, outrageous even to make that connection. On the conscious level she was complaining of not being penetrated; she was not connecting between that and the early occurrence in childhood. She hated men and at the same time desired them and had voracious sexual desires that were never satisfied. This would spill over into her personal life, affecting her ability to make ends meet financially.

Other problems were also ancillary to this. She gradually saw the patterns of her life as being recreations of the childhood scene, albeit decelerated—the childhood scene lasted 30-45 minutes, whilst the adult scenes lasted a year or two in their cycle. When she saw it, there was great pain; great recognition and great relief then replaced the feeling of resentment and her case against the universe. Soon she accepted her fate and the cancer that she had created. The acceptance and the taking of responsibility for the misuse of pleasure apparently had an effect on her body which removed the cancerous cells entirely.

Did this person enjoy this experience as a child, only to decide later as an adult that she should not have enjoyed it? And is this what created the problem? Yes, but you are not taking into consideration the entire scope of what happened. Let's see if we can reconstruct it and explain it point by point, since the explanation of this will help so many other people understand their own distortions and ensuing negative manifestations:

1. She had this particular experience in childhood during which she was brought to orgasm without being penetrated.

2. Since she was brought to orgasm, she views this experience as being a peak one. She sees it as the ultimate

of pleasure. She, therefore, confuses it in her psyche, albeit unconsciously, with the feeling of bliss she had when she was at-one with God before she started her cycle of incarnations.

3. Even if she were not brought to orgasm, she would feel the same way about it since this was the first time that she experienced these feelings. In their pure form, these feelings are always seen as the ultimate.

4. Since this experience is the ultimate, it became the goal, the one state to be sought, the way a Buddhist seeks nirvana, or the way a Christian seeks the Christ within and without.

5. So she grew up, still seeking that peak experience, albeit unconsciously. She attracted life patterns that provided the re-creation of this experience.

6. However, the experience itself, as pleasurable as it appeared to be, was incomplete. Without penetration the adult does not experience the ultimate of sexual pleasure. Furthermore, the experience the way it was first gone through was not natural then and is even less natural now that she is an adult. This disconnection from nature creates guilt. Add to this the guilt that exists for wanting an experience that is essentially crassly physical and which, therefore, excludes fusion on the emotional, mental, and spiritual levels, and you have an enormous amount of guilt being manufactured.

7. The battleground for this conflict between her nature and what she wants from her personality becomes her vagina, the seat of her sexuality. The physical manifestation of that battleground is the acceleration of the growth of some of the cells in that part of her body—cancer.

8. The realization of the whole pattern of behaviour that she developed in order to recreate this initial experience

Individual Will and Determinism

makes her conscious of the childishness, the futility, the falsehood of what she has been pursuing all of her life as if it were a god.

9. The apprehension of this first on the spiritual level and second on the mental level influences the emotional level where the desire for this is reduced or dissolved, making room for new, more mature and adult desires that satisfy the entire person.

10. To the degree this is an integrated experience, to that degree there will be a consequence on the physical level. That consequence is the cessation of the rebellion of the cells that would like to find nature once again. You see, the cancerous cells were merely nature's attempt to come back. The manifestation is negative but the intent of these cells was positive. If it were not for this cancer, she would never have been able to resolve this entire negative trend.

I believe that this is not the first time she has manifested this. It is obviously a deep pattern that has come back in this lifetime. The proof of this is that the genesis of the whole problem was in her childhood. All childhood problems are inherited from past lives.

Now, healing like this is possible for everybody, but we are not making claims of being able to heal anybody. We are merely saying that if you apply this material to your life you will heal. **You** will heal; **we** are not healing you; **you** are healing yourself by removing the barriers to the Universal Life Force and the Universal Consciousness. It is as simple as that. It is not any more difficult.

Had there been penetration would there have been a different reaction? Yes, there would be the worshiping of a different type of situation. But the problem is not that there was not penetration, the problem is that she remained fixated on recreating an experience that happened in the past. That is a problem because she is not living in the now and, therefore, is not at-one with nature.

PREDICTIONS

If you want to know what your future is going to be like, all you have to do is to look at yourself today. Indeed, that which exists on the mental and emotional levels today will be on the physical level tomorrow. Your thoughts and your feelings today are constructing tomorrow's manifest reality. The great implication of this: if you want to build a better future, change your thoughts and your feelings today; take responsibility for your entire self today; anything you think today will find itself as a feeling tomorrow and as a physical reality the day after.

Here again is the element of free will. Nobody is forcing you to think in any other way than the way you think today. However, when you see the results of it tomorrow, you will not want to establish the connection between today's thoughts and tomorrow's "reality."

FREE WILL CONFUSED AS LICENSE

The gluttonous child we have described above considers free will as "I can eat as much candy as I want." He will blame the universe for giving him a stomach ache. Later, when he grows up, he will see that free will also encompasses the consequences of what he has done. With the raising of consciousness, he will know better and say, "If I eat in a gluttonous manner, I will get sick. I am free either to eat in a gluttonous manner, in which case I will get sick, or to eat reasonably, in which case I will be nourished, energized, and healed." With the raising of consciousness and with the connection between cause and effect, free will, freedom, is seen as inseparable from responsibility, i.e., from the Law of Cause and Effect.

The person who does not accept this wants freedom from the Law of Cause and Effect. He wants the advantages of doing as he pleases, but he does not want to face the consequences of it. He, therefore, favours an unjust universe. That's how he will create injustice.

Justice is a function of the Law of Cause and Effect. For every action, there is a reaction. Now he has violated justice. Later, when he experiences the tummy ache, the consequences of his license, he will feel unjustly treated. He forgets that he himself did not want the Law of Cause and Effect in the first place. The injustice that he perpetrated on the universe through his double standards backfires. He then experiences the same injustice directed at him. Having been the victimizer, he now becomes the victim.

People sometimes believe that they are "forced" to obey the laws of God. So they rebel, believing that they can arrogate what they please, when they please. Having created their own laws—anarchy—they now have to live in accordance with these laws. So they suffer from them. Nobody is forcing you to obey God's laws. It is something that you have to come to realize by yourself. **You must learn that it is in your best self-interest to be responsible.** That is the only way you are going to change. You are not going to change in any other way. You cannot be altruistic unless you experience that it is in your best self-interest. With the raising of consciousness, you will get to the point where devoting yourself to total service, surrendering everything you have to it will be experienced as conquering the universe. You do this and the universe is yours.

God did not create evil. Evil was created when people wanted to arrogate to themselves that which did not belong to them. The fall of the angels occurred through double standards, through saying, "I am better than you and I will take what you have." This, then, as we have seen, sets up the situation where the reverse is going to be true. Thus, the self-created hell is going to exist until the time comes when we have the courage to realize how we have first created it for ourselves. Then, we will voluntarily want to get out of it and finally obey the laws of God.

The process of rejoining the laws of God is a gradual one. This is what true faith is all about—the gradual removal of the barriers, the re-energizing of that which has become numb, the continuous realization of new and fundamental truths, the continuous rediscovery of the same truths on higher levels of development.

In what way do you find it difficult to obey the laws of God? For instance, do you find yourself irresistibly attracted to dishonesty, to stealing, to telling lies? Do you find yourself irresistibly attracted to being cruel or to imposing your will on others, or to letting others impose their will on you? Where do you want to get something for nothing?

PUNISHMENT

Is the tummy ache punishment for gluttony? It depends upon your degree of evolution. If you are a child who needs limits, then the concept of punishment inflicted by a superior being helps you build your inner authority, your inner conscience. Eventually, as an adult, the concept of punishment becomes unnecessary, as do laws. You can see that the tummy ache is not punishment anymore; it is the logical effect of your lack of responsibility. The child needs to be told as a first step that "God punished you for overeating." Eventually, by internalizing this concept of an authority out there, self-authority is built and the person realizes that within himself he has the power once attributed to an outer level God.

The difference between the adult and the child is, therefore, the difference between this religion of ours and the conventional religions. Respectively, one is an adult religion and the other one is a child's. Applying a child's religion to an adult situation is as ludicrous as is the opposite. Therefore, we need to tolerate these people in their primitive state. What is intolerable is when an adult wants to pretend to be a child, desisting responsibility and attributing it to an irrational God. What is also unacceptable is when a child arrogates too much responsibility. This occurs, for example, in some New Age teachings where the notion of freedom is pushed past natural law into license and where the lower self is never really looked at as an ever-present reality in human existence.

AN UNEXPECTED BLESSING

It may seem that the more you "sin," i.e., violate the laws of God, the further away from God you are. It seems also that the less you violate the laws of God the closer you are to God.

In effect this is only true in one sense. In another sense, the more you violate the laws of God, the more pain you create for yourself. The prodigal returns, only after having drunk the cup to the fullest. He wants to return to his Father when the bad ways have been so great that he gets outraged by them, wanting to renounce them. Any premature return is not enough, and is best discouraged.

The greater the pain, the greater the desire for resolution of that violation and, therefore, the closer you are to God. Thus, people who are in crisis are closer to God than people who are not. That is why Christ preferred to be in the company of those who were admitted sinners. The experience of pain these people were going through was making them a lot closer to God than the others who were still caught in the goody two-shoes status quo. Those caught in the false life, desperately pretending to be good and pretending to uphold all of the values that exist in the Higher Self are, therefore, further away from God than those who blatantly violate Spiritual Law and, therefore, are experiencing the painful consequences of having done so. The pain means the desire for a better state and, therefore, a readiness for self-improvement. Lack of pain and the maintaining of the status quo contain a lot less desire for self-improvement.

Does that mean that one has to murder, rape, pillage and plunder in order to find spiritual reality and the Path? No, not at all. These actions create incredibly painful karma. However, one can experience the murderer within, the rapist within, the thief within through the controlled circumstances we provide here. Thus, the soul is gradually cleared of these negativities without ever having to act them out. This then constitutes our way.

Resist not evil. Fully experience the evil within you. The pain that will come from this will propel you into looking for and finding the ecstasy of at-onement with God.

All of this can be done with your free will; you must choose to do all of this. God cannot make you do it, nor can He make you want to.

DEPENDENCY ON OUTER LEVEL REALITY FOR HAPPINESS

A person who has accepted this way and who has unified himself with the decision to experience all of his pain and thus open himself to the experience of ecstasy is happy inside no matter what happens on the outside.

Here we recall Viktor Frankl and his concentration camp experiences. In the midst of horrendous outer level conditions, he experienced the ecstasy of contact with his wife. He says himself that never had he found such happiness before than in those moments when he was able to experience the ecstasy of those dialogues with his wife on the subliminal level. This was happening in the midst of incredible physical suffering.

Let's consider the opposite situation—an individual who is depending on outer level conditions for his happiness. He will not feel happy until he gets a particular house or a particular car or unless he marries a particular type of person. When he gets it, the happiness he experiences is temporary. Soon thereafter he will want something else because inside he is still escaping from at-onement with himself. Furthermore, since that condition exists on the inside and has not been resolved, he will create on the outer level negative circumstances that will prevent him from having all those material things that he desires so much. Thus, he will undermine himself and never be happy.

If he experiences the truth he will learn that he must accept that he is powerless in certain situations on the outer level. Here we are reminded of the Serenity Prayer:

> God, grant me the serenity
> To accept the things I cannot change,
> The courage to change the things I can,
> And the wisdom to know the difference.

It is not some outer deity who is punishing you by not allowing you to have a better car or a better home. It is your own disconnection from the Law of Cause and Effect, your own violation of the laws of God, your own disregard of your task that is creating those conditions. If you at-one yourself with all of these: (1) You will lose your desire for that particular car or that particular house. (2) You will have the power in your hands to get them if you want them.

This may seem contradictory, but it is a Spiritual Law which applies to our world of imperfection. One has to give up that which one wants the most in order perhaps to have it.

INNER WILL AND OUTER WILL

There are three types of will:

1. **The outer will, the will of the little ego.** This is where we experience our wants and where we do not understand why they do not come about, why we do not get what we demand.

2. Inner will, which is divided into two parts:

a. **The will of the lower self,** often contradicting the will of the little ego in (1) above. The lower self, in spite of all of its childishness, may have a very strong message that we need to heed which would prevent us from fulfilling the need of the little ego. Say, for example, that the little ego wants to have a Lexus. The lower self may undermine that desire for a Lexus. Even though that undermining is manifested through negativity, there is a very important message there. Perhaps it is that the Lexus is wanted for the wrong reasons. The harmful volition/negative intent of the lower self sometimes has a positive message behind it.

b. **The Greater Will, the will of the Higher Self.** Here is where what we really want exists. If the ego is resilient enough to heed the message that comes from this level, it will want to ally itself with it and together dissolve the little will of the lower self. If the message is not heeded, then it is communicated through crisis, and that which the ego has constructed, no matter how positive it seems to be, will be destroyed so that the true message may be received. The destruction of the status quo is such a crisis.

It is true that you can will anything you want. However, if you will something that is unnatural, i.e., against the will of God, you are willing something that is obviously against your task as well. Thus, you will create conditions wherein you will want to destroy what you have created even though the desire to do so is an unconscious one.

You can test it. Ask yourself what the motives are that exist behind that which you want. Suppose, for example, that you want to succeed in your profession. There is nothing wrong with that; it can be part of the Plan, and it can be in accordance with nature.

However, if it is motivated by greed or by a desire for approval, or by a desire for one-upmanship of others, then it violates natural law and is doomed to fail.

What you want may be unnatural for inner reasons. You may have to experience something else, go in another direction, simply because there is a lack, a gap, or a fault in you that needs correcting. That deeper need may be enough to thwart any of your attempts. And that deeper need may be unconscious. Make it conscious.

Even if you temporarily seem to have what you want and even more than you want, the existence of the harmful volition and not working to expose and resolve it will create a situation in which you will eventually destroy what you have.

You can deduce whether a desire within yourself is in accordance with the will of God or not by experiencing its nature. If it is forced, heavy, contrived, pushing, or if it cannot tolerate the possibility of failure or of contradiction, i.e., if it is steeped in demands, then you can be sure that it is not the will of God and that you are disconnected from your soul.

A desire that comes from the soul or from the Higher Self is different. It is calm, persistent, it tolerates frustration and learns from it. It tolerates the opposite situations as long as they need to be experienced, without complaining and without demanding or despairing. One of the properties of the mask and your Higher Self is that you will find the difference between a false desire and a real one.

The contrived quality of the false desire can come from two levels of distortion:

1. You can demand it from your emotional self, from your astral level, being fixated on it, experiencing it as an addiction.

2. You can demand it from your mental level, being fixated on particular sets of thoughts. Thus it is not given that because you have a feeling or an emotion of desiring something you are connected with your soul. This is a great misinterpretation of the truth. Feelings can be just as distorted as thinking.

The natural soul need contains all of those together—thought, feeling, action, experience, activity, receptivity, all are there, harmoniously balanced and confident that in the last analysis, what is right will come about. When this occurs, then your will and the will of God are one, your will and nature are one. It is inevitable that you will get what you want.

RAISING CHILDREN

Just as any other area of our lives, raising children has been influenced by the prevailing glamours of society. In Victorian days, a strict discipline was imposed on children, stifling them, killing their Instinct of Enquiry. In reaction to this, Dr. Benjamin Spock took us to the far side of the other spectrum where children were deprived of discipline—and I say deprived purposefully.

The consequence of the two extremes has been the formation of either rigid, knowledgeable people with no capacity for pleasure or self-indulgent illiterates. As a result, there is a great gap between those who were educated during the Depression years and those called the "baby boomers." Of course, this creates great conflicts, misunderstandings, destruction of standards, etc.

The correct way of raising children is a resilient one residing somewhere between the two extremes. Dr. James Dobson has extensively and very wisely written a few books on the subject, appropriately giving them titles such as *Dare to Discipline* and *Parenting is Not for Cowards*. Rather than launch into an extensive description about what should or should not be done in what circumstances, I would rather refer you to these books which I find to be excellent.

There are a few points, however, that need to be understood about raising children.

1. The first problem the child encounters is his conflict with authority. Indeed, he experiences authority as restrictive. There is no way a child can understand why it is that he cannot eat an infinite amount of cookies or candy, why it is that he cannot play with fire or why it is that he cannot fly off the fifth floor balcony. Thus, as children, we have all submitted to authority for the wrong reasons. We obeyed because we could not do anything else about it or because we needed and sought our parents' approval. We did not obey because we understood it or its purpose.

Consequently and inevitably, the pleasure principle became associated with that which was forbidden. Since pleasure is God and since life has no purpose without pleasure, the forbidden—as well as pleasure—was sought dishonestly. Furthermore, all the child's resources were focused on the seeking of pleasure in a dishonest and unlawful manner.

The parent who understands this will know how to do two things at the same time: (1) On the one hand he will allow the child to sometimes violate his directives and, (2) he will at the same time set very strict limits which eventually will form a healthy conscience in the child. The greater the maturity of the parent, the more easily he will know how to stay on this tightrope; in fact, it will appear more like a wide road than a tightrope, and he will comfortably be able to walk it. The more the parent is stuck in his own childhood, the more difficult it will be for him to do this. Thus, he will fluctuate between over-permissiveness and over-control.

Thus, parenting becomes a great test of growth for the parents involved. Another conclusion that can be drawn here is that we can now understand why grandparents make much better parents than parents do. So, the proximity of grandparents is a great healing factor for everyone concerned, children, and parents.

2. The child is primitive. As cute, as innocent, and as lovely as he is his Life Force is very rough, primitive, cruel. Furthermore, their consciousness is very limited. Consequently, it is not enough merely to reason with him. In fact, reasoning with him is sometimes contraindicated. Because of his primitive state, primitive forms of punishment have to be administered to him. Spanking, therefore, is the only way to enforce the law at that level. It is the same with humanity. Wherever humanity was and still is primitive, the only language understood must be force. This happens to be Spiritual Law. If you try to reason with the disobedient child, he will interpret it as your apology to

him for depriving him of his pleasure. It is the same for the hoodlum or with the tyrant. You do not reason with these people. You use physical means to prevent them from harming themselves or others.

So, dear spiritual reader, let's no longer have any of this pacifistic glamour that you call non-violence. You are doing much more harm than good by preventing yourself from using the specific methods you need to apply in the raising of your children. You are being a coward under the banner of loving them. Harmlessness is to be found through the just administering of physical punishment when it is needed.

PRAYER IN SCHOOL

When will the United States learn to separate church from state? Its European parents have been doing just this for a century or two, depending upon which country is considered. This concept was imparted to humanity during the Age of Enlightenment, the eighteenth century. It is high time that it be applied in this country.

Those who advocate prayer in school have the hidden agenda of proselytizing Christianity. *Indeed, when the great majority of the students are Christian, what do you think a prayer is going to sound like in a school?* No matter how neutral anyone is—and nobody is, least of all the teachers—some bias is going to be expressed.

It is also fallacious to believe that prayer can be initiated by students and that it thus constitutes freedom of speech. *Suppose there is someone in the classroom who happens to believe that sex orgies are holy, how would you like your child to be exposed to a prayer exalting orgies? That certainly would constitute freedom of speech, wouldn't it?* Christianity becomes just as offensive to anyone who is not Christian when it is expressed in schools.

Prayer does not belong in schools. It belongs at home and in churches.

SYSTEMS OF EDUCATION

As long as every county in the United States has the "freedom" to create its own school district, you will have an extraordinarily and unnecessarily expensive school system that will not make any sense and that will mess up, confuse, and divide the country.

The education of a nation cannot depend on the local and parochial ignorance of parents. It must be centralized and conducted by wiser and more enlightened people. It must also have nation-wide standards. A high school graduate in Texas or in California or in Minnesota must pass through the same exam, must have been exposed to and have learned the same level of material. Without this, the universities would be reduced to Towers of Babel where no one understands what anyone says.

When will this country learn that what they are doing is not freedom but license? When will they finally reach the educational wisdom of their parents in Europe? Until then, we will regress in terms of education. It is already shameful and sad that we are number forty-eight on the list of nations in terms of literacy.

HOMOSEXUALITY

No matter how much defense there is against believing the following, nevertheless it is true: homosexuality is a distortion. Why? Because a key does not fit into a key and a keyhole does not fit into a keyhole. Homosexuality is a distortion of the nature of the individual.

Warning: As much as it is a distortion, there are other

distortions that exist in the heterosexual world. If by being heterosexual, you believe that you are superior to homosexuals you are very much mistaken. You are committing a great spiritual error.

Many souls need to undergo the experience of homosexuality in order to find their individuality. Indeed, homosexuals, through being rejected, find out what it is like to rely on their own resources. They much more easily transcend the problem of selling out to their parents and, therefore, become a lot more open to material emanating from their soul and from their Spirit. It is no wonder then that there are so many of them who accomplish so much in the world of art, music, acting, and in many other subjects, too. It is extremely important to understand all of this and to beware of judgment.

In many religious organizations, it is erroneously believed that being a homosexual "distorts the alignment of your energies" and thus disqualifies you as a priest or a monk or a person who graduates to the higher titles of spirituality. We at The Church of the Path® do not believe this way. Every one of us has distortions. Spiritual growth is the process of gradually neutralizing those distortions, filing them away. Promotion to positions of responsibility—minister, master and other titles in our Church—are wide open to members of the homosexual community who simply do their work on this Path just like anybody else.

CHAPTER 20
THE SPIRIT AND THE SOUL

THE SPIRIT

It is otherwise called the Higher Self, the Monad, God Within. It contains all that is already purified within us. It includes the "will of God," or the "greater will." It is not all knowing, but it can access other Higher Selves for any information or capacity it needs.

Thus, if we can access our spirit, through our personality and soul, we can, "ourselves"—our little ego—access infinity through it.

Everything grows. God, the Christ, our Spirit, or Higher Self all grow. The entire purpose of creation is growth. When an aspect or attribute is purified, it becomes integrated by the Spirit which is thus augmented in its capacity for power, pleasure, creation, love, and intelligence.

FORMATION OF THE SOUL

Right this minute you are preparing for your next incarnation by the way you think, feel, and act. The sum total of your belief systems, the ones that you have chosen to digest, and the others that you have chosen to keep in spite of your best self-interests, all determine right here and now what your next incarnation will be, what your future is going to be.

Just as it is true to say that you create your future by what you are doing in the present, it is also true to say that you create your next incarnation by what you are doing right here and now.

Before birth, your spirit, your Higher Self gets together with many spirit guides and together decide what it is that you are going to do and how it is that you are going to shape your next life. They then construct your soul. Your soul is, therefore, the repository of that which will be released into your personality and into your life experience in your next incarnation. The soul is, therefore, a seed with a plan to gradually release at specific times and places after incarnation that which needs to be experienced and worked on. So the contents of the soul decide what your incarnation is going to be like. These contents contain:

1. **Some unresolved aspects, negativities, etc., that need to be resolved.** These are decelerated parts of you that weigh heavily on your spirit and prevent it from movement. The decision to resolve a particular negativity does not just serve you, it serves many others around you. It also adds to the experience bank of humanity your particular method of resolving a universal problem. Thus, by resolving a particular problem in your life, you program humanity just as you program a computer, with your particular brand of resolution. Other souls may then access what you have done, helping themselves to achieve their own process of purification.

2. **A lot of individual unfinished businesses.** For instance, you may have a karmic debt with somebody which you repay through undertaking a particular role in this person's life in your incarnation. So, from one incarnation to the next we meet each other in different roles—fathers become sons or brothers, daughters become wives or husbands and so forth. We also change sexes from one incarnation to the next so as to experience humanity in its

totality. In resolving this unfinished business, we re-establish connection with the Universal Life Force. Thus, we not only perform a service to ourselves, but we also perform a service to humanity.

It is obvious from the above points, but worth repeating, that the ultimate purpose of incarnation is service. Also, it is extremely important to see that service can only be accomplished through the resolution of our own problems and not through the avoidance of them.

3. **Talents, abilities, capacity to experience beauty, wealth, pleasure, etc.** Sometimes these are made available to the person immediately upon his birth so as to make the other tasks more easily handled. However, sometimes an individual may make the wrong decision. He chooses, for instance, to be born into too much wealth. This, then, corrupts him and he wastes his life. Or, he may even take too much talent, behind which he protects himself and avoids dealing with the more negative aspects of himself.

So, as you can see, mistakes are also made outside of the body. You can also see that your choice, good or bad, also exists outside of the body.

A good exercise here would be to read biographies from this point of view. When reading a biography, ask yourself, *"How did this person prepare his soul? What are the mistakes he made in preparing it; what are the issues he avoided dealing with during his life; and what is it that he has contributed to humanity? What is it that he needed to overcome in order for that contribution to finally be revealed in his life?"*

NAPOLEON—AN EXAMPLE

Let's take some individual and global examples to illustrate this point about preparation for incarnation and the life that follows. We have used Mozart in other contexts, so let's take somebody else this time—Napoleon, for example. His task was obviously the synthesizing, the consolidation of the destruction created by the French Revolution. Indeed, the French Revolution had destroyed the old order which had been in existence since the end of the Roman Empire with its systems of kings, cardinals, popes and emperors. Napoleon's leadership, as dictatorial as it was, re-established a sense of order and authority, this time with a new world order as its base. His conquests of the whole of Europe and Egypt resulted in the reawakening in every single one of these countries a sense of nationalism and individuality. He brought with him the need for reform, the idea that all men are created equal and the necessity to destroy and topple the existing corrupt monarchical systems of government. Thus, he generalized, universalized, the French Revolution and its ideas. That was his task. He saw himself as a liberator and he announced himself as such.

The destruction of the French Revolution became with him synthesized in the idea of modern nationalism and individual freedom.

Thus, he could not be born to high nobility. However, he had to benefit somewhat from the advantages of status and title. Had he not been born with them, he may not have benefitted from the military training he so very much needed. So, he was born of very small and poor Neapolitan nobility.

Although his destiny was to be unraveled in France, "no one is a prophet in his own country." Thus, he was born in Corsica, "fatefully" one year after Corsica was annexed to France. I firmly believe that Choiseul, unconsciously acting under the influence of France's collective soul, annexed Corsica to France *because* Napoleon was going to be born in it. I also believe that Napoleon waited to be conceived and to incarnate *after* Corsica was annexed to France. Napoleon's Corsican origins made him a stranger in France. Indeed, if you travel through France today, you will find that the Corsicans are still seen as strangers. People humour them for their accent, for their boasting, etc.

So Napoleon was born into a huge and poor family. As a child he was ridiculed because he was small and physically weak for his age. He was not exactly your handsome, wellborn, healthy, son of a marquis with a silver spoon in his mouth. This made it possible for him to develop his own style of military warfare and his own ideas about the future of Europe, its unification, etc. At the beginning, he was very clear about his task, and, therefore, extraordinarily successful. However, his successes were too much for him. Past the year 1800 and fueled by his ongoing military victories, megalomania took over. He lost contact with his task and converted his powers to his own purposes, thus regressing.

Napoleon's personal life was a mess. In true Ray One fashion, he did not trust anyone and no one trusted him. He put his ineffectual family on every possible throne in continental Europe, did not support them, and was thoroughly disappointed by every single one of them. He fathered about thirty children, only one of whom was legitimate, the Duke of Reischtat. His wife, Marie Louise of Austria, was the niece of Marie Antoinette of France who had been beheaded during the revolution. This union was an incredible reversal. How could Napoleon, the personification of revolution, reverse himself so much so as to marry the ultimate representative of the old regime that had been destroyed at such incredible expense? He lost himself into the glamours of his time and sold out to them. His sellout was his demise. Some of Napoleon's critics demonstrated that his emblem, the bee, curiously resembled the ancient fleur-des-lis, only reversed. This in itself epitomizes Napoleon and his reversal. Napoleon in reverse very much gives you the feudal system.

Nevertheless, Europe as it is today is really Napoleon's Europe. It is unified, it is democratic. Even England has joined it, which, of course, was Napoleon's dream. He tried to do this militarily, but was thwarted.

THE CONFEDERACY
OF THE AMERICAN SOUTH—AN EXAMPLE

The huge glamour of empire which took hold in Napoleon also took hold in his nephew, Napoleon III, and his illegitimate grandson who later became Maxmillian I of Mexico. The entire Mexican Empire was an attempt at regression to the pre-French Revolutionary feudal system that existed in continental Europe. Semi-secretly, the Mexican Empire was allied to the Confederacy during the American Civil War. The Confederacy itself included many reincarnated souls of French nobility. These pre-French Revolution nobles, some of whom were beheaded during their revolution did not accept their crisis and did not interpret it in the right way, so they reincarnated in the American South and tried to recreate the same situation there with the slaves, the mansions, the manners, the mannerisms and so forth.

Listen to some of the battle hymns from the South and compare them to some of the ones from the North. The hymns of the North were drawn from American folk music. They have survived, and we still know them today. However, those from the South are hardly ever played or heard. They very much resemble baroque and rococo music. They were really the recreation in the second half of the nineteenth century of the fashionable French court music—an anachronism, of course, as was the entire exercise of the Confederacy.

So Napoleon's soul carried a task that was partially accomplished. His egocentricity and lack of purification made it possible for the forces of darkness to gradually take hold of him and lead him to do exactly the opposite of that which he was supposed to do. The consequences of this were considerable. The soul of the Confederacy which was made out of reincarnated ancien regime French nobles became the ally of the soul of the Mexican Empire, of the Austrian Empire and of the descendants of Napoleon. Those were strange bedfellows, strange allies indeed. Think of it—they sold out to each other in order to maintain a status quo that was already defunct.

LINCOLN—AN EXAMPLE

Abraham Lincoln's task was accomplished in spite of his extraordinary personal difficulties with this coalition. I believe that it is because of his Sixth Ray personality that he prevailed in his faith in his fight against slavery. Economists want to reduce the Civil War struggle to merely an economic one in which the North's industrial protectionism was at odds with the free exchange policies of the South.

This struggle was only one of the outermost reflections of the true struggle; it is not the deep one. The deeper one was the ideological struggle, the struggle between two ways of life, the old and the new. The old one was trying to regress us to the ways of the eighteenth century, ways of feudalism, versus the new one which was trying to propel us into the progress of the twentieth century.

In this, we also see the soul of the United States, its task, and its purification process in the making. We can say that the problem of slavery existed at the time of the creation of the United States. However, the country was not as yet ready to deal with it. This problem was released in its personality in the middle of the nineteenth century for the purposes of resolution.

KNOWING THE CONTENTS OF YOUR SOUL

From microcosm to macrocosm we have traced the formation and the manifestation of a soul, on an individual and on a global level. *What are the contents of your soul, what did you put in it, what is yet to be revealed, can you feel those states already existing on the mental level descending into the astral level and then on the physical level?* **If you are able to see this, you will be able to predict your future, avoid barriers to your task, and manifest your genius.**

CHAPTER 21
REINCARNATION

IN THE BEGINNING

Consciousness breeds energy. Energy follows thought. In the beginning was the Word and the Word created the world, as the Word was God. The Word, the thought, the consciousness incarnates in the body. Acceptance of the existence of an original consciousness which creates the body and the physical level immediately involves acceptance of the following:

1. **Incarnation:** spirit creating a body and energizing it, using it for specific personal and cosmic tasks at incarnation.

2. **Reincarnation:** when the task is finished or when a particular body is used up, whichever comes first, the spirit, the idea, the consciousness looks for and energizes another body. The idea is immortal; the body is mortal, finite.

When your car is too old, you buy a new one. When you change consciousness, you also change your outer life, including your friends and your possessions, to suit the new consciousness. This is reincarnation.

Rich people who are afraid to die and abandon their material wealth undergo excessive rejuvenating techniques. Pharaohs had their bodies embalmed and buried with all of their wealth so as to take it beyond their lifetime. Old establishments stifle new ideas and new life in order to eternalize themselves. All of this comes from insecurity, as does all bigotry. It also comes from the refusal to open up to new ideas, to think.

Now look at yourself. *To what extent do you really want to face all of yourself? To what extent are you petrified? To what extent are you holding on to lines of least resistance, protecting your little skin?* To that extent, you do not really believe in reincarnation or in life; you believe in petrification. But to the extent you want to face all of yourself, to that extent you believe, really believe, experientially believe in reincarnation and you lose your fear of death.

Reincarnation is a good reality—a reality in which we can rejoice. It is the confirmation and assertion of eternal life.

Look at Mozart. When he was three years old, he had to be lifted up onto the bench to play the harpsichord. How could he possibly have developed this skill? At age six or seven, he picked up a violin and played it. The violin happens to be a very difficult instrument, and there is no way, without training, that you can put your fingers on a violin and know the note you are going to play. By age ten, he had composed an opera. Where did he get these skills and more? From incarnating and reincarnating as a musician much the same as Plotinus did with philosophy.

REINCARNATION AFTER ACCIDENTAL OR PREMATURE DEATH

If there is an accident or a premature death, can there be a quick reincarnation? Yes, men die in wars and people die in accidents that were not meant to happen, so they come back. In some cases, spirit guides help them to find a body they can inhabit.

In the case of death happening prematurely, the soul, aided by spirit guides, will look for an opportunity to reincarnate as quickly as possible in conditions that are approximately the same as in the life that was just interrupted. Depending on the degree of development of the individual, he will have available to him help to find a new situation and inhabit it.

However, in other cases, the premature death is not an accident. It may seem to be for those who have become attached to the person who dies. However, his death was very part of his task. He needed to die the way he did. He was born to meet death in that particular way. An example that comes to mind is of a ten year old child who was killed by a car while crossing the street. I worked with the parents to guide them through their grief and in the course of this work they eventually related some very significant things. For instance, the day before his death the child was talking as if he was going to die the next day. In retrospect, he was saying things that were presaging his death. Obviously, the "accident" was no accident.

This entity came in, went through a particular portion of life for a specific purpose and died a painful death, also for a specific purpose. The gift he gave to his parents by dying could clearly be seen in the work they were doing with me. They had to come to terms with the greatness, the grandness of the universe through the very tragic crisis of their son's death. They could either embitter themselves for the rest of their lives and destroy their marriage by blaming the world or take the opportunity offered for them to begin to realize the greatness of the Law of Cause and Effect and the true meaning of incarnation and reincarnation.

THE RISK INHERENT IN INCARNATING

How can unexplained accidents be explained from the point of view of the Law of Personal Responsibility? If you create your own reality, how could accidents occur? From the point of view of absolute reality, yes, you create your own reality. However, from the point of view of the relative, in the process of creating it, you may make mistakes. To the degree you are removed from absolute reality, you are also removed from determining your future. There is always a risk involved. There is always the existence of contrary forces that want to impede the process.

Let's consider the most important of all incarnations, the Christ. When He incarnated, He took a risk. He did not know what the outcome was going to be. He immersed Himself in a human body, losing, albeit temporarily, His consciousness. This consciousness was gradually regained. It was not given that He was going to succeed in His battle against the forces of darkness.

It is the same with us. When we incarnate with a particular soul, we do not know whether or not we will be able to achieve all that we have planned before we incarnated. Also, we do not know what the forces of darkness have in store for us. We can only guess by the shape and the nature of our own lower self, provided of course that we are in a process such as this one, which is rare.

Furthermore, you may have overestimated or underestimated particular factors in this process. You may have bitten off more than you could chew, or less, both of which
possibilities would lead to regression.

The cultivation of consciousness makes it possible for you to anticipate what may happen and prevent negativities while pursuing that which is positive. This comes from the fact that with consciousness you are able to know the nature of your lower self. Once your faults are known, it will also be known to you that the forces of darkness will intervene in the precise quality and quantity represented in your lower self. Say, for instance, somebody has a great insecurity in terms of his or her sexual self-worth. The forces of darkness will monopolize the situation by creating events wherein the person is willing to sell his soul for the purpose of sexual gratification. Integrity will be impaired for the sake of experiencing a particular aspect of sexuality. Now, before birth, this problem may very well be underestimated or overestimated in which case it will lead to distortions and to unplanned events in a person's life. This constitutes accidents.

WHEN DOES THE SOUL INHABIT THE BODY?

It is a question in the context of abortion. The soul hovers over the life conditions that have been chosen to be inhabited and with the infant's first breath, it enters the body. Some of you may have a knowledge of what I am saying about hovering over the life conditions before birth. You are going to have dreams concerning this because some of you have retained this memory. Be open to your dreams concerning it.

MEMORY OF PAST LIVES

The trauma of birth will make you forget many of the memories of a past life, but it is not the only thing that will make you forget them. There is another process that the entity goes through before incarnation which is a process of voluntarily erasing the memory of past lives so as to start a new "tabula rasa." Tabula rasa is a theory that people who do not believe in reincarnation talk about. They say all children start fresh with a "level table," there is nothing on it; they are all the same at birth. We do not believe this.

As puberty sets in children lose memory of their previous life. With the coming in of the inferior function, the soul releases into the personality the adult task. This new influx obliterates the memory of the previous lifetime. Look at your life as you were as a girl or boy before puberty; if you remember, you will find karmic memory. I invite you to search for it. The loss of memory of past life is temporary. It is recovered through the process of purification. At the same time, it is sometimes re-experienced in the form of dreams or in an inexplicable attachment to a part of history, a certain mode of dress, a certain type of music, a certain habit of thought.

EXPERIENCE BETWEEN INCARNATIONS

Let's go now to the cases where it takes a longer "time" between death and rebirth.

1. Outside of the body you will find yourself at the beginning on the etheric and astral levels. If you died a violent or traumatic death, you are terrified, and the shape of your subtler bodies is still espousing the shape of your physical body at the time of death, which is a mess. You have not had, as yet, the presence of mind to know that you can create whatever body you want to create. You have to undergo a healing process in hospitals in the other world in order for you to come back to being yourself.

It is not given that you will go through the tunnel that is spoken about in the material on Near-Death-Experiences. Your terror of death and your lack of belief in reincarnation may keep you around for awhile as a discarnate soul. Cemeteries are full of discarnate souls who still do not believe that they are dead. They stay around as ghosts or become poltergeists.

2. Once you leave this plane, the etheric and astral plane, you enter the mental and spiritual planes where you meet people you have known in this life who have died. You also

meet people who you have known in other lives who you start recognizing and, at that point, you recover the memory of those past lives.

If you are helped through your death, then you immediately inhabit a shape that somewhat resembles that which you had when you were in your twenties, at the peak of your physical health. Psychics have verified this, and I saw it myself when I helped my father leave his body. All of a sudden he looked the way he did at twenty-seven, his age when I was born. He was smiling and had all his hair and teeth, including the separation between his two front teeth. I was not expecting it, but there he was. Our prayers set up the situation where his mother and his sister were there to help him out. It was a smooth type of death, but had he died in an accident, it would have been very difficult.

TIME BETWEEN INCARNATIONS

When you die, you find yourself on another level of existence where life goes on. Things are different. A lot of souls are there, and you can stay there for a long time. You do not have the body to limit you, and, depending on the types of faculties that you developed while in the body, you create, evolve, enjoy, etc.

The levels of art and music that exist in these realms are immensely evolved and make us look very primitive. You are in that sphere with the skills that you have purified and attained. You want to develop some of those skills even more. That is why you want to reincarnate. You confer with your spirit guides and you choose an appropriate time in humanity's history in which to reincarnate.

Sometimes the wait is decades, sometimes centuries, sometimes it is millennia, sometimes it is root races—entire root races with particular types of people with a particular task.

For instance, the Semites came from the last solar system to reincarnate in the middle of the Atlantean period, waiting all that time. The other souls, who were living at the time the solar system was under the Third Ray of Active Intelligence, evolved and did not have to incarnate anymore. Those who remained waited until the middle of the Atlantean period to reincarnate for particular reasons. If you recall, the middle of the Atlantean period marks humanity's individualization. The thought "I am me, an individual," could not occur before. These souls did not want to reincarnate before. It would have been painful and redundant for them before then.

In some cases of great lives, when there is "time" between incarnations, spirit guides go on field trips to study the terrain for a particular incarnation and then come back with a report from which they determine what type of life a particular individual is going to have. Also with great lives, a lot more protection is provided to prevent accidents that could result in premature death. I remember, for instance, an example Peter Caddy of Findhorn in Scotland told us. He was getting messages telling him not to drive so fast because his guides had to spend a tremendous amount of energy preventing his accidents.

There are different levels of protection depending on the importance of a particular life. There are some spirit guides who will stay with you permanently while others will come and go. Let's say that you have an eminently successful situation and that you are doing a tremendous amount of good. Because your importance has increased, additional guides come in to help you. You know the phenomenon of attracting guidance when you are aligned with the truth. I know this is what happens when I get my guidance for the sermons or to dictate this book.

THE PROCESS OF PURIFICATION

Our process of purification is not just interested in clearing the negativities of a particular lifetime, it extends itself and attempts to clear those negativities that were not planned to be purified in this particular lifetime. The acceleration of the process by the Path makes this possible. We encounter many people who, when faced with new problems later in life say, "I didn't bargain for this; this is a lot more than I expected to have to deal with." In many cases this is true, because these other, greater problems are made available to them since they are now ready to handle them. The acceleration of their process of growth has made this possible. Of course the good news is that by dealing with these unexpectedly difficult problems, they get to experience unexpectedly great states of bliss and pleasure and to attain powers they thought they never would acquire as well.

Clearly, it is impossible for the overwhelming majority of people to finish their process of purification in one lifetime because they have to purify outrages that were committed through hundreds if not thousands of incarnations on this Earth. Could this be done in one lifetime? Impossible. The process of reincarnation for the purpose of removing all of those barriers that we have created to God becomes, therefore, a logical and inevitable reality. It is ludicrous to believe that this lifetime is the only opportunity that I will ever have to get my act together.

Do all fixations originate in childhood? A guarded yes. It is conceivable that a fixation may originate as an adult who then does not work it out in that incarnation and carries it over to the next.

For the sake of argument let's use a positive example. Say that you lived at the time of Christ and you met the Christ. That is something that you will carry with you forever. But if you met the Christ as a child, you might not understand the significance of the meeting. As an adult you are much more likely to have your soul substance impressed with such a momentous occurrence. That impression will stay with you from one incarnation to the next as a peak experience that you will try to recreate. That is "positive." If that first impression remains pure, then your seeking it is pure. But the first impression is darkened by your own misperception of what the light is, by your own desire to change the nature of the light in order to make the seeking easier.

And so, gradually, what you are looking for is no longer what you experienced, but something entirely different. You are no longer seeking for the Christ, and you are still living in the past. Even the seeking of a positive experience becomes negative with time and necessitates change.

So, people who surround gurus could be those people who are looking for that Christ experience again. The positive aspect of this is that they are still looking for that peak experience. The negative aspect is that in their hope that they have found it, they project onto teachers powers that these people do not have. To the degree there is lack of process in those teachers, there will be counter-transferential response and collusion with the followers. And then it becomes a cult. That is why it is so important to stay in process and be aware of what goes on.

SOULS AND THE EVOLUTIONARY PROCESS
OF NON-HUMANS

Do animals, vegetables, and minerals have souls? Do they

have consciousness? Every atom of creation has a task, and, therefore, has a soul. However, there are different levels of consciousness for various kingdoms of nature. For example, there is a difference between the consciousness of a mineral and that of a vegetable, an animal, a human, and superhuman. The progress of consciousness heightens in accordance with the elevation of the being from one kingdom to the next through the process of evolution. One judges the increasing consciousness in (1) motility, and (2) the ability to separate the self from the rest of reality. For instance, in science, "life" starts with the vegetable kingdom. Scientists have been able to prove that even plants move. They all do. The ability of plants to move, their propensity for change through the seasons and through their functions, means that they have greater freedom than the minerals, thus they have attained a higher level of spiritual development. It is also true if we were to compare the vegetable kingdom to the animal kingdom, or the animal to the human, or the human to the superhuman, etc.

Does that mean that we as humans have gone through the evolutionary process just described? Yes, certainly from the physical point of view. However, we have also been influenced in our evolution by the spirit realms that never fell. There has been interaction, intermingling, intermarriage between higher and lower beings, creating humanity. Beings from other planets have intermingled and intermarried with beings of this planet, thus heightening their process of evolution. There are strong suggestions of this in the Aztec and Mayan civilizations through their artistic representations as well as through aerial photographs that have shown patterns suggesting the existence of landing strips. The Theosophists believe that the primates are a degeneration of humans, not the other way around. According to them, some humans have regressed, thus reversing their process of evolution and became trapped once again in the animal kingdom.

Is there parallel development? For example, can a vegetable being make it to the Kingdom of God without passing through animal and human kingdoms? That was not the way it was planned originally. The original plan was for the vegetable kingdom to go through the animal and the human before reaching the world of spirit. However, because of the great regressions experienced in the human kingdom, the vegetable has earned the right to pass from its state to the transcendence of three-dimensional reality (the equivalent of superhuman-hood for us) through the world of the devas—leprechauns as they are called in some countries in the West. Let's not forget that the vegetable kingdom is the only one that is ruled by three rays, the three Rays of love—Rays II, IV, and VI.

CHAPTER 22
INITIATIONS

WHAT IS INITIATION?

We will talk about initiations, taking into consideration four elements:

(1) The idolized self, the lower self and the Higher Self, (2) The Seven Rays, (3) The five earthly initiations and how they relate to (1) and (2), and, finally (4) Maslow's Hierarchy of Needs. We will also bridge to historical and cultural examples so as to better explain humanity's relationship to its own initiations. This will help you understand yourself individually and globally.

Your growth as an individual is meaningless unless you consider it from a global standpoint. What you do for yourself, you also do for humanity, even though in the beginning it may appear as if you are self-centered, focusing on your best self-interest.

Your true best self-interest and humanity's best self-interest are one and the same. We will also assume that you have a rudimentary knowledge of the mask, the lower self, the Higher Self and the Seven Rays.

Initiation is a process of return to God, therefore, it is a divestiture of defenses. It is a lot more an undoing than a doing. It is also a liberation. At the same time initiation makes more consciousness, energy, knowledge, love, faith, etc. available to the individual. Every time he takes a higher initiation, he experiences states which are closer to God, greater knowledge, etc. Therefore, initiation is freedom with responsibility. The greater the freedom, the greater the responsibility.

An initiation can be compared to the advent of puberty in a person's life which is the release of particular energies coming from the soul into the personality, creating a new body, a new state of mind, a new voice, a new task and a reversal of the old one.

A word of warning: beware of glamourizing initiations. The minute you glamourize anything, you are back to pre-initiatory humanity. Just as you can instantly place yourself in the state of mind of a master, you can also instantly place yourself in the lowest spheres of development.

The pretense of being spiritual, or having attained initiation, therefore, constitutes the most damaging, the most dangerous and the most seductive of regressive tools of the devil. Initiations are not doled out to you because you have been a good boy or a good girl nor are they arrived at by sitting on a bed of nails meditating or being positive.

INITIATION ONE
Birth
Ray Seven
Instinct of Self-Preservation

The individual experiences a desire to improve himself. He is reborn. Prior to this state he is basically a human wreck, not much better than an animal, perhaps with a bit more consciousness.

Before the first initiation, he is under the control of his senses, his basic desires, his basic instincts. A detailed and accurate description of this state can be found by studying the key words of astrology[8] as they apply to ordinary humanity. The individual before initiation is a seeker of form, of the deceleration of energy.

After the first initiation he starts taking command of his life and he accelerates it, disengaging himself from form. Before initiation, he does not seek to understand the meaning of his struggle. He collapses into it in despair. This state is very often confused with initiation four, the Renunciation, particularly by the Catholics who idealize victimization. By contrast, an initiate will seek the meaning of the struggle as the first step towards its resolution.

Before initiation, the person is thrown to and fro between the pairs of opposites, i.e., over-activity and over-passivity, fear and cruelty, despair and demand, and many others. He cannot, nor does he want to distinguish between the harmless and harmful. He allows himself to be a victim of this situation, trying to steal himself a little corner of sanity out of the chaos which his life has become. The individual is also isolated before initiation. No matter how many people exist around him he still feels alone and does not see the light. At the time of initiation, he begins to see the light which he cultivates.

Before initiation, this person will abuse any power available to him. Let us remember that people who are not initiates can have psychic power. They are experiencing the lower psychism that was available during Atlantis and that they have not as yet given up. Therefore, they are inferior to those who have given up their psychic power and have finally joined the Fifth Root Race.

---

[8] Bailey, Alice A. 1951. Page 653. *Esoteric Astrology*. New York: Lucis Publishing Company.

Ruthless abuse of power can also be a result of regressive process. Indeed, somebody may have, at some time, been an initiate but then allowed himself to regress to lower levels of human existence, thus reversing the initiatory process.

Somebody who is an initiate will know who he is, will be able to identify himself and identify others for who they are. He will claim his authority but he will see to it that his claim does not interfere with anybody else's authority.

Before initiation there will be a desire for matter and non-movement. This is the manifestation of the negative aspects of matter and of mother. As an initiate, this state will become the awareness of the potential within the individual or the entity to create, to give birth.

Before initiation, choice is made for you by circumstances that seem to be totally outside of your control. The way out of this is to recognize the point of tension that exists between the pairs of opposites and try to toe the line of this point of tension. This is what happens when somebody becomes an initiate.

Maya, illusion and glamour[9] are rampant before initiation. The person is totally lost in illusions which he follows one after another.

A good example of this is to be found in the hippies of the 1960s and 1970s becoming yuppies in the 1980s and 1990s. They are actually chameleons, going from one glamour to another without ever taking the trouble to consciously realize what they are doing. They sell out to the highest bidder and to the highest manifestation of power at

---

[9] Illusion is to reality (thinking) what glamour is to feelings (love) and what maya is to action (will).

a particular time and place.

The initiate who discovers this harmful condition must reach what we call "the point of disgust" in which he feels outraged at the situation and enters into battle against glamour. The warrior aspect in the individual is born through the initiatory process.

Here we recognize knighthood as a spiritual pursuit. The laws of chivalry, the search for the Holy Grail which were so very well understood during the beginning of medieval times find their place here.

This is also the opportunity to challenge and dissolve once and for all the glamour of pacifism that exists in spirituality and in religion. There is nothing vainglorious about pacifism. War must be waged when it must be waged and there is no other way about it. Only war will destroy the glamours. The character has to be attacked and broken in order for consciousness to finally emerge.

Before initiation the person is engaged in feeding himself. No matter what else exists in the universe, the first and foremost focus for this individual is to feed himself. Gandhi used to say that you cannot talk about God to a hungry man. In other words you have to give him first a bowl of food and perhaps talk to him about God later. Here we find a parallel with the Maslow's Hierarchy of Needs. The initiate will raise his goals higher and higher, elevating them from the physical through the emotional and mental to the spiritual.

Before initiation ruthless ambition is rampant. Initiation transforms that voracious ambition into surrender and dedication. The individual or the entity becomes a channel for the light on which "he turns his back." Before initiation, desire takes over. Addictions abound and multiply. After initiation, the person is able to shed his personality and become like water in Aquarius. Before initiation, the person or the entity descends into matter. After initiation, he cuts the umbilical cord with his parents and becomes a saviour as in Pisces.

Most of the incarnations of an individual are experienced before the first initiation. They number in the hundreds or even in the thousands in some cases. When an individual enters into the first initiation he may spend many lives in that state, in the time between the first and the second initiations.

The contrast between the pre-initiatory state and the post-initiatory state gives you an idea of the function of the first initiation. At the time of rebirth as experienced by many millions of people at this point in humanity, the person is interested in self-improvement. He wants to better himself. He is, pardon the expression, empowered. He begins to start examining and discrediting some of the glamours to which he has heretofore been a slave.

Many who take the first initiation have to go through a stage of questioning their religious affiliations. Many others take the first initiation and remain within their own religion, becoming born-again Christians, for example. In spite of their desire to improve themselves, they are very much in conformity to their environment. They subscribe to the glamours that exist around them. They believe in positive thinking.

All of this is ruled by the Seventh Ray of Order and Ceremony. The person is fascinated and, toward the end of this stage of events, obsessed with things being done right and in order. Perfectionism sets in.

The huge weight of superimposition makes this person vulnerable again to addiction, particularly toward the end of the phase between the first initiation and the second. As the person becomes ready to enter the second initiation a resistance to the drive to improve himself becomes superimposed. It becomes a glamour in and by itself.

The weight of this glamour creates an equal and opposite condition in the lower self which brings on the necessity for liberation. Since the individual does not know any better, liberation has to come through addiction, through substance abuse, through sex addiction and so forth. So the very well known activities to control addictions—Alcoholics Anonymous, twelve-step programs, churches built around twelve-step programs—are all manifestations of the period that exists between the first and second initiations. The addictions are particularly intense as the person gets close to entering the second initiation.

We can, therefore, say that the first initiation is concerned with the mask. The emergence of the knowledge of the lower self marks readiness to enter the second initiation. However, this entrance is fiercely resisted.

Even in twelve-step programs, ways have been found to make the addictions a function of victimization. For example, it is now a fad in Alcoholics Anonymous to say that it is a chemical imbalance that propels people into alcoholism. This is putting the cart before the horse, of course. The chemical imbalance is the result of alcoholism and itself becomes a cause of alcoholism later. The body does not create the soul, the soul creates the body.

An addiction is a soul problem, it is a function of the lower self. It creates physical conditions.

The defense against entering the second initiation also creates numbness. The person will find himself petrified into positive thinking numbness, or will become petrified in his addiction to a twelve-step program which keeps him from emerging as the full individual he really is. This self-protection and self-destruction come from a fear of success. Since addictions have been the result of the abuse of success, the individual is afraid that success will bring with it a return to the addictions.

One of the causes of addiction is the substitution of approval for love. For example, if as a child I am a good artist, I draw well and get my mother's approval for it. When approval replaces love and is pursued, it does lead to temporary success. If I improve a particular ability for the sake of approval, I will improve the ability and I will get approval. But approval is still not love, which is what I wanted to begin with. The fact that it is done in contradistinction to my desire for love is something that will occur to me later, after success has been achieved. In the meantime, achieving success for the sake of approval will get me approval. There is no freeze involved. It will work. The freeze[10] is *approval = love*. I am operating under "approval brings success and success brings approval," which is not a freeze. The problem occurs when success is achieved. Then: (1) the success that is achieved far surpasses what is expected, and (2) it still is not satisfactory.

However, at that point the person does not know what is going on. He has forgotten that he
chose to pursue approval in contradistinction to love. He expects approval to give him the satisfaction that love would give him, which is an impossibility. So, there is a gradually

---

[10] A freeze is a wrong conclusion. Wrong thinking on the mental level *freezes* energy, petrifies it and creates a block, preventing the flow of the Universal Life Force and the Universal Consciousness. See Rev. Dr. Albert Gani's book *Know Thyself* for the chapter on *freezes*.

increasing sense of despair in the soul. It has all been for naught. The edifice must be destroyed.

The defense against this is found through the hyping of self-improvement, of being a good boy, of seeking even greater amounts of approval, of superimposing even more the glamours and the expectations and the demands that are made on the self and on others. The heaviness of this construct is unbearable. The person needs temporary relief from it, so he drinks, or he becomes promiscuous and for a little while he gets great relief, the relief that he would get if he were to discard the entire false contraption which constitutes his life. But in order to do this, he must enter the second initiation of baptism and he does not want to do that because it is painful. See here also the concept of the Law of Repulse, the concepts of premature healing, the concept of the distortion of emotions.

The first initiation is also connected with the Instinct of Self-Preservation, the basic instinct in humanity. Indeed, the simple going about earning one's living or making sure one has enough to eat, or taking care of one's physical needs is very much involved here. However, it has a higher meaning than the crass pursuit of physical needs that is to be found before initiation. It is connected in our mind to the safety and security level of needs as it is found in Maslow's Hierarchy. The person in this phase is concerned with fairness, being treated fairly, with having a roof over his head and so on.

One can see here also the social level of needs as dictated by Maslow—the desire for approval, the joining of clubs, the selling of one's soul for advancement in a firm or a company, and so forth. If one considers the next Maslovian level of need, the need of the ego, one also finds parallels with this initiation. Indeed, the person is self-motivated but in a selfish manner. He does not as yet have a sense of his needs being at-one with the needs of humanity. He is beginning to have glimpses of this but he is mostly focused on what it is that he is interested in and nothing else.

So we can say that the passing from the Maslovian deficiency values (physical, safety and security, and social needs) to being values (ego and self-actualization) is the passage into the second initiation. All of the mundane motivational workshops are, therefore, attempts at raising people from the deficiency to the being values, i.e., to raise them from no initiation to the first. They stop there. They do not go any further. They are not interested in going any further. They know very well that advancing beyond this point would bring to the individual a level of integrity that may be detrimental to the company.

Indeed, the self-actualized individual who is into the greater initiations may question the unethical ways of the company, the quality of the product that he is supposed to sell, the unjust practices that are undertaken for the sake of greed or for the sake of expediency. In actuality this is a perceived detriment because being ethical will ultimately benefit the company not harm it.

INITIATION TWO
Baptism
Ray Six
Instinct of Procreation

Here we enter into the most difficult period of an entity's career on the human level. Baptism by fire—and not by water as it used to be prior to the great flood that put an end to the Atlantean civilization—propels the individual into the discovery of his lower self. This explains the huge amount of defense experienced prior to the entrance into the second initiation. People simply do not want to experience their lower selves. They hate the idea. This church, The Church of the Path®, which takes people through the second initiation and beyond, is thoroughly disliked and resented by the overwhelming majority of human beings. It pushes the buttons of people who do not want to enter into the discovery of the negative sides of themselves. We have seen with the fall of the angels that the exaggeration of goodness is what creates the lower self. It is in wanting to be "gooder than good" that one becomes cruel, afraid, dishonest. The great dissatisfaction that comes from the artificial acceleration of process ends up in the formation of the worst possible aspects of humanity. We find here the recreation of the story of Herem who seduces people into being good and very good but who ultimately brings them to his brother Satan with his cruelty, greed, dishonesty, fear and other negativities.

One can say that the lower self has, therefore, been created by the glamour. Or one can say that the destruction of the glamour reveals the existing lower self that energized it in the first place. Whichever one you choose to believe, chicken or egg, the fact remains that at the second initiation the individual enters into a stage wherein he has to look at and deal with the negative aspects of his personality. No one can do this unless he has already acquired a certain amount of faith. This is achieved during the first initiation, particularly during the first stages after the first initiation. This faith is the reason why the Sixth Ray is involved at the second initiation.

The whole process of looking at our negative side is intolerable without being convinced of the existence of something positive within us which was realized in the first initiation. The worst possible aspect with which we come in contact within ourselves is our harmful volition.

What is most difficult for a person to believe is that he desires the negative. He intends for the negative to happen; he takes pleasure in manifesting the negative. He uses the negative for his own selfish purposes. As monstrous as this appears, no progress is possible unless one comes to terms with this harmful volition. It is not enough to say that one has a shadow, that one has a negative side which was absorbed by osmosis at the time of birth and that maybe with some goodwill one can do something about overcoming. Nothing of the sort will happen unless the person sees the negative volition behind the lower self. So we can talk about two negative elements, one distinctly different from the other:

1. The lower self, itself, with its contents: cruelty, dishonesty, greed, sloth, fear, etc.

2. The harmful volition: the *desire* to be cruel, the pleasure in being cruel, the rationale whereby cruelty will get me what I want, the desire to be afraid, the desire to act out one's fear, the desire to see that fear will get me what I want, etc. We have here the commitment to maintaining and sustaining those negative elements within ourselves.

Neither Carl Jung, nor Bioenergetics, nor all the healy feelies that exist in the New Age talk about this harmful volition/negative intent. You can find the concept of intentionality in Freud (*Beyond the Pleasure Principle*), Adler in many of his works, Bretano and Husserl.

The bringing to light of the negative intent transforms it into healing intent. And it is with the transformation of the negative intent that the dissolution of the lower self can occur *and not before*. The harmful intent is the negative inner volition; transformed, it becomes good will.

The beginning of this phase of spiritual growth is merely

concerned with the identification of the most superficial levels of the glamours and the idolized selves. However, even the identification of that is extremely precious and constitutes a lot more than anything else achieved in psychotherapeutic modalities. The intent in pursuing and cultivating these glamours is identified. The mask is identified for what it is—a mask, an aspect of the self that is further removed from God, from the Higher Self, than are the more crassly negative ones such as cruelty, fear, etc. The beginning of this period of growth is one in which the person experiences deep despair. It is the beginning of the entrance to the long dark tunnel. It is the beginning of the dark night of the soul. In spite of this, the individual pursues his task patiently and diligently. I personally believe that this is his finest hour.

In the midst of one's worst negativity, it is the most noble of all undertakings to still have faith in the positive and pursue the light no matter how far away it seems to be.

Inside himself the individual then travels from the outermost regions of himself, the glamours and the idolized selves, into the more negative parts of himself. In traveling in that manner, he also recovers memories which he lost—volitionally, of course. The real meaning of his childhood is revealed to him. The re-interpretation of this from the point of view of awareness and responsibility becomes his task. A teacher, a teacher, a guide is essential for this pursuit. However, having said that, it is very easy during this stage of development to look in the wrong way and find the wrong teachers.

It is so easy to be flattered by false teachers, who are interested in subjugating a lot more than they are interested in showing a person how to heal himself permanently. There are some misguided "guidances" that say that at times spirit guides will disappear and then the individual will be lost; for a while there is nothing one can do to progress. This is nonsense. It flies in the face of anything that makes sense at all about the universe. Granted, there are times when spirit guides no longer manifest. However, if the person has good will he will find teachers on the human level who will do just as well if not sometimes better than the spirit guides who are further removed from humanity.

Beware of "guides" who talk about glamorous notions of teachers from other planets and of being totally at their mercy when it comes to your spiritual development. This type of notion is not only false but regressive. It leads to belief that the individual is a victim and not in charge of his own process.

At the same time, having said that, remember that when the teacher is found, it is important to maximize time spent with him or her; the time together is limited. The period that will follow is one during which the student will be on his own and will be tested in his ability to teach what he has learned, to give what he has been given and to find new guides, new entities that are more developed than he, to recognize them, and to follow them. These entities may be found on the human or on the superhuman level.

So, as the individual progresses through this difficult time between the second and third initiations, he also acquires the capacity to regress into his past and re-experience the ways in which he has alienated himself from his Higher Self, thus creating the lower self, the mask, the glamours, etc. You can see here how the integration, resolution and assimilation of the experiences of the past prepare him for the future. The "now" expands into the past and into the future as he progresses.

The deeper the individual goes, the closer he comes in

touch with the original longing for God. These glimpses of existential longing are intermittently experienced with glimpses of finding God and at-onement with God. However, the individual is still unable to maintain or remain within these states. He is still struggling to find the truth. He is still in the process of discovering and identifying the lower self, therefore, he is still to a great extent identified with the lower self. This will remain true until the end of this very difficult period.

In the second half of this period, when the person is learning how to increasingly master his lower self, a new kind of defense emerges. This time, instead of fearing and resisting pain, the pain of the lower self, the pain of the guilt created by the lower self, the pain of past experiences that one resists to re-experience—the individual now resists pleasure. Resistance to pleasure is much greater than resistance to pain. In resisting pain, one resists the finite. In resisting pleasure, one resists the infinite.

When we investigate our lower self and the way that we have created pain for ourselves, we discover its finiteness. In the beginning, while we are still struggling with its identification, the lower self appears as infinite as the Higher Self appears later.

The fear of abandoning oneself into the exploration and the re-experiencing of the lower self is the same fear of the infinite that is experienced at the other end when the person is ready to experience the reality and the ever presence of the Higher Self. Only the pleasure is a lot greater than the pain in terms of experience. Consequently the fear and the resistance to it will be far greater.

The forces of darkness know this very well and they are intensely interested in converting this person to their uses.

- "Those Saints whom God loves best the Devil tempts not least."
  —Robert Herrick, 17th Century

The end of this period, therefore, marks the entrance to the first real initiation, the third. In that respect the forces of darkness will put up their greatest fight then and there. The Dweller on the Threshold appears at the door of the third initiation more powerfully than ever before. The temptation to join the forces of darkness is more powerful at that point than it ever was. The lure of the forces of darkness is that the disciple, having achieved the most difficult part of his process, is ready to receive powers that transcend three-dimensional reality. He is about to be clairvoyant, to be clairaudient, to experience the reality of the superhuman creation, the reality of angels, to communicate with them. Having freed himself of the grips of his lower self he is able to do this. That is why he is so desirable to the forces of darkness. The benefits of all of this difficult work are about to be reaped.

One might think that having been able to govern the lower self, the person is less susceptible to the forces of darkness. This is true. However, his emerging capacity to have power, to have clairvoyance, to communicate with the astral plane is an invitation to the forces of darkness to use him for their own evil purposes. Furthermore, let us remember that he is not quite free of the lower self as yet. There are ways that he can rationalize that which he has already given up and bring those things back.

One can observe this process of regression with those people who reach a certain point in their development and who then decide to quit the Path. They are the most dangerous. In their regression they take others with them.

They take those who are their students. Furthermore, what they have learned on the Path is now put to the service of the lower self and the forces of darkness. For instance, clairvoyance can be put to the service of knowing what the stock market is going to do. Magnetic power can be used for the purpose of sexual seduction or for the acquisition of money, or for deceit.

Just about every great historical personality in politics and in religion has experienced this aspect of regression and fall. Jesus Himself experienced it in His despair on the cross, "Why hast Thou forsaken me?" However, He did not act it out the way Moses did, the way Mohammed did, the way many others did. For notorious acting out of this aspect, check out Rasputin who misused his spiritual powers to have orgies with nuns and finally seducing and subduing the vulnerable and besieged Romanoff dynasty.

Interestingly, the instinct identified with this period is the Instinct of Procreation. You can see here the close connection between the Sixth Ray and sexuality. The healing of the idealism of the Sixth Ray is through union in sexuality. Religion is a function of union through sex. The dissolution and resolution of the lower self correspond with a desire for union with the opposite. Even Jung knew this when he talked about the shadow and its function in the state of being in love. He did not say it as precisely as this, but he said it nevertheless.

So the emergence and purification of the most despicable aspects of the self result in the opening to the greatest possible pleasures that humanity can offer, sexuality. Also, it opens the door for creativity. The union with the dark side results in the beginning of creativity.

Another significant development that occurs during the period between the second and third initiations is atheism.

The person temporarily loses touch with the existence of God. This increases his faith, not decreases it. Faith in God is the rediscovery of the Law of Cause and Effect, the laws of nature as operating on an inner level. What is being abandoned and what is commonly called atheism is merely the relinquishing of old time religion, the religion that was necessary at the beginning of the history of humanity, when it was going through its infancy and needed the discipline of a punishing God. Nihilistic philosophies such as Nietzsche's or Jean Paul Sartre's are also to be found emerging from these states wherein one discovers the lower self and its mechanics.

Towards the end of this period, however, the reality of the divine becomes increasingly apparent. With this, the initiate will feel as if again embracing the reality of God is a betrayal of nihilism, existentialism, atheism. At that point one can see how all of these beliefs have become glamours in their own right, just as old time religion and being a good boy or a good girl was a glamour at the time of the first initiation. The passage into the third initiation requires the dissolution of the glamours, or at least in the beginning the ability to identify them and not to identify with them. It takes several incarnations to undergo this painful step. I would venture to say that it takes fewer incarnations to go through this step than to go through the previous one for two reasons:

1. It is easy to stay complacent after one has undergone the first initiation. By contrast the pain that is experienced between the second and third initiations motivate the person to want to get on with it. He is more alive even though he experiences more pain.

2. It is a higher state of development, therefore, it is more accelerated. The passage into the third initiation

makes it possible for an individual to make it to the fifth by the time he dies. Some do, some do not.

INITIATION THREE
Transfiguration
Ray Five
Herd Instinct

From the point of view of the superhuman kingdom, the passage from the second to the third initiation corresponds to the first initiation. It is the first real initiation. The person has now successfully "made it" through the worst temptations of the forces of darkness. He can be trusted. He can give and teach and heal. He gathers around him people who follow him. It does not mean that he is through with the process of purification. He still goes through the battle that has been started but is now at a point where it can be governed. The process was begun during the second initiation with the dissolution and resolution of the lower self. He finds himself still in duality. However, he is able to volitionally identify the negativity within him without identifying with it. That is why he can be trusted as a teacher. That is why he is given power, he is given guidance. He gets clairvoyance to the degree that he can take it, and to the degree that he is not blocking it by the still existing unresolved lower self. For him, acting out on the outer level is minimal if at all existing; however, it is existing on the astral level. He still has negative thoughts and feelings which he can identify and not identify with, if he wishes to do so.

His capacity to stay disengaged from the forces of darkness is still not total. He finds himself at times saying, "I have had enough of all of this goodness. It is now time to collapse." He does this out of choice, likewise choosing to raise himself out of these states whenever the situation calls for it. Unlike the mask which is the imitation of the Higher Self, at this stage he can volitionally open his channel to the Higher Self whenever he wants. We can say that this person has achieved a level of self-actualization as is known in Maslow. He can attain states of grace and happiness. However, he is not quite happy as yet. He finds himself lonely. He still is susceptible to betrayal. He knows that the hurt that he experiences during these times is still a function of the degree to which he is seeking people's approval or affection. He is also able to disengage from this and not to allow it to interfere with his work. However, this condition still exists, albeit latently.

He has no problem identifying his harmful volition and that, by the way, is his "secret." He who is able to always know his harmful volition has reached the third initiation. In fact, if there is anything that is the mark of the third initiate it is his ability to do so. Doing that, of course, gives him instant motivation to bring himself out of his problem.

Third initiates can be found in just about any state. There are very poor third initiates, there are very rich third initiates, there are third initiates who are wanderers and there are others who are well established. However, all of them experience a sense of loneliness, disengagement and sometimes despair. The existential despair that Jesus experienced on the cross before he took the fourth initiation characterizes the person who has taken the third.

He has not quite made it into the realm of the superhuman, so he finds himself surrounded by those to whom he has to give what he has received and isolated from those who have reached his particular level of development. As difficult as this seems to be, it is not nearly as difficult as the process that has gone on between the second and third initiations. This is because the person in this state, however difficult his leadership role may be, can find solace in bringing about the states of grace, the states of at-onement, the energizing presence of the Universal Life Force and the Universal Consciousness. His friends are his deep states of at-onement. Sometimes in those states he is able to correspond with his spirit guides, some more than others, thus ending forever the fear of being alone as experienced in the lower states of development.

There is in this person a stubbornness, a persistence, an impatience which is quite different from the perfectionism to be found after the first initiation and before the second. In this case, it is the pursuit of a better state that he very clearly perceives. Of course, his despair and his impatience are a function of his still existing lower self. They are also a function of his demand that it happen immediately. One can, therefore, say that in a sense this is also perfectionism returned. But it is a perfectionism that sees the ever increasing presence of perfection, as opposed to the perfectionism that pretends to see the ever increasing approach of perfectionism. It is a perfectionism that is in a hurry to accept and purify as many negativities as possible in contradistinction to the type of perfectionism that denies the existence of any negativity.

The third initiate is a person who will have no problem blatantly telling you that which he feels about you with total honesty. This total honesty will appear to be cruel to you. However, from his point of view it is a giving and not a cruelty.

If you want to experience a third initiate, see if you can have an interview with somebody who has achieved something extraordinary, a great inventor or the head of a huge corporation which he has created or a great innovative composer or scientist. Once you are in his presence ask him what he thinks or feels about you and be ready for being struck across the face. Your glamours are going to be instantly attacked by this person who will seem to you to be totally insensitive to your pain. From his point of view, he sees your pain as progress. One day you will be able to see the same thing.

Interestingly enough, this initiation of transfiguration is associated with the Herd Instinct. It is through the Herd Instinct that one achieves self-actualization. No leader can exist unless he takes into consideration the good of the group. All individuality is to be found through the good of the group. The influence of the Fifth Ray here means that at this stage the person has a great wealth of knowledge. This also is a peculiar mark of a third initiate. It seems as if there is no end to what he knows and the degree to which he can dig up stuff and remember things and so on.

At the end of the period between the third and fourth initiations this person must give up what he has built. In order to go on to greater work, he has to renounce. This is why the forth initiation is called the initiation of renunciation.

A person who is a third initiate has now entered and is a member of the Hierarchy, who see to the growth of humanity from the point of view of the light. He is now a trusted member, part of the personnel of the Hierarchy.

INITIATION FOUR
Renunciation
Ray Four
Instinct of Self-Assertion

This initiation corresponds to the crucifixion. Indeed, at that point the person has crucified the ego. The difficulties that Jesus encountered at the cross, feeling lonely and feeling as if all was for naught, is the type of despair that precedes the initiation of renunciation. This is why it is energized by the fourth Ray of Harmony Through Conflict. It is the final conflict, the final battle with the lower self, the unification of the self once and for all. The individual faces his final battle. For some it is difficult, for some others it is not, depending on the degree to which their task is a big one—the Christ's task was the biggest of all. It also depends upon the degree to which he has tasted the cup of karma and drunk it to the fullest. The degree to which he is still attached to what he sees as unfinished business, to an insistence that those he taught be perfect, that his teachings not be distorted and misused, to that degree he is going to find it very difficult to take the fourth initiation of renunciation and go on. But to the degree that he has learned to accept this he will pass through the fourth initiation.

I believe that Gandhi passed through the fourth initiation while still alive. Here is a man who was able to teach and also disagree with those whom he taught. Indeed both Nehru and Jennah, who were respectively prime ministers of India and Pakistan, contradicted a lot of his teachings. He was able to let go of this and only interfere when he felt that his influence was going to have an effect. He knew when to disengage and let people make their own mistakes.

When Jesus said, "It is finished," He was instantly invested with the fourth initiation. Let me remind you of something. Jesus took the fourth initiation, the Christ took the sixth on the cross. The Christ was already a fifth initiate before He decided to incarnate in the body of Master Jesus.

The surrender, the relinquishing that is required here is not new. The disciple has prepared for this throughout his history. Every day he surrendered in his sleep, in his meditation, in his sexuality, in his process, in his admitting and accepting the existence of the lower self and of the negative intent behind it. He is now able to totally surrender to the will of God. Many people take this fourth initiation at the time of their death, the same as Jesus did. These days many more people are doing so.

This brings me to an extremely important point concerning this initiatory process. We have within ourselves all of the initiations already effected since we are connected with God and we have a personal Higher Self. We can, therefore, experience those initiations in parts of ourselves. So, when we talk about an individual achieving those initiations, we are talking about those aspects that he brought in during a particular lifetime achieving those initiations. The I Am consciousness in each one of us has already achieved all of the initiations; it is the infinite consciousness of God.

A person who has taken the fourth initiation and who still lives in the body takes on fewer students than a person who has taken the third initiation.

This is due to two reasons:

(1) There are fewer students who can be receptive enough to take in his light.

(2) He himself is engaged in greater and deeper work, whether on the field of humanity or in other fields. For example, he may be deeply engaged in training spirits on the astral level or in influencing humanity on the subliminal level.

It is very interesting to note that the Instinct of Self-Assertion which brings self-actualization is identified with the fourth initiation of renunciation.

Indeed, one has to renounce in order to assert. The act of self-assertion is an act of renunciation because it renounces the seeking of approval and the false value systems to which we have sold out in the past. No assertion is possible without that. Meditate on it.

INITIATION FIVE
Revelation
Ray One
Instinct of Enquiry

At this stage the person has reached the point where he can enter or leave the material world at will. He materializes and dematerializes for the purposes of his task. He no longer has to reincarnate. He no longer has to sleep or to eat or to have bodily functions the way humans still need to have them. He is completely purified and at-one with the Higher Self.

This does not mean that he does not grow any more. His growth, however, is totally involved in the positive. Since the Higher Self and God are totally revealed to him at this point, the Instinct of Enquiry is at work.

Again it is interesting to note how the Instinct of Enquiry which is so prevalent and powerful in early childhood and which is lost at the time of the formation of the ego, reappears in all of its force and its childlike qualities in the fifth initiate.

At the fifth initiation the person also has a choice to remain in his eternal youth. On Earth we have experienced Babaji, a fifth initiate who always appears a youth in his early twenties while his disciples continue to grow old and die.

There is not much to say here. If you have achieved the fifth initiation, then you should teach us. We have nothing to teach you anymore. Please come and see us. We need you.

INITIATION SIX
Decision
Ray Three

The same is true of the sixth initiation of Decision. We are told that at that point the person decides whether he wants to stay in the service of humanity or go on and be a server on the many other paths that exist. This is ruled by the Third Ray of Abstract Intelligence. Indeed, imagine the amount of intelligence that is needed to make that type of decision!

At that point it is also inaccurate to speak of instincts. To put it more precisely, we do not know what instincts are involved at that level of development. Surely the five human instincts have been totally experienced and integrated by the time the fifth initiation is reached.

INITIATIONS SEVEN, EIGHT AND NINE

Let us mention them briefly. **Initiation Seven, Resurrection. Ray Two.** We get a vague idea of resurrection being connected with total love. **Initiation Eight. Transition.** This initiation is identified with all of the Rays of Attribute, IV, V, VI and VII. You can see here that the entity is finally integrating all of the lower rays. Finally **Initiation Nine. Refusal.** Here the entity leaves our sphere of existence and goes to another universe. At that point he is under the influence of the three Rays of Aspect, I, II, III and integrates all of them.

CHAPTER 23
THE CALL TO YOUR TASK

WHAT IS THE CALL?

The call is the seed plan existing in the soul. The seed of a pear hears the call to create a pear tree and heeds it. The tree then follows the call to create leaves, blossom and fruit. And the cycle starts all over again.

Before the acquisition of consciousness, there was no blockage to the hearing of the call. It is the emergence of consciousness and its existence in a limited form that temporarily interferes with the flow of nature. As consciousness grows, it becomes increasingly harmoniously blended with the energy it shapes. Before it grows it goes through a stage of conflict against that energy. The function of adulthood is the acceptance and surrender to one's true nature.

The call is the call of nature. Here is where we can understand the veracity of the call being present and being expressed in our soul on a permanent basis. God is calling us all the time. God is calling the seed of a pear to create a tree all the time. If you understand this about a pear tree you will understand the same thing about yourself.

There is here also an explanation of "in the beginning was the Word." The Word is the call, it started everything. We are the Word of God. Creation is the Word of God which is still being uttered and will continue to be uttered until all of creation has rejoined God in at-onement. The vibrations of the Word create the universe and create each individual.

Therefore, hearing the voice of God, hearing one's task is as natural as life itself; the state of disconnection from one's task is the unnatural state.

The search for the Word of God is a process of divesting oneself, of unlearning those falsehoods that have been accumulated through the ages, eventually to find the inner state of all knowledge that already exists.

If we do not hear the call it must be because we are blocking it. The blocks to the call constitute our immaturity. Removing the blocks results in the recognition and practice of maturity and wisdom which were always there in the first place.

BARRIERS TO YOUR TASK

Here we find the true meaning of "God waits until you are mature to reveal your task." It depends upon your deciding to make it happen. God wants nothing more than to release this material to you and to show you what your task is. However, it is your decision whether or not to remove those barriers which prevent you from hearing it, or more precisely, when to do so. Consider the part of you that says, "I am not ready." It is as though you are waiting for some magical event to take place and make you ready. If you decide to be ready, you will be ready and you will be ready now. It is a matter of decision.

Since God is nature and happiness and grace, to the degree that we follow the call, to that degree we will be in a state of grace and happiness because we will be in God. Therefore, the smallest dissatisfaction in any area of your life is a function of your resistance to the call. Also, the dissatisfaction itself is the key to the manner in which we resist the call. It is the sphinx that stands at the door of

Thebes and presents Oedipus with the riddle through which he recognizes himself, vanquishes the sphinx and enters into Thebes, i.e., the next phase of his task.

Let me explain. The full experience of the dissatisfaction provides us with a blueprint to the resistance to the call as well as the way in which we can respond to it. For instance, if I am a painter and I am also penniless, the experience of my need for money will lead me to get a job in which I earn it. The call may very well be for me to acquire the humility to have a job and not to demand that my paintings be instantly and unconditionally accepted by the public. The call may also be a need to look at my paintings critically and see whether I have to improve them. If improvement is needed I must grow as a painter before I am able to sell my artwork and live on it. If I were to blame my lack of money on the stupidity of the public, I would not hear the call. I would feel neither the need for humility nor the need to improve my trade, my chosen profession. Thus, the experience of the dissatisfaction makes it a blessing rather than a curse.

Let's take another example: a writer with writer's block. Here we have an inner obstruction. The full experience of the inner obstruction will reveal to him the reason for its existence, why his creativity is being blocked. The block may be there because he abused his earlier writings, or he may have rested on his laurels, or his writings may have had a defect which is now trying to be corrected by his soul, or his spirit is propelling him into a period of gestation which will eventually give birth to a greater or wiser writer. A writer caught in this situation must ask himself how he has created this block. Is he too proud to realize that what at one time was valid for him as a writer is not valid any more? Is he too stuck in his ways, nursing the same old pet peeves that he creates over and over again in his work? Does he feel guilty about something? Is his guilt real or false?

For some examples let's go to seventeenth century France, the Golden Age of French writing. Let's consider several contemporaries and compare them in terms of their blocks. Moliere never had any writer's block. In fact he got better and better until he died on stage in 1673 playing "The Imaginary Invalid." He could write in beautiful Alexandrine verses without any strain. Racine was tighter in his ways. Towards the end of his life he was not as prolific, even though what he produced had a lot more wisdom than what had come earlier.

Boileau, the critic, the judge of that era, became increasingly rigid and stuck in his ways. He was able to clearly see the great talents. For instance, he is the one who recognized that Moliere was the greatest of them all in every respect. However, because he rigidified himself, he came to a point of total dryness. For the last ten or twenty years of his life he practically wrote nothing and died in 1710 very dissatisfied with what he had done. He became so glamoured by his own criticism, so obsessed with trying to fit all art forms into the ancient Greeks mold, that he dried up. Now, if we had talked to him and said, "Listen, Nicola, you're stuck in your ways. You need to let go of all of this Greek stuff. It was good for an era but now we are ready to change and enter into a new century, an new way of thought, the Age of Reason." He would have resisted. He would not have wanted to give up any of this because he totally identified with it, glamourizing it and, therefore, petrifying in it. He listened to his call and responded to it in the beginning of his life. When it was time to change, he was not willing to do it.

Other writers have been able to change. Consider, for instance, the many stages of Goethe's life. Consider Victor

Hugo's changes, reflected even in his political allegiances—progressing, uncharacteristically, from the right to the left, opposite to what we usually see.

THE CALL IN FLUX

That demonstrates another property of the call: the fact that it is in continuous flux. Your call may tell you one thing today and a different thing tomorrow. And you must have the resiliency to change your ways accordingly or else you will miss the boat.

OUR DISSATISFACTIONS ARE THE CALL

There is an ongoing voice that is continuously calling us to our task. Our Higher Self registers this voice, hears it very clearly. However, the lower spheres of our development have become deaf to this call. On the outer level we wonder what is our task, what is God calling us to do, we seem not to find the answers. All we find around us are dissatisfactions, sometimes vague ones, sometimes specific ones, all of which seem to be antithetical to the voice inside that will show us the way and that will take us away from those unpleasantnesses and dissatisfactions.

The fact is that the dissatisfactions themselves are the call. The call heard clearly by the Higher Self and blocked by the lower self is experienced on our level of consciousness through dissatisfaction, through the point of tension created by the disconnection between the Higher Self and the lower self. Dissatisfaction, therefore, is an indication that the call exists. In fact it is a manifestation of the call itself.

Dissatisfaction means longing and aspiration. Lack of dissatisfaction means accepting the status quo and decelerating into death. The state of dissatisfaction is, therefore, a very precious one on our dualistic level of existence. It vigorously wakes us up to listen and heed the call within. That is the only way that dissatisfactions are found and resolved. Sometimes the mere finding of the dissatisfaction itself immediately floods you with great pleasure. When, for instance, you make an important connection about how you have created your unhappiness, you are immediately flooded by pleasure and happiness. The subsequent resolution of the distortion itself and its consequent pain automatically increase the capacity for happiness and pleasure.

The satisfaction found through avoidance of pain is a dead one. It is satisfaction of the mask. It is regressive. So we have three states.

    1. **The idolized self.** On the outer-most level there is an attempt at convincing oneself that one is satisfied; the line of least resistance "copes" with the present condition in false acceptance. False equilibrium is created, false life is pursued. This we call the idolized self or the mask.

    2. **The lower self.** The dissatisfaction is experienced first in its vague form and then in increasingly clear ways. The person is motivated to seek and find the cause of the unhappiness which always lies at the bottom of the pain. This we call the lower self.

    3. **The Higher Self.** The capacity to accept and experience the pain in its worst form reveals its cause and makes it possible for the person to dissolve it. This is how we search and find our Higher Self. The dissolution of the pain through the resolution of the misconceptions and of the lower self reveals the true nature of the call. The person instantly experiences hope and acquires faith.

SPIRITUAL PROGRESS

The great barriers to the hearing of the call are doubts, rationalizations and excuses on the lower self level. They all interfere with the call. Perhaps the most insidious of all is the search for peace. Peace is often a euphemism for escape from dealing with one's problems. Thus, the search for peace becomes a banner under which escape and duplicity are rationalized. Nirvana is seen as a place of immobility where nothing happens. Might as well be dead or be an inanimate object as to live in this kind of "peace."

The reality is that nirvana is a state where activity and receptivity have been so accelerated as *movement* that they have become one infinitely vibrating whole. The person in nirvana, far from avoiding problems, is continuously taking on problems and resolving them, continuously in the process of purifying the inanimate and making it animate.

So, if you think that spiritual progress means being free from problems, you are very much mistaken.

Spiritual progress is a function of the ability to deal with and resolve problems in an accelerated fashion. Settle down; you have an eternity of problems to face. Might as well start enjoying them because they will never go away. Your task is the solving of problems.

What do you think the Christ is doing, what do you think Babaji is doing up there or in there or wherever They exist? They are continuously considering and resolving problems thereby Themselves growing. For these beings, the definition and resolution of problems constitutes creativity. Since They are free of lower self this then is a blissful, pleasurable creative process which nourishes others and nourishes Them at the same time.

CHANGE

So, one of the prerequisites to hearing the call is acceptance that the nature of life is continuous and perpetual vibrant change, not stasis and death. The search for peace in its distorted way is, therefore, foolish. There is no peace the way you want it. The only peace to be found is the at-onement within which we accept struggle and proceed to resolve it, accept conflict and proceed to harmonize it.

That is why it is also foolish to believe that renouncing life is accomplishing one's task. The swamis, the monks, all of those who retreat from life and deprive themselves of the pleasures and of the pains of life are not progressing at all, they are regressing into stasis and death. They believe they are the servants of God; in reality they become the agents of the devil instead. You are a servant of God when you live your life to the fullest. Be a servant of your life and you will hear the call.

SPIRITUAL DEVELOPMENT AND THE CALL

The greater the spiritual development of an entity, the stronger is his call and more difficult his task. Conversely, the less he is developed, the smaller is his task and the weaker is his call. It follows that the lesser developed individual may have heard his call and achieved his task, therefore, arriving at a state of great happiness, abundance, strength, fulfillment, bliss in his life. At the same time, someone else whose spiritual development is greater may find it much more difficult to hear the call because it is strong and frightening; his task may be immensely more difficult. This person will be in a state of anxiety, misery, lack, creating problems of all kinds and of all dimensions in his life.

So, it is foolish for anyone to compare himself to others.

Whenever you find yourself looking at others and saying, "Why is he so much wealthier than I am or much happier than I am?" you might then be tempted to conclude that the universe is unjust. Little do you know that your spiritual development may be much greater than his and, therefore, much more is demanded of you than is of him.

Moses, Jesus and Mohammed all went through times of despair during which they compared themselves to people around them who seemed happier and had more than they. Yet those other people were a lot less aware and intelligent. These great souls, too, succumbed to the temptation of seeing the universe as unjust, of believing that God had abandoned them. Consider, for instance, Jesus' "Why hast Thou forsaken me?" which is one of the last things He said on the cross. He, too, fell into this trap. The higher purpose of His undergoing this experience was to demonstrate that doubt is a human condition, that it is OK to experience it but that it can be overcome, that it is a temporary situation. He, Who was the most developed of created spirits, had to go through this error of doubt and of preparing Himself. If a being as high as He went through this, why not you?

YOUR TASK

Look at your situation and then consider that it is very possible that your task is different from others. See your jealousy of others' "easier" lives as a misguided set of feelings and thoughts. Also see your contempt of others who are beneath you, who cannot achieve what you have achieved, as the equal and opposite misguided state. Accept, then, your task as being *your* task, your difficulties as being your own and your call as being unique. Rather than comparing yourself to others through the outer manifestations of life, concentrate on the inner state of life so as to open yourself to the call.

What is expected of you first and foremost is the purification of yourself: the removal of the barriers that prevent you from at-oneing yourself with your Higher Self. Thus, the answer to the question, *"What is my task?"* is very simple: your task is to purify yourself; your task is the Path of Purification, the dealing with your negativities.

Therefore, your task is facing you squarely here and now. You do not have to look any further than right here to find it.

Gradually, this purification, as it removes layer upon layer of negativities, misconceptions and error, eventually reveals a higher purpose to one's life. At that point the person is ready to give and to actively contribute in a positive manner to the growth of humanity.

If you are not quite happy, if you are not in a state of bliss then it must mean that you have not quite followed God's call, i.e., that you have not quite purified a particular aspect of yourself. Therefore, another effective method of looking for God's call is to ask, *"How happy am I; how harmonious is my life inside and out; what are the areas of dissatisfaction in my life?"* This is the barometer, the yardstick that determines how much of your task you have undertaken, where your task is and how to accomplish it. Ask yourselves these questions in every possible aspect of your life—consider your body, your mental capacities, your emotions, your sexuality, your professional ability, your financial capacity, the skill with which you handle your money, your ability to love, your openness to the experience of pleasure, your willingness to experience pain, etc. Facing the negative aspects of our lives is God's call. Thus, it is ludicrous to try to escape them. Escaping our negativities is escaping God's call.

Can you do it alone? No. It is impossible to do it alone since you are dealing with material which is by definition unconscious. To deal with it alone will only result in falling prey to the tricks of your lower self, as you have in the past. It is, therefore, essential to: (1) avail yourself of the help of those people who are a few steps ahead of you on the Path; they are called teachers; (2) be involved in a group of people who are undertaking the same type of goal. Thus, you will gain the support of the group. Also through identification with the members of the group it will be a lot easier for you to accept your own shortcomings. Basically, the two activities described constitute the practice of our religion and the fundamental outer level activities of our training programs.

Other activities that you do on your own are equally essential, such as meditation, prayer, Daily Review, note taking. However, one activity cannot exist without the other; they support each other. So, you cannot do it alone, nor can you do it only through activities with others. The work alone, and the work with other people compliment one another and create a whole.

SACRIFICE

What needs to be sacrificed in order to hear the call is the false life, the false call, the false motivation, the false aspiration, the seeking of approval. When humanity was in its infancy, sacrifice was expressed by killing animals and surrendering them to the gods, or abandoning some goods for the use of the gods. All of this is a primitive expression of the true meaning of sacrifice which is the surrendering that which has become petrified, the letting go of that which we have created so as to create more.

The first undertaking in the finding of the call is the

tearing off of the mask, i.e., the pseudo-call. This is a painful process which reveals the conceit with which you have held on to the false life. It forces you to experience humiliation. This humiliation is there only to the degree conceit exists. Once the conceit is given up, humiliation becomes humility and eventually is transformed into dignity. Indeed, there is a lot of dignity in the tearing off of the pretense and the mask. Eventually it even becomes a humourous process as it is so very often experienced in group when we can freely and lovingly make fun of each other. This is the way to true peace, the only true peace.

How much are you willing to sacrifice for the sake of the truth. What is it that you are willing to surrender? Consider your little habits, your little comforts, your possessions, your pet feelings and emotions, your pet ideas and beliefs, your inheritance, your titles, your indulgences which are euphemistically called your rights. Consider those and consider more. Consider everything that constitutes your life and ask yourself whether you are willing to sacrifice it for the sake of the truth. If you are not, then you have not really surrendered to the will of God and to that extent you will not hear the call. If you are willing to sacrifice everything, you may temporarily lose it, only to regain it or something else much more precious in another form and from another angle.

In the last analysis, nothing is lost. Only that which has been disconnected from serving God will be lost. Only that which is not essential to the accomplishment of your task and to the contribution to the Plan of Salvation is what needs to be sacrificed and what will be lost. Anything that has any validity or that yields any pleasure will be found again by the individual, through correct means this time, not in the old ways.

As you can see, you may not be ready to hear your call. You may need to take all of this one step at a time and not delude yourself about your readiness when it is too soon. This is the process. In and by itself it is blessed and needs to be respected.

MIMESIS

Let us look at anyone who incarnates with a great task. In the beginning, he does not know that he is invested with this great task. He undergoes the same challenges that are presented to everybody else. As he overcomes these challenges—a lot more easily than others do—new and more difficult challenges are presented to him. The new challenges are greater and greater, more so than for anybody else. They, then, call forth the capacities with which he incarnated.

The challenges themselves draw out of him the material with which he has been invested, initiated or given. He approaches these problems in new ways. He makes available to humanity new information. Until he appeared, these greater challenges were seen as insoluble, impossible to overcome. He shows how to overcome them through new inventive ways that have never been seen before.

However, his followers, rather than undergoing their own challenges, will undergo pseudo-challenges that resemble the ones undergone by their leader and teacher, automatisms recreated to suit this purpose. This is mimesis. The original experiences of the leader are flattered into meaningless rituals, endlessly repeated by the followers in their attempt at obtaining the power, creativity, greatness that their leader once had.

The state of knowing, when the process of transformation is arrested, reverts to automatism in a sudden regression. Thus, what was once knowing, as originally taught by the great teachers becomes reduced, through mimesis, to automatism.

CHAPTER 24
SACRAMENTS

PURPOSE OF SACRAMENTS

The sacraments, or the creation of permanent energy forms, fulfill many needs:

1. They fulfill a deep human need for order and ceremony. Consciously or unconsciously those who celebrate the Mass in conventional churches know this. When you attend a Mass you have a deep sense of order and ceremony which communicates and triggers a profound sense of security.

2. They also fulfill a deep need for cleanliness and purification. You will notice that in the celebration of the Mass that there is a cleaning of the cup from the inside and from the outside. This refers, of course, to the Christ's admonishment to clean the cup not only on the outside but on the inside as well, i.e., the purification process, which is an inner process. This must be done with a lot of love and care and at-oneing. By doing so, we get a sense of participation in the process of cleansing. This is a very reassuring process which brings people together.

3. They offer the possibility for people to create chapels in their own home. Indeed, you can create a corner where you will accumulate energies by celebrating the Mass, praying, meditating. This place will then build up and have

available for you to take in the energy forms whenever you need them.

TYPES OF SACRAMENTS

A sacrament is something regarded as having a sacred character or mysterious meaning. Under this heading we have all of the known celebrations. At The Church of the Path® they constitute the acknowledgment of a passage, an initiation. Thus, we have a baptism, a confirmation, a marriage, a last unction, remembrance day.

However, there are many other types of sacraments. Every single moment of our day can become a sacrament. We must celebrate and fill with God's glory every moment of our life. For example, daily prayer, work, intimacy, sex, etc. can all be seen as sacraments. The fact that they are practiced every day must not diminish their importance.

One of the most celebrated events in Judeo-Christianity is the Mass. One also finds its origin in many other civilizations. It is extremely important to study its process and to understand and thus restore it to its universal meaning.

THE MASS

The human experience creates a storehouse of information and patterns which then shapes the soul and the personality of the future generations. For example, consider the fact that we are the inheritors of millions of years of established patterns of behaviour which repeat themselves. Let me explain one pattern and show how it has resulted in creating what is called the sacrament of the Mass.

Consider a primitive society in which there is a dominant leader who is strong and inspired. People will depend on this person and develop patterns of submissiveness and rebelliousness towards him. They will admire him and resent him at the same time, and for the same reasons—what he brings, what he teaches, how he handles the law, etc.

Eventually his "sons" become stronger, coalesce, kill him, eat his flesh and drink his blood. This is done so as to "incorporate" him. It is an attempt to become like him, to be him, to acquire his power, his wisdom, his strength and so forth. Then they feel guilty about it and "totemize" him, deify him out of guilt. They also try to emulate him, try to look like him, try to act like him, try to sound like him in an attempt to bring him back.

This process has been repeated for millions of years and is deeply encrusted in the human soul. As such, it creates rituals that are now repeated. One of them is the Mass. The Mass as it is known in the Catholic Church is a reflection of many other similar ceremonials that are to be found in religions all over the world. Thus, the celebration of the Mass, the blessing of the elements, the sacraments, correspond to a reality which has its roots in the beginnings of humanity.

When entering a cathedral or a church where the Mass is celebrated, one feels an extraordinary sense of peace. This is because energy forms created by the celebration of the Mass are maintained in that place and are built upon century after century. The deep sense of holiness that is experienced, this magic of deep peace, is very specific. It is based on ancestral behaviour. Indeed, remember that the Mass is the celebration of killing the father, eating his flesh and drinking his blood, an act that we as humans, prehumans and even animals have repeated for millions and millions of years. It is the memory of this emotion-filled set of events, encapsulated in the celebration of the Mass that creates in these churches those healing energy forms. When a group of people goes through the process of remembering those events and of healing their guilt for the cruelty contained in this behaviour of their ancestors, they create energy forms that are as real as if they were material. These energy forms linger in the churches and have a healing and soothing effect on whomever enters these places of worship. The encapsulation of the entire act is an exercise in cause and effect and, therefore, in the experiential understanding of the Law of Karma, which means the experience of the guilt-producing behaviour, of the ensuing guilt and of the restitution of that guilt which creates healing.

Many believe and many psychologists believe that religion originated with the guilt for killing father. Out of that guilt, primitive humanity would build totems, reminiscent of the father. Gradually, the totem which was originally meant to represent the slain father is invested with all kinds of powers, wisdom, omnipotence, healing, etc. There is a lot of merit in seeing guilt as the restoration of nature and, therefore, the search for God.

Is the killing of the father the Fall, since it is the incorporating, through eating his flesh and drinking his blood, of him into ourselves? In essence, we become the father/God. Yes, it is the fall, bringing on conceit, self-will and fear. However, it is also the rise since it is the beginning of taking full responsibility for ourselves, thus starting on the path of finding God again. It is on one hand a usurping of the throne of God and on the other hand it is a surrender to Him.

The bigots totally misrepresent this. They only see it one way. They see the negative side of it, thus negating growth altogether. At best, they, through the Mass, see themselves obtaining instant grace. There is no room for process, for individual growth. Growth and any attempt at pursuing it become evil.

The eastern philosophies, in contradistinction, completely disregard the entire process of the Fall, of killing the father, eating his flesh and drinking his blood. They make the exact opposite mistake of wanting to see too rosy a picture, too facile a process of growth.

One day in the future there will be scientific proof of all of this. For the time being the celebration of the Mass or of the sacraments can be seen as a mechanical device that creates this deep sense of peace and at-onement. What we are at-oneing with, actually, is our deepest archetypal experiences.

Is this also at-oneing with violence and murder? Of course, there is violence in patricide. But that really does not count. It disappears in the context of the attempt at emulating, assimilating, taking in the father or the guide or the wisdom. Evil is finite, it goes away; goodness is infinite, it perpetuates itself. The primitive aspect of the Mass does not have to remain primitive. The blood does not have to be referred to as blood any more. It can be seen as spirit, as the flowing of spirit. The assimilation of the symbolic wine can be seen as the assimilation of the spirit of God, or Christ. The eating of His flesh can be seen as the incorporation of the aspect of adaptability, taking in God the Mother, and can be accompanied by a commitment to do so, or a prayer to do so.

We at The Church of the Path® add a third element—water—to this. By adding water to the wine and by blessing the water, we introduce the link between spirit and matter, the flowing purity of love, the Son aspect. Therefore, for us, we celebrate spirit, soul and personality;

spirit, soul and matter; will, love and active intelligence.

A person deeply anchored in this process of purification, when exposed to these energies, whether in a cathedral or by celebrating the Mass in The Church of the Path®, will not direct these energies to "magical thinking." He will not expect these energies to do for him the work that he does not want to do for himself. A person deeply involved in this process will have his faith in the process renewed by the assimilation of these energies.

This is exactly what I have experienced whenever I have gone into a cathedral. The pilgrimage to France which four of us took in June of 1994 confirmed what I am saying. The visiting of holy places, even small ones, always resulted in our renewed commitment to our process. It acted as an encouragement. We would come out of these churches dedicated even more to the work that we were doing on the Path. By contrast, for someone who is not committed to the Path, these energies can be regressive. They can lead him into superstitious types of behaviour. They can bring him healing before he understands the reasons for his discomfort or disease. This is premature healing and will eventually lead to unhappiness, deeper pain, deeper distortions, deeper distress. The individual ends up rejecting the Mass and everything associated with it; he quits the church which has the right methods of triggering positive energies but which misuses them since they are not put in the context of the process of purification. The person becomes an atheist and eventually through his atheism and his taking responsibility, joins the Path and rediscovers the value of the Mass and sacraments, this time from a different place, from a deeper and much more meaningful place.

It is extremely important to remember that in no way are we trying to establish here automatisms which would lead us to doing the work of the devil rather than doing the work of God. When an energy machine is used for negative purposes or for selfish purposes then it does the work of the devil. When it is used in the context of purification it leads to great creativity, permanent healing and service to humanity. So, beware of how you use this energy machine, the Mass, which is put at your disposal.

BUILDING ENERGY FORMS

What we build on the three-dimensional level, the building of a house or of a church for example, is an inadequate representation of what already exists in the world of spirit.

The building of energy forms through prayer prepares for you the edifice in which you are going to live in the future. This can be extended to include every word, every thought, every action you take. All is geared towards building your future home—near or distant, depending on how constant and continuous it is that you accumulate these energies. The act of praying and the act of going through rituals is a great builder of energies. The more you practice it, the safer you will be here and in the future. Obviously, you are also building negative energies, consciously or unconsciously. Those are also your future homes.

Consider the shape of cathedrals. They all imitate the shapes of the energy forms that are created during prayer. That's why there is such a desire "to reach the heavens," a desire to defy gravity which can be found in all the cathedrals that were built, particularly in the twelfth and thirteenth centuries in Europe. The incredible investment of energy and resources that went into construction of those cathedrals demonstrates that we are talking about a reality. Why would people in the middle of the Middle Ages invest such vast amounts of time, effort and money into building so many cathedrals if they were not receiving a genuine benefit from their labours? At this point you may ask, "Why did it stop at the end of the thirteenth century and for the best part of 100-150 years?" Very simply. Western Europe experienced a great amount of abundance during the twelfth and thirteenth centuries. Then, for some reason, at the end of the thirteenth century and through the fourteenth and fifteenth centuries, Europe was plagued by all kinds of problems, including an extraordinary amount of bad weather.

Nobody knows why this was but it not only thwarted the building of cathedrals, it also brought in plagues, the Hundred Years War and all kinds of other calamities. It was as if there was an ebb and flow experienced, where for a while there was peace, there was abundance, there was building. Then came a time of great strife and great problems which ended it.

Compare the form of cathedrals to the form of mosques. You will find them to be amazingly similar. Indeed, there is a main center which becomes the nave in the cathedral and there are turrets which become minarets in the mosque. There is a central place for prayer, therefore, surrounded by four turrets or four minarets. The Turks later constructed the Blue Mosque with six minarets. However, all other mosques have four minarets.

So we have a universality to the shape of this spiritual form that is created through the mechanism of prayer, or through sacraments. This universality of form is deeply embedded in the human soul and the human experience. This is what we refer to when we pray. These are the energy forms that we create when we meditate, when we go deep inside of ourselves.

Consider the Taj Mahal—same shape, same dome, minarets. However, it was built for the purposes of love. Mumtaz Mahal is its real name. It means "the house of Mumtaz," the princess who was so very much loved by her fabulously rich husband that he had built in her memory this fantastic edifice.

Therefore, the longing for somebody with whom one is involved in an intimate relationship corresponds precisely to the longing for God and creates precisely the same energy forms. Here you have proof positive of this principle of oneness between the love that is to be found in the greatest of human experiences, sexuality, and the love that is to be found through prayer and through the sacraments.

INTIMACY

The taking in of the body of Christ, the incorporation of God[11], the Father principle, is a very intimate experience with God. The sexual act has a great deal of this taking in aspect, of absorbing the other person with their taste, their smell, and of giving out of your own. The need for intimacy with God and with the Christ in the Mass is a very important experience, a holy one. So is the need for intimacy with another just as holy an experience. Therefore, praying before the act of love is extraordinarily enhancing of

---

[11]Although the Christ is the Son aspect, He plays the role of the Father in the Last Supper. He later loses His brotherly aspect for a more fatherly one, and, in fact for many Christians, Christ is God incarnate, is the Father. We do not believe this way. We believe that Christ is our Elder Brother, not our Father. However, in the Last Supper He symbolizes Father, He takes Father's place for the sake of teaching us. Thus, He becomes the father who was killed, eaten and identified with.

closeness, of pleasure, of giving and of taking.

SACRIFICE

In the Mass what is being celebrated is the sacrifice. Indeed, the Christ sacrificed His body, His lower self. So did the father in the tribal story that I told you above. Think, for example, of Christ's intent to stay with us until all of us are saved, including the worst of us, including His brother Lucifer. This sacrifice of staying with us is reenacted in the offering of His body for incorporation and assimilation. We commit ourselves to Him by taking Him in, He commits Himself to us by staying within us. So, here is another aspect of the Mass that must be remembered. Eventually, as we become teachers or givers, we, too, have to go through the act of sacrifice. A mother, in giving to her child, sacrifices herself to an act of selflessness. She does it completely and entirely for the welfare of her offspring. So did the Christ come in and manifest His parenthood of us, He representing God. In turn, each one of us in positions of leadership must manifest the same aspect and must surrender to others to be absorbed by them.

WORK

What we do on the Path is work. Our work is purification. *Laborare est orare*. This very well known Latin phrase means "to labour is to pray." Prayer is work. We cannot pray if we have not purified.

Some people are incapable of praying. Sometimes you will find yourself incapable of praying. This is particularly true if you are overcome by guilt, by shame, or by both. Consider also being overcome by greed. When you are in these states you will find yourself incapable or unwilling to pray. Prayer is the invocation of the Universal Life Force and the Universal Consciousness. One has to be open in order to pray and, therefore, one has to work towards opening oneself in order to pray. The process of opening oneself is the process of purification as it is practiced on the Path.

Therefore,

1. To have prayed well is to have worked well. Wherever and whenever you are able to be open to the Universal Life Force and Universal Consciousness, you will be able to do good work, no matter what your field of endeavour. Consider, for instance, being a real estate agent. If you are able to pray well and say "I commit myself to doing the work of God today. Dear God, help me find this person a house." You will be doing good work. You will have surrendered your own will to the will of God. You will find the right house for that person, not the one that will give you the greatest commission. You will be willing to refer this person to somebody else who may be better qualified than you to give him what he wants.

Eventually, in the long run, this will result in greater and greater abundance for you because you will start positive ripples that will build up and gradually emanate from you to the rest of the universe as a prayer does, as an energy form does, as a cathedral does.

2. To have worked well is to have prayed well. Work is prayer. If I completely lose myself in what I am doing, no matter what it is, even a simple task like filing or a menial task like cleaning up, I am in the act of praying. The act of surrender to a task is a prayer. I become a channel, I am able to invoke energies in me that I find are greater than I thought I had. I am able to then release and give all of these energies. The more I give of them, the more open I am to receive them and, therefore, the more I progress, the more

I am close to and intimate with God.

Other conclusions that can be drawn from this: working is like taking a good meal. So is prayer. We understand the process of being nourished by a good meal. We may even understand the process of being nourished by prayer, but seldom do we understand the process of being nourished by work. Indeed, work can be very nourishing and very satisfying.

The total surrender to giving something always results in greater and greater energy because giving creates the necessary vacuum for more energy to come into you. The Universal Life Force and the Universal Consciousness have nothing else to do but to penetrate you. All you have to do is to create a vacuum for them. How better can you create a vacuum for them than by giving out what you already contain within yourself? So giving is receiving, working is re-energizing.

Of course, if work is done for selfish purposes, to get or to merely receive, then you will stop energizing yourself, there will be no room for the Universal Life Force to penetrate you. You will have no use for new ideas coming from the Universal Consciousness since you are continuously stuffing yourself with outer level realities and creations that have already been created by somebody else or by yourself. The devotion to giving and working and creating always creates freshly, always gives out and is life.

CHAPTER 25
PRAYER, MEDITATION, ATTUNEMENT AND INTERVENTION

DEFINITIONS
One has to differentiate between the following:

Attunement. An attunement is a short time during which we still our minds, concentrate in silence and prepare for whatever spiritual work we have scheduled to follow the attunement, such as prayer, meditation, a class, a group session or an individual teacher hour, for example.

Prayer. This is made of three parts:
a. *Invocation.* Here is the more traditional form of prayer, the one in which you draw in, long for, express your need for the presence of God, for the strength necessary to deal with a particular problem, for an answer that you do not seem to be able to find, for a state that you do not seem to be able to relinquish, or for a state that you do not seem to be able to reach. Much distortion exists in the practice of invocation. People pray for God or for Christ to rescue them. As I have said so many times, no self-respecting God or Messiah or prophet will ever rescue you from anything, since you have created your own reality, your own calamities. Therefore, praying for that release is wrong. You should pray for the openness to realize the ever-presence of God and of Christ, for the strength, the courage and the dignity to sustain the

presence of God or of Christ, or of an emissary of God, an entity of Light. You should pray for the fortitude and the willingness to implement in your life that which readjusts you to the Universal Life Force. Last but not least, you should pray for the natural state of loving and giving. Outside of this state, guilt is manufactured automatically.

Therefore, most prayers which are to be found in organized religion are wrong. Some of them, however, are gems, wonderful examples of invocation. Whenever I have found those, I have put them to use in our church. Some I have modified to suit our philosophy of life which is a lot more sophisticated today than it was when they were written.

b. *Evocation.* This is the affirmation, the assertion of the goodness of the universe, the claiming of what is actually our birthright, i.e., total fulfillment in every area of our life. This form has also been distorted by the positive thinkers who bypass the process of purification and claim in an arrogant way results that they have not earned through the painstaking labour of dissolution of the lower self. They call those "affirmations." Unless preceded by the process of purification all affirmations are regressive.

c. *Instrumentality.* There is a third aspect here which I call instrumentality. The instrument is you. You invoke and you evoke. This work on the Path is the cultivation of the instrument. Some of these prayers take you through the process of purifying your instrument. You will find them to be hard only if you resist the process. This, too, has been distorted by the atheist psychologists for whom all that exists is the "systemic"—as they call it—manipulation of your soul substance. They do not say soul substance, however; they call it unconscious, which is incorrect. Thus, they discount both the value of invocation and of evocation, limiting themselves to the manipulation of the instrument in order to achieve their goals. This is the way of the atheist. And this is also a distortion.

Meditation. Meditation is not the process of numbing as practiced by so many misguided New Agers. It is a process of heightening consciousness. It is a method of penetrating a problem. Its five steps are universal in their nature. I was stunned to have found how similar are the five steps of meditation that I teach to Francis Bacon's *Novum Organum*. His five steps of approaching and resolving a problem are as universal and as eternal as the five steps of meditation that you find in this book. Meditation is a tool for increasing the reality of the here and now, not escaping from it. Practice it and enjoy it.

I refer you here to the *Prayers and Code of Conduct on the Path* for more on this subject and for a more extensive description of the five steps of meditation.

INTERVENTION

Can we help others solve their problems? Can we be helped by angels to solve our problems? Can entities from other realms intervene in our realm for the sake of helping us? Yes to all of these. However, unless we create a condition within ourselves wherein we have taken full responsibility for our sins and wherein we long for, desire, call for assistance from others to come and alleviate our pain and sorrow, the help coming from outside will be regressive and not progressive. However, if we do fulfill the condition of taking responsibility, the help will be progressive, it will assist us accelerate the process of our growth, resolve endless vicious circles, etc.

Thus, group prayer is very much recommended because

the whole is greater than the sum of its parts in terms of healing. However, again, if group prayer is used to heal somebody who has not taken responsibility for himself, then the healing is regressive, it will go into energizing the negative. Where negative symptoms are removed such as an illness or a cancer or a negative emotional condition, the healing thus obtained will create other and greater negativities in the future. The person thus "healed" is rendered powerless towards his own problems. He becomes dependent upon others to save him, never sinking deeply enough to experience the pain of his own guilt. This pain itself, when experienced, is the only healing medicine that has ultimate validity.

Many of the prayers of The Church of the Path® begin, "Eternal Father, Mother and Son?" What about daughter? If feminists who ask that question knew more about the English language, they would not ask it. One refers to mankind and one includes women. The son aspect is not an exclusively male aspect. It is female or male. Feminists are committing the same error as male chauvinists when they build cases such as the one represented by the above question. The study of English will remedy the situation.

CHAPTER 26
BAPTISM

WHAT IS BAPTISM?

Baptism is the second initiation. It is the entrance on the Path of Purification. It marks the time that the individual has decided he is ready to look at himself and his negative aspects which he needs to reveal, purify and transform.

It is to be distinguished from the birth initiation. The birth initiation is the time when the individual becomes aware of the desire to improve himself. He is not ready yet to realize that self-improvement must also involve self-purification. For him, self-improvement is a linear striving towards the positive. Those who belong in this category, those who have taken the first initiation of birth can be found in the born-again Christians, the positive thinkers of Unity Church, those who practice the Course in Miracles, etc.

When someone is ready to take the initiation of baptism, there is a defense against it. The defense manifests in the individual's becoming fanatically reborn, fanatically a positive thinker. When that occurs, it means that the person is ready to look at what is negative within himself and overcome it. That is immersion in water, immersion in the unconscious, i.e., baptism.

Therefore, baptism is an initiation that must be entered into voluntarily. An individual must say, "I want to be baptized; I want to devote myself to the process of purification." At The Church of the Path®, we provide a baptismal ceremony for those who desire to take it. There are specific exercises involved in it, and there are specific oaths that apply to it.

In contradistinction to the linear direction which is taken after the initiation of birth, baptism indicates the readiness to go in two separate directions: (1) digging inside to reveal the negativities, and (2) going forward towards self-improvement. Thus the process acquires a new dimension. Not everyone is ready to take on this new dimension. However, when one is ready, if defense is manifested, misery and crisis will occur, which will perforce propel these people into the process of purification.

A good example of this is to be found in the twelve-steppers who are really first initiation people, having discovered the linear process of self-improvement. One has to dig deep inside and find the negativity that has created their addiction. The twelve-step program is a good initiatory process; it leads to the Path of Purification

MAGICAL THINKING ABOUT BAPTISM

The whole notion that the mere sprinkling of water on an infant makes him blessed and guarantees that he is going to heaven constitutes the height of magical thinking and brings on disastrous results. Indeed, if I am guaranteed that I am going to heaven because I am baptized, what prevents me from becoming a monstrous murderer?

Furthermore, this type of fallacy has brought incredible suffering. For example, if a choice has to be made between saving the expectant mother's life or that of the unborn child, Catholics have chosen—sanctioned by the Pope, practiced today in Catholic hospitals—to save the child rather than the mother. After all, the mother is going to heaven, having been baptized, but the child is not since he has not been baptized as yet. This is absolutely insane—the sacrifice of a grown woman with developed consciousness and with the capacity to have other children, for the sake of an infant who has not as yet been born and whose soul can easily incarnate again in another body. This is practically murder, murder by bigotry, murder through false belief.

CHAPTER 27
MARRIAGE

POWER AND BLESSINGS
OF THE MARRIAGE CEREMONY

Love is the most powerful force in the universe. The love that brings two adults together is the most powerful love in human experience. Lovers who declare their mutual commitment publicly, openly, frankly and generously, enormously enhance the force of this love and increase its pleasure. Thus, marriage is a commencement much like a graduation. It is a beginning, not an end as many people make it.

Many people live together and believe marriage to be a meaningless ceremony, that it does not really matter. However, the decision to get married, the event of marriage, the blessing of a couple by a community, by their friends and by the authorities of their community has an immense meaning. Imagine how the new union is strengthened by the bounty of blessings from the spirit guides of everyone attending the marriage, not to mention all of the souls who are there! The effect is incredibly strong. Anyone who has undergone this ceremony can attest to that.

My first marriage was effected under unhappy circumstances. Indeed, I was much too young, my wife was pregnant and my mother and my mother-in-law both were there, resenting the entire situation. However, when the judge married us, there was a magical feeling to it. It was as if the sky opened and released incredible blessings on us. And yet there was nothing religious on the outer level about this ceremony. It was merely a judge in New York effecting it in his office.

THE WAY IT WAS IN THE PAST

Historically, marriage has been grossly misused for every possible negativity. Since it is the greatest event it also engenders the greatest distortions. Indeed, marriages were concluded even before the births of the espoused. People doing business with each other could agree that one's daughter would marry the other's son or vice versa before they even had a son or daughter. A king would promise his son to another king's daughter for the purpose of military alliances, for the purposes of subjugating people, commerce, industry, etc. (The papacy is certainly not immune to this situation. Look, for example, at the Borgia popes.) Of course, the result of this is that it would influence souls to enter particular bodies or choose particular lives that were already predetermined by parents. Thus, you had a collusion based on greed that even preceded birth. The collusion includes the parents, the souls, as well as many other beings who are not purified. This has contributed to the deceleration of the Plan of Salvation.

Thus, a marriage based on love between two people was seen as undesirable. In fact, it was seen as evil, the height of stupidity or concupiscence. It was the marriages of convenience that were seen as more desirable and more spiritual, i.e., carrying with them the delaying of gratification—the grown up thing to do. Here is an example of a gross distortion of a spiritual principle, spirituality and delaying gratification used to the service of greed in order to denigrate love between two people, the greatest possible love known in human existence.

To a great extent, this is still around us today. For instance, to my astonishment, I heard a few days ago at a Hindu temple, a person who was called a saint say that America was much better off a hundred years ago when marriages were arranged.

The abuse of the forces of love, Cupid and sex and the subjugation of them for the purpose of greed and approval is commonplace. It can be found everywhere in all old time religions. It is the consequence of Sixth Ray control. Indeed, in the past it was necessary to "control" sexual forces because they had become rampant. Surely today this is not the case. On the contrary, we are ready to restore the forces of love, Cupid and sex in their rightful place—as expressions of divinity, as the highest form of at-onement with God in the human experience. So, involuntary/forced monogamy occurs for various reasons:

1. Marriages of convenience.

2. Subjugating love, Cupid and sex for the purposes of greed, approval.

3. The woman is chosen by the man because she would enhance his financial or social position in society. To the extent the great force of Cupid is demeaned, to that extent Cupid, pleasure and love disappear. To what extent is this still the case in your life?

Allow yourself to be in total truth and honesty with your partner. Cultivate Cupid in your relationship. Bring that in-love feeling back in your lives. Be in love. Be in God.

WHY PEOPLE FALL IN LOVE

People who want to get married or who long for the blessed state of matrimony need to examine the reasons they choose to be attracted to somebody. We may think that we are free of some of the greed that used to motivate unions in the past. Actually, we are still subject to it. Now it is our own greed as opposed to our parents' in the choice of a mate or of a partner. The dictum, "It is as easy to fall in love with a rich man as it is to fall in love with a poor man," has been internalized by a lot of women who act it out deliberately, by choice. They find themselves magnetized by men who have money or who have power or who have a capacity for affluence.

This inner state is very comparable to prostitution. The difference is that a prostitute is a lot more honest about her intentions of selling her body. In the case of the person who has conditioned himself or herself to be attracted to and to fall in love with specific features of another, such as abundance or position, they are committing prostitution on the physical and emotional levels.

The prostitute does not fool herself in the selling of her body. She does it consciously, she knows what she is doing. The sin here is a lot less than the person who has convinced herself that she is doing the right thing by falling in love with a person with money or power. The same can be said of men who fall in love with measurements, with a mother figure who will take care of them, or with money or power. It is once again, the same problems encountered in earlier human history, only now elevated to higher levels of development.

The forces of love, Cupid and sex operate from the involuntary, from the infinite, from the cosmic Life Force. We do have a choice, of course, to fall in love with whomever we want to fall in love with. However, this choice itself can be put to the service of evil, such as greed, etc. Left on its own and by itself, the person finds the right mate, the mate with whom he is most likely to at-one himself and accomplish his task.

HANDLING THE BLESSINGS OF MARRIAGE

The blessings given to the couple must be received and assimilated by them. It is extraordinarily important for them to work to acknowledge and identify, to dissolve and resolve the negativities in them that would misinterpret these energies, misuse them or even block them. Let's look at what can mar this happiness.

1. Can all the pleasure be accepted? If you look closely at yourself, you will find difficulty in taking the pleasure. However, remember that this pleasure, this state of grace, is reality. The grayness that is usually experienced in everyday life is illusion.

2. Falling from this grace, misconceptions set in:

a. Marriage is a tender trap. It may be tender, but it is still seen as a trap because pleasure is still seen as a function of diversity of partners. Not true.

Pleasure is a function of mutuality, of give and take—the freer the mutuality, the greater the pleasure. You can see this with your friends. The freer you are to share yourself with them, the more you enjoy yourself. It is the same with couples. The more intimate they are with each other, the greater the pleasure that they experience.

b. Intimacy is weakness. In marriage, intimacy occurs on the physical level, on the emotional level, on the mental level, on the spiritual level, whether we want it or not. As children we were never taught this. Instead, what we saw about marriage was mostly one-upmanship, father and mother each desperately trying to be right while making the other wrong. Each tried to be on top by making the other be on the bottom. They also tried to be on top by pretending to be on the bottom. Women were trained to make men feel good by always marveling at their strength, their great minds. In this way, they thought they would have the upper hand, "they knew how to keep a husband." Husbands, on the other hand, had to live up to that expectation. So, there was no room for them to be insecure, to admit their lack, their deficiency. And women could not admit their strength, intelligence, knowledge, superiority. So, on the emotional and mental levels, the marriage was increasingly loaded with lies. The partners felt more comfortable with their friends, since, in that context there were no lies, or fewer lies.

Sex was, therefore, the only refuge of intimacy. However, when there are lies on the emotional and mental levels, when there is discomfort about honesty, then physical intimacy suffers. Pretty soon, it becomes a duty, a marital duty. Then it disappears.

Therefore, in order to keep the in-love feeling alive, partners should cultivate the truth on all levels. By doing so, there will be a continuous self-revelation to the other and a continuous search into the other.

This will solve the problem of

c. Needing diversity, another wrong conclusion. Diversity will be found within the safety and openness of the relationship. We are all infinite. We have within us infinite aspects that need a safe place to allow themselves to be revealed.

COMMITMENT/VOWS

It is important that each participant compose his or her own vows which will be recited during the ceremony. This is just about all that is required in terms of ceremonials. The rest is up to the celebrant and up to the individuals getting married.

The marriage commitment is a gift that each gives to the

other, not shackles that are imposed on the other. There are many prerequisites for a successful marriage. First and foremost is the willingness and ability to say and practice the commitment. A few of the others are the freedom to:

1. Make autonomous decisions.
2. Experience all the pleasure that is possible between the partners.
3. Make mistakes and learn from them; not be perfect.
4. Grow into a wiser person at one's own pace without judgments.
5. Be entirely truthful, holding no secrets on the mental, emotional and physical levels; the self-idealizations, pretenses, masks must be shed (the conscious ones and the unconscious ones).

A marriage based on these commitments cannot come at an early age. A certain amount of maturity must be developed before it can be successfully undertaken and a huge amount of honesty and goodwill is required to maintain it.

FOR BETTER OR FOR WORSE

The fulfillment of this part of the commitment ensures the permanence of the love feeling. If I marry for better or for worse, I commit myself to love and accept *all* of you, not part of you.

Your revealing your dark side is not just OK, it is a prerequisite of marriage, an insurance against boredom, against falling out of grace. Yes, it will bring on fights, but they are healthy. If we train ourselves to be in total truth and honesty with each other on all levels, we will get closer to each other.

I give you the right to tell me truthfully all you feel about me, no matter how painful it may first seem for me to receive it. I ask for permission to do the same with you. Together, we will be for each other harbours for all that we fear, all that we find unacceptable in ourselves. Together, we have faith that nothing within us is unacceptable, nothing within us cannot be transformed.

If we can create this island of safety for each other, then our relationship will be a source of enormous strength which we can tap for any purpose and a place of replenishment in which there is as much pleasure to give as there is to receive.

For this, we commit ourselves to total honesty with each other on all levels, learning how to totally love each other, for better or for worse, for richer or for poorer, in sickness and in health.

MARRIAGE AND COMMUNITY

In a community such as this one, an uncommitted marriage constitutes a threat to the rest and a danger for them. Indeed, here are two possible harms that can be inflicted on the community by an uncommitted marriage:

1. Sexuality and cupid, removed from the marriage, gets transposed onto other members in a predatory fashion. If, because of the community's high degree of purification, this can't be done, the transposition, will occur outside of the community.

2. The lack of commitment creates guilt. In turn, guilt creates a reluctance for transparency and therefore an unwillingness to confront. The unexpressed confrontation in the marriage becomes vicious hostility against those outside the marriage.

DIFFERENCES BETWEEN SEX, CUPID AND LOVE

SEX
1. There is here a great urge to merge opposites.
2. Sex creates spiritual life and ideas.
3. Sex creates the human shell (body).
4. By itself it is very selfish, animalistic.
5. It fades without Cupid, particularly in women.
6. Otherwise it is permanent.

CUPID—IN LOVE STATE
1. Cupid is a great urge (as sex).
2. It has power and a powerful effect.
3. It is of short duration.
4. It carries a person from sex to love, therefore, it is a bridge.
5. It disappears if a person does not know how to love.
6. It can happen to anyone, developed or not, mature or not.
7. It will remain alive if the person knows how to love.
8. It is the closest emotion to love for the undeveloped.
9. Its selflessness is a function of adulthood.
11. Through Cupid a person surpasses himself.
12. It urges the soul to surge and burst out of itself.
13. It leads one from selfishness to selflessness.
14. It leads one from inertia to motion.
15. It is a foretaste of unity, leading to marriage and to God.

LOVE
1. It is a state, an atmosphere.
2. It is permanent
3. It must be learned.
4. The capacity for love increases through the Path of

Purification.
5. It is a function of consciousness and wisdom.

CONDITIONS FOR CUPID TO REMAIN ALIVE IN A RELATIONSHIP

1. Learn how to love.
2. Maintain alive the Instinct of Enquiry. If you feel that you know all there is to know about your partner, or that your partner does not need to know more about you, you will kill Cupid.
3. Change. Believe in Cupid, be willing to risk it.
4. Ability and willingness to experience pain.
5. Ability and willingness to accept the other as he is.
6. Total truthfulness.

Cupid is a great urge for adventure, for exploration of the soul of the other—out of separation. Both Cupid and love inspire altruism.

Therefore, wanting to get married is not a function of love. It is a function of Cupid (the "in love" state). It says, "this seed that was planted within me, this ecstatic foretaste, I want this forever." And so they get married. Staying married is a function of knowing how to love. And if you know how to love, then Cupid permanently will stay in your marriage.

CUPID RELATED TO CLEANSING

Cupid is the great adventure. As long as you feel that there is something new to discover in your partner, then Cupid will stay alive. The minute you decide that you know everything there is to know in him, or he knows everything you want him to know about you, Cupid leaves. The mistake is believing that you and your partner are limited. That is where "for better or for worse" comes into the picture. Why? Because:

1. You have already exhausted the "for better," or at least that which you call the "for better."

2. You do not want to get into the "for worse."

And here is the test of a marriage, going through the "for worse" and transforming it is real love. Here is where the pretenses start, walls are built. And nature is blocked. Dulling the "for worse," kills Cupid, dulls the relationship.

SOULMATES

Your only soulmate is God. Every time someone wants to betray his wife, he says that he has just found his soulmate in his mistress. First of all, the likelihood of that being true is very remote. Second, if it were true, it does not justify the betrayal of a commitment.

There is an incredible amount of nonsense being spouted by those erroneously called New Age teachers concerning soulmates. It is true that each one of us has a soulmate. It is not true that we will find that soulmate by betraying a commitment. As true as it is that we have a soulmate, our mates contain within themselves, and we contain within ourselves, infinite possibilities of unfoldment. When we become all that we can be, we are capable of attaining at-onement with whomever is our partner at that time in our life. We can do it. When there exists between two people good will and the desire to continuously transform, that is good enough.

DIVORCE

If one or both partners do not practice a Path of Purification, their relationship petrifies and putrefies. It becomes a detriment for both of them. For instance, instead of encouraging one another to develop the areas in which they are weak, they continue to compensate for each other, protecting one another from growth. The absence of growth and the absence of change preclude the existence of the in-love state, Cupid. Eventually, without Cupid, sexuality is also gone on the physical level. What is left? Do they really love each other? Not exactly. They unhealthily depend on one another.

There comes a time when the perpetuation of this negative situation becomes absurd. Divorce is necessary. Far from sending people to hell, when one partner, or both of them, have tried everything under the sun to revive the relationship and have failed, divorce is a liberating and blessed event. When a marriage is no longer valid there are issues that justify its dissolution. Then, the marriage has to be dissolved because it is regressive. If it is not, it becomes a function of self-idealization, a holding on to a dead form which is obsolete.

With the acceleration of energy it is very possible that there is the need for a new relationship because the old one has served its purpose and needs to be dissolved or because one of the mates is no longer interested in the unfolding process that exists on a path such as this one.

Of course, there are invalid reasons for divorce. Promiscuity, sexual incontinence are perhaps the major ones. However, there are others. Furthermore, promiscuity and sexual incontinence never exist in a vacuum. There is always a reason why a person is promiscuous or incontinent. These reasons are to be found in defects and problems that exist in the marriage. It is the not facing of these problems that triggers the promiscuity and incontinence. In these situations the problems are getting worse because they are not faced consciously.

Sex has been so misused by humans that its expression and experience became associated with guilt. Marriage, through commitment, exposure, and blessings, removes this guilt, thus making sexuality more pleasurable and Cupid more present. Thus, the destruction of interest in a spouse occurs to the degree there still is association of sex with all of its misuses and distortions in the past.

It is the return to the bad old ways, and with them guilt. It means that there is an obsessive "marriage" between sexual pleasure and guilt. And it means that there is commitment to their distortion. Otherwise, marriage would be and would remain more pleasurable, due to its guiltless context by definition.

When two people are tied in a marriage, they must follow a Path of Purification such as ours. If they do, divorce will become unnecessary. On the contrary, they will come to feel closer and closer to one another, no matter how difficult have, in the past, been their troubles.

CHAPTER 28
DEATH

FEAR OF DEATH

Dying is an act, a natural act. It occurs everywhere around us. Accepting it, when our time has come, makes it easier. We then enter a state of grace. If dying is accepted as part of living, fear of dying disappears and yields immortality.

Fear of death is fear of life. Fear of death is fear of change. Since life is change, then fearing death means fearing life. Therefore, knowing how to live is knowing how to die. *Preparation for life is preparation for death.* Illumination in life makes death a very happy and easy experience to go through.

The manner of death prepares the manner of birth.

DEATH AND THE SURVIVAL INSTINCT

If death is such a liberating experience and if being imprisoned in the body is so agonizing, then why do we have an Instinct of Self-Preservation that prevents us from dying and that makes us fight death tooth and toenail? The answer is that it could not be any other way. If it were different, people would not be able to penetrate this three-dimensional reality and accomplish their task. So, God created this condition wherein the Instinct of Self-Preservation is a "ring-pass-not." Once you are born, the Instinct of Self-Preservation keeps you from going back.

However, you would rather return.

If you look at any infant after its birth, you can see that it wants to go back. The worst day of your life is the day of your birth. It is unhappy in this new state. But as its life progresses, as the soul releases into the personality the task that is to be accomplished in this three-dimensional reality, the personality involves itself in the accomplishment of this task; it becomes "a matter of life or death" to accomplish this task. In view of this, as you read this material you might want to meditate on the futility of your defense against doing what you must do, which is looking at all of yourself and accomplishing your task.

When a task is accomplished and the person has looked into himself and has developed the necessary defenselessness, which brings with it true fearlessness and harmlessness, then the Instinct of Self-Preservation relinquishes its fear of death. It happens at this point because the personality has understood the reality of immortality.

When you have looked at all of yourself, you feel immortal and you lose the fear of death.

When you have accomplished your task, you feel the link with infinity and with immortality and, therefore, you no longer fear dying.

The existence of the fear of death in an individual is proof positive that he has not looked at himself thoroughly and that he does not want to accomplish his task.

Preparation for death and understanding of death is very much part of life. That's why the capacity to put one's life on the line, in moments of heroism, is seen as such a noble, elevated thing to do: because it, indeed, requires a state in which the task has been accomplished. It is a state of high spiritual development to be able to risk one's life.

This becomes distorted into the fanatical self-sacrifice of the terrorist. However, that sacrifice is no longer true surrender. It becomes the suicide of the coward who doesn't want to accomplish his task.

WHY DEATH?

It is not just people who die; plants die, animals die, and to a certain extent death can also be experienced in the mineral kingdom when a crystal or stone loses a particular magnetism or energy. Death is the relinquishing of the physical body. It occurs to the extent an individual has a lower self.

There is an increasing point of tension between the parts of the individual that continue to progress and the parts of the individual that continue to regress due to lack of focus and evolution. If the lower self is not worked through, the person dies only to be reborn into three-dimensional reality in another body in order to develop that which has heretofore been undeveloped. In reality there is no death.

ACCIDENTAL DEATHS

In many cases a person comes into a body with a particular plan which is interrupted by an accident or a war in which he loses his life prematurely. As accurate as a plan is from the point of view of the Forces of Light, some circumstances cannot always be anticipated. Furthermore, many people will take on a life knowing that there is a possibility of death in a war or an accident. They still go ahead with incarnation, trying to complete their task. Their success depends upon the degree to which they are able to liberate themselves of their own primitive self or lower self which attracts particular evil circumstances. It would be perfectionistic for souls to request before birth a perfect set of conditions in order to incarnate.

The greater the development of an individual, the more he has control over his destiny no matter what the dangers. To the extent a person has "cleaned up his act," he will have determination over the course of his life and can avoid all accidents. The great majority of humanity is not developed and has limited consciousness. Thus, many people are magnetically attracted to particular physical situations over which it seems they have no control This accounts for a great deal of what is called "accidental" death.

HIGHER SELF, LOWER SELF AND IDOLIZED SELF (MASK) DECISIONS TO DIE

It is almost true to say that the Higher Self decision to die is the only decision to die that counts; the lower self and mask decisions to die are mostly ineffectual. The Higher Self decides that it is time to disconnect from the body when the energy used to keep the body, i.e., the personality, alive is getting diminishing returns. It is, therefore, in the best self-interest of the individual to no longer squander his Life Force equity in this particular personality manifestation. Death is then instituted through the removal of the faculties.

Lower self decisions to die can be found in suicide, despair, or false interpretations of the nature of spirituality.

Suicide means refusing to live the life given to you. It squanders the Life Force. It makes demands for perfection. Suicide can be found, and is experienced, in daily microcosmic form: any refusal to deal with a problem is a form of suicide. Any seeking of expediency is suicide. Any wrong answer is suicide—the three wrong answers being aggression, subservience, and disconnection.

Inflicting personal death is the ultimate form of wrong answer. So we arrive at a contradiction:

1) Death, the ultimate frustration, is the ultimate humiliation.

2) In order to escape frustration, which is humiliating, I inflict upon myself the worst possible humiliation: death.

Idolized self decisions to die are found in the myths of some cultures. For example, the German mythological characters seem always to die in glorious battle. In dying, they glorify their own cruelty, and thus avoid feeling the pain of guilt. Other examples of lower self types of death are people offering themselves to be crucified or as human sacrifices, etc.

Idolized self/mask decisions to die mostly come through the manifestation of the affected conscience.

The affected conscience is that part of the mask which is a false conscience, which has an exaggerated or false sense of guilt about the existence and the nature of the lower self, and which is out to destroy the lower self, thus destroying itself. From the point of view of the mask, there is a desperate attempt to escape revealing what is in the lower self. At the same time the lower self appears to be the Real Self, the real nature of the individual, since seeing past it into the Higher Self is impossible. These people are, therefore, left with the following two unwanted choices:

1. There is a continuous and perpetual super effort to maintain mask forces. The energies that are invested in this never regenerate since they are invested in falsehood.

2. Reveal the lower self and feel that they are totally bad. This seems to be the worst possible scenario even though it is one to which they feel irresistibly attracted.

Furthermore, if the lower self is perceived as the Real Self by the mask, then the mask will not want to let go of the lower self since it would lose its identity entirely. The decision of the mask to die has to do with putting an end to this incredible nightmare. This nightmare is a lot more painful than the clear revelation of the lower self.

OUT-OF-BODY AND NEAR-DEATH EXPERIENCES

It is possible for an individual to leave his body behind and to travel through different realms of reality. This has been abundantly demonstrated in a great number of books that have been written on the subject, from Shirley MacLaine to Robert Monroe. We also experience this in dreams. The only difference between this state and death is that in death the "silver cord" which ties the soul to the body is cut.

There is also a great deal of material that has been accumulated on this subject by Dr. Raymond Moody, Dr. Elizabeth Kubler-Ross and many other reputable scholars. They gathered their facts from people who had undergone a Near-Death-Experience. These individuals seem to go through several phases that can be roughly described as follows:

1. A disconnection from the body. In this state they find themselves aware of their body, aware of everybody else in the room or wherever their body happens to be, and able to defy gravity. They see everyone, but no one sees them.

2. A long dark tunnel experience which takes them from their previous state to "the other side." This long, dark tunnel is our passage through the astral plane, the plane on which evil resides. It is the Christ who frayed that tunnel for us. However, it is still our responsibility to purify ourselves enough to enable us to pass through it without being lured by temptations and without deviating and getting stuck in

the world of evil. Literature and mythology have a number of excellent examples symbolizing this process of the long, dark tunnel.

The one that I like best is Ulysses' attempt to come home from the War of Troy. During this voyage he got lost and he was continuously being tempted, particularly by Circe. He successfully overcame those temptations. He even went to the trouble of being tied to the mast of his ship in order to resist the voices of the Sirens and of the temptress Circe. The wonderful thing about his story is that he had his crew tie him to the mast, thereby exposing himself to the longing, to the pain of frustration and to the loss of consciousness, while at the same time protecting everyone else on the ship from the experience by seeing to it that they put wax in their ears. He wanted to be fully conscious of the temptation, and he wanted to go through the ordeal without protection. So did the Christ during His incarnation, and so should we as we go through the trials and tribulations of our lives. The full experience of the pain, of the temptations, of the agonies, of the longings, of the frustrations, elevates us to maturity. It brings wisdom and raises our state of consciousness.

However, I am not sure that this experience of the tunnel is available to everyone. In fact, many people who have gone through the Near-Death-Experience do not describe going through the tunnel. They merely stay stuck on the physical level, i.e., in their etheric body, the one immediately past the physical body on the way up the scale. Therefore, in order to go through the long, dark tunnel, you must have attained a certain level of development. You must be able to identify the majority of your lower self and thereby deactivate its negative, magnetic power.

3. The meeting with the Being of Light. At the exit of the tunnel a Being of Light awaits you and asks you to review

your life. Actually, it is not a question of asking at all. In the presence of that light, one is compelled to instantly examine every single moment of one's life. It is the brightness of the light that shines on the individual which is the cause of the clear and instant vision of the entire life.

The individual then becomes aware of several things.

a. What counted in his life is how he loved, how selflessly he served, and who benefitted from his help.

b. What of the life plan with which he came in at birth was not started or left undone.

c. The harm that he did and whether or not he made restitution for it.

The more unresolved harmfulness there is within the individual, the more unbearable the light is going to become for him and the more likely it is that he will want to return. He will want to go back either to the sphere of Earth and humanity or to another place more suitable for his state. There are many other spheres that, outside of time and space, permeate and interpenetrate our reality. If the guilt is enormous, in order not to feel the pain of it, the person will want to disconnect cause from effect. So, he is relegated to a world in which cause and effect are even further removed than on the level of our three-dimensional reality. There, cause and effect are so separated from each other than they seem not to exist. You can imagine the extraordinary amount of time that it will take for a person in a place like that to regain the privilege of being born again as a member of humanity.

Take, for example, gang members, members of the SS during World War II, or Stalin and the communists who committed more killings and outrages than anyone in Germany. These people will not incarnate on the human level for a very long time. The result of this is going to be a separation between those who purify and those who do not. This is because those who do not purify cannot stand the light of the presence of those who do.

There were a number of predictions in the 1960s and 1970s, according to which the Earth will cease to be a sphere of purification. It will become a sacred planet. Humanity, or more of it anyway, will be a lot less subjected to evil, to being the dumping ground of negativities emanating from the evil plane.

What is the connection between these predictions and the separation between those who do the work and those who do not? At the present time both those who do the work and those who do not, physically live in the same place, planet Earth. The predictions announce a new era whereby those who have not done the work will no longer incarnate on Earth. They will incarnate in another sphere which will take over the role of the purifier which Earth has held for so long. The Earth will then become a sphere of development which is much closer to the Hierarchy as well as to other planets where more developed beings live.

4. The person now meets with people he knew during this incarnation who preceded him in death, as well as with people he had known in past incarnations. They are there to greet him and receive him if it is the time of his death; they are also there to tell him to go back if he has not finished what he must finish in this lifetime. Many people describe an unwillingness to return to their bodies, since they found such utter pleasure and bliss in the presence of the Being of Light. Others see the wisdom and necessity of returning to complete what they started.

5. Those who have undergone this experience and re-entered their body have found that their attitude toward life changed drastically. In the book, *Heading Toward Omega*, Kenneth Ring, Ph.D., Professor of Psychology at the University of Connecticut and President of the International Society for Near-Death Studies, clearly demonstrates this. Dr. Ring submitted questionnaires to people who had undergone a Near-Death-Experience. He found that after this experience, their lives changed drastically and their values were totally different. It was no longer important for them to have success, to have money, or to dress in a particular way. Their primary focus became caring and giving and helping and serving. Their focus shifted from the physical to the spiritual because they were no longer afraid of death.

I think that we have a duty as human beings to read this material, to be aware of it, and to impress our soul substance with it. Doing so will help to dissolve our fear of death.

6. If the soul remains out of the body, i.e., if the individual dies, it takes up another task. The new task depends on the soul's ability to teach, to give, to instruct, to share experiences, to educate, to prepare others who are ready for incarnation, or simply to create beautiful energy forms, as in music and other forms of art. Everything that we know on the three-dimensional level is a poor imitation of what already exists outside of the body.

A few decades ago, for instance, Rosemary Brown received Beethoven's *Tenth Symphony* in dictation from Beethoven himself. The musical experts recognized that, had Beethoven been alive, he would have composed a Tenth Symphony in that fashion. It was the natural progression of his thought process from the point of view of music. Ms. Brown was not a very good musician. She was asked why this was given to such a mediocre musician as she was, when it could have been given to a great number of excellent ones who could have done it better justice. Ms Brown said that she herself had asked that question to the spirit of Franz Liszt. His answer was that she was chosen because she was the least likely person to write such a piece of music. This would demonstrate the veracity of the communication.

7. In the case of a young person, if the body is so mangled by disease, accident or surgical intervention that the soul cannot stay in it any more, the soul then disconnects from the body and looks for another body to incarnate in as quickly as possible. Among us are an incredible number of people who have reincarnated very quickly after World War II. An astonishing percentage of the Baby Boomers are such people. In working with them it is not very difficult to perceive how they died, if they died a violent death, etc. Of course, not too many of them are open to receiving this type of information.

IS DEATH THE END?

In order to answer this question one has to focus on the nature of the individual and the process of birth. The Monad, or the Higher Self, puts together a soul with positive and negative aspects and attributes to enter a personality in the dualistic world which we call physical reality. The person has a choice. The choice is to go through his task or not to, to act in accordance with Spiritual Law or to violate it. To the degree the individual chooses to violate Spiritual Law, to that degree when he dies he will reincarnate under worse conditions. On that level, death is merely death of the physical body. But, if there is a continuation of violation of

Spiritual Law, then the individual as a consciousness disintegrates—explodes.

This is real death—the death of the soul. The continuous violation by the soul of the laws of the universe, the continuous choice made for the forces of darkness ends up creating a condition where the soul itself explodes and dies. Fear of death as we know it on Earth is based on fear of this possible event and on the knowledge of this event. In fact, fear of death on Earth is fear of what would happen in this particular case, i.e., the loss of identity, the loss of consciousness, the loss of existence as an individual.

SURRENDER

The capacity to surrender to sleep demonstrates the ability to surrender to death. It is also true of the capacity for sexual surrender which is a demonstration of surrender to pleasure and ecstasy. It is interesting in this context to note that representatives of great evil have always had much difficulty falling asleep. Emperors such as Nero, Caligula, Caracalla, Justinian all kept incredibly odd hours. They were never really able to sleep; they would finally fall asleep out of exhaustion. This difficulty in falling asleep was due to the fact that the minute they slept they were reminded of all the outrageous karmic debt that they were accumulating.

Consequently, a person in this condition is terrified of reincarnating. Having abused the powers and advantages that were given to him in this lifetime, every time he falls asleep, he gets a glimpse of what is going to happen to him in the next lifetime. Without his power as emperor or without his riches, what will he do? If he has abused his power and money in this lifetime, then being deprived of his power and money is death of the worst kind. So, he becomes the archenemy of the notion of reincarnation and even of the notion of God.

This is why Justinian eliminated any notion of reincarnation from the Catholic Church. It is very much to the discredit of the Catholic Church to have consequently followed the dictates of such a corrupt person as he. It is true that Justinian and his wife, the whore Theodora, saw to it that the pope who opposed them was poisoned and a more sympathetic pope elected. However, this does not excuse the church from removing from its catechism the teaching of reincarnation and never reinstating it—a mistake which has continued to perpetuate a huge and grave falsehood throughout Christendom.

In terms of the life of the conventional churches, one can draw the same conclusions as we would for an individual. For example, the incredible outrages performed by the Catholic Church throughout the centuries, including the one just mentioned, weigh heavily on its soul. It must take steps to drastically change those beliefs, to replace them with more sane ones, and to make restitution for all past outrages, or it will disappear.

SUPPORT OF THE DYING

Death is a crisis. It is the ultimate destruction of the defense mechanisms. Therefore, it is the ultimate crisis in a person's life. So, anything that can be said about crisis applies to death and to the death process. For example, it is important to be with the dying person and to listen to what he has to say with a minimum of editorializing and a minimum of confrontation. In fact, there will be very little need for confrontation since the defenses are shattered. What is important is to help the individual release and reveal as much as possible of what is on his heart. This is the reason for confession before death. At this time he is asked if he has any secrets which he wants to tell the priest before he dies. This is an extremely valuable exercise which will greatly help at the time of meeting with the Being of Light. Admitting a guilt is the first step toward restitution. It is a huge step which alleviates the karmic debt to a great extent. The sins that have been committed on Earth need to be left on Earth, even if merely on the conscious level. This process is much easier if the person knows that he is going to die than if he does not.

Support for the dying person consists of just being there and doing a lot more listening than talking. Support is also to be given by imparting as much information as possible to the dying person that physical death is not the end. This can be done by bringing the facts of life after life to the person's attention. If he can read, it would be good if there were reading material relating to this available to him. If there is a lot that you need to say, it is not a bad idea to put it in a video. This is particularly valuable if you believe that he will not be able to listen or that he will not have the patience, etc. With this method he will have control over turning it on and shutting it off at his own pace.

Do not lie to somebody who is dying. Do not try to spare him or to protect him against the pain of his own death. He has chosen his crisis. You have no right to rescue him from it. This is the work of the lower self and mask, not the Higher Self. If you lie and conceal things from someone who is dying, you are really being very selfish. You are doing it out of your own desire to be loved by the person. The dying person is really in as great a need as is a baby. Remember, it is his crisis not yours. Your duty is merely to be in truth. Soon he will be with his Maker. What counts is what will happen to him when he is again in full possession of his consciousness and finally discovers the truth. What kind of communication will you have with him at that point if you have lied to him? What kind of karma do you accumulate by doing so? By telling him the truth you may temporarily incur his displeasure, but you will receive his gratitude when he regains his consciousness and realizes what you have done for his sake.

The reason people who are in the process of dying do not want to hear the truth is like that of a child—they do not want to undergo the pain of facing reality. Except for birth, which remains the most painful experience in human life, they are right now in the worst possible condition.

PREPARING PEOPLE
TO MAKE THEIR TRANSITION

The most important thing is to encourage him to reveal as much as possible of himself before he dies, to be as straightforward as possible with everyone around him and to leave no stone unturned.

This process would be facilitated if it were done in the presence of someone he trusts such as a minister or teacher. He may not have reached the point where he has the courage and honesty to tell these truths to other people or to reveal these things to the people who are involved. Nevertheless, it is extremely important to convince him that he should talk to someone who has taken vows of keeping things private such as a priest, a minister or a teacher.

Once this is done, and preferably while the person is conscious, a ceremony of last unction should be performed with him. Prayers should be said for his soul to be committed into the hands of God, for his lower self not to hook into any of the astral plane forces, and for him to fully benefit from the experience. A process of prayer and healing should also be undergone to protect and seal all of the chakras except the crown chakra. This is done in order to avoid, if possible, the departure of the soul from the other chakras and also to avoid the entrance into those chakras of undesirable lower entities looking for a vulnerable vehicle. Oil should then be put on the crown chakra in the form of a cross or in the form of a symbol that has spiritual significance be used. However, the important thing is to follow what the person believes and what the celebrant believes because that is what will carry the soul out of the body without difficulty.

It is very important to refrain from hindering the departure of the soul from the body. The ones who are close to the person dying will be tempted to implore him to come back, to not go, etc. They will perceive this as an act of love. True love would be expressed by letting him go. Actually, by doing so, one gets closer to him, not farther away from him. It must be understood that physical death is a great liberation. It is a time of celebration rather than a time of grief. This state of euphoric joy can be sometimes attained if we can dissolve the defenses and misconceptions in the way.

It is also important not to touch the person leaving, unless he requests it. In the latter case, it may be enough to hold his hand. However, do not touch his head from which he is exiting. Touching him there will impair the exit.

When the soul is about to leave the body it is very helpful to have someone present who can actually see and experience this on the etheric and astral levels. Others who are in the sick room with the dying person should be urged by the celebrant to try to tune into these levels of reality.

What I have observed is the struggle of the soul as it tries to come out of the body. At that point I have also experienced the presence in the room of many entities amongst which were to be found the dying person's relatives who had already passed on. They were there to help him out of his body and to convince him that it is all right to die. The spirit guides were also there.

At this point it is important to actually visualize the soul leaving the body through the crown chakra. As you do so, you will gradually be able to see that you are helping this process along. You may even have glimpses of what this person looked like in his mid-twenties, for this is the state that he recovers. You may even urge him by saying, "You no longer have to look this way, the way your body looks now. You can go back to looking your best." I, for example, recognized my father the way that he looked when I was a very young boy. I was born when he was twenty-seven.

There will come a point when you will feel that the soul is clearly out of the body, and you will see the cord. At this point it is important to silently ask the person who is dying if he would like to have his cord cut, and if so, who he would like to cut the cord. The person who has been appointed should imagine himself actually cutting the cord. You may use any method to cut the cord. I visualize using scissors because this is the only way that I can conceptualize cutting something. I used an imaginary pair of scissors to cut my father's cord. After the cord has been cut, the body dies in about thirty minutes.

After the silver cord is cut, all that is left in the body is the lowest part of the personality. It attracts negative occurrences, tapping into the lower selves of those who are present. Thus, assisting the death of someone requires a great deal of spiritual purification on the part of whomever is assisting.

To facilitate the process of surrender of the body, the

colour orange should be emphasized in the room. For example, orange candles may be burned and orange paper may be used to cover the lights. In addition, it is important to softly play organ music in his room. The dying person may even request particular music that he would like played.

For a few days after someone dies, many people who were close to the person will experience him in dreams or in visions. These are real experiences not to be discounted and not to be relegated to the realm of illusion or imagination. It is important when this happens to acknowledge the person, to open your heart to him, and to tell him that it is OK, we are closer now than ever. The person should also be encouraged to go on to his task.

DEALING WITH SOMEONE WHO DENIES HE IS DYING

My father was. I think that the last thing that my father said to me was, "Don't worry Albert, I'm not going to die." Do not press the point. Sooner or later they will sink into unconsciousness. At that point you can silently tell them. "You are in the process of dying. It is good if you just accept it and if you release your body." You will find them still to be defensive at this stage of the game. It does not matter. You just continue to communicate to them silently that they are dying, that it is OK to die, and that it would be a lot easier if they just let go of their body, etc.

LIFE SUPPORT SYSTEMS

On a temporary basis, to facilitate a surgical intervention, life support systems can be used. However, they are *not* to be used to prolong the process of death when it is known that the person is afflicted with a terminal illness and is about to die. Life support systems for people who are in comas is an absolute aberration. It serves only one purpose —the enrichment of hospitals and doctors. Life support systems to prolong the life of someone who is already gone for all intents and purposes is a gross act of greed and a gross violation of the will of God. A person on the Path must make it very clearly known in his living will that no life support systems should be used at the time of his death. Thus, it is of primordial importance for those on the Path to have a living will, lest their wishes be violated by the next of kin who may not be on the Path.

DISPOSAL OF THE BODY—CREMATION

The Earth is a huge cemetery in which for millions of years dead bodies have left their diseases. The major diseases of today are inheritances from the past. The Lemurians gave us the venereal diseases while the Atlanteans have left us the viral infections such as cancer and probably even AIDS. Cremation is the only logical, practical, spiritual solution to this problem. It kills once and for all that which is diseased. The body is returned ashes to ashes and dust to dust, the way that it should be. This is the only way that the body should be disposed of.

A body that is buried or embalmed continues to be tied to the soul. The desire to have one's body embalmed and buried is a function of the fear of death. The fear of death is fear of life and, therefore, a violation of Spiritual Law. When the soul is still tied to the dead physical body, it is extremely difficult for the soul to be liberated and go on to its new task.

What about this nonsense concerning the belief that one should not cremate the body, because at the time of last judgment, those who bodies have been cremated will not have one in which to resurrect?

Of all the nonsensical beliefs that exist, this must be one of the most ridiculous. Indeed, even if the body is not cremated, isn't it going to decompose? What about those Christians who have been buried and whose only remains at this point are in skeletal form? Are they going to inhabit their skeletons when they resurrect? What about the Egyptian mummies? Does that mean that those Egyptian pharaohs have a better chance of resurrecting than the Christians who have merely been buried "earth to earth and dust to dust?"

By holding such childish beliefs, those who call themselves Christians or Jews or Moslems regress to the worst expressions of the Atlantean civilization—the attachment to and the veneration of form, the worst kind of death. I do not feel that this subject should be dignified with more comments than this.

FUNERAL CEREMONY

There should be a procession from the crematorium directly to the place where the eulogy will be given. It is best if the eulogy is given in a church, as in The Church of the Path®. The individual's spiritual teacher should give the eulogy. If it is done in the presence of someone who is higher in the hierarchy of the church, then the higher person should introduce and conclude the eulogy. The ashes should be scattered in a natural place of the choosing of the person who has died. There should not be a specific place where ashes are scattered, otherwise, with our limited consciousness, we again create a cemetery. The scattering of the ashes should first be done by those who were closest to the person who died. This sequence should be determined by the celebrant. The ashes should be scattered after the eulogy is concluded.

Very important: if there are feelings of joy at any time during the ceremony, it is extremely important that they be expressed rather than hidden behind false and destructive guilt. Death is a liberation. It is a commencement of freedom, not an end. This is true on the Path more than in other places.

YOUR WISHES FOR YOUR FUNERAL
VERSUS YOUR FAMILY'S WISHES

This is an extremely important consideration for people on the Path. Once again, we are ushering in a new religion with new rituals and new attitudes toward death which are not widely accepted by others. In fact, others view what we do as evil. It is extremely important for a person to clarify his wishes while conscious and in control of his facilities. Dissenting members of the family must be put in their place which means away from the process that we have chosen to undergo.

OLD MORBID BELIEF SYSTEMS
ABOUT FUNERALS

This whole business of displaying the body, embalming the body, having fainting fits around the body, wearing black clothes for eons following a person's death, having great displays of grief at the time of someone's death, hiring professional criers and wailers, paying enormous amounts of money for burial places and luxury coffins, paying priests and rabbis to do special services for years and years to come, insisting on being buried at a particular place, is utter nonsense.

These are the products of the limited consciousness, of greed, of the primitive self in action, of cruelty, of insensitivity, or of over sensitivity. All of this must be avoided.

It is unfortunate that one has to go through funeral homes in order to have one's body cremated. It would be preferable if access to the crematoriums were available without having to deal with the thieves and con artists that are to be found in the funeral business.

CEMETERIES

Cemeteries are very unhealthy places indeed! They are full of discarnate entities who have not resolved to let go of their bodies. They wander around and create a great deal of mischief for themselves and for their loved ones. Avoid cemeteries at all costs.

WILLS AND INHERITANCE

It is extremely important for us to have our wills written and to appoint the correct people for the disposition of their body. At this point our belief system is not very well accepted. It is inviting trouble not to have all of this very specifically done before the process of death starts.

Inheritances are mostly debilitating. People who inherit money use it as a way to regress into childhood. It is a way for them to still be supported by their parents without having to do their own work and without having to accomplish their task. Very few people are ready to receive an inheritance.

It would be much better to completely eliminate the whole concept of inheritance from our society. Think of the incredible amount of money that would be available if this were done. This money could be used for the purpose of providing free and universal education, free and universal health care, free and universal re-education of the soul, etc. Instead, huge amounts of money are given by parents when they die, to their children. This serves the purpose of protecting their children from discovering their own task and from pursuing it. This they call love!

Actually, it is the height of selfishness and shortsightedness—in short, stupidity. On the contrary, each individual should manifest and give from himself to the universe. In return money and other expressions of abundance will come to him naturally and to the degree that he gives to the universe.

The world is full of people who have inherited incredible amounts of money and who do not know what to do with it, thus wrecking their lives royally.

LIFE AFTER LIFE

After physical death what type of work will people on the Path do? They will continue the work of purification. The extraordinary experience of being on the Path while being in the body, impresses on the soul methods of working and methods of dealing with life circumstances which must be taught to others. This teaching continues after death perhaps to an even greater extent than it was being experienced while in the prison of the physical body.

Upon death, a person who is on the Path is received with much greater care and protection than a person who is not on the Path. His work on cleansing opens for him the possibility of receiving greater help from the Hierarchy. One has to remember that those who are on the Path and who dissolve their negativities, increase their power, their effectiveness and their influence.

As a result, they become the target of negative entities. The forces of darkness try to attack people on the Path more often than they try to attack people who are not on the Path. The worker on the Path protects himself against this through continuous purification of motives, etc. This makes available to him greater and greater numbers of protecting agents.

The Hierarchy is looking for the opportunity to engage in battle with the forces of darkness. The worker on the Path in his process makes this engagement possible. This is true of life in the body and also at the time of death when the person has to pass through the sea of darkness. Having protected himself by dissolving his negativity and through cultivating defenselessness, the worker on the Path earns the protection of the angels of God. That is why it is so important to undertake your battles and to never compromise. Fight the injustices, go against the line of least resistance, renounce and denounce.

What happens after death to people who are not on the Path? The deliberate attempt at conscious purification of one's negativities creates a sharp distinction between those who do this work and those who do not. Those who do the work give permission to the Forces of Light to protect them from the attacks of the forces of darkness. Thus, they are expected, protected and guided past the long dark tunnel into the light.

Those who do not do the work run a great risk of being caught on the astral level by the forces of darkness. These forces will be able to trap them through the elements that have not as yet been purified or at least identified for the purpose of purification.

Are there people who are not on a Path of Purification and who are able to make it through the long dark tunnel? Oh yes. Examples are to be found in those who have only taken the first initiation and are concerned merely with the linear process of self-improvement. However, those who have gone to that stage have been ready to embrace the

Path of Purification and avoided doing so, run a great risk of being caught on the astral level by the dark forces.

Many ordinary, run of the mill people have been able to go past the long dark tunnel, meet the Being of Light and go beyond. This is clearly demonstrated in the books on life after life. However, they remain the minority. And, even if they make it to the other side, having not gone through purification, they have to come back and go through it in another body.

PAIN KILLERS

They are necessary for those of us who have not made it to the point where we are able to do without them. It is ludicrous to submit yourself to the excruciating pain of a surgical operation without pain killers.

Jerry Lewis brilliantly portrayed the humour of such a situation in the film "Cracking Up." In this film he is an Indian guru with long hair, long beard and a robe. He refused anesthesia for an operation because he was a master at mind control, Hatha Yoga, meditation, Tai Chi, etc. However, the minute the doctor was about to use the scalpel, Jerry Lewis jumped off the operating table and ran out of the operating room screaming over and over again, "It hurts! It hurts!".

Don't be that ridiculous. Be who you really are. Take advantage of the wonderful progress of medicine which is very much a part of the progress of humanity.

Concerning the more common medicine—aspirin, antacids, etc.—one must try to get to the point of not needing them. However, they may be essential, in moderation of course, for those who have not learned how to heal themselves.

The taking of vitamins and herbs is very highly

recommended. There is no way, given our lifestyle and given the quality of our nutrition, that we can avail ourselves of the vitamins we need. Furthermore, herbal cleansing is very conducive to spirituality.

However, we are very much against pain killers that keep people from experiencing pain that they can withstand. This is particularly true when it comes to emotional pain. It is ridiculous for psychiatrists to prescribe tranquilizers to people undergoing psychosis or even neurosis.

The pain is the cause, the consequence and the healing. Pain killers remove the medicine. The pain is the self-manufactured medicine which would solve the problem. Pain killers regress the person to the point of no return in many cases.

Pain killers are a way of escaping pain and inducing pleasure or artificial peace of mind. When pleasure is sought as an escape from pain, it is a violation of Spiritual Law. Soon, the pleasure is felt in diminishing ways, and then the pleasure disappears completely, leaving the person in total and constant pain. This is true of addictions as well as any other escape.

We on the Path believe in suffering the pain and in allowing ourselves to be as conscious as possible of the pain on every level. When we do this, the pain lessens and even disappears in some cases. The pain increases through the defense that we put up against it. The pain decreases when there is defenselessness.

ORGAN DONATION AND ORGAN TRANSPLANT[12]

An organ represents the sum total of a person's Higher Self, lower self, and mask self. When someone is not on the Path, his organs are not undergoing a process of purification. Therefore, their nature on the etheric level is quite different from their condition in a person who is on the Path. Organ transplants should not be done even between people on the Path. If you take someone else's organ, you take with that organ his karma which you add to your own. Haven't you got enough difficulties as it is? Why add someone else's? The person on the Path should accept the fact that he is dying and that there is very little that can be done to save this particular body. It is all right; it is no big deal. If he wants another body, he will get one soon.

Organ donation is not recommended for Renewers. If you leave one of your organs for transplant, you will stay attached to that organ and you will find it difficult to disconnect from it.

ATTENTION TO THE PHYSICAL BODY

Many people believe that if they focus on their physical body and keep it as healthy as possible, they will avoid the process of death or at least prolong their life. They also erroneously believe that focusing solely on the physical body will result in the prevention of disease. Both notions are

---

[12] Recent scientific studies prove that organs carry the karma of the donor: Parsall P, Schwartz GE, Russek LG. *Changes in heart transplant recipients that parallel the personalities of their donors.* Integrated Med. 2000; 2(2):65-72. Broccolo M, Favez N, Karam O. *Perceived changes in behavior and values after a red blood cell transfusion.* International Journal of Clinical Transfusion Medicine 2018:6.

untrue.

The body is the precipitate of what happens on the mental and emotional levels. Suppose that you have misconceptions on the mental level. Those misconceptions will create wrong feelings and wrong movements on the astral "emotional" level. Those in turn will create a dis-ease in the body or a reduction in the immune response which will attract diseases on the physical level.

Now, this can be dealt with temporarily on the physical level. The symptoms can be treated with diet, surgery, medication, etc. However, if the condition persists on the mental and on the emotional levels, the physical body will continue to be assaulted by disease coming from these levels, becoming more and more vulnerable. It will seem that the more attention is given the body, the more sensitive it becomes.

Those who idealize their body and their physical condition escape the work that needs to be done on the emotional and mental levels by taking the easier road of dealing strictly with their body. They rationalize the increasing sensitivity of their body by believing that they are becoming more subtle and that the increased sensitivity means that they are becoming more spiritual. Nothing could be further from the truth. They are merely wasting away into death. They are more dead than they know. They are embalming their body. They are closer to the Egyptian pharaohs than thriving human beings.

Conversely, if the individual focuses on the problems he is having in his life, on the problems of the astral level, on the understanding and on the education of the primitive self, on the causes of these problems as they are found on the mental level through the limited consciousness, then this whole process is reversed. The health that is created on the mental and emotional levels will help greatly in creating a healthy physical body since there will be less and less precipitation of negativities onto the physical level. Then and only then can the process of health—eating right, exercising, etc.—become valid. One must remember that healthy physical habits are the simplest and crassest modes of purification. They should not be mistaken for the highest and most revered modes to obtain spirituality.

Sometimes people decide to die while they are very healthy, for example, Yogananda. Yogananda knew that he was going to die, and he died without being sick. Now, Yogananda was overweight, and he did not exercise. However, he did not die of any disease. He died clearly because he wanted to. It was time to go.

Many other examples can be cited to disprove the simplistic theory of equating focus on physical health with longevity, without taking into consideration the other levels of existence. On the Path, we are primarily concerned with the health of the soul, the health found on the spiritual, mental and emotional levels. It is only secondarily that we stress physical health.

The goal of humanity is to reach immortality. The basic, most powerful, and most fundamental instinct, the Instinct of Self-Preservation, has for goal and for divine consummation immortality.

This is immortality in the body not just immortality of the soul. Eventually, humanity will find this. In the meantime, those who have achieved the fifth initiation while still in the body have been able to demonstrate the reality of immortality in the body.

The most notable example of this was the Count of Saint Germain whose reappearance was documented in the memoirs of the Marquise d'Adhemar. She saw him periodically for a period of fifty-eight years; however, he always appeared to be forty years old! He did not obtain immortality by going to healy-feelie healers, by being fanatically vegetarian, or by exercising. Remember that Christ, the greatest incarnation of all, ate meat and drank wine, while Hitler, the lowest possible representation of evil in today's humanity, was a vegetarian and teetotaler.

USE OF DOCTORS, NOT BEING USED BY THEM

You may want to use doctors, you may want to use chiropractors. We all do. The progresses in the medical profession are staggering, are wonderful, are extraordinary.

We need to take advantage of them. However, it must be accompanied by our way of taking responsibility for yourself. In some cases, the medical profession can be completely bypassed. In fact, it is bypassed most of the time. We do not know the degree to which we are healing ourselves from one moment to the next by practicing the Path. We only know when we are sick and when perhaps the sickness has gone too far, when the destruction has already taken root.

For example, I may drink a lot to the point where I have irreparably damaged my liver. Then the distortion has gone too far. At the same time I may be in a process of healing where many other problems are being prevented. Nevertheless, my liver problem continues to get worse, leading to my death. However, this by no means is to say that I was not healed of other maladies. If one of the links in the chain breaks, the whole chain is obsolete; the person dies.

Healing is experienced in our church on a daily basis by people who come in for morning services from 7 to 7:30 AM. In a short thirty minutes people come in with colds and leave without them, come in with headaches and leave without them, etc. And there is no telling how many other healings have occurred that have not been reported because they have not been felt.

It is at times necessary to accept that it is better to let go of a body through death or to let go of some possessions through another form of crisis rather than achieving a Pyrrhic victory by overcoming the problem in another way. The loss of a life is sometimes more healing than the saving of a life. This is why people sometimes choose to die early deaths. They have done what they came to do. The energy that would be spent sustaining a particular body which has outlived its function is a lot more expensive than letting the body go and forming another one, or simply letting it go and living on the other planes of existence.

CHILDREN WITH TERMINAL DISEASES

This is an area where doctors and hospitals make fortunes. They try to keep alive a body that either is in the process of death or that should die. This person was born with that condition for a reason.

The purpose may be that this entity needs to undergo a particular pain such as the one that is experienced by their deformity or their illness. Then, they should be left alone to die.

Many fortunes and many lives of wonderfully functioning adults are ruined by doctors and hospitals who insist on keeping alive young entities who should die. These entities are kept alive for the purpose of lining the pockets of the doctors and hospitals. All of these evil intents will completely disappear if there is universal health coverage and if it does not necessarily profit the hospital or the doctor to keep someone artificially alive in this fashion.

A couple who were Episcopalians and who came to me for counseling spent their entire savings as well as the entire power of their medical coverage to maintain the life of a deformed baby who was born to them. This child died any way at age two and a half. They ruined their lives in two and a half years of senseless attachment to a little body that was deformed and whose task was not to linger as long as it did. This is but one of numerous examples to be found.

This nonsense is a result of a very misguided belief of the Judeo-Christian tradition. According to this belief, one must do everything that one can possibly do to maintain life because it is God-given. They fail to recognize that the Lord giveth and the Lord taketh away. The Lord gives life and the Lord also gives the conditions under which life is taken away. It is just as sinful to prevent one as it is to prevent the other.

SUICIDE

Suicide is a function of despair and, thus, is an expression of a demand. Basically, the individual is saying, "I demand that life be different than it is; and if it isn't different, then I am going to kill myself." Other demands may involve shame and guilt about aspects of themselves that the individual wants to hide. For instance, the lack of acceptance of certain areas of the lower self or the lack of acceptance of certain sins that have been committed will create a desire for self-destruction.

Another cause for suicide can be the unwillingness to go through the pain of injustice—what they consider to be injustice, of course.

However you look at it, a person who commits suicide is in despair and is making a demand on life. He wants life to be different from what it actually is. He has not made the connection between what is inside of him and what has happened outside in his life. When the actor George Sanders committed suicide, he left a note saying that he was bored and that he was leaving all of us in the cesspool that we call life. If you have ever seen films by George Sanders, you will recognize his huge mask of conceited boredom which eventually killed him.

Suicide is the ultimate violation of Spiritual Law. It is the most destructive act one can possibly commit. It is better to be a murderer than to commit suicide. The person who commits suicide will find himself in a world of extraordinary deceleration. In a book called *The Bright Light of Death*, Annabel Chaplin described what happened to a friend who committed suicide. Through her psychic abilities, she found the person completely engulfed in a sea of mud along with other people who had also committed suicide. It was very difficult to distinguish one person from another. They were moving very slowly. The person who commits suicide will find himself in this decelerated state indefinitely or at least for a very long period of time.

I suppose that the situation should be lessened in the case where a Dr. Kevorkian intervenes and administers death to someone who is suffering. I am not sure, however. In any case we do not advocate this course of action. The pain experienced by the individual at the time of death is extremely valuable for his process of purification. The Higher Self uses the pain of death as a way to overcome many problems.

For example, we know for a fact that our friend Don overcame his vanity through the process of death. At The Church of the Path® we were able to witness this very graphically and very precisely. With the disappearance of his vanity, Don's defenses also disappeared; he became wonderfully open, generous, giving, warm-hearted and loving—more than he ever was before. He was able to give the truth with great courage and honesty. This is something that he had great difficulty doing before his terminal illness.

Death is an opportunity for acceleration and advancement. The by-passing of all of this with suicide is a grave mistake which takes untold pain to correct later.

CATHOLIC HOSPITALS

Beware of Catholic hospitals. Stay away from them. This is particularly true if you are going to give birth. They will save the child and kill the mother because the mother is baptized. The mother is baptized, she will go to heaven after death, whereas, the unborn child is not and, if he dies in childbirth, will not go to heaven, the Catholics believe. Needless to say, this is the height of stupidity and does not belong in our belief system. A child is blessed when he is born. He may undergo a ceremonial baptism, if the parents desire it, but this does not necessarily make him blessed by God. He has already been blessed when he was born.

The life of the mother at the time of childbirth is infinitely more important than the life of a baby. Through the process of reproduction, a baby can be recreated. Furthermore, a soul who was planning to inhabit the body of the child who will not be born can inhabit the body of another child through exactly the same process. However, terminating the life of a functioning adult who is loved, who loves, who performs many purposeful and useful things in society, and who is in the process of accomplishing her task, is murder. They condone that murder by making the excuse that she has been blessed by the questionable sacrament of Catholic baptism.

CHAPTER 29
SYMBOLS

SYMBOLS ARE EVERYWHERE

Everything that happens in your life is a symbol of the way you have used energy and consciousness. Thus, your body is a symbol, your dreams are symbols, incidents from the most minute to the most eventful are all symbols that reflect how you have used or abused the Universal Life Force and the Universal Consciousness, i.e., God.

All of these symbols are more than just God's creation. They are God's creation and they are your creation of God's creation.

Material reality is deceleration of unexperienced emotions. Material reality is, therefore, a symbol of emotions. Material reality is, therefore, a mere symbol. Collectively, the unexperienced emotions of those entities inhabiting Earth have created this material universe, including Earth, as well as their bodies. Also collectively, they have invoked the intervention of higher beings whose task it is to guide them in their career on this plane of existence. Collectively they have also created holy spots, investing them with their faith, their prayers, the Universal Life Force that was available to them.

ILLNESS AND DISEASE

Any illness or dis-ease is the result of the misuse of the Universal Life Force by the limited consciousness. It manifests in the body when it has not been attended to on the mental and on the emotional levels. Thus, an illness is a symbol, a *symbol of an unexperienced emotion.*

There would be no illness, however, if there were not a point of tension between the desire to decelerate and become matter and the desire to accelerate and to find God once again. Indeed, an unattended thought becomes a feeling; an unattended feeling becomes matter and stays matter until it is revived by a desire to go the opposite way. Thus, disease can happen in two ways:

1. The Higher Self trying to prevent the deceleration into matter;

2. The Higher Self trying to reaccelerate matter while the lower self is trying to prevent it and keep the ongoing process of deceleration.

Sometimes for the purposes of letting the individual learn a lesson, the Higher Self will not intervene in the process of deceleration. The process of birth is thus unimpeded by the Higher Self. The Higher Self, and the soul for that matter, stay in the background while a part of the soul descends into matter and energizes a particular body.

However, at some point when appropriate, the Higher Self may prevent this from happening in its battle against the lower self. This battle occurs on the astral level first. Thus, disease, the consequence of those points of tension, can be observed first on the astral and etheric bodies before it descends on the physical body. Furthermore, the healing of a physical disease can be greatly accelerated by understanding and dealing with the energies of the astral and etheric levels. Thus a good and wise healer works.

The same is true in the second instance given above. In the cases in which the individual is ready to re-energize matter, accelerating it and raising it to the levels of the

Higher Self, there will be obviously an opposition from the line of least resistance, from the forces of darkness that will try to maintain the status quo and the deceleration process. Again, there will be a conflict created on the astral level which will be at some point or another experienced on the material level.

MENTAL ILLNESS

A "mental" illness is a conflict that has not descended on the physical level. From the point of view of mundane psychology and psychiatry there are two types of illnesses—neurosis and psychosis. From our point of view, the neurotic is saner than the psychotic because he is much more in touch with his lower self. The psychotic person is no longer in touch with his lower self. He is entirely in his mask. So, then, the psychotic is suffering from a double distortion on the astral level whereas the neurotic person is only suffering from a single distortion.

MEANING OF PAIN

Healing has occurred in our church not only on the mental and emotional levels, but also very powerfully on the physical level. Indeed, diseases that had been treated by medical doctors for decades without any results were healed fairly quickly through this process of purification. This is also true in some cases of terminal illnesses, eradicated in a few weeks through the deep personal responsibility and re-experiencing of that on the astral level which caused the disease in the first place and which was maintaining it.

We should avail ourselves of the services of modern medicine. However, if we do not accompany this with the deep experience of whatever it is that exists on the astral level and that has created this illness, we would be retarding the process of healing, or even worse regressing it. The healing itself will then become a weapon of regression, used for prematurely preventing the person from experiencing the consequences of his illness. This is where suffering is holy.

Pain experienced through a disease is a steppingstone to finding out the real meaning of that disease and, therefore, to the eventual healing of it permanently.

HOLY PLACES

In and by themselves icons or holy places or "consecrated" churches are nothing special. They are material reality. However, invested with the astral and mental energies of the people who pray around them, they "become" holy.

This process can be used fruitfully by every one of us. It is not necessary to have anyone come and consecrate these places. You can do it yourself. Of course, it helps if a person who is more evolved than you were to invest some of his own prayers and energies to a particular place or a particular home. Indeed, if we create a space in our home where we pray, a space that contains objects that have particular significance to us, this place will acquire energy; it will attract elemental spirits; it will create an aura of healing around it.

However, no matter how evolved are these energies and no matter how holy is your person, your misuse of this powerful energy remains a possibility, remains a function of your harmful volition. Therefore, the work is to resolve and dissolve whatever creates and maintains the harmful volition within you. If this is not done, these energies merely serve to energize the unattended negativities and the unidentified harmful volition. If this happens, these energies which are neutral in and by themselves become servants of the devil in your life and in other people's lives around you. Take, for instance, the worshipping of the "holy places." Incredible misery has been perpetrated in the name of these holy places and their liberation during the Crusades and in modern times in the formation of the Jewish state. The notion of chosen people and/or chosen places precipitates acts of barbarism in the name of religion.

MUSIC

Music is the most evolved expression of western civilization. Music inspired by the search for God is, therefore, the most beautiful. Thus, it would be a great pity indeed to deprive ourselves of the extraordinarily beautiful liturgy created for misguided churches. As misguided as the churches are, perhaps the best thing they have produced is the music that is performed within their walls. Perhaps the purest expression of invocation and evocation in the Christian churches has been effected through its music. And the best of this music is to be found in the Baroque and Rococo era, the apogee of western civilization reached in a parallel fashion during the Age of Reason with the philosophers and with the composers.

The seventeenth and eighteenth centuries represent by far the height of western civilization. Let us not forget, however, that this period also represents the height of secular humanism, not the height of Christianity. Secular humanism grew in spite of Christianity. Musicians composed for the churches not necessarily because they believed in all of their ritualistic nonsense. They composed for the churches because they were hired by the churches and because that was where they could express their own honest, genuine search for God.

What we are saying here was not foreign to the enlightened monarchs of the time, such as Frederick the Great, or Catherine the Great, or Louis XIV. Those are obvious answers if you take the trouble to think for yourself and to arrive at your own conclusions.

CELEBRATIONS OF THE SEASONS AND OF NATURAL CYCLES

It is a good thing to respect the rhythms of nature and attune with it through prayers at appropriate times such as the solstices or the equinoxes. These are necessary activities but not sufficient ones. They must remain a sideshow. The main show, the main event must remain the work of purification, the work of dissolving the barriers. This is ongoing and is indifferent to seasons. In fact, a point will be reached in a person's development when seasons and cycles that are manifestations of the material world will no longer matter. This is the goal. Thus, the celebration of seasons is a relative function, not an absolute one as erroneously presented by the Catholic Church and by other obsolete religions.

How about the ebb and flow, the expansive and contractive states to which we have to surrender both in our lives and in the life of the universe? Yes, indeed, there are some times when you must expand and other times when you must gather yourself together and contract. However, this also is a cyclical manifestation that is created by the fact that we belong to material reality. Once we are free from reality, expansion and contraction no longer become separate. They occur at the same time and in the same "space." Of course, it is impossible for us to conceive of that. We have glimpses of it once in awhile, when in a state of supreme and sublime awareness the notions of expansion and contraction become moot. For example, when you make a beautiful connection and you feel yourself in a state of immortality, the notions of expansion and contraction are immaterial so is the full moon, so are the seasons, so is Easter or Christmas moot. You can have that connection at any time, at Christmas or at other times. However, in the relative world, it is necessary to temporarily take seasons into consideration.

CHAPTER 30
PSYCHIC POWERS, THEIR MISUSE AND PREMATURE HEALING

ASTROLOGY

We believe that the only valid approach to astrology is its utilization as a tool for personal growth. Any use of astrology for predictions, for avoidance of experience, for determination of behaviour, prostitutes astrology and puts it to the use of the forces of darkness. Let us mention in passing that this is true of tarot cards, of *The Book of Runes*, of the *I Ching*, and of all other crystal ball types of magical thinking.

The fact that there are different types of energies that affect us at different times of the year is a reality. The configuration of the constellations and of the great bodies of matter in the universe will have different effects on the personality, and to some extent on the soul, to the degree that the soul is decelerated, Earth-bound. To the extent that we are free of problems, that we have reactivated the process of acceleration of energy, i.e., the process of the return to God, to that extent we are no longer influenced by any of these forces, whether astrology, the runes, tarot, or whatever. However, even if we are influenced by some of these forces, what happens to us is still our responsibility.

MISUSE OF ASTROLOGY

In what way would we want to use these forces? Do we

want to use astrology for selfish purposes, for egocentric self-aggrandizing ones? Do we want to use it to protect ourselves from some of the issues we have to face within ourselves? If this is the case, then we are misusing those astrological forces. However, if, while still being under the influence of these forces, we see to it that they are used for higher purposes, for giving, for constructiveness, for happiness, for contributing for the betterment of the universe (which never interferes, by the way, with our personal happiness) then we are putting those forces to good purpose. This ethical taking of responsibility and being accountable constitutes spirituality, and is the real work of the Path. The attempt at by-passing this instantly puts you in the service of the forces of darkness.

So, is the astrologer who predicts your future working for the forces of darkness? Yes.

PAST LIFE REGRESSIONS, THE HEALY-FEELIES, ETC.

Here again the same thing applies. If any healing art, clairvoyance or talent is used to bypass the process of taking responsibility for one's life and finding intentionality as it exists in everybody's soul or personality, it instantly puts these arts, abilities and gifts under the jurisdiction of the forces of darkness.

People obtain these powers by following the Forces of Light, of course. However, there comes a point when they find the process too difficult. They *make* the process too difficult because they no longer want to follow it. They also fall prey to all of those people who worship them; having not purified enough themselves, they become susceptible to the adoration of their followers. This is reminiscent of the mutual seduction of parent and children.

Suffice it to say here that each individual has a desire to

be unconditionally loved. This desire has never really been satisfied. It can only be satisfied by God. However, when one's child or follower looks at them with complete devotion and expresses to them their total trust, they will capitulate since they see in this the love of God. They will not want to listen to the Forces of Light that caution them and that are trying to call them back to reality and the necessity to continue their process of purification in humility.

The Romans knew this very well. When a general came back from his victories, he was given a hero's welcome. In this hero's welcome he was paraded in the streets of Rome. He was showered with flowers, dancers preceded him and followed him, he could have practically anything he wanted. However, on the same chariot as he there always was placed a wise and old man who did two things: (1) he held a crown of laurel a little bit over his head and (2) he kept repeating, "Remember, you are merely a man." In other words, do not let this go to your head.

The same must be practiced by anybody who has been able to develop any type of skill, particularly a skill that would be seen as magical by those who benefit from it. This includes doctors, scientists, presidents, politicians, anybody.

The abuse of any of these powers will result in the eventual loss of them. Unfortunately, in the meantime incredible damage is done, not only on the outer level but on the inner level as well, causing people to lose faith in spirituality.

Perhaps the greatest damage is caused by convincing people that they do not have to go through the painstaking process of purification. Indeed, they can go to a healer, an astrologer, a psychic who will predict their future, who will reveal their past lives. By not doing this work for themselves, removing the barriers that they have created themselves, they become even more dependent and depleted.

The artificial removal of the barriers sets individuals back in a more heavy manner than ever. Indeed, if the blocks can be removed by somebody on the outside, the motivation to remove them yourself will be lost. Thus, you will travel away from acquiring these skills, not towards acquiring them.

PRIMITIVE PSYCHIC POWERS

Up to the second half of the Atlantean Period humanity was psychic. Clairvoyance, clairaudience, powers to heal, powers of materialization and dematerialization were available to humankind.

Unfortunately, in spite of the fact that humanity had all of these powers available to it, its consciousness was limited. As a result of this, the powers were abused. Having been abused, it was necessary for humanity to lose them. In order to regain them, we must take responsibility for and dissolve all of the negativities that have blocked these powers.

Many entities have retained some of those primitive powers. We can find them in the Indian chief, the aborigine, the shaman, etc. It is a grave mistake to believe that these people are superiors or teachers because they have these powers.

On the contrary, they are inferior to all of us who do not have them. They have not allowed themselves to let go of them and to join humanity's attempt at regaining those powers in a new way, through the increase in the level of consciousness. The powers in and by themselves are of course not primitive; they are available to everyone.

COMMUNICATION WITH HIGHER SPHERES OF DEVELOPMENT

Communication with higher spheres of development is

not only possible, but is also desirable and beneficial. To make this connection, one has to fulfill certain conditions of purification: one has to be free enough of negativities in order to put aside the lower self and to become a channel for the greater forces which can only come through the Higher Self. In other words, the ego function must be used to consciously set aside the lower forces within and make room for the higher forces.

Note that the conditions do not stipulate that one be free of negativities; this is not required for communication with higher spheres.

What is necessary is to have developed the ability to disengage from one's negativities, albeit, temporarily. To that extent, one is temporarily able to contact the higher spheres who will then be more than happy to give their guidance which is part of their task.

CHANNELING

Like anything else it can be used for good or for evil. We are all channels. In fact, we are multi-channels similar to a radio or a television which can be tuned to different channels at different times. Most of us have lost touch with the entity with the remote control.

So we channel surf unconsciously, going from one mood to another, from darkness to light sometimes without even knowing that we are doing it. The loss of this volition is a result of excesses, abuses, lower self.

The whole point of spiritual growth and of the Path of Purification is the regaining of the control of this volitional entity.

Every thought, every feeling, every note already exists in higher spheres of development. We merely descend them.

As an example, someone I knew was a channel. The

channel manifested through them because they underwent a specific process of purification that prepared them for it. This process involved living a life as a drug abuser and dying of an overdose of drugs in their immediately preceding incarnation. The negative aspect of this was the loss of a life; the positive aspect of this was the destruction of their ego defenses which made it possible in this lifetime to be a channel.

So beware of judgments. Do not judge. Instead, take in what is coming to you and deliberately and volitionally sort it out, deciding what you want to keep and what you want to reject. This is the only way to deal with your channel, i.e., with all of the information that is constantly flooding you. This is also the only way to deal with other people's channels and with all of the good and bad material that comes through them.

Each part of us attracts entities and forces that are commensurate to its development. For example, the lower parts of us attract spirits and forces from a lower level of development, whether from the forces of darkness, or spirits who are discarnate and floating around trying to find someone to be attached to.

Let's not forget that part of those lower forces are the glamours. The glamours will then draw to themselves flattering spirits and energies, resulting in messages of self-aggrandizement and self-idealization. Many mistake this to be God's guidance. They call guidance from the Divine what their glamours, masks and idolized selves receive, when it actually comes from very deceptive spheres of development. These forces will seduce the individual and subjugate him to the forces of darkness. The world is full of "channels" who not only receive, but give flattering material while being totally taken over by those duplicitous and negative forces.

Here we find the reason conventional churches have been so reluctant to accept channeling and other similar New Age practices. It is this irresponsible aspect of channeling that gives it its bad name—deservedly so. One very important element to remember here is this: it is not because you hear an inner voice that you are hearing the truth. This "inner" voice may very well have been called by an unconscious lower self or idolized self aspect in you. However, there is no point in throwing out baby with bath water. Just because the majority of "channels" are frauds does not mean that channeling itself has no validity.

One must also consider the possibility that someone may have undergone a process of purification which then created a channel to a lot of good and powerful material. However, later in his life he distorts this current, using and abusing the material that he has received for egocentric purposes instead of for what it was meant, i.e., the healing of humanity and the raising of its consciousness. Examples of this can be found in the story of J.Z. Knight who channeled the spirit called Ramtha. Ramtha gave wonderful teachings in the beginning. Unfortunately J.Z., once she had achieved success and notoriety was overcome by her glamours. Apparently, Ramtha left her and the later trance sessions are said to have been faked. Since she did not allow any purification instructions to come through, her work deteriorated for her and for everybody else. The people who followed her are just as responsible for a false teacher as she is responsible for her blocking of her good information that she needed. One also thinks here of Baghwan Rajneesh's oft-mentioned Rolls Royces.

True spirits will always begin by pointing out to you aspects of yourself that you do not want to see. Those are the authentic messages which are to be heeded, particularly at first. Furthermore, it is no use trying to receive guidance for somebody else when you have not as yet started your process of purification. In such cases, the majority of your guidance will be motivated by your own negativities and line of least resistance. The same is true of feelings. People believe that just because they have feelings, these feelings must be true. People say "I have a gut feeling about this or that," implying that the gut feeling must be right. Nothing could be further from the truth. A gut feeling, or a feeling, may just as well be wrong as is a thought. There is nothing vainglorious or magical about feelings. It is only that having repressed feelings for so long, we are now idealizing them.

We say to you as we say to everybody else, do not believe anything that you do not experience. This includes what we tell you. Take everything and weigh it, experience it, give it a try. If it is not true then discard it and go to the next issue. At the same time, keep an open mind to the possibility that you might be wrong. Strength is found in the ability to be open and resilient. Weakness is to be found in the pseudo-strength of rigidity that does not allow any information in. This rigidity is always compensated for by an overmalleable place somewhere else. Find the two extremes in you; identify them and choose to let them go and to find the true receptivity, resiliency and malleability that will allow you to be healthily and harmoniously reactive.

PREMATURE HEALING

The line of least resistance will seduce us into misusing all subjects described in this chapter. Because we defend against the experience of pain, we will resort to premature healing through abuse. Mental pain created by uncertainty will, for instance, resort to the predictions of astrology, rather than to the healing inner search for the causes of the pain. Emotional pain will be avoided by attributing it to a past life. So will physical pain be avoided by quick and facile healings. However, when used in the context of maturity and self-responsibility, all of these subjects become beneficial.

CHAPTER 31
SPIRITUAL LAWS

UNIVERSALITY OF THE LAWS OF GOD

In creating His worlds—and there are many, many worlds and many spheres of development—God unified them through His laws. Indeed, the laws of God are common to all the worlds of creation. What differentiates one world from the other is the degree to which its inhabitants choose to follow or to violate the laws of God.

Every single atom of creation is in perfect order and conforms to specific laws. That which violates laws is illusion. The first principle of logic is the principle of non-contradiction. It says that "A" and "non-A" cannot exist at the same time and under the same ratio. Life cannot be non-life, reality cannot be non-reality; that which is not true is false. Falsehood does not exist since it is not part of life.

No matter how different are creations, the laws of God, Spiritual Law which is natural law, apply to all of them. This is also true for different types of matter, different levels of energy or consciousness. For example, in some worlds of creation, matter is so dense and so compact that it seems as if it would never behave the way our matter does. Actually it does, though in a much decelerated manner. It takes a much longer time to connect cause to effect. At the other end of the spectrum, matter as we know and experience it through the senses does not "exist." The energy is so accelerated and cause is so close to effect, that it is difficult for us to perceive or even conceive of how this works. Nevertheless, the laws still apply to that level.

Baby consciousness may believe that Spiritual Law does not exist.

For example, when we are disconnected from the Law of Cause and Effect, we may be convinced that what we think, feel, or do has no consequence. Children are known to believe this. And it is not true.

The Law of Cause and Effect still exists even though it is not perceived by the people who are disconnected from it. They create a reality in which there is a delay between cause and effect. That does not mean that the effect will not someday come. When it does, having disconnected, they will feel that they are the victims of something arbitrary and irrational, like waking up somewhere without knowing how we got there.

What people do not realize is that when they disconnect cause from effect, it may temporarily seem to suit their getting away with a thought, feeling or act. However, it works both ways. Having disconnected cause from effect in order to victimize, they themselves become victims of their own disconnection, never understanding what is really happening to them. Disconnection decelerates energy because it goes counter the nature of development. Example: say that I commit murder and refuse to take responsibility for it. I disconnect cause from effect. I decelerate my reality. Meanwhile, the festering guilt within me, from which I also disconnected, will unconsciously draw to me a situation in which I, too, will be killed. I will then feel like an innocent victim. However, it is my own disconnection that is now killing me.

Let's see if we can enumerate and define some of the major laws that govern the universe. The following discussion relates the laws to the Seven Rays.

LAWS PERTAINING TO THE FIRST RAY: WILL OR POWER

1. The Law of Return.
Everything proceeds from God and will return to God.

2. The Law of Repulse.
a. *In order for anything to be built or constructed, **destruction** of the old and obsolete must occur.* This is law and it is a healthy, positive part of nature. Look around you and you will see nature destroying the old through the bursting of the new. The new petals burst open in the universe and violently destroy the bud. The new fruit does the same thing with the petals, etc. That is why the First Ray is also called the Destroyer of Form.

b. *Every organism will reject a body that has become foreign or obsolete.* **Anything that has a negative component to it must either be cleansed of its negative component or be destroyed.** If you think of the crises in your life, you will understand this principle and it will help you a great deal. On the physical level it is easy to understand why a body would reject a transplanted organ, for example.

Let's take the life of a successful businessman, architect, etc. Originally he practiced his profession because he loved it, because he felt a sense of task towards it, because it brought balance to his life. To the extent there were ulterior motives to the pursuit of his profession, to that extent there is a splitting, a lack of commitment, or a partial commitment invested in that profession.

Let's say he used it for the purpose of obtaining

approval, or for the purpose of making a lot of money, or for the purpose of acquiring sex or power over others. Gradually, the interest in the profession itself wanes as it becomes a mere tool for obtaining the fulfillment of the more basic and frustrated needs. The need for love becomes the need for approval or the need for sex or the need for power or the need for money.

There comes a point when the Higher Self cannot tolerate this situation, so it destroys it through the creation of a crisis. When that crisis occurs, if the person is on a Path of Purification, he will become aware of the ugliness of his creation. He will reach the point of renunciation, as we call it, in which it will be easy for him to let go of his creation and start anew. Or, it will be difficult, but he will compel himself to do it.

The repetition of the same violations without working on them creates physical consequences which can't be ignored. Thus, although, for us, the physical is the lowest level, manifestation on that level raises consciousness, compelling us to change our ways. This is the one reason why we live in this physical world.

So, in a sense, the refusal to work on a problem also brings on an acceleration of sorts: the descent of the problem on the physical level; the acceleration of demise, the actualization of it so that it can no longer be ignored.

The repulsion of anything in your life is, therefore, a necessary step before you can start anew. If it did not exist, there would be no progress. There would be a continuous deceleration into dissatisfaction and unfulfillment. The Law of Repulse is a great liberator.

3. The Law of Initiation.

Whenever an organism is prepared and receptive the

First Ray will penetrate it and will "initiate" it with energies, powers of creation, initiative, genius, insight. This is very often experienced and talked about as a spark. We say of this person that he is illuminated, he has a spark, a light bulb as it is depicted in cartoons sometimes.

When we invoke the Life Force or the Christ, we become receptive to the initiation of these energies into our system.

LAWS PERTAINING TO THE SECOND RAY: LOVE/WISDOM

1. The Law of Attraction.

This law has to do with mutuality, reciprocity. The more you give the more you receive. It has been talked about by the Christ in His sayings, "give and you shall receive," "seek and you shall find," etc. One has to remember here that loving is a natural selfless current, a need. Any love that is contrived or forced is not love at all, it is pretense. The Law of Repulse will take care of destroying it. However, the natural giving movement of nature is a real need that has to be respected and fulfilled.

Trees generously give, animals generously give, even infants, who are supposed to receive, generously give when they love you; they want to give you something, and they do. The Law of Attraction basically says that if you follow that instinct, you will receive. You will receive a lot more than you give. This law is the key to abundance.

The giving that we talk about here has a lot more to do with *quality* than with *quantity*. What counts is the quality of your giving, the intent behind your giving.

For instance, I may generously and humbly give $5, or in a conceited or reluctant or sensational manner give $500. The $5, because it is given with quality feelings, with good will and good intent will have a much greater effect than will the $500. The effect of the $5 will be itself a cause for my getting a much greater reward than the $500. Of course, I am using this example so as to illustrate that you can give one hundred times more in quantity and yet you have not given as much from the point of view of quality.

Stinginess and avarice are to be found behind the sensational false giving. If I have a lot of money and I only give $5, falsely claiming quality and humility, I am stealing and lying. If I give $500 while expecting approval, I am also stealing. In the latter case, I am stealing people's good feelings; in the former case I am stealing money that could be given and is not. Having said the above, I do not mean to encourage the stingy person who only gives $5.

2. The Law of Magnetism.

Through emanation, love acts like a magnet, attracting love. However, the Law of Magnetism also works with negativity. Like attracts like.

3. The Law of Brotherhood, which is sharing.

The positive aspects of communism are to be found here. The reason why communism did not work is, of course, because it was practiced in circumstances where people were not ready for it. The "enemies" of communism in the twentieth century came much closer to manifesting the ideals of communism than the communist countries themselves because of the Western world's greater readiness and greater consciousness. Sharing must be done freely.

4. The Law of the Builder.

Each individual consciousness has for task the

continuous building of new energy forms, new ideas, new implementations that enhance and accelerate the implementation of the Plan of Salvation. Remember, though, that the impulse comes from the First Ray; the idea is generated by the First Ray. The Second Ray follows through with the aspect of the builder.

LAWS PERTAINING TO THE THIRD RAY: ACTIVE INTELLIGENCE AND ADAPTABILITY

1. The Law of Adaptability

This law says we must be receptive and accepting of all experiences in our lives, positive and negative, in order to understand them and to reverse them through the other rays.

For instance, let's say that I need to become aware of anxiety inside of myself. What will facilitate this awareness on all the levels of my being is the Ray of Active Intelligence and Adaptability, Ray Three. Once I am aware of my anxiety, the Seventh Ray will want to see disorder in it, the Sixth Ray will want to see the lack of faith, the Fifth Ray will want to specify precisely that which I am anxious about, the Fourth Ray will want to see the thesis and antithesis operating in my anxiety, the Second Ray will want to see the love and the wisdom behind the anxiety, and the First Ray will want to do something about it.

The same example can be applied to a positive realization. Say, for instance, that I need to become aware of my capacity for pleasure. The same mechanism will apply.

In Ray Three is to be found the capacity to experience pleasure and pain, both of which are goals for a disciple on the Path.

2. The Law of Greater Understanding, Acceptance and Non-judgment.

All in life must be accepted if we are to accomplish our task and to live happily. The slightest non-acceptance creates the hardening of defensiveness, and, therefore, brings us to crisis.

3. The Law of Cause and Effect.

This great law, oft-mentioned, and so thoroughly explained by us elsewhere, needs no more elaboration here.

There may be doubt as to whether the Law of Cause and Effect belongs under Ray Three. As far as I am concerned, it does. However, if you disagree with me it is really all right. As far as I see it, when the Law of Cause and Effect is put under the triad of Intent/Commitment/Causality (causality meaning the Law of Cause and Effect), then it becomes clear that intent is a function of the First Ray, commitment a function of the Second Ray and causality a function of the Third Ray.

LAWS PERTAINING TO THE FOURTH RAY: HARMONY THROUGH CONFLICT

1. The Law of Harmony.

Every single creation in the universe will eventually harmonize and unify with every other creation. All alienation is, therefore, temporary. The task of each individual is to bring together, unify, different aspects of himself that he brings in with him which are in a state of disharmony. Here, it is important to mention the following: aspects or attributes turned negative cannot merge. They develop with one another relationships of negative dependency and mutual hatred. They can only merge—find peace—when they transform themselves into their positive components. By contrast, aspects or attributes that are positive and natural merge and unify without losing their individuality.

For example: two seemingly contradictory negative feelings will not merge with each other. Fear and cruelty cannot unify. They contradict each other and they feed one another, but they do not merge. When I am in a state of fear I cannot be cruel, I am incapable of even thinking of cruelty. It is seemingly somebody else's cruelty that is creating my fear.

Later I realize that the cruelty is really mine. So I sink into that state. In the state of cruelty it is impossible for me to feel fear. Yet, it is fear that fuels my cruelty. If I were not afraid I would not need to be cruel. The two hate each other and feed each other at the same time, but cannot merge. The person experiencing one of them is bound to experience the other and in the process feels as if he is in hell.

Two positive feelings seemingly contradictory—laughter and sadness can merge. Yes, sadness is a positive feeling. One can feel sad from the Higher Self for some of that which happens to us; sadness needs to be differentiated from despair or depression which are negative states. Sadness is positive in that it comes and leaves us easily, despair or depression stick to us and do not want to leave.

The best examples of this can be experienced through the genius of Charlie Chaplin's movies. The Little Tramp is at the same time poor and hopelessly in love—sadness—and funny, comical—laughter. We experience both feelings at the same time, we cry and laugh all in the same mood. The two positive feelings are blended in one.

Here is another example of two positives merging together: wisdom and awe. A very wise and extremely intelligent scientist, full of wisdom, can be in childlike awe in the face of a new discovery or in the face of all that which is still to be discovered.

The wisdom which is erroneously identified with an attitude of blasé adultism is usually seen as incompatible with the childlike awe and joy in discovery. In reality, true wisdom means openness to new discoveries and makes it possible for the experience of the new and, therefore, for the experience of continuous and perpetual wonderment. Only the eternal youth can be wise, being always in awe.

Consequently, all positives can be integrated. All negatives are at war with one another and cannot be blended.

2. The Law of the Pairs of Opposites.

This is a law particularly applicable to our sphere of existence, the sphere of duality. For human beings in particular, this law is very important. Each one of us still lives in duality, a duality characterized particularly by the split between our mother and our father. This mother/father split and its resolution is the fundamental kernel of the Path. Each side of the pairs of opposites contains positive and negative aspects.

And here is the rub. The idea is to detect the unholy alliance of positive and negative aspects in each side and disengage them one from the other. All conflicts are created because of this type of confusion. The wars of the sexes are nothing else but an outer manifestation of this. The different cycles undergone by a civilization are simply an out-picturing of the wars of the sexes. For instance, one can say that the 1980s and 1990s have been a father period, whereas the 1960s and 1970s were a mother period. That was preceded by the 1940s and 1950s being a father period and the 1920s and 1930s being a mother period. In the previous century, the energy was slower. The first half of the nineteenth century, permeated by Romanticism, can be seen as more of a mother or feminine time; it was preceded by the Napoleonic Wars and the destructive—not necessarily negative—forces of the French Revolution which can be seen as a father aspect.

History provides us with a continuum of this fluctuation from one end of the spectrum to the other. This, of course, is the attempt of humanity to find the balance. At the time of this writing, for instance, we are going through the apogee of a father manifestation. A conservative type government has just toppled the liberal grip on the houses governing the USA. Heartlessness, repression, fanaticism, bigotry are now rampant. However, if we were to examine the causes of this manifestation we have to go back to the 1970s during which the opposite was rampant—chaos, permissiveness, license, etc. It is the 1970s that have created the 1990s. One must not forget this in terms of the examination of the development of a civilization or of an individual; one must always look for the roots of what is happening to us by examining what we have done when we were on the opposite side of the spectrum.

3. The Law of Conflict.

This is a law of the first duality, the lower one. No harmony can be found unless conflict is risked. This reminds us of what we found in the First Ray whereby nothing new could be built unless the old was destroyed. Here then is the connection between the First and the Fourth Rays. The Law of Conflict of the Fourth Ray reminds us of the Law of Destruction and the Law of Repulse of the First Ray. They are connected.

It says in the *Mantram of Fire*[13], "Naught in me seeks the way of peace, naught in me yearns for Earth." The seeking of conflict is indeed a commendable search. We must seek the places that are at war. We must seek war in order to experience peace, even if it is merely to consider the conflict between that which needs to grow and that which resists growth.

The way to find peace is to become at-one with ourselves and decide that we are going to wage war. This conflict within ourselves is also a conflict outside of ourselves. Thus, we find harmony inside while conflict is undertaken on the outer level. The refusal to fight the battle on the outside internalizes the problem and creates a war inside. Thus is Spiritual Law.

4. The Law of Good versus Evil.

This is a law of the second duality, the higher one. Once the first duality has been conquered, the duality between mother and father in which evil and good have not been quite defined —remember that there are positive and negative aspects associated with both father and mother), one has to undertake this second conflict, the conflict between good and evil. On both the father side and on the mother side, the positive elements are differentiated from the negative ones. The positive aspects are then unified and the negative aspects are purified.

This is called the crucifixion of the ego. One must differentiate between the two dualities as follows: the first duality, the one between mother and father, the duality of

---

[13]Bailey, Alice A. 1955. *The Light of the Soul: The Yoga Sutras of Patanjali.* New York: Lucis Publishing Company.

the aspirant is defined with a vertical line dividing a circle.

The second duality is defined by a horizontal line dividing good above and evil below.

The combination of the two lines together, of course, creates the cross, the crucifixion of the ego.

The clarification of the issues of good and evil in an individual is extremely valuable. Granted, anything can be good in some cases and evil in others. However, every individual should be able to gauge within himself what is evil and what is good. This is one key element in spiritual growth and development.

Once these issues are clarified, the individual moves closer to discipleship. Indeed, when goodness is unified within himself, he opens himself up to the infinity of goodness, which becomes increasingly dominant over the finiteness of the negative, also experienced by him. At that point there is a wonderful sense of confidence. One knows that the battle has to be won. Nevertheless, we fluctuate between knowing this and forgetting it. Jesus Himself fluctuated between the two. Indeed, on Palm Sunday when He entered Jerusalem, He was confident of victory. Even though He knew He was going to be crucified, and was going straight towards His arrest, He courageously confronted many people who were encrusted in corrupt authority. Then, in the midst of His excruciating suffering on the cross, He doubted the existence of God. He got lost again in the lower duality. In doing this, He brought every one of us great hope because if He doubted, so can we. Undergoing doubt, therefore, is no sin, it is part of the process, part of the war that we need to wage. Illusions can be powerful.

LAWS PERTAINING TO THE FIFTH RAY: CONCRETE KNOWLEDGE

Knowledge of matter and of the handling of matter are very much a part of spiritual life. There is a general misconception according to which concrete knowledge and science have absolutely nothing to do with spirituality. Nothing could be further from the truth. Scientific thought comes from the exact same source as does spiritual thought. Scientists are channels in the very exact same way as are spiritual leaders or musicians. The search for the truth in science undergoes the same exact process as the search for the truth in any other endeavour in a person's life. It is a spiritual search. The good scientist surrenders himself to the same process of self-exploration and purification as does the good aspirant or the good disciple on the Path. Indeed, the good scientist asks himself why it is that he is not getting a solution to a particular problem. He probes inside himself to see whether he has any mental blocks, whether he is not open enough to a new idea or to a new way of proceeding.

And, sure enough, the universe cooperates.

There are innumerable discoveries that are made through mistakes. Penicillin is a notable example of this. We know that there are no mistakes. Mistakes themselves are attracted by intent, unconscious as it may be. Thus, the process of individual purification and group purification will yield scientific discovery.

1. The Law of Enquiry.

The Instinct of Enquiry is the highest instinct in humanity. Indeed, it comes about and manifests itself harmoniously when the other four instincts are themselves harmoniously functional. Let's remember the other four instincts: 1. Instinct of Self-Preservation, 2. Instinct of Procreation, 3. Herd Instinct, and 4. Instinct of Self-Assertion. Notice how the first and the second instincts can be and sometimes are in conflict. The same is true for the third and the fourth instincts. When harmony is established between those conflicts, then finally the Instinct of Enquiry manifests itself. Nothing is holier in human existence than the honest curiosity of the mind. The figuring out of three-dimensional reality leads to God. Indeed, great scientists have discovered God through their work. Therefore, the most material endeavours, when undertaken honestly and courageously, always lead to God. This is the basic Fifth Ray law.

The pursuit of alchemy, the seeking of the philosopher's stone as it was called, enters into this. Indeed, the Arab chemists (al-kimi, as chemistry is called in Arabic) were mystics, pursuing the transformation of matter into gold, or seeking the philosopher's stone. The transformation into gold, i.e., into the higher expression of minerals, is itself a process of purification and of spiritual growth which is sought through the study of matter. We see in the pursuit of alchemists the attempt at acceleration of matter.

2. The Law of Release of Energy in Matter.

Here we get into another law of the Fifth Ray, which is the necessity for matter to find a way to accelerate itself. Inherent in every atom of creation is the desire for betterment. This is the true nature of all that is. It is this desire to better itself that turns matter into life, raising it from the mineral kingdom to the other higher kingdoms until it reaches God. Every atom has to find its explosive power. It is extremely important to understand that the discovery of atomic energy and the explosion of the atom bomb were the greatest events on the three-dimensional level in human history. A lot of people misinterpret this because they see it only from the point of view of negativity or of destruction. However, from the point of view of the release of energy into the universe, from the point of view of the dissolution of matter, it is an enormously important event. Humanity will discover how to do this in a safe way and harness this type of energy with positive results in the future. We are not there yet. We are trying and we will get there. It would be a grave mistake to abandon this type of pursuit just because we have little baby boomer father fixations, images and freezes that associate this energy with militarism.

LAWS PERTAINING TO THE SIXTH RAY: IDEALISM AND DEVOTION

Here we have the laws of total devotion which have to do with commitment.

1. The Law of Commitment.

This law very much pertains to the Sixth Ray. The more we are committed to something the more we achieve it and the closer we are to God. The less we commit to something the less important is our achievement, and the more harmful volition or splitting or dualism is involved. Thus, commitment and harmful volition are precisely tied in a relationship of inverse proportionality.

2. The Law of Sacrifice.

One has to sacrifice. Sacrifice what? Sacrifice the lower self, sacrifice the masks, sacrifice the false life. In this catechism we talk of the false life and the creators and the perpetrators of the false life. The root of the word sacrifice is "sacred, to make sacred, holy." In order to make holy, one has to let go of something. Here we find parallels with the Law of Repulse and with the Principle of Discrimination, which is a First Ray principle.

The asceticism that was necessary during the Age of Pisces, ruled by the Sixth Ray, was a manifestation of this law. It was a necessary phase because of the excesses that were found to exist prior to this time under the Romans, etc.

3. The Laws of the Absolute: the Absolute versus the relative.

The only real world is the world of the Absolute. The world that we live in, the world of the relative, is illusion. However, as we travel towards becoming at-one with the world of the Absolute, we have to learn how to accept and live in the world of the relative. In our Absolute pursuit of the truth, we sometimes must negotiate ourselves through the traffic of the untruth. Christ did and so must we. Nevertheless, through our life and our tolerance of the relative we must have the one-pointed focus of the Sixth Ray idealism in order to find God. That's law.

4. The Law of the Positive Aspects of Duality.

Every negative aspect, thought, feeling, deed, attribute is a distortion of a positive one. In our dualistic world, the only way for us to recover the positive inherent in the negative is to experience both positive and negative side by side. This is the positive aspect of duality. In the Sixth Ray, this differentiation is central. In that Ray, one finds the positive in contradistinction to the negative and one has to tolerate the two side by side. From that point of view we gain from duality. If it were not for duality we would not be able to appreciate the positive, nor to look for the positive in the negative.

The disciple has a dual life. On the one hand, he searches for the Absolute. On the other hand, he negotiates in the life of the relative. The art of being a disciple consists of being able to sustain this paradox. The life of Jesus Himself, indeed the entire Christian experience, is a training in doing just that. It characterizes the nature of spirituality during the last 2000 years, while under the influence of the Sixth Ray.

LAWS PERTAINING TO THE SEVENTH RAY: CEREMONY, MAGIC AND ORDER

1. The Law of the Perfect Universal Order.

The universe is in perfect order down to its minutest detail. The disorder that we encounter is of our making, out of our own limited consciousness and out of our own disconnection from the laws of the universe.

2. The Law of Inherent Ritual in Creation.

Here is the necessity for ceremony and ritual. We have to respect the rituals of nature. We must find and practice the rhythms of the universe and respect them with humility. But we need also to establish rituals for the emotional body, rituals of purification such as Daily Review, confrontation and support of others, the practice of love, the release of anger, etc. The practices of our church provide us with such outlets.

The same is true about the mental body. Mental rituals consist of nourishing your mind with stimulating thought processes that are positive. The exercise of the mind used to be widely practiced in our western world. It has been on the decline lately, resulting in functional illiteracy and ignorance. Perhaps the advent of computers will remedy the situation. It is gratifying to see the reemergence of the Instinct of Enquiry in younger people through computers. The practice of our religion, therefore, consists of attending those groups and those sessions during which we do these rituals. Unlike other churches or spiritual paths, our activities are intellectually stimulating, involving history, mathematics, music, etc.

Other rituals, of course, include the rituals of prayer and meditation. As you can see, rituals are in no way limited to those which have traditionally been associated with religion.

3. The Law of Good Habits.

The good habits that are thus acquired through the practice of our religion and its rituals align us with the order of the universe. Then magic happens. It is "magic" because we do not as yet know the causal connection that brings us this unexpected abundance. It comes to us when we are at-one with the forces of nature. In reality there is no such thing as magic the way we expect it, as in a desire to win the lottery, for example. The pursuit of magic in this particular mode is a violation of the Law of Order. One has to continuously find within oneself the cause that creates a particular effect. If we start believing that something can happen to us without our having created it, then we will start becoming victims and will live in illusion. Therefore, magic is brought about by reality, not by unreality. Unreality blocks the manifestation of magic. It is through the connection with the infinite goodness of the universe and with the Creator that magic occurs in peoples' lives, that unexpected goodness happens. This is Spiritual Law.

SPIRITUAL LAWS CREATE US

These laws create us, they make us, we do not make them. They in turn have been made by our Creator, God. However, even if you do not believe in the existence of a creator who has created those laws, it behooves you to experience their veracity. Not experiencing them means that there is a harmful volition to experience their opposite.

For instance, it may serve your lower self to believe that there is no such thing as the Law of Cause and Effect. Thus, you can rape, pillage and plunder, seduce and manipulate without any consequences. Only at the other end of the line, when you are raped, pillaged, plundered, seduced and manipulated you will complain that there is no justice in the universe. Having been unjust to others, the Law of Cause and Effect will manifest in spite of yourself and make you experience the very injustice that you inflicted on others.

However, if you have decided to forget your own outrages, you will appear to be victimized which will then make you want to justify even greater outrages; "If that is done to me, then I can do it to others." In saying this, don't you see that you are obeying the Law of Cause and Effect.

The minute you say, "since that was done to me, I have to do it to others," you are yourself obeying the Law of Cause and Effect. It is by making those obvious connections that one finally realizes the existence of that divine law.

AUTHORITY

The word "law" is associated with authority. Thus, when one hears "law" one rebels instantly. Authority, being the first problem we ever experienced in life, is the last problem we will ever resolve.

Indeed, equating authority with destructiveness, cruelty and general negativity is a universal problem. Thus, the knee jerk reaction from second nature (not from first nature) is to refuse the very notion that there exist laws that govern the universe. In spite of those resistances, however, these laws exist. *Eppur si muove*, as Galileo said under his breath as he was forced to retract his teachings in the presence of the Pope.

CHAPTER 32
A COMMENTARY ON THE UNIVERSAL DECLARATION OF HUMAN RIGHTS

SECULAR HUMANISM

It took the philosophers of the eighteenth century to successfully challenge the legal anachronisms of antiquity. Until then no one had ever dared raise his voice against such outrageous practices as the absolute right of the father over his family, or the superiority of men over women, or the "Biblical" authority of slavery. Up until then, the "Christian" world was engaged in perpetuating all of those outrages in a wholesale fashion. In fact, those who called themselves Christians were dead set against the new ways of thinking that the eighteenth century philosophers brought about—secular humanism. Furthermore, they are still dead set against it, still ranting and raving about this secular humanism which they see as evil.

If it were up to the so-called Christians, we would still be back in the Middle Ages buying and selling our daughters or sons, mistreating women and owning slaves. Also, we would still be under the tutelage of a king whose absolute power was blessed by the church and whose hereditary rights were to continuously and perpetually commit any outrage his little heart desired.

The Declaration of Human Rights, which has its roots in

the philosophical movement of the eighteenth century, was first implemented at the time of the French Revolution. It was necessary then to destroy not only the nobility, but also the power of the church. This great impetus had its origin in the great release of energy into the human personality around 1725 by the Hierarchy. This release of energy created the philosophical way of thinking which then precipitated the French and the American Revolutions towards the end of that same century. Of course, the pendulum swing unfortunately had to go to the other extreme. This explains the great cruelty perpetrated on nobility and on the high clergy in France during their revolution. If you visit the great cathedrals of France you will invariably see inside and outside of them many statues of saints and kings without heads. This beheading occurred during the French Revolution. Just as the guillotine beheaded humans during that period, statues befell the same fate, though by way of hammer and chisel. You will not find this information in many guidebooks. You will also not find a similar manifestation in England, for instance. There the saints' statues were left intact.

The necessary destruction made way for a kind of life that has become universal at this point. The declaration of human rights devised by the philosophers, became the Declaration of Human Rights of the United Nations. Instead of relegating Absolute law to ignorant and backward fathers in individual families, a universal law was created for the human family, founded on freedom, justice, equality, and promoting peace in the world.

This Declaration of Human Rights is for us as important as was the dispensation of the Ten Commandments at the time of Hammurabi, repeated by Moses. It rightly connects disregard and contempt for human rights with the barbarous

A Commentary on The Universal Declaration of Human Rights

acts and outrages perpetrated by mankind. In this connection there is a strong indictment of all those who call themselves Christians. Nor are other world religions exempted of this indictment. The barbarous practice of cutting off adolescent girls' clitorises in Arab countries, for example, is a gross violation of human rights and should be ended immediately, forcefully if need be.

The preamble of this declaration stresses freedom of speech and of belief, and freedom from fear and want as aspirations of the common people. Indeed, merely printing this is a liberating act in and by itself. Making it part of the belief that nations are supposed to uphold makes it even more powerful.

It also legalizes rebellion against any tyranny that curtails human rights. In the not too distant future, this type of tyranny will no longer be tolerated in the human world. There will be military intervention to end these abuses whenever and wherever they occur. At the time of the writing of this catechism, the United States has the opportunity to lead the world in such a cleansing action against, for example, China who is the most notorious violator of human rights. Failure to do so will encourage the forces of darkness to regroup and attempt again to subjugate the entire human race.

INTERVENTION OF ONE NATION OVER ANOTHER

Is the intervention of one nation over another a violation of these human rights? For example, my suggestion of intervening in China for the establishment of the natural human rights of the Chinese could be seen as an attempt on our part to curtail the freedom of the Chinese, to interfere in the internal affairs of a sovereign nation. This misconception can be immediately dispelled if you consider the fact that some nations are more mature than others. And the more mature must behave towards the less mature as a parent behaves toward a child, limits must be set, boundaries have to be erected. The child needs those boundaries; children confuse freedom with license. The parent has to recognize that only through the demonstration of responsibility can the child earn freedom. Thus, through the boundaries, he is taught the great connection that exists between freedom and responsibility. So we can conclude that:

1. **Not all nations are ready for the type of democratic freedom that can be practiced when maturity exists.**

2. **Those nations who are mature must have the strength and the will for the successful intervention in the countries that need the type of discipline that will guide them to their eventual maturity.**

3. **If this is not done, the less developed nations will—and have in the past—steal power from the developed ones, create great military strength and overcome the precious freedom that has taken so long to develop in humanity.** The regression which would then result for humanity is incalculable. The loss of life involved in correct military intervention is much more easily remedied than the loss of freedom and spirituality. The latter subjugates and kills the spirit; it takes much, much longer and is much more painful to regain.

4. **Responsible and developed nations must find a way to bring their forces together to bear upon those nations that need their help.** This help must be given whether or not it is requested.

5. **Only when this happens will it be possible to promote the development of friendly relations between**

nations as suggested in the preamble of the charter.

6. The little egocentric concerns of nations must give way to the greater need of humanity.

No nation, particularly those who are the most developed, can today afford to be isolationist. There is at hand a great participation in the final destruction of the political evil that has enslaved humanity since the beginning of time. Losing this opportunity will create another crisis.

THE UNITED NATIONS

The United Nations is suffering today from the "ills of the disciple." Indeed, lack of effective, vigorous action is its weakest point.

The UN subscribes to the world freeze that says weakness is good and strength is bad. This must be reversed. To the degree that it is reversed, freedom will be enjoyed by humanity. To the degree this freeze is perpetuated, it will lead backwards to a time of enslavement and materialism, to a new Dark Ages, this time cloaked in technology.

UNIVERSAL DECLARATION OF HUMAN RIGHTS

Adopted and proclaimed by General Assembly resolution 217A(III) of 10 December 1948

Preamble

Whereas recognition of the inherent dignity and of the equal and inalienable rights of all members of the human family is the foundation of freedom, justice and peace in the world,

Whereas disregard and contempt for human rights have resulted in barbarous acts which have outraged the conscience of mankind, and the advent of a world in which human beings shall enjoy freedom of speech and belief and freedom from fear and want has been proclaimed as the highest aspiration of the common people,

Whereas it is essential, if man is not to be compelled to have recourse, as a last resort, to rebellion against tyranny and oppression, that human rights should be protected by the rule of law,

Whereas it is essential to promote the development of friendly relations between nations,

Whereas the peoples of the United Nations have in the Charter reaffirmed their faith in fundamental human rights, in the dignity and worth of the human person and in the equal rights of men and women and have determined to promote social progress and better standards of life in larger freedom,

Whereas Member States have pledged themselves to achieve, in co-operation with the United Nations, the promotion of universal respect for and observance of human rights and fundamental freedoms,

Whereas a common understanding of these rights and freedoms is of the greatest importance for the full realization of this pledge,

Now, therefore,

The General Assembly

Proclaims this Universal Declaration of Human Rights as a common standard of achievement for all peoples and all nations, to the end that every individual and every organ of society, keeping this Declaration constantly in mind, shall strive by teaching and education to promote respect for *these rights and freedoms and by progressive measures, national and international, to secure their universal and effective recognition and observance, both among the peoples of Member States themselves and among the peoples of territories under their jurisdiction.*

COMMENTARY ON THE ARTICLES

Article 1
All human beings are born free and equal in dignity and rights. They are endowed with reason and conscience and should act towards one another in a spirit of brotherhood.

This means that the great majority of humanity is in violation of this basic and fundamental right. The subjugation of women in Arab countries, the buying and selling of young children in underdeveloped countries, the enslavement of people, these are all violations of this basic human right. The gross and blatant indifference of the West towards this treatment of our brothers and sisters has attached to it a huge price tag. Someday this bill will be presented to the West which may not be able to pay the price. By looking the other way, the West is participating in the continuous and perpetual violation of these rights. By colluding, it is doubly guilty: (1) it participates in the crime, and (2) it knowingly averts its eyes while having the power to stop these crimes against humanity. The spirit of brotherhood here commands the putting an end to all of these outrages, forcefully if need be.

Article 2
Everyone is entitled to all the rights and freedoms set forth in this Declaration, without distinction of any kind, such as race, colour, sex, language, religion, political or other

opinion, national or social origin, property, birth or other status.

Furthermore, no distinction shall be made on the basis of the political, jurisdictional or international status of the country or territory to which a person belongs, whether it be independent, trust, non-self-governing or under any other limitation of sovereignty.

This article identifies any kind of discrimination of human rights. Here again is an invitation for us to do something about those violations as they occur in other countries. Not doing it will perpetuate their backwardness. In a shrinking world, we will very quickly pay the price for this omission.

Article 3

Everyone has the right to life, liberty and the security of person.

This article refers to the fundamental responsibility of every government—to provide for the safety and security of its citizens and to defend their freedom within and without the country.

Article 4

No one shall be held in slavery or servitude; slavery and the slave trade shall be prohibited in all their forms.

The prohibition of slavery in all its forms can extend, can it not, to religious slavery, for example. Indeed, the time will come when the manipulative and enslaving practices as perpetuated by the conventional religions will be seen as violations of human rights.

We certainly can start by denouncing the attempts of the bigots to teach creationism in schools, for instance. This is a form of enslaving our children's minds into believing an anachronistic theory. Article 4 will one day be extended to the astral level. On the Path, we are already extending Article 4 to the astral level when we reveal the parts of us that want to enslave others and when we confront people who are enslaving their masters or their families or their friends. One can say that there are all kinds of enslavements: emotional, mental, financial, spiritual, sexual, etc. An enslavement can appear in any area of life. For the person on the Path, Article 4 is something that needs to be continuously monitored as it relates to himself and those around him.

Article 5

No one shall be subjected to torture or to cruel, inhuman or degrading treatment or punishment.

For the majority of humanity, this article is violated in a wholesale manner. Again, the developed nations of the West accumulate guilt every time they look the other way.

Article 6

Everyone has the right to recognition everywhere as a person before the law.

This article does away with the privileges of nobility. Indeed, everyone is equal before the law. An interesting note here about England. It is peculiarly backwards of England to still maintain that the lords—the members of the House of Lords—are exempt of this equality. Indeed, they can only be judged by their peers, i.e., by other members of the House of Lords.

Article 7

All are equal before the law and are entitled without any discrimination to equal protection of the law. All are entitled to equal protection against any discrimination in violation of this Declaration and against any incitement to such discrimination.

This article is violated everywhere, including in the so-called developed countries. Indeed, there is substantial discrimination on the basis of money. He who has the most money benefits by the best defense vis-à-vis the law. It is obvious that you can get away with murder these days. We are witnessing it in the incredible publicity given to trials and to courts.

The unconscionable focus on such matters is falsely attributed to our mere desire for sensationalism. There is a lot more to it than that. There is a huge concern about the mounting injustice of the American legal system. The enormous fees charged by lawyers to defend someone, the preferential treatment given by judges to lawyers who would otherwise sue them is systematically destroying the legal system from top to bottom. Indeed, one can say that there is less and less justice in the United States, and perhaps in other countries as well.

In order for people to be equal before the law, legal services must also be equal for all people. No preferential treatment should be given for anyone. Thus, lawyers should be regulated and paid by the very same state that gives them their license. If this were so, they would have to do their job and do it properly or else lose the right to practice their profession. Lawyers are mistaking freedom to be license. They do not have the truth as their goal. Thus, they violate their oath as well as human rights.

Article 8

Everyone has the right to an effective remedy by the competent national tribunals for acts violating the fundamental rights granted him by the constitution or by law.

The commentary for Article 7 applies also to Article 8. Indeed, "competent national tribunals" may no longer exist.

Article 9
No one shall be subjected to arbitrary arrest, detention or exile.

This article is another one that is continuously and perpetually violated for the great majority of humanity. Again, we see the guilt of the West by omission.

Article 10
Everyone is entitled in full equality to a fair and public hearing by an independent and impartial tribunal, in the determination of his rights and obligations and of any criminal charge against him.

Unfortunately, "in full equality" no longer applies. It has been violated through the privilege of money.

Article 11
1. Everyone charged with a penal offence has the right to be presumed innocent until proved guilty according to law in a public trial at which he has had all the guarantees necessary for his defence.

2. No one shall be held guilty of any penal offence on account of any act or omission which did not constitute a penal offence, under national or international law, at the time when it was committed. Nor shall a heavier penalty be imposed than the one that was applicable at the time the penal offense was committed.

This article is being grossly abused by the rich who are literally getting away with murder.

Article 12

No one shall be subjected to arbitrary interference with his privacy, family, home or correspondence, nor to attacks upon his honour and reputation. Everyone has the right to the protection of the law against such interference or attacks.

The interesting aspect of Article 23 is "nor to attacks to his honour and reputation." Indeed, that refers to our admonitions against maligning and dumping, the character assassination that occurs by slander, untruth and disinformation.

Article 13

1. Everyone has the right to freedom of movement and residence within the borders of each State.

2. Everyone has the right to leave any country, including his own, and to return to his country.

This article is continuously and perpetually violated, once again, by those states that still have totalitarian regimes

Article 14

1. Everyone has the right to seek and to enjoy in other countries asylum from persecution.

2. This right may not be invoked in the case of prosecutions genuinely arising from non-political crimes or from acts contrary to the purposes and principles of the United Nations.

This article guarantees the right of a person *to take refuge* in any country of his choice. This, however, is being continuously violated by those greedy people who, not being persecuted in their own countries, pretend to be in order to make more money in another country. The abuse of this privilege has resulted in the closing of borders of such countries as the United States and France, who up to recently had their doors wide open to whomever wanted to come. Here, again, one can see that the necessity for limits—thou shalt not—exists in the places where consciousness is still undeveloped. Thus, commandments take the place of rights for people in those states.

The story of my youth is a very good illustration of the need for this article. I was born in Alexandria, Egypt of Jewish parents who were themselves born in Alexandria, Egypt of parents who came from the old Ottoman Empire. My grandparents fled the Ottoman Empire at the time of the arrival of the Christian Greeks who were a lot less tolerant of the Jews than were the Turks. Egypt at that time, having acquired the Suez Canal, was seen as the land of opportunity, a kind of America of the Middle East.

In the beginning, no one, including my grandparents, ever thought of changing his nationality or acquiring a new one. While Egypt was under British protectorate, there was a great deal of justice there. However, when nationalism took over Egypt in the 1940s it became necessary to re-examine the situation. My father, who had been an active Zionist when it was tolerated in Egypt, found himself in big danger of being arrested and tortured when the first Israeli-Arab war erupted in 1947. He was never arrested for reasons that we will never know—probably the loss of the list of Zionists in Egypt by the inefficient Egyptian government. However, as a result of that and from sheer cowardice, my father took his old Ottoman papers—which could have been converted to Turkish citizenship which would have been of more use to us than what he did—and applied for Egyptian citizenship. He got his Egyptian citizenship and everybody celebrated and congratulated him. Becoming an Egyptian citizen opened doors for him professionally; at the time he imported radios from Europe. However, by the time 1956 came around—the Suez Crisis—it was obvious that an Egyptian Jew was an oxymoron. Indeed, anyone who was not a Moslem Arab was discriminated against. This included the Copts, the Egyptian Christians, whose existence in Egypt predates Islam. So there we were with a nationality that did not make any sense at all. We were Egyptian citizens but we could not benefit from the protection of the Egyptian government. For that matter, anyone could have attacked us in the streets and the police would not have protected us—a fact that occurred to many other Jews in Egypt at that time.

To add insult to injury, it was clear that my father's business which had been taken over by the Egyptian government, would not survive for long. We had to leave and also leave behind everything that had been achieved. For all intents and purposes, we were worse off than people in Egypt at that time who did not have a nationality. They were being welcomed in many more countries than the Egyptian-citizen exiles. Thank God, a cousin of my mother guaranteed us and after many trials and tribulations we were able eventually to make it to the United States.

Upon arriving in France, where we spent three years waiting for permission to come to the States, we gave up our Egyptian citizenship and got refugee papers from the French government. At that time France was very liberal in its immigration policies. Later, after having been thoroughly abused by immigrants who called themselves political refugees in a dishonest manner, the French government did the right thing and closed its doors to refugees[14].

There is a staggering number of refugees in the world, people without a country, without the protection of any government and without any identity, withering away in refugee camps. The plight of the Palestinian people, for example, is an outrage. The whole idea of Zionism, the appropriation of lands that do not belong to you, just because 3000 years ago your ancestors happened to live there, is a tremendous disgrace that has heretofore been tolerated by humanity. The consequences are incredible amounts of homeless people who were never absorbed by the neighboring Arab states for political reasons, i.e., to build a case against Israel. Two wrongs do not make a right. Now they are both implicated in the outrage. They deserve each other's company.

By the way, what is erroneously called the Holy Lands, is no longer holy. It has not been holy for a long time. Aside from its historical value, there is no longer any energy left there. God help those people. God protect them from the karma that they have accumulated for themselves. A second holocaust can indeed happen because of this.

How does the formation of Israel compare to the United States or Australia being settled by the Europeans? At the time of the colonization of the United States, the indigenous populations represented moribund civilizations that were dying anyway. Indeed, their population was decreasing and they were living in very primitive conditions that had nothing to do with the task of this root race. One has to remember that the American Indians are the descendants of the

---

[14]French policies towards refugees have liberalized dramatically since the 1996 publication of this book.

Atlantean root race. Their practices are the ones that were known then and are now obsolete and need to be replaced. The Aborigines in Australia are even older in their origin, belonging to the Lemurian root race. It is time for them to be assimilated in the new progress of humanity.

This situation is quite different from the Jews taking over Arab lands. Jews and Arabs are both active participants in our civilization today. Neither of them represents the Atlantean or the Lemurian races. If any comparison is to be made, the Jews should have assimilated in the countries where they lived. They refused to do so, stubbornly and proudly claiming their specialness, arrogantly alienating themselves from the neighboring populations who they thoroughly provoked. The provocative character of the Jewish people is particularly evident in Israel where their bellicose ways are rampant.

Why should the Jews need to create a theocratic state? By doing so they have joined the fanatical Islamic countries that are so antagonistic to them. Theocracy is an anachronism. It will fade away as did communism.

The history of the Jews, and I am one of them, is a tale of countryless people. It is not that they were deprived of having a country, it is that they did not want to have a country. Take my ancestors for example. You can trace them back to the Iberian Jews who lived in Spain and Portugal in peace and prosperity under Arab domination. In came Ferdinand and Isabella with Christianity and without tolerance. The Inquisition then persecuted the Jews who fled to several parts of Europe, particularly Holland which was thriving in riches. And wherever they went, they always developed professions that were footloose and fancy free, where they could pick up and leave, pack up and go. The Jews never wanted to integrate themselves in any of the countries in which they lived. In addition to this, since they cultivated their minds and developed their intelligence to a high degree, they accumulated wealth at a much quicker pace than anybody else.

So, suppose you have in the midst of a classroom somebody who denies belonging to the classroom and who also does fairly well, being in the top five of a thirty member class. He would create enemies very quickly because he alienates himself and by the fact that he is among the best. He continues to play his cards close to his chest. Eventually he is chased out of the class. Is he a victim? No. He is, in fact, a victimizer. He lived in that class, he benefitted by what was given to him, he took what he wanted. He created a situation where he had to leave and he left. This is blatant arrogance, disregard for nationalities, for the hospitality that is given to him. And so it is with the Jews.

In addition to this, they believe that it was right for Joshua to exterminate in holocaust fashion every man, woman, child and animal that lived in eight cities of Palestine just because they were not Jewish. It is in the Bible. This belief in the holocaust has a price tag at the end of it. The price was paid in the middle of the twentieth century with the Hitleric holocaust. We are not here condoning Nazi extermination techniques. They were perpetuated not only on the Jews, but on the gypsies and on anybody else the Germans considered to be an inferior race. Had the Nazis occupied countries in Africa, they would have done the same thing there. However, there are no victims, and this is the way the Jews created their own reality.

It is outrageous to realize the incredible amount of wealth that is being diverted from the United States to Israel by Jewish Americans. This is done through a secondary false guilt for not immigrating to Israel, for staying in the United

States out of greedy purposes. However, it is not right; it is wrong. It is the financing of a thorn in the Arab side, aided and abetted by the United States.

What the Jews did was to abuse the "right to seek and to enjoy in other countries asylum from persecution." This abuse is being perpetuated by many other people today, including for instance the Mexicans who are ruining the underbelly of the United States. Not that the United States is a victim, since it continues to illegally employ the cheap labour that comes from south of the border. By profiting from cheap Mexican labour, Americans are aiding and abetting their own disintegration.

Article 15

1. Everyone has the right to a nationality.

2. No one shall be arbitrarily deprived of his nationality nor denied the right to change his nationality.

Today there are many people in the United States who refuse to change their nationality. They live here, they work here, they profit from this country. Yet, they continue to have contempt for this country, not wanting to change their European nationality, holding on to it with conceit.

Those are cases where it is not at all a question of right of nationality, it is a question of duty. It is, therefore, people's duty to become American citizens if they live here for a certain number of years.

Article 16

1. Men and women of full age, without any limitation due to race, nationality or religion, have the right to marry and to found a family. They are entitled to equal rights as to marriage, during marriage and at its dissolution.

2 Marriage shall be entered into only with the free and

full consent of the intending spouses.

3. The family is the natural and fundamental group unit of society and is entitled to protection by society and the State.

Numbers 1 and 2 of Article Sixteen are being grossly violated in the overwhelming majority of countries of the world. Marriage is "free" only in the West. In other countries, fathers sell their daughters, men buy wives, children are promised in marriage before they are born. These acts of barbarism have not as yet been stopped by the United Nations, nor have they been thoroughly and categorically condemned publicly during any of the sessions that I know of. Indeed, the guilty parties are very well represented at the UN. They get the benefits of being part of that organization, yet they continue to violate the very same articles to which they pay lip service.

Article 17

1. Everyone has the right to own property alone as well as in association with others.

2. No one shall be arbitrarily deprived of his property.

This article was thoroughly violated by every single communist country on the globe. It is today being violated by China, North Korea, Cuba. Thank God for the destruction of the Evil Empire so people can now own property there the way human beings should. Where was the United Nations from its creation in 1945 to the destruction of the Evil Empire in 1989? How much collusion was there with those countries who were perpetuating such outrages? Everyone looked the other way. The voices of truth were indeed a minority until finally in the 1980s there was enough demonstration of strength under the Reagan administration to topple the balance.

Article 18

Everyone has the right to freedom of thought, conscience and religion; this right includes freedom to change his religion or belief, and freedom, either alone or in community with others and in public or private, to manifest his religion or belief in teaching, practice, worship and observance.

The infiltration of local school boards by bigoted Christians results in the teachings of such anachronistic theories in science class as Creationism. The civilized peoples of this world should be outraged, as most certainly would have been the founding fathers of this country. Creationism is entirely an aberration of Judeo-Christianity. It has nothing to do with scientific reality.

How many more outrages are there out there in the world? And what is the United Nations doing about it?

Article 19

Everyone has the right to freedom of opinion and expression; this right includes freedom to hold opinions without interference and to seek, receive and impart information and ideas through any media and regardless of frontiers.

Again, this has been thoroughly and consistently violated by all the dictatorships in the world, particularly through Soviet disinformation. This was never addressed adequately by the United Nations until it was too late.

Article 20

1. Everyone has the right to freedom of peaceful assembly and association.

2. No one may be compelled to belong to an association.

This also has been violated in the same manner.

Article 21

1. Everyone has the right to take part in the government of his country, directly or through freely chosen representatives.

2. Everyone has the right of equal access to public service in his country.

3. The will of the people shall be the basis of the authority of government; this will shall be expressed in periodic and genuine elections which shall be by universal and equal suffrage and shall be held by secret vote or by equivalent free voting procedures.

This is very nice, except that it only applies to those who are ready for it—those who are literate, those who have had an education, those who have a full belly and are not swayed to and fro by people who promise to fulfill their basic needs. It cannot possibly be applied in primitive countries where it would create incredible anarchy and chaos.

How was the paragon of democracies, Athens in its Golden Age, created? People forget that before Pericles, before the Golden Age of democracy, was a time of enlightened despotism. Indeed, in the previous century, Peisistratos was an enlightened despot, a dictator who saw to it that education was universal and widespread in Athens, that streets were kept clean, that people were disciplined and did their duty. As a result of that discipline, the Greeks found themselves ready for the democracy that followed. So it is and so it will have to be in those countries that are not ready, whether we like it or not.

Enlightened despotism is a dangerous business. It is very difficult under an enlightened despot to have the type of complete justice that exists in a democratic country such as the United States. However, when presented with a choice between overwhelming safety under a dictatorship, anarchy, chaos and physical danger under a democracy that does not work, people will always choose the former and reject the latter. Unfortunately, in some cases this results in the outrages created by fascism. However, in other cases, the enlightened despot brings with him a lot of positive elements which are necessary to bring in democracy. Take, for example, Franco, in Spain who was a fascist. At his death, Spain reverted to a democracy. It was then able to join the European community. This experiment worked. Some others did not work. Iran, for example, would have made it into the Twentieth Century under the leadership of the Shah. The Persians are now a century backwards again because of giving in to a religious line of least resistance.

There is no mention in this article of the enlightened despot. There should be. A word of warning here for the democracies, including the United States. Democracy is an earned privilege which comes with self-responsibility, so is freedom. Self-responsibility is becoming a forgotten art and virtue in the West. So we are moving at an accelerated pace, at an alarming pace towards the possibility of a dictatorship. Soon we will resemble Mexico where they could use a dictatorship; they may have one before we know it.

Article 22

Everyone, as a member of society, has the right to social security and is entitled to realization, through national effort and international co-operation and in accordance with the organization and resources of each State, of the economic, social and cultural rights indispensable for his dignity and the free development of his personality.

Here is the good side of socialism in action. Indeed, not only does the citizen have a right to social security, but he also has the right to medical care and to education which should be provided for by the government. This also must include legal protection which would end once and for all the plethora of nonsense which exists today in American courts and the courts of the world.

Article 23

1. Everyone has the right to work, to free choice of employment, to just and favourable conditions of work and to protection against unemployment.

2. Everyone, without any discrimination, has the right to equal pay for equal work.

3. Everyone who works has the right to just and favourable remuneration ensuring for himself and his family an existence worthy of human dignity, and supplemented, if necessary, by other means of social protection.

4. Everyone has the right to form and to join trade unions for the protection of his interests.

What Article 23 does not take into account is the line of least resistance and the lower self. Sure, everyone has the right to work. But does everyone *want* to work? That is a different question. Most people do not want to work. Their numbers are increasing. The work ethic is being systematically destroyed by the welfare state. Indeed, if you are guaranteed food and shelter if you work or not, why should you work? Furthermore, if you work, you have to be taxed, so that your taxes can pay for those who do not want to work and who get food and shelter. That adds one more argument against having to go to work. This productivity is unfortunately being replaced by slave labour in underdeveloped countries. For a short time, we in the West will benefit by this, relying on our superior technology and on the short-lived greater value of our currency. However, soon those who do the work—the slaves, as in the Hegelian master/slave relationship—will take over. And at that point we will pay the price for not wanting to work.

Developing a work ethic should very much be a part of the curriculum in schools. Ethical development is perhaps the most forgotten about and yet the most important element in anybody's education.

Article 24

Everyone has the right to rest and leisure, including reasonable limitation of working hours and periodic holidays with pay.

What are we in the West and what is the United Nations doing about the millions of people who are still in sweatshops, in China particularly?

Article 25

1. Everyone has the right to a standard of living adequate for the health and well-being of himself and of his family, including food, clothing, housing and medical care and necessary social services, and the right to security in the event of unemployment, sickness, disability, widowhood, old age or other lack of livelihood in circumstances beyond his control.

2. Motherhood and childhood are entitled to special care and assistance. All children, whether born in or out of wedlock, shall enjoy the same social protection.

This can only be true in a country where there is personal responsibility exhibited by individual citizens. If a country regresses into the line of least resistance of wanting to be taken care of, those measures are counter-indicated. It is preferable for people to experience lack of food and lack of shelter so as to finally trigger their Instinct of Self-

Preservation. This way, work will be valued.

There is an interesting distinction between those people who were born during the Depression and lived through World War II, and those who are their children. The former category, having experienced lack of food and shelter, are hard workers and have developed an Instinct of Self-Preservation. Thus they have created abundance for themselves. Most of them have money and wealth and leisure. Their children, however, who were born in the lap of luxury have not developed their Instinct of Self-Preservation. Consequently they have not wanted to work hard, creating a decline in the standard of living which we are experiencing today. Had the Instinct of Self-Preservation been triggered in the baby boomers, or had they been given the necessary ethical training and discipline there would be no decline in the standard of living. Indeed, it would steadily increase, as it should.

Article 26

1. Everyone has the right to education. Education shall be free, at least in the elementary and fundamental stages. Elementary education shall be compulsory. Technical and professional education shall be made generally available and higher education shall be equally accessible to all on the basis of merit.

2. Education shall be directed to the full development of the human personality and to the strengthening of respect for human rights and fundamental freedoms. It shall promote understanding, tolerance and friendship among all nations, racial or religious groups, and shall further the activities of the United Nations for the maintenance of peace.

3. Parents have a prior right to choose the kind of education that shall be given to their children.

We are in complete agreement with (1) and (2). We would like to extend it to any type of education, including graduate education. This should be available to anyone who wants it and should be paid for by the citizens.

National exams should be available for anyone who wants to enter them. They should be completely impersonal—colour-blind. No special favours should be given to anyone for any reason. The standards for qualifications for professions should be the same for everyone.

Under the present system, with quotas and all kinds of societal pressures existing, standards of excellence have been forgotten. If they are not restored, we will continue our descent into lower and lower common denominators.

If there is a need to equalize conditions, it should not be done by lowering the standards of the exam or by favouring people on the basis of race, colour or creed. This is complete violation of everything this country stands for and everything this declaration stands for. The equalization can be done through helping the students during their years of training. As long as all of this is done before the exam it is acceptable, even desirable. The exam itself should not be subjected to this type of manipulation and unfairness.

Number 3, however, needs a caveat. Parents have a prior right to choose the kind of education that shall be given to their children. Yes. But the majority of parents should not impose over the minorities the type of education they want for their children. This is particularly true when religious education infiltrates itself under the hypocritical guise of science or history in the textbooks.

Religion belongs in churches. If people want their children to be educated in a religious manner, they should send them to religious schools and they should leave public schools alone.

Article 27

1. Everyone has the right freely to participate in the cultural life of the community, to enjoy the arts and to share in scientific advancement and its benefits.

2. Everyone has the right to the protection of the moral and material interests resulting from any scientific, literary or artistic production of which he is the author.

We agree with (1). However, (2) poses a problem. Indeed, when it is extended to ownership of ideas then it is in violation of Spiritual Law. Ideas do not belong to human beings. They are the property of the Spirit and they are given generously from the spirit world to the world of humanity to be distributed as generously as they were received.

There is currently a battle, a trade war between China and the United States, over China's pirating of copyrighted material developed by big American firms. In the first place, the battle should not be over copyrights, it should be over human rights which are being continuously and perpetually violated in China. It is outrageous indeed that we should have a most favoured nation status for China when it is perpetrating such flagrant violations of human rights. It is also outrageous that we should buy her products which are products of slavery and injustice. In the second place, are not the well-paid, fat American corporations paying for their disregard of those violations of human rights perpetrated in China? Indeed, they have no hesitation to opening up McDonalds or branches of IBM or other great corporations in China in order to make money. But when it comes to human rights, they look the other way. Is not the pirating of their products one way for them to pay for this disregard? We are not condoning the pirating or the theft. We are merely saying that it is a direct consequence of another theft committed on a higher level of development by the West.

Article 28
Everyone is entitled to a social and international order in which the rights and freedoms set forth in this Declaration can be fully realized.

So, who is going to enforce it? Where is the force of arms that will ensure this? Who is taking the lead to do this? Those who have already been able to achieve this in their own countries and who are selfishly closing their eyes to the demise of everyone else in the world will have a very steep price to pay in a future that is not too far distant from today.

Article 29
1. Everyone has duties to the community in which alone the free and full development of his personality is possible.

2. In the exercise of his rights and freedoms, everyone shall be subject only to such limitations as are determined by law solely for the purpose of securing due recognition and respect for the rights and freedoms of others and of meeting the just requirements of morality, public order and the general welfare in a democratic society.

3. These rights and freedoms may in no case be exercised contrary to the purposes and principles of the United Nations.

Yes, absolutely. The concept in (2) here was developed in the eighteenth century. It is a very valid one. A new world order is being visualized here. We pray that it comes to pass.

Article 30
Nothing in the Declaration may be interpreted as implying for any State, group or person any right to engage in any activity or to perform any act aimed at the destruction

of any of the rights and freedoms set forth herein.

Same as for Article 29.

CONCLUSION

This is part of our religion. We believe in this Declaration. We believe it is our right and our duty to see that it come to pass. This will not be an easy task. Every citizen in the world is called upon to contribute in that respect.

This Declaration has even more religious significance and relevance than the Ten Commandments. The Ten Commandments were meant for a humanity in its childhood or even infancy. The Declaration of Human Rights addresses a humanity that is coming out of adolescence and is contemplating adulthood.

CHAPTER 33
POLITICAL SYSTEMS

There are three types of political systems that are representatives of the first three rays. In any organization all three of them will be found in one degree or another.

MONARCHY

This was a necessary phase in human history. In the beginning, particularly at the time of Atlantis, the kings were enlightened, inspired to guide humanity. They were superior beings who incarnated for that purpose. The primitive state of humanity required that such great beings would come in and become and be their leaders.

The hierarchical feudal system that ensued was a necessary phase. Of course it became rigid and obsolete later on, when through greed it was enshrined in heredity. Here we encounter the fallacy of inheritance. For example, a person achieves. Through the process of regression, which we have studied elsewhere, he now enshrines his achievements, having forgotten how he got there. Enshrining those achievements, he wants his offspring, who have done absolutely nothing, to benefit from the fruits of his labours. This corrupts the development of the children who are now invested with rewards that they have not earned. In this process is to be found the demise of monarchy and feudalism. This demise is obviously due to the excesses that come when benefits and privileges are given to people who have not earned them.

So here you have the positive and negative aspects of monarchy and feudalism. Obviously, we are talking here about the First Ray of Will or Power in manifestation.

The forms of government that we name dictatorial, including fascism, actually belong here. The dictator acts as if he is enlightened from above, as if he had been given divine powers to guide others, to guide his nation, to make laws, etc.

DEMOCRACY

This is a function of the Second Ray. Here everyone has an equal start. May the best person win. Here is cultivated the respect of other people's freedoms. They must say as did Voltaire, "I may disagree with what you say but I will defend to my death your right to say it. Only in this type of climate can democracy succeed. Therefore, it is ludicrous to believe that democracy can be successful in underdeveloped countries. Only enlightened monarchy in one form or another will succeed there.

For democracy to succeed, inner authority must be developed and, therefore, responsibility must be respected. The destruction of democracy comes through the abuse of capitalism. A person may work hard and in his own right achieve a great deal of wealth and power.

He then forgets the way he got there and enshrines the wealth and the power, trying to monopolize the market and to enslave people.

This evil gets further compounded with the process of inheritance.

The Law of Cause and Effect is usurped and the result is slave labour, the abuse of people, outrageous ostentatiousness and indecent wealth. And the equal and opposite—abject poverty.

SOCIALISM

This system can only happen when humanity has given up greed and is willing to share its three-dimensional wealth with everybody. If it is undertaken too early, i.e., before the problem of greed and selfishness has been resolved, it becomes a pseudo-solution to the problem of poverty. With greed still present, instead of the voluntary sharing of wealth which it is supposed to be, communism becomes "I want what you have and I do not want to work for it, either."

This is exactly what happened in communist countries. From the start it was corrupt. The communists wanted to have what the monarchical system had. It was not at all a question of sharing, it was a lot more a question of stealing. What occurred next is a story in the continuous lowering of motivation. Instead of bringing greed out in the sun and getting it to work for you as in capitalization, thus resolving it and dissolving it, greed was seen as anathema. This created massive apathy. The greedy unevolved masses decided that since they did not have to work for it anyway, they would give a minimum in order to get the share that they were supposed to get.

It did not work. In fact, it created millionaires, it negated the basic human rights of freedom of expression, of speech, of travel, etc. It plunged these countries backward into systems that were much more feudal and monarchical than the ones they had originally destroyed.

The frustration that was born out of this failure created a desire to conquer the world. This then is why there was a voracious desire to infiltrate and convert one country after another to their communistic philosophy. It worked to the degree that the countries in question themselves were still under an obsolete form of monarchical or dictatorial rule (which is the same thing).

On the positive side, a certain amount of help, welfare, equalization and charity should be practiced in all countries. Indeed, we have to provide the poor and the deprived with an opportunity to re-establish themselves as respectable and respected individuals. Thus, welfare, helping others, sharing of the wealth is a necessary undertaking. However, it is not a sufficient one. By itself, it collapses. It is a temporary measure, and an opportunity given to people on a limited basis to help them join others in becoming productive, earning a living and accomplishing their task.

COEXISTENCE OF THREE SYSTEMS OF GOVERNMENT

In any system of government or in any organization you will find a combination of the three systems. Depending on its degree of development, one system will be favoured over the other. At different times in its history, as it progresses or regresses, one system will work and the others will not. Take Greece, for instance. In its Golden Age, around 450 B.C., it was a democracy. It later became an oligarchy, a dictatorship, and finally became part of Alexander's empire.

Take Rome. Once again, at some point there was a viable democracy that toppled the old monarchy, the kings of Rome. With the plethora of slaves and with the corruption of the Roman spirit through material conquests, the system degenerated into the empire which was the only thing that could work under such circumstances.

It is not given that a country can sustain democracy forever. One hopes that it is possible but there is no guarantee. In turn, the country itself has to recognize when strong leadership is needed and when it should be relaxed.

If consciousness is raised continuously and perpetually, capitalism will enable people to self-actualize and lose their greed. With the loss of greed there will be a greater striving towards sharing and, therefore, towards greater socialism or even communism.

This socialism will be a voluntary one and not an imposed one. It comes from the innermost self of the individuals instead of being imposed from the outside. One can see this system already existing when one considers the life of evolved individuals. An evolved individual does not need much to live on. The more evolved he is the less he requires. As long as he can be fairly comfortable and accomplish his task, he is perfectly happy. It is the unevolved individual who accumulates, amasses in the hope of self-protection or for the sake of approval, etc. All of which are evil practices.

True socialism and true communism also mean doing away with outer level human law. Only because inner authority and the instinctual obedience to law have been cultivated and achieved. Any attempt at establishing this utopian paradise too early results in abject anarchy and destruction.

SECULAR HUMANISM VERSUS THE FEUDALISM OF THE CATHOLIC CHURCH

The constitution of the United States, the Declaration of Human Rights and all of the other political dispensations of the eighteenth century are enlightened indeed. They represent enough of an ideal—a realistic one—for humanity to follow at this point.

Let's not forget, however, that they are the product of secular humanism, not of Christianity. Christianity, if anything, has been the archenemy of this type of democracy. This can be very easily verified historically. Indeed, the entire church hierarchy is a duplication of the feudal system. The pope is the correspondent to the Holy Roman Emperor, the cardinal is the correspondent to the king, the bishop to the duke, and so forth. The destruction of the monarchical and feudal system also destroyed and rendered meaningless the hierarchy of the church. It became then an anachronism and still is, a lingering dying one.

Let's not forget, also, that this feudal system is not medieval, but Roman. It was set up at the end of the Roman Empire when Christianity became the official religion. That is how antique and obsolete it is. It dates back to antiquity, not just to the Middle Ages. The word "pontiff," which these days is applied to the pope, was applied both to pope and emperor. There is a misguided thought process in the United States that equates democracy with Christianity. True, democracy is a product of the essence of Christianity. But democracy has not been brought about by Christianity itself. Indeed, Christianity as I said before, has tried very hard and still is trying to destroy democracy, to destroy human rights.

CHAPTER 34
REFLECTIONS ON HISTORY

According to Robert Eisenman, the Dead Sea Scrolls demonstrate that Christ's purpose was to restore Judaism to its original purity.

Although I do not agree completely, I certainly see that what Christ was actually trying to do was quite different from Paul's interpretation of it. Paul eliminated the revolutionary aspect of Christ, creating a poor imitation of Him in order to be acceptable to the Romans. The destruction of the Jewish revolt in 67 A.D. (Masada) destroyed the followers of James who was the true successor of Christ. (*The Gospel of Thomas*.) Thus, the attempt to regain the Semitic identity of Palestine was defeated and repressed.

Mohammed and the Arab Conquest constitute a return of the Semitic rebellion against the Romans, and the final victory over them.

Master Jesus reincarnated as Mohammed. This would make sense, since He then completed in the Seventh Century A.D. what was started in the Sixth Century B.C. What reincarnated was the Jesus part of Jesus Christ, the Sixth Ray part of the Saviour, His personality, not His soul. Indeed, the Christ did not need to reincarnate; however, Jesus did.

Now, isn't the Arab Conquest, Islam, a resurgence of this desire to revive and purify the Jewish tradition? This time it was victorious, reversing Masada and vanquishing Christianity in Asia—except for Asia Minor, in North Africa and in Spain.

According to the Belgian historian Henri Pirenne, the Roman system of commerce, industry and communications survived the barbarian invasions of the Fifth and Sixth Centuries. It is a misconception to believe that the barbarians destroyed the Roman Empire. They were absorbed by it, Christianized, i.e., Romanized, made to fit into an essentially Roman system, which later became the feudal structure of the Middle Ages. Pirenne shows that it is the Arabs who finally destroyed the Roman Empire. Indeed, after the Arab Conquest, the Roman system of commerce, industry and communications no longer survived. This is not only true of the countries invaded by the Arabs, it also applies to all of Europe, which even though not physically conquered by the Arabs, was plunged into the darkness of the Middle Ages. It is as if Jesus came back to deal the final blow to the oppressive Romans who had been victorious at Masada.

The subsequent blossoming of the Arab civilization bears this out. Indeed, the flourishing of Arab culture, commerce and life in the eighth and ninth centuries is an out-picturing of the blessings that came through their dispensation. *They* achieved what Jesus and James wanted to but did not. Having done so, they were blessed. Amazingly and independent of the Arab Empire proper, Spain under the jurisdiction of the exiled Omayyads, also flourished. The blessings came because they were both in truth, bringing in the much needed light, demonstrating the wrong ways of Christianity which sank into medieval barbarism and stupor. Europe was to be awakened centuries later by an anti-Christian, humanistic movement, the Renaissance.

CHAPTER 35
THE DEBT OF CHRISTIANITY

THE REPRESSED ASPECT OF THE CHRIST

The aspect of the Christ that has been repressed is that of the overturner of tables, the rebel, the rabble rouser. It was He Who was repelled both by Roman excesses and by Pharisaic hypocrisy, the hypocrisy of His own Jewish religious background. This aspect is well preserved in the *Gospel of Thomas* which was unadulterated by the later "gospels" of the Bible or by Paul.

Christ, in the *Gospel of Thomas*, clearly is quoted to say that His followers should "turn to James the Just" after His death (Saying #13). James and his followers were closer to the revolutionary Christ than were the Apostles or Paul. In the writings of the Dead Sea Scrolls, one can see what those followers really believed.

They believed in a forgotten aspect of the Christ; they believed in a Christ who was militantly opposed to the status quo imposed by the Romans and by Pharisaic Judaism. This militancy was accepted neither by the Jews nor by the Romans. The coalition of them resulted in the death of the Christ. It also resulted a generation later in the wiping out of James the Just and of his followers.

CHRIST AS GOD

The whole idea of presenting Christ as God was a Roman notion that resembles more Nero's pretensions than it does the teachings of Christ. Christ, the most highly evolved human, the greatest of all creations, was a creation of God, and as such, inferior to Him. Paul and the Apostles fabricated a type of Christianity that was palatable to the Romans, thus selling out the true teachings of Christ.

DILUTION AND PAGANIZATION OF CHRISTIANITY

Paul and his followers converted Christianity into paganism for personal power and satisfaction. Instead of the religion of innovative teaching and purification, it conformed and followed, thus perverting the purpose of Christ. Conventional religion stopped being Christian when the gospels of the Bible and Paul's writings were adopted as the word of God.

Paul, who had a Christ experience on the way to Damascus, was originally a convert to the following of James. In fact, Qumran, the seat of the Dead Sea Scrolls, was in the region of what was at that time called Damascus. Damascus then was not merely a city, but a region. Paul was obviously on his way to Qumran. He was on the right way. Therefore, he experienced the Christ Who led him to go there. Apparently, his hypocrisy and deception forced those in Qumran to throw him out.

He is referred to as the Liar in their literature. What he wanted to do and what ultimately he did do was to water down the teachings of Christ and to blend them with existing pagan creeds so as to make the Christian religion palatable to everybody. He invented it for everybody. Every single sharp and challenging aspect of the Christ was turned into its opposite—challenging became accommodating; confronting became colluding, etc.

Paul himself in his hypocrisy is very reminiscent of a lot

of the false teachers of the New Age who go from city to city preaching their own style of the line of least resistance. They cannot stay in one place because they do not have enough teachings to do so. So, Paul established little nuclei of "Christianity" just about everywhere in the Mediterranean basin, particularly on the eastern side of it.

Thus, no real Christianity existed beyond the first couple of centuries, except for the break-away "heresies," for some of the Gnostics, for the Cathars, and for other enlightened peoples who, openly or secretly, continued the correct interpretations of the teachings of the Master Jesus Who carried the Christ. The most extraordinary story of these heresies has to be the history of the Cathars who were massacred by the Albigensian Crusade in the beginning of the thirteenth century.

The destruction of Masada in 67 A.D. by the Romans was, I believe, an answer to the threat posed by the rebellious Jews, stirred up by the Christ, and who were denouncing the Roman and Jewish corrupt status quo.

Consequently:

1. The Bible gospels, all written by those who had never met the Christ, were diluted to suit the Romans. Of Matthew, Mark, Luke and John, John is the person who could have met the Christ but, of course, it is not given that he did.

It is impossible, however, for those who actually transcribed these documents to have met the Christ since these writings were done in the second or the third century. In those days, there were many other gospels available. The ones that were chosen to be part of what ended up as the Bible were the ones which merely conformed to Paul's teachings.

2. Paul's teachings certainly constitute an even greater

and more outrageous sellout. He represented Christ as a namby-pamby, non-threatening victim. "The Liar" in the writings of the followers of James the Just peculiarly reminds us of Paul.

3. **The Earth reacted as well.** Consider the two eruptions of Vesuvius around that time. The first one—a warning—occurred in 63 A.D., prior to Masada. The second and final one occurred soon thereafter. I believe that the hand of God is to be found here, as surely as it is to be found in the destruction of Atlantis thousands of years ago and of the Evil Empire in 1989.

4. **The diluted and paganized Christianity became the official religion of the empire.** It proceeded to eliminate violently any and all opposition. This has gone on for nearly two thousand years, interrupted somewhat by Humanism and by the Age of Reason and the Enlightenment. It is now gaining momentum again. This time the violence is done on the mental and astral levels, with the outrages about contraception, abortion and sexuality in general. However, it is already trickling down to the physical level with the abortion clinic murders of doctors by fanatic bigots who call themselves Christians.

5. **The seductive religions created by Paul and his followers are easy ones to pay lip service to.** It is the seductive religion of Herem, the brother of Satan, he who is in charge of the mask, the glamours, and of materialism. Those who subscribe to these religions will find themselves under the hoof of Satan at one point or another. Condoning them occurs through "good intentions." Good people and people who want to be good, but who do not want to exert themselves too much and who do not want to really dig into themselves to find what the truth actually is, get taken in.

TRUE CHRISTIANITY IS THE PATH

The teachings of the Christ are the Path. It is their tradition that we uphold here at The Church of the Path®. We are the real Christians. We tolerate the false ones. We do not object to them calling themselves Christian, but we resent their saying that we are not, that we deceive them by calling ourselves by their name and that we had better refrain from doing so. Their intolerance itself is proof positive of the fact that they are not Christians, for Christianity is above all the religion of brotherhood, sharing, and, therefore, tolerance. Thus, we are the Christians and they are not. They are the bigots, similar to the ones who discriminated against and tried to eliminate our predecessors.

They are still accumulating an expensive karmic debt. The bill is about to be presented and John Paul II's planned "apology" in the year 2000 will be a travesty, too little, too late. God help them!

QUESTIONS CHRISTIANS SHOULD ASK THEMSELVES

What do we learn from this? Plenty. Ask yourself.
1. *To what extent do you sell out?*
2. *In what way do you sell out your faith, your genius?*
3. *How do you extinguish, demean, infantilize your fires?*
4. *Who do you avoid confronting?*
5. *What character traits do you avoid expressing?*
6. *Where do you find your mask that wants to compromise and materialize everything? Compare it to the Pharisees and the Apostles.*
7. *How much truth do you vulgarize to make it palatable?*
8. *What motives lie behind this?*
9. *How about your greed, your selfishness, your*

dishonesty and behind these check out your insecurity, lack of faith, your despair?

10. Do you know, know as an experiential reality, that true happiness is only to be found in at-onement with your innermost self, not in selling out and splitting yourself?

TWO CONTRADICTORY ASPECTS OF THE CHRIST

We have to consider the two contradictory aspects of the Christ taken up by two different factions.

(1) Christ the rabble rouser. The rabble rouser appears so clearly in the writings of James the Just. He had to have been like this if He were the messiah. James the Just was the true inheritor of the movement that Christ created. His teachings resemble a lot what Christ and His followers believed and were ushering in.

(2) The loving and accommodating Christ. Paul took this aspect and used it to create a religion, outside of the context of the original Christ teaching, that would be accommodating to the Roman Empire. That is why it survived. It was much easier for the Romans to tolerate the non-threatening doctrine of Paul than to tolerate the radical challenge of Christ and James.

The same is true about the Jewish religion. Rabbinical Judaism the way it is known today in the world is really the Pharisaic one, the one that was palatable to the Roman Empire. That is why it survived. The Judaism which disappeared was a combination of a religion and a political movement which was looking for the independence of the Jewish state. The destruction of the Temple of Jerusalem and the history of Masada put an end to that Judaism. Those who were left sold out to the Romans and changed their beliefs in order to do so. Thus, they were tolerated and survived.

Would Christianity have disappeared if it had not sold out to the Romans? I do not think so. Through the process of reincarnation, those souls would have come back and continued their work. This process of reincarnation can powerfully be felt in our day and age. For example, consider the resurgence of Neo-Nazism in young people in the 1980s and particularly in the 1990s. Consider also that those who were born in hippie families became yuppies, right wingers. The hippies themselves came in to bring back the romanticism of the first half of the nineteenth century, aided of course, by the forces of the Aquarian Age.

The Romans themselves reincarnated into the British, creating British imperialism. This explains the extraordinary affinity the British have for Italy. They do not have it for France, they have it to some extent for Spain, but not nearly as much as they have it for Italy. There is a great romance between the Englishmen and Italy which still survives up to today.

Consider Nazis being reincarnated as Zionists, creating the bellicose state of Israel, armed to the teeth, provoking and continuously frustrating the Arabs and robbing their lands under the banner of religion. This argument is very convincing if you happen to have visited Israel in the 1960s and 1970s. In the 1980s and 1990s a new generation of yuppie Israelis is coming around that does not much care for all of these old issues. However, through indoctrination and wrong teaching, a lot of hatred has been preserved in the Israeli soul, perpetuating in that way the cycle of violence that exists in the Jewish karma.

CHAPTER 36
OUR PATH OF REBIRTH AND PURIFICATION

THE PEOPLE OF GOD

The "people of God" as they are called in the Catholic Church are people who by their own definition are reborn. As in John 3:3, "Jesus answered him, 'Truly, truly, I say to you, unless one is born anew, he cannot see the kingdom of God,'" and John 3:5, "Jesus answered, 'Truly, truly, I say to you, unless one is born of water and the Spirit, he cannot enter the kingdom of God,'" rebirth is what is needed.

REBIRTH

Rebirth can only happen through the ashes of crisis. Osiris resurrects, as does the Phoenix, out of his own ashes. This is very powerful symbolism. It means that one has to experience crisis in order to be reborn. Sometimes the crisis must happen on the outer level, but this is not necessary. One can bring about crisis through our process, through the re-experiencing of undigested thoughts and feelings and bringing them to a head in controlled circumstances before they can create a shattering on the outer level. When the crisis comes and the unnecessary superimposed layers are destroyed, the person is able to see once again the truth. He is reborn.

After rebirth there is still a lot of work to do. One has to see to it that he not return to the bad old ways that existed prior to his rebirth. That is the Path; that is indeed what distinguishes him from other people and makes him a member of The Church of the Path®. The work, as explained by this church and by the sermons and by the process that we practice, is what distinguishes this person from others and makes him a God-blessed person.

DISTINGUISHING BETWEEN PEOPLE WHO ARE ON THE PATH AND PEOPLE WHO ARE NOT ON THE PATH

Immersion in water is an outer level ceremony. It and all of the other "sanctified" and petrified practices of conventional religion cannot possibly create rebirth. In fact, belief that they would do so regresses the individual away from the necessary crisis and pain that he must experience in order to be reborn, and in order to let go of his little ego.

The magical thinking that leads people to believe that baptism shortly after birth distinguishes them from everybody else is a product of the forces of darkness. It encourages people to follow their line of least resistance. It leads them to conceit and elitism. It leads them to claim privileges that they have not earned. It leads them to seek premature and undeserved salvation.

It is the surrender to the process of purification in humility that makes a person on the Path a true noble. We are constructing the new and only nobility through the following of the Path. Nobility or title arrived at in any other way than this process of purification is worthless and regressive. People who practice this process in one form or another, even using other words, are indeed on the Path.

Where are they? Where are you, oh brothers of our soul? We seek you; we want to find you. We want to embrace you. We want to participate with you in our process. We want to unite with you. We want to learn from you. We want to teach you. We want to share with you what we have.

We are indeed exclusive. We exclude those who avoid the process of purification with whatever subterfuges. However, we bless, we accept, we want to unite with whomever in the world wants, as we do, to take full responsibility for their lives, discover the truth and the power of the Law of Cause and Effect, believe that they determine their own reality and also believe that the experience of this truth is what will lead them to true altruism and to at-onement with God. These principles are at the root of every religion at its inception.

Thus, in every religious group there are people who are genuinely seeking. However, they are blinded by their own thirst for approval and that is why they do not have the guts to challenge the false teachers who still have power over them. We urge them to read this catechism and to open their minds to the eternality of the teachings that we are trying to follow and to the fact that we seek the essence of all religions instead of membership in a particular club.

So, yes, we are exclusive but we are also inclusive.

CHAPTER 37
THE CHURCH OF THE PATH® HIERARCHY

CHURCH HIERARCHY

When The Church of the Path® was founded there were only two levels of hierarchy.

1. On the first level one received, one was taught, one learned, one assimilated and one went through the process of removing one's defenses. This was just about all.

2. Later a person developed readiness to give. This, too, had to be attentively discerned and heeded.

These basic two phases were each then divided into two others. In the first phase are to be found the novice and the aspirant. In the second phase are to be found the disciple and the teacher.

Alongside these, there has to be a leader. The position of minister was created. The first minister of The Church of the Path® was Albert Gani. He held this position since the time of the founding of the Church December 21, 1986, in McAllen, Texas until his death in 2018.

When he left McAllen for Austin, it was necessary to create ministerships in McAllen. Robin Bates and Siobhan Polvado were ordained as ministers at that time. This perforce created the necessity to elevate Albert Gani to a higher level. The position of Master was created at the suggestion of Dorothy Sanders, who thought, rightly so, that these titles should be patterned after the Hierarchy. So, Albert Gani was confirmed as Master of The Church of the Path®.

At the time of this writing, therefore, we have the following sequence in the hierarchy of the Church: (1) Master, (2) Minister, (3) Teacher, (4) Disciple, (5) Aspirant, and (6) Novice. The titles were created out of a raising of consciousness and out of necessity. More titles will be necessary in the future as the expansion of the church becomes a reality.

BOARD OF EXAMINERS

There is a Board of Examiners consisting of anyone who has arrived at the rank of disciple and above that will receive applications for teachership. The board may accept or reject the application, and the board will give final authorization for taking the Oath of Teachership. This board will also examine complaints about teachers and will take appropriate action, such as dismissing a teacher, removing the responsibility of a teacher to a particular worker and assigning that worker to a new teacher.

If a person violates the requirements of his position and if he is incapable or unwilling to take responsibility for it, the Board of Examiners demotes that person. No one is or should ever be immune to demotion. Taking an oath means demonstrating that one should keep it. The subsequent betrayal of this oath in a repeated fashion results in dismissal. In some cases if there is a gross and blatant violation of the oath, then demotion is immediate. One does not wait for further outrages to be committed in order for dismissal to occur. These are the types of judgments for which the Board of Examiners is responsible.

CHAPTER 38
OATHS AND COMMITMENTS

TAKING IN AND GIVING OUT

There are two stages in a person's life on the Path. In the beginning, one joins the Path with the intention of self-improvement. The person's entire focus is on making his life better, on obtaining happiness and on chipping away at his problems. At some point, however, this process of taking in must be reversed to a process of giving out.

There are abundant signs that it is time to give. Some people are too eager to get into this state. This usually occurs when they are no longer willing to look at themselves and to purify themselves. They do not understand that even when you give out help, you still have to continue the process of purification. This attitude can be found in people who believe that they have gone through and are complete with the process of purification. They are false teachers. They can be found in New Age circles, in conventional churches and in psychotherapy.

Other people may go the other way. They may very well be ready to give, but they resist. These are the people who overprotect themselves. They rely on past achievements. Some of them depend on money that they have inherited or that they have earned in their own right. The perpetual abuse of these advantages will lead them to lose these advantages so as to finally come to terms with the fact that they are ready to help and must give to others what they have received. This transition from taking in to giving out is marked in our commitments as the transition between aspirant and disciple. You will, therefore, be able to see the differences between that which is required of an aspirant or novice and that which is required of a disciple.

This is the choice one must face when passing from the second to the third initiation and having to choose between the Forces of Light and the forces of darkness. Wanting too quickly to become a disciple or resisting passing into discipleship both are an embracing of evil. They are on a path of regression. The aspirant who does so is either pampering himself or is being dishonest and escaping the process that has not been completed.

In a group process such as ours, the readiness of someone to pass from one stage to the next is obvious to other people. It is much more obvious to other people than it is to the person concerned. This, of course, demonstrates the great value of the group. The person himself cannot merely blame his teacher for accusing him of being ready or of not being ready. There are other people to contend with who are saying the same thing.

In defining all of this we are slowly but surely discovering the true meaning of group consciousness and group initiation, which is the task of this Path.

NOVICE

The novice is the beginner. Oaths are not necessary for him, only the conscious awareness and adherence to the following five points:

1. This is not psychotherapy. It is a spiritual path.
2. He enters into it out of his own choice.
3. It goes beyond the dissolution of personal problems into challenging of old belief systems and replacing them

with new ones.

4. He should, therefore, keep an open mind and consider any new eventuality as far as the universe, creation, his life, his fate are concerned.

5. He should not believe anything he does not experience or anything he does not wish to believe.

ASPIRANT

The aspirant takes an oath to:

1. Understand, respect and adhere to the five points made to the novice.

2. Be on this Path for the sake of his purification, not for any other ulterior motive.

3. Forswear any and all collusions and maligning, by an oath to expose the one who maligns to the one who is maligned, by also challenging a person who says anything negative about a third person. This should be done by the three parties involved, openly revealing what was being said, thus verifying truth or falsehood and dissolving any cowardly character assassination.

4. Face any and all negativities he finds within himself so as to dissolve them, without exception.

5. Not resist any confrontation by his brothers and sisters on the Path, superior or inferior, and before rebuttal, seriously, honestly and courageously consider whether there is a grain of truth contained in the confrontation, accepting this truth with gratitude. This is to be done no matter how unpleasant the confrontation seems to be.

6. Confront honestly and courageously any negativity he sees in his brothers and sisters on this Path, superior or inferior, without displacing onto that confrontation any of his own cases, irrationalities or vendettas. It is understood here, since no one human is perfect, that this can only be

respected in a relative way. It is further understood that no matter how imperfect is a confrontation it is preferable to its omission and repression.

7. Work honestly and courageously toward revealing and dissolving all negative feelings and thoughts, knowing that they constitute harmful, poisonous energy forms for everyone concerned. These are worse in their effect when their exposure is omitted.

8. Understand and dissolve the difference between owning up and revealing the lower self—a Higher Self act—and dumping negativity—an act of the mask. This is to apply in group, individual sessions or in casual, everyday life.

9. Study and apply the material given in the sermons.

10. The practice of Daily Review and daily prayer.

11. Attend the activities of the training program, i.e., individual sessions, group, conceptual format, or sermon transcription, weekly services.

Baptism can be taken from the grade of aspirant on up.

DISCIPLE

A disciple begins to give what he has received, teaches what he was taught. He qualifies for a position of responsibility, leading a committee or representing the Path community to the world around him. Therefore, if he still feels any of the following and he cannot master that feeling, he does not belong in this category; he is still an aspirant and not yet a disciple:

1. Shame of The Church of the Path®.

2. Fear that it might be a cult.

3. Fear that it has ulterior motives towards him, such as robbing him of his money, brainwashing him, forcing him to do what he does not want to do.

4. Superiority due to his worldly position or his wealth.

As a disciple, he is able to recognize all of these, if they still exist, and not allow them to be acted out. It is understood that, although he may still experience their existence, he is able to master them.

The difference between an aspirant and a disciple is, in a way, the same as between an adolescent and an adult. The adolescent has the body of an adult but has not as yet mastered his lower self. He, therefore, cannot be trusted with responsibility. The adult may still have a lower self but he has learned to manage it. He is still in the process of educating it. However, he can be trusted because he can be depended upon to manifest his Higher Self when the need arises, or when discharging his responsibilities. Therefore, as a disciple, he:

1. Commits to the requirements of the aspirant.

2. Commits to clearly defining his lower self concerning any of his responsibilities.

3. Commits to do his utmost to put aside his lower self—not repress it—while discharging those responsibilities.

4. Commits to serve individual and group, knowing that what is good for one is always good for the other.

5. Commits to finding whatever is preventing the manifestation of (4) on an individual and on a group level.

6. Commits to confronting this problem until it is resolved, using Spiritual Laws, meditation, and the help of all concerned.

The following is an example of a disciple's commitment:

"I commit myself to daily prayer to God, to Christ, and to my spirit guides to help me in cleansing these motives and in exposing them in the supervisory formats that are appropriate.

"I dedicate myself to my work of purification on myself which I know is a fundamental prerequisite for the discharging of my duties as a teacher.

"I commit myself to becoming a model in all possible ways to the people I help.

"I commit myself to working continuously on any authority problems that I may still have. I realize that it is impossible for me to be an authority as long as I still harbour authority problems. I also realize that on the irrational level I still harbour these problems and that they have to be kept in check continuously and assiduously.

"I commit myself to willingly go through the inevitable negativity, hatred and maligning from those whom I help. I understand that this pain is a necessary experience. I also understand that the pain remains minimal as long as I am not involved and dependent. The pain, therefore, becomes a yardstick for me to use in order to know how involved I am with the people I help. I commit myself to using that yardstick in my work on myself and in my supervisory formats.

"I commit myself to refrain from colluding with the people that I help and to expose all of my desires to collude no matter how subtly they still exist in my soul.

"I commit myself to keep confidential all of the material that comes up in private sessions. I understand that it is entirely the responsibility of the worker to divulge or reveal this material to other members of the group or to the public. I also commit myself to lead this person to make restitution for whatever harm he has done which has been admitted to me confidentially during a private session.

"I commit myself to the building of the Path community. I understand that this is a spiritual Path whose task is to form a community of people who live under the same Spiritual Laws. I commit myself to that community and I commit myself to contribute my utmost to its building and to its thriving.

"I commit myself to continue and persist in my work as a teacher with as much integrity as I can possibly muster. I understand that by taking this oath I establish a strong bond with those people that I help. The dissolution of this bond on the outer level is very harmful to them and to myself. I commit myself not to do so."

CODE OF CONDUCT AND OATH FOR TEACHERS

In order to qualify as a teacher, one needs to have taken discipleship commitments and to have shown a capacity to respect them and to abide by them for an acceptable period of time.

The amount of time is determined by the Board of Examiners, and it varies with each individual. It cannot be set in terms of time, space or other three-dimensional consideration, rather it is something that is felt when someone has abided by his commitments for a while.

It is understood by the teacher that not only is he responsible for the cleansing of his own soul but that he is also taking responsibility for the cleansing of other people's souls. Each one of these souls is as important as his own. Therefore, he has a responsibility to continue his work of purification on this Path, perhaps even to accelerate it.

If he does, then his work as a teacher with other people will magnify his own process and his progress will be that much more intensified. If he does not, his teachership will become a burden. Those he helps will add to his woes and to his problems, hooking into his problems through the process of transference and counter-transference.

It is, therefore, very important at this point of entrance into teachership to recommit to this Path. If he does not, perhaps it is time to leave. He has gotten everything that he could get here, and it is time for him to say, "This is not for me."

If he does want to continue with earnestness and good will, the Oath for Teachers as found in our Code of Conduct, must be taken.

DUTY OF THE TEACHER

If a teacher has negative feelings for a worker and is unable to clear them, the teacher has the responsibility and the duty to resign as a teacher of that particular person.

For example, if a teacher is tempted to respond to a worker's sexual feelings or if a teacher himself has sexual feelings that he seems to be unable to dissolve, resolve or neutralize, he must immediately resign as the teacher of this person. It is important that this resignation be done before any acting out. This acting out, or precipitation of these feelings from the astral level to the physical level, would take the form of passes, flirtation, verbal suggestions or anything that might communicate seductiveness in any way.

Failure to conform to this will result in immediate dismissal of this person as a teacher not only to that person, but also to others that he helps.

The above example which is used from the field of sexuality for clarity also applies to any other situation, such as collusion concerning an addiction, financial involvement, etc.

CHAPTER 39
BUDDHISM
A REINTERPRETATION FROM THE POINT OF VIEW OF THE NEW DISPENSATION

COMMENTARY ON EARLY TEACHINGS OF BUDDHA

Just as it is very valuable to study the life of Christ and to learn from it, it is valuable to study the life of Buddha. He was born a prince to fabulous wealth and opulent life conditions. His father wanted to protect him against the experience of anything negative. It is almost tempting to say that his father must have belonged to a positive thinking church. So, the little prince grew up to be a handsome young man, developing nicely in all of the arts and sciences, learning the skills of war, marrying a beautiful princess and having a child. Essentially, he lived in paradise. We can make a connection between this and the state of Adam and Eve before eating from the Tree of Knowledge.

At age twenty-nine the Buddha and his charioteer ventured out of the palace property. They encountered old age, misery and death. This came as a shock to the young prince. The charioteer told him that life was like this and that some day this was going to happen to him. He returned to the palace full of disillusion and despair.

Now this is where the story that is told conflicts with reality. The story says that he decided to leave. This does not make sense. Before he left, he must have had a huge fight with his father, his mother, his wife and everybody around him who had so desperately tried to keep him in illusion. He must have been in an enormous dilemma between maintaining the status quo as he had known it in the palace on the one hand, and pursuing the truth on the other. His decision to leave was not an easy one.

This element of doubt and struggle is not talked about when this story is related by Buddhists. Nevertheless, it represents the most significant of all struggles, the most difficult of all passages in a person's life. It demonstrates the destruction of the umbilical connection and shows the necessity to do so if one is to find wisdom or enter the Path. It corresponds to what every single person who has entered a Path of Purification has experienced. Indeed, everyone on the Path has had to break the status quo, the negative contracts established with his family and his old connections. He has had to denounce and renounce all that was taught to him, rethink it all and discover the truth or untruth of it through the Path. He has had to go through and experience hatred of parents, the way it is expressed by the Christ in the Bible and in the forgotten Gospel of Thomas. He has had to experience the reality that his task does not bring him peace but a sword.

I feel that the Buddha actually had his little trip outside the palace at age twenty-eight. For a year, he experienced the destruction of everything he believed in. This destruction was going on inside of himself. The decision to leave was merely the bringing to the outer level that which had already been accomplished on the inner level. By breaking his ties with everybody, he put it into motion. This is what happens on the Path. This is a necessary step for anyone who undergoes spiritual growth.

By removing the whole element of crisis and of pain, the Buddhists are creating a new status quo, the Buddhist status quo. Having become themselves the authority, the Buddhist organizations are now suffering from the same mimesis as the Christians. (See the section on Mimesis in the chapter entitled "The Call to Your Task.")

So he left and sought enlightenment. He wandered from one ascetic teacher to the next, following another form of status quo, the antithesis to the previous one. Whereas there was opulence and materialism in its exaggerated form in his previous state, there now was asceticism, denial of form.

At some point at age thirty-five (here again I think it is thirty-three, corresponding to the Christ's final teachings and death) he sat under a tree and discovered that what he had been doing by pursuing asceticism was just as negative as what he did throughout his youth. He realized that one escaped the truth either by being too attached to form or too attached to anti-form, erroneously called the inner life. So he decided that the truth was to be found through the middle way. He saw this clearly by attaining a state which he called nirvana, we call it cosmic consciousness.

BUDDHISM

In that state, he put together the teachings that now consist of the Buddhist religion. They are divided into the following sections:

A. **The necessity to recognize the omnipresence of the Law of Cause and Effect.**

This is a sine qua non condition for entering the Path. It is for the Buddhists as well as for us here at The Church of the Path®. Indeed, he had to recognize the Law of Cause and Effect when he, for the first time in his life, came in contact with old age, disease and death.

This recognition of the Law of Cause and Effect is the

fundamental prerequisite of the Path. This requirement must be respected. If anyone is not ready or willing to accept this as a prerequisite, he does not belong on the Path. From this necessity comes another one that we hold here at The Church of the Path®. And that is

B. **The willingness to be open to any possibility of change in your innermost set of beliefs.** You must be ready to put in question anything you have learned. You must be willing to place it on the chopping block, to abandon it, to change it, to dissolve it, or to re-experience it in new ways. This does not mean that you are forced to believe in anything that you do not experience. On the contrary, we stress the fact that you must not believe in anything that you do not experience. However, you must be open to the possibility that there might be a new way of thinking.

During his meditation, the Buddha brought to clarity the teachings that he later imparted. He first devised the doctrine of the Middle Path.

C. **The Doctrine of the Middle Path.** The Buddha experienced two extremes before enlightenment. The first was the extreme of ostentatiousness, the illusion created by material possessions and by the bourgeois status quo. The second was the illusion of asceticism and of total abstention, disconnection from life. His great realization, which significantly put him apart from the Hindu religion existing at that time, was that spirituality was to be found somewhere in between those two extreme illusions. As the key word says for Libra: "I choose the way that leads between the two great lines of forces." Anything that is pursued with intensity is a violation of Spiritual Law, and, therefore, brings unhappiness. It is a function of demand and, therefore, it brings despair.

We agree with this position. They both represent

glamours. They cater to the idolized self whether it be bourgeois or ascetic. We very much agree with the Buddha that one has to live reasonably. However, we also believe that a certain amount of luxury is necessary if one is to be able to afford spiritual pursuit.

We also believe that succumbing to the pursuit of bourgeois ostentatious material possessions or of the ascetic life constitutes a line of least resistance, a laziness. In both cases, the individual settles into a life of no struggle, no risk, no resiliency, no flexibility, no creativity. Thus, in both cases, there is no growth. Both extreme positions lead to regression.

How does one find the Middle Path? By adhering to the Four Noble Truths as follows:

D. **The Four Noble Truths.**

1. **Attachment to things and to people and to the environment brings suffering.** In our teachings, we find this to be true only when we talk about the false life. As we have seen in so many lessons, the false life is created by: a. the abandonment of our real instinctual needs, and, b. opting to become that which we are not in order to please our parents, society and the environment.

The type of desire which is created in this way is intense, forced, demanding, obsessive and addictive. There comes a point in a person's life when this has to be abandoned. Surely, in the life of the Buddha himself that point was reached when at age twenty-nine he realized that his life as a prince in the palace, marriage, fatherhood and all was a function of the false life. It was not rooted in reality. Therefore, he had to abandon the whole thing. His entire lifestyle, having been so thoroughly permeated by falsehood, having been created by falsehood and being a function of falsehood had to be destroyed.

The suffering that he experienced through this is not a function of the nature of marriage or of success or of abundance. It is a lot more a function of having made those positive aspects into the enemy of his Real Self and of reality, thus creating duality. It is creation of duality through illusion, untruth, that brings about suffering. Being anchored in reality cannot and will not bring suffering, it can only bring happiness.

Is there guilt involved in Buddha leaving his family or in Gauguin leaving his to pursue his task in the South Seas? Is there guilt involved in the Christ denying His mother and saying that one has to forsake his family in order to be a follower? Just about everyone who has done anything significant in his life has had to, in one way or another, burn his bridges. The answer is there is no guilt. If there is, it is false guilt—and false guilt is capable of leading to real secondary guilt. What is being abandoned is the lie, the illusion, falsehood, duality. To the degree those attachments are based on falsehood, to that degree breaking them does not create guilt. On the contrary, continuing to maintain them would create guilt—real guilt. The guilt for abandonment is false guilt.

Every single person who has embraced the Path has had to do what Buddha, Christ, Gauguin and the others have done. Every one of us has had to disengage from the negative contracts that we had with our parents and our parent substitutes. Sometimes, even our children are our parent substitutes and we have had to separate from them for the same reason. To the degree these people from whom we disengage are connected to this falsehood, to that degree the disengaging becomes a necessity, a condition of entering the Path. If these people want to abandon their negative contracts and to join us on the Path, then we do not have to leave them. We can continue our relationship with them. However, it will not be the same. It will be more of an equal to equal relationship. In some cases it will be a teacher to student relationship which may seem unfamiliar.

For example, a person on the Path may become his parents' teacher. How does that sit with the parents? How much will they like it? To the degree they do not, they are still attached to the old negative contract which is obsolete and which must be broken.

2. **The cause of suffering is desire, craving for sensual pleasure, continued existence, and annihilation; for happiness in all places, accompanied by joy and covetousness, which lead to rebirth.** Again, here one must differentiate between positive desire and negative desire.

Nothing exists without desire. The universe was created because of desire. Any act of creativity, including the Buddha bringing out his teachings, is a function of desire. He desired the teachings. Later, with Brahma's exhortations, he desired to give them because he had received them. One desires unity away from duality. Negatively one desires duality. That is the desire that is negative and must, therefore, be given up. Giving up desire is worse than death. It is the death of the soul. As long as there is life, as long as there is consciousness, there is desire. Consciousness desires energy to mold it; energy desires consciousness for guidance. This is a law of the universe, God's law.

Let's distinguish between two things, sexual pleasure and sensual pleasure. Sexual pleasure is one of the sensual pleasures. Let's deal with sexual pleasure first. Sexual pleasure, when integrated is the most powerful force in the universe and the most pleasurable. People find God in sexual pleasure. The orgasm, the at-one explosion of two people giving and taking with each other is God manifest.

How did the Buddha feel about women? When the Buddha was asked how to respond to women he advised that we should not see them, that we should abstain from speech with them and that we should keep wide awake around them. Here is the unfortunate cruelty towards half of the human race perpetrated as advocated by Buddhism. It is as bad, if not worse, than Christianity as advocated by Paul in I Corinthians.

Are women entitled to spiritual development on an equal footing with men? According to Buddha, no. Women are decidedly inferior. There is almost a sense of derision about them and a definite sense of mistrust.

Needless to say, we do not agree with any of this. Women are just as entitled to respect and spiritual development as are men. Granted, in those days, women kept themselves in an inferior position in order to be taken care of. However, two wrongs do not make a right. It was very much part of the Buddha's duty to make it possible for women to grow, as the Christ did. Here is, then, where the Buddha is inferior to the Christ. Christ never put women down. His followers did. And Buddha did.

Other sensual pleasures. *What's wrong with the ecstatic enjoyment of food or swimming or an occasional candy?* The enjoyment, the pleasure, the joy, the bliss involved is God's healing. It has been made by God, we have to respect it and we have to practice it. There is nothing wrong with any of this.

So why did Buddha in his ultimate wisdom name craving for sensual pleasure as the cause of suffering? Because in his days there was so much abuse of sexuality and sensuality that it was necessary to disengage from it in order to find spiritual reality. This is true of the Christian faith as much as it is true of the Buddhist faith.

Humanity has had to undergo a period of time during which the finding of spirituality, being on the Path, required disconnection from sexuality and sensuality. However, we are way past this point now. As a matter of fact we are very much into the result of this repression—apathy and numbness.

Why are we so apathetic, having become couch potatoes in seeing our pleasures in a passive way rather than in an active way? Because, for so many hundreds of years pleasure was seen as a problem, forbidden. In actuality, pleasure is connected to movement. If there is no pleasure there is no movement. So, people have become numb to the point where they had rather not move from fear that they will do something evil.

It is high time that this change. If there is one affliction that can be attributed to people on the Path it is apathy, inertia. It is time to move and enter a vigorous path that unifies and illuminates those human activities. There can be no unity unless people integrate sexuality and sensuality into their path.

A path that disconnects from sexuality and sensuality on the physical level advocates duality; it creates a dualistic situation by definition, which is exactly opposite to what the Buddha is trying to teach. Thus, new Buddhism and new Christianity must be inclusive of those sexual pleasures, not exclusive. The old exclusive religion must be given up for the new inclusive one.

Now let's deal with "desire for continued existence." There is a positive aspect to wanting continued existence, it is called the Instinct of Self-Preservation. Its divine consummation is the realization of immortality. Continued existence is a very positive thing indeed. The most positive thing ever. Thus, the desire for continued existence must be seen as such. One loses the fear of death by not having given up the desire for continued existence. The giving up the desire for continued existence is the giving up on life. It is done out of fear of life.

Fear of death is fear of life. Fear of life and fear of death lead to the false giving up of the desire for continued existence. They lead to the escape into abstinence and the denial of life, euphemistically called "renouncing life" by the swamis.

These days there is a way to achieve this state of no fear of death. It is through the activation of the Instinct of Self-Preservation to the point where we realize that there is immortality, that even the death of the body is a temporary situation that reveals to us the immortality of the soul. We must also understand that the ultimate goal of humanity is immortality in the body, not just outside of it. One day it will be achieved. There is no reason why our body cannot be on a program of continuous maintenance where it maintains its eternal youth. The Masters of Wisdom have gotten to that point. They have achieved this ability to create a body that has transcended disease and death. In that sense they have—through the acceptance of reality, not through the denial of it—achieved what Buddha's father wanted for him as a prince. Instead of hiding the "facts of life"—old age, disease, and death— it is through the facing of these problems, and the transcending of them, that one finds the eternal youthful state and the eternal happiness that Buddha's father sought for his son.

What about annihilation? It says here, "the cause of suffering is desire, craving for continued existence and annihilation." Well, the desire for false existence, the dualistic one, the one that denies the problems rather than facing them, the faithless one, will bring desire for annihilation. We have seen this so many times, particularly in the lectures on instincts and needs. The false existence, the false life to which we have attached ourselves, denies and contradicts the real life and the real needs which have been denied and repressed.

Thus, at some point we are bound to want to destroy the false life, since its existence is a continuous reminder of the denial of our real needs and of our Real Self. This is what the Buddha experienced at age twenty-nine. This is the type of annihilation that he desired. The desire for this type of annihilation is positive, it will happen to all of us. We call it the point of relinquishing, the point of outrage. However, in this new age and in this new dispensation it is the annihilation of what is false in the false life and the preservation of what is true and good in it. Thus, it is not either the false life or the new. It is the new life preserving what is right out of the false life and re-energizing it while discarding what is false.

"Desire for happiness in all places, accompanied by joy and covetousness, which lead to rebirth." In our days, this has become a dualistic statement. The "desire for happiness in all places, accompanied by joy" is positive. It is what God wants for us. The pursuit of happiness was sought when the precursors of the new dispensation gave us the Universal Declaration of Human Rights in the eighteenth century. The pursuit of happiness in all places and in joy is not just an option, but a duty. It is our duty to God to find happiness in all places, happiness accompanied by joy and bliss and ecstasy. As I have said so very often: anything short of total happiness and bliss which is greater than you ever expected means the existence within you of a desire to violate the laws of God and to live in duality?

So the first part of the sentence "for happiness in all

places, accompanied by joy" does not belong to the second part of the sentence that says "and covetousness which lead to rebirth." Covetousness is antithetical to happiness and joy in all places. Covetousness is a function of duality. If I am covetous, it means that I am intensely desiring something. I can only intensely desire something and demand fulfillment in this way if I have limited myself in my concept of fulfillment. It is only when I try to squeeze the infinite into the finite that it becomes obsessive. If the infinite is allowed expression as it really is, it will be experienced as light, as joyous, as hopeful, but also as capable of sustaining rejection and non-fulfillment. It is the decision that we are going to experience a particular pleasure in one way and not in another that makes us covetous. It is the decision to control the universe and not surrender to it that brings on the intensity and perfectionism and, of course, the consequent despair and death which leads to rebirth.

Let's take an example. If I am obsessively desirous of a woman, it means that I have seen neither her nor myself in reality. This obsession is a product of what I want her to be and what I want myself to be for her. Perhaps I want to be a knight in shining armor and see her as a damsel in distress, in which case I will be addicted to this role and addicted to finding a woman who, herself, is addicted to the role I have assigned to her. This is dualistic in that it excludes all of the other aspects and facets that belong to her, not to mention myself. If I am to include who she is in infinity, and if my perception is allowed to come from my own infinity, then there will be unity in my movement towards her and my desire for her is not going to be covetous; it is going to be a longing, a loving, a creative desire, an open energy system.

In this open energy system I will create happiness in all places accompanied by joy. Covetousness does not belong in such an open and honest system. In it I will also find the immortality which will preclude rebirth, not lead to it.

3. **Extinction of suffering is the total elimination of craving, abandoning it entirely, being liberated from it and having no attachments.** It was so 2500 years ago. It is not so today. Extinction of suffering today is the total facing and experiencing the craving, abandoning ourselves to that experience entirely, not abandoning the experience entirely. The experience of the craving does not have to include the indulgence in it. We can own up to it without acting it out. In fact, as often said in our religion, owning up to it diminishes the chances of acting it out, not the other way around. He who tries to quickly eliminate craving or abandon it entirely will find himself compelled to act it out in the worst possible conditions. He will be creating duality. He has to drink the craving, the cup of karma, to the fullest. He has to experience it fully, albeit on the astral level in order to come to the point where he will dissolve it. He will see that by dissolving it there is no loss, there is everything to gain.

So, "being liberated from it and having no attachments" will be reached through the full experience of those negative attachments, the taking responsibility of what it is in us that has created those negative attachments and the redressing of those mistakes. Then, we will be truly liberated from those attachments once and for all.

Consider little children. You can tell them not to eat candy until you are blue in the face. They will continue to desire candy and want to eat it. It is through the total experience of this greed and infatuation and through the experience of the effect that it has on their bodies that they will finally want to give it up, see the light. Gradually, they will find out that the same sensual pleasures can be found in other places which are a lot healthier and a lot more at-one with their adult task. They will see that there is no difference between the craving in its original form, which is nothing else but positive desire, and the task, with its fulfillment. No task can be achieved as long as it is dualistically separated from pleasure.

Thus, we arrive at a general common denominator throughout these three Noble Truths:

Only through living life to the fullest can one achieve liberation, true detachment and enlightenment. Escape from those desires through the artificial elimination of them, through a tour de force, as it were, is what precisely leads to our worst possible problems.

4. **The Eightfold Noble Path is the Noble Truth of the Path to the Extinction of Suffering.** This, too, has to be reworded. The Path has not for goal the mere extinction of suffering. The goal of the Path is happiness, the pursuit of happiness. Bliss, ecstasy, joy, pleasure, happiness, fulfillment, creativity must be found in a total fashion. This, then, is the Path.

THE EIGHTFOLD NOBLE PATH

a. **Right View.** This means right perception. In order to reach it, one has to clear one's self of the desire for the wrong perception. Indeed, this desire is present in us practically from the minute we are born. In order to escape the suffering of disconnection from God experienced at birth, we have made our parents into gods. This is wrong view. It still is around us. This retreat from pain by creating easy solutions is still being done by just about all of us. It nurtures the wrong conclusion—that the three-dimensional world creates suffering. If I hold that belief, it then becomes in my best self-interest to see the world out there as a negative world that will make me suffer so I can justify my escape from it. This escape may have been valid at the time of Buddha. It is no longer valid today. In fact, doing today what Buddha did 2500 years ago is the same as burying ourselves in asceticism. It is not the Middle Path.

The Middle Path today must be perceived as the integration of three-dimensional reality, the penetration of it, the purification of our outer-level life. The removal of the ways that we have wanted to think wrongly will reveal a good and benign universe.

b. **Right Thinking.** On our Path of Purification, we adjust our mental level to the laws of God that are to be found on the spiritual level. Right thinking becomes the detection and the dissolution of all of our wrong conclusions.

One of them has already been addressed under the heading of Right View. It is the belief that the world out there is negative and, therefore, in order to stop suffering, I have to disconnect from it. In fact, there are two misconceptions here: (1) That the world out there is negative, and, (2) In order to find happiness, I must disconnect from it. We have dealt with both misconceptions in the previous sections. Let's deal with some others in this one.

Take, for instance, the disconnection between love and power. It creates in our thinking self a multitude of misconceptions. Let's try to list a few of them:

1. Power is devoid of love and, therefore, always negative.

2. Love is devoid of power and, therefore, always vulnerable even though positive.

3. Strong is bad.

4. Weak is good.

Of course, none of this is true. Power without love is

negative power. It eventually disappears and dies. There is no power without love. Power without love is illusion. Also, love is the most powerful force in the universe. There is no love without power. Love gives you power and makes you creative. You do not have to be submissive when you love or when you want to be loved. Furthermore, loving sometimes must be expressed through anger or unpleasantness which do not make love any less valid.

    c. **Right Speech.** Words have power. They are an act. They are the crystallization of the combination of thoughts and feelings. Much harm can be done by speaking in a wrong way or by using the wrong words. Therefore, it is essential for a person on the Path:

    1. To carefully choose the words that he speaks, making sure that he uses the right coinage for whatever it is that he wants to say.

    2. To continuously be in the process of enriching his vocabulary, being open to new expressions, new words that are coming through with the new dispensation.

    3. To refrain from negativity, harmfulness in words which can come either through hostile expression or through pseudo-positive ones which, of course, hide hostile intent.

    4. To heed the messages behind the way he misspeaks, making full use of the opportunity that those mistakes bring to him in terms of finding out what are the inner negativities that have created them.

    The continuous practice of this type of discipline will bring the individual to the point where he will finally be able to express himself spontaneously and harmlessly at the same time. To the degree a person lives the Path, to that degree his expressions are spontaneous, coming out harmless and harmonious.

    d. **Right Action.** This is perhaps the most misunderstood

requirement on the Path. It is particularly misunderstood by those who believe they are spiritual. Erroneously, action is seen as a priori negative by those disciples. Non-action is seen as preferable in most cases. One talks about non-participation, non-cooperation, non-violence. Of course, in some circumstances, non-violence is very effective. It was against the British when Gandhi practiced it.

However, what would Gandhi have done in Auschwitz? What would have happened if Gandhi had been in Churchill's position? Or in FDR's? The answer to this is very simple—the Nazis would have taken over the world and we would have been set back into dark ages that would have lasted another thousand years.

Right action, right violence, right military intervention, right anger, right overturning of tables, right disciplining must all be restored to their legitimate position. They must be seen as valid expressions of love, as the implementation of the will of God.

Guilt by omission—non-action—should be seen as worse than guilt by commission. Indeed, if I am witness to a murder without doing anything about it, I am doubly guilty. I am guilty of murder since I participated, albeit vicariously, in the murder in question. I am also guilty for not doing anything about it.

When will those who call themselves spiritual, ever understand that action is a function of the First Ray and it has its place right alongside love/wisdom and active intelligence?

e. **Right Living.** It is important for the disciple to develop good habits in his life. Taking it from the physical point of view first, the disciple must bring his eating, drinking and exercising in line with the Path. He must practice harmlessness with himself. He must also be a good husband, father and citizen, discharging his duties in a harmless way, which means in a way that contributes to the welfare of everyone concerned. Therefore, any negative occurrence in any of these matters, whether it is on the level of friendship, on the level of romantic relationships, on the level of parenting or on the level of profession must be seen as an opportunity to become fully aware of the harmfulness that he creates accordingly.

When this is realized, right steps must be taken to redress the situation. It is not by being celibate, by renouncing the world, or by sitting under a tree and meditating that any of these experiences will be undergone. By not going through them we never grow. We never have the opportunity of releasing and purifying our insides.

Part of our task is to bring with us at birth some negative aspects that we are to dissolve during a particular lifetime. The dissolution of those negativities adds to the bank of experience of humanity. By dissolving my negativity, I make my experience available for others to tap into and emulate. If I do not bring any negativity with me, or if I refuse to partake of life, and, therefore, do not resolve those negativities, what is the point of my life? My life has no meaning. I am a mere parasite on the universe.

Thus, abstaining from life, from sex, from struggling, from having a job is the coward's way out. Far from being superior and spiritual, those people are inferior and regressive. Again, it was not always this way. At the time of Buddha things were different. It was necessary to "renounce life" in order to find spirituality. It no longer is today. Right living today is the penetration of all of life, the integration of it.

 f. **Right Effort.** We often refer here to the swimmer as an allegory to the way we handle life. Indeed, like the swimmer, a certain amount of effort is required to stay afloat and to swim. However, to a large extent we surrender and we trust the waters of life, the Universal Life Force and the Universal Consciousness. We swim with them.

Right effort is always light, elegant, devoid of affectation and of demands, trusting and willing to undergo frustration. Right effort, nothing else, is what the ego must do to put the rest of ourselves in sync with nature. Any more would bring less. *Le mieux est l'ennemi du bien.* (The better is the enemy of the good.)

g. **Right Memory.** The reason we do not remember is because we do not want to. The loss of memory represents the intentional block to the full experience of the Law of Cause and Effect. It simply is too painful—we have decided—to take full responsibility. We would rather see ourselves as victims of chaos. So we opt for amnesia.

The dissolution of the intent to have amnesia makes it possible for us to re-establish our capacity to remember. We will understand what is happening to us now in a way that is equivalent to the recovery of the lost memory or we will remember. New experiences will be finally interpreted in the right way. Thus, we may not have to recover memories of past lives, for example, where the same occurrences have been experienced. So, what needs to be recovered is quality of memory not quantity.

For instance, a doctor may treat hundreds of patients who have the same ailment. He may not remember each one of the patients he has treated. However, he remembers the pattern of circumstances that he must treat and reacts accordingly.

By focusing on the aspect of quality, memory, combined with cause and effect, makes our life a lot easier. This mechanism of apprehending cause and effect necessitating memory in terms of quality not quantity constitutes the progress that we have achieved over our Atlantean predecessors. Their memory was far greater than ours. Through quantity they had to remember and reconstruct the Law of Cause and Effect. For example, two plus two equals four was for them a matter of memory. They had to see two objects coming together with two other objects and, therefore, creating four objects, instead of memorizing the concept alone once and for all. This greater efficiency on our part will make it possible for us to eventually achieve greater progress than the Atlanteans.

So, right memory for us is different than right memory for the Atlanteans. It is necessary to remember on the qualitative level not on the quantitative level. Therefore, past life regressions and past life memory are reduced to very secondary importance—if important at all—in the progress of the individual.

Is there any difference between memory now and memory at the time of Buddha? People at the time of Buddha were a lot closer to the Atlanteans. They had phenomenal memory, much greater than ours. As recently as the Middle Ages, in spite of all the darkness in terms of intelligence, people had extraordinary memory, far greater than ours. Nevertheless, they were still in their infancy in terms of their development. The capacity to remember on the qualitative level in no way means a superior mind or person. The capacity to make connections on the qualitative level constitutes a far superior ability, one that is serving us well in this day and age.

h. **Right Meditation.** It is very important to realize that meditation is not an exercise in meaningless pleasantry. It is not merely sitting mindlessly while nice music is playing in the background. If you are going to do that, might as well get drunk—at least you would be a lot more honest in your intentions.

Meditation is a very specific process which has five steps to it.

The first step is concentration, the emptying of the mind.

The second step is the stating of the problem and the desired solution as we see it at that point.

The third stage is the consideration and the experience of that which contradicts the fulfillment that we desire and the weighing of the merits and the demerits of this contradiction.

The fourth is a stage of surrender to the universe, allowing it to guide us, since we have done all the work required.

And the fifth is the stage in which visualization, the right blueprint of what needs to be done, thought, or felt occurs to us in minute, exquisite detail.

Thus, a meditation can take a minute or a year. One can enter into meditation about a subject and leave it an hour later, merely having gone through the first two stages, or not even have gone through the first. Gradually, through the right practice of meditation, the disciple learns how to accelerate this process. The first steps come to him quicker and quicker as he masters life to the point where they occur to him automatically, first on the emotional level and then on the mental level. Finally, on the spiritual level his life becomes a continuous process of meditation. This is the goal on the Path.

INTENT

It is extremely important to bring up the principle of intent as a huge factor in the ability to be on the Path and to implement the eight rules.

Particularly in Buddhism, the Law of Cause and Effect and its implementation is understood as primordial, essential. In order to understand and implement the Law of Cause and Effect, commitment is necessary. That, too, is understood. However, what is not understood is that positive intent must exist in order for commitment to be possible and for the Law of Cause and Effect to be totally apprehended.

Harmful volition is in existence to the degree commitment is not. For example, if somebody is committed at 80% to a task, 20% of him negatively intends to go the opposite way.

If we were to consider the eight rightnesses that we have considered above, in order to fully implement them, the person must ask himself, *"How is it that I want not to have right view, not to think rightly, not to speak harmlessly, not to act in the right way, not to live right, not to exert effort, not to remember, and not to meditate? What are the specific ways that I do this in my life? What are the consequences in accordance with the Law of Cause and Effect for not doing this and for intending not to? And how do I mask that harmful volition? How to I pretend to be practicing right view, right thinking, right speech, right action, right living, right effort, right memory, right meditation? How do I force all of those rightnesses on myself while negating, refusing to face the part of me that has harmful volition?"* All of this is totally omitted from Buddhism, as well as from all the Hindu disciplines.

We encounter this in its distorted form in Christianity, through the concept of evil. However, the way it is presented there is in a very static fashion, one that is not conducive to progress, to the dissolution of these negativities.

So, the modern Buddhist on the Path must do the work we are doing in order to achieve the Eight Fold Noble Path of his religion. If he does not, he will never be a Buddhist.

THREE STAGES FOR EACH NOBLE TRUTH

In Buddhism they also talk about the three stages needed for each noble truth. They are described as follows: (1) Theoretical understanding of the truth, (2) Putting the truth into practice, traveling the full path, knowing pain and its nature, (3) Theory and practice are at-one. The person is ready for the highest enlightenment.

This describes the process of penetration of problems as we practice it on the Path. For instance, if I am involved in wrong speech, I must first theoretically understand that I am involved in it in order for me to straighten it out. I must also understand why I should practice right speech. The understanding of it at first is theoretical. I have not experientially made the causal connection between all of these truths and the actual experiences in my life.

This brings us to the second stage in which I put the truth into practice. The "knowing pain" is the process of discovering how I create the pain through my harmful volition, through my negativity and through my lack of commitment. Harmful volition and lack of commitment result in pain. That then is the manifestation of the Law of Cause and Effect. If I speak harmfully, I will inflict pain and experience pain.

In this stage I understand the true nature of pain. Pain is the consequence of wrong thinking and wrong feelings which result, for example, in wrong speech. Any wrongfulness, anything anti-nature on any level of myself creates pain. This is the true nature of pain. Conscious or unconscious, my pain exists. As those connections are made, that unconscious pain becomes conscious.

Thus, we reach the third level where theory and practice become one, where I am in the state in which I experientially know that the practice of harmlessness protects me from pain, makes me ward it off. For instance, even before I speak I am conscious of the fact that I need to speak harmlessly. When theory and practice are at one, I speak harmlessly in a spontaneous manner.

CONCLUSION

The Buddha brought a new wave of enlightenment to the existing religions. He was to the East what the Christ was to the West. It is interesting to note that Buddhism is far more successful east of India, Buddha's birthplace. It is the Chinese and the Japanese who have taken up Buddhism, not the Indians. This, once again, confirms that no one can be a prophet in his own country.

CHAPTER 40
THE TEN COMMANDMENTS
A REINTERPRETATION FROM THE POINT OF VIEW OF THE NEW DISPENSATION

1 Corinthians 13:11:
> *When I was a child, I spake as a child, I understood as a child, I thought as a child: but when I became a man, I put away childish things.*

It is time to approach the Ten Commandments as grown-ups. This means that we must raise them to the inner level, being concerned with inner deity, as we, as children, were concerned with outer.

Commandment I
Deuteronomy *5:7:Thou shalt have none other gods before me.*

Looking at this on the inner level:
(a) One must be anchored in the belief in the One True God, the Divine, not the idols, which are many.
We have made our idolized self our God. Looking at your idolized self, you will find that it consists of many idols, colluding and/or contradicting one another. This is the source of all unhappiness.
Cultivation of faith in The One God must, therefore, include the detection and dissolution of all idolized selves.

This is our Faith. Worshiping one God destroys all idols, inner and outer.

(b) The dissolution of idols also dissolves the harmful volition that has created them and that lies—pardon the pun—behind them.

(c) The devalued self (depreciated self), also created by the formation of the idolized selves, will consequently show itself and die as well.

Commandment II

Deuteronomy 5:8: *Thou shalt not make thee any graven image or any likeness of any thing that is in heaven above, or that is in the earth beneath, or that is in the waters beneath the earth.*

Islam, by limiting itself to the outer level meaning of this, deprived its civilization of portraits or paintings of God's creation. However, in spite of this rigidity, we find, in Islam itself, a high degree of understanding of the problem of images, for example in Mulla Sadra, as well as in many other philosophies.

The true, inner meaning of this has to do with substituting reality with its **image**, reducing it and petrifying it, thus creating falsehood.

The formation of images, freezes, petrifies us in falsehood and compels us to evil.

Deuteronomy 5:9: *Thou shalt not bow down thyself unto them, nor serve them.*

We obey our images and our idolized selves by patterning our lives after them, consciously or unconsciously. We attract situations that prove our illusions and repel those that prove reality. Any obedience to falsehood is a betrayal of God.

Deuteronomy 5:9: ***...for the LORD thy God am a jealous God ...***

God's jealousy has nothing to do with Him being hurt by your betrayal, the way your lover would be. So, don't go play power trips with Him by betraying Him the way you betrayed your father or your husband, your wife or your mother.

This brings up the motivation behind betrayal of authority: taunting authority, thus demonstrating power over it. This is an addictive, automatic reaction meant to get attention in a harmful way, out of the inability to captivate, total benign—loving—attention in an exclusive way. This false interpretation of God's jealousy is therefore a function of immaturity.

In reality, it has to do with cause and effect. Violate reality—God's creation—and you create your own unhappiness.

But there is another meaning here. God's jealousy means that He will not let you get away with it. The consequences of your violations will not be removed. You must suffer them. That is God's punishment. It is implacable. He will not remove causality for the sake of your distorted self, or of your other selves. Were He to do this, He too would be obeying the evil that you have created.

When you do not want to pay the price for your transgressions, God will appear vengeful and jealous.

When you pay the price, God will be seen by you as merciful, loving, compassionate, and forgiving, which is His real face.

When you do not want to pay the price, **you** are mean, jealous, vengeful, and egocentric. Seeing God that way is the result of your own projection of your own distortions onto Him. You do this because you do not have the courage to face this evil within yourself. So, you accuse God of the very evil that you create. This is an abomination, a double and triple distortion. You have seen children or friends behave this way towards you. You have seen yourself enraged by it. Why should God's reaction be any different?

Deuteronomy 5:9: *...visiting the iniquity of the fathers upon the children unto the third and fourth generation of them that hate me...*

This refers to the evil we inherit from our parents when we worship them, emulate them, rebel against them, then compulsively obey them.
It refers to your astonishment when you found yourself having become the worst of your parents—both of them, one at one time and one at another.
It refers to your astonishment when your children display the same defects as you and your parents; when you find those same problems in your grandparents or great-grandparents.
It is God punishing you if, as a child, you look at it merely on the outer level. It is you punishing yourself if you look at it on the inner, as a self-responsible adult. No one can punish you but yourself.

Deuteronomy 5:9: *...of them that hate me ...*

This refers to this projection onto God of what I find so unacceptable within myself.

Deuteronomy 5:10: *And shewing mercy unto thousands of them that love me and keep my commandments.*

Here it is: His mercy which comes through restoring all your selves to your original state, which is your love of God. Loving Him means cleansing on all levels, restoring yourself to Him. Then, causality can only bring happiness. We become God. So, the first step to Godhood is cleansing. By doing it, I place my destiny in God's hands, my hands. My hands become God's. God's hands become mine.

Commandment III
Deuteronomy 5:11: *Thou shalt not take the name of the LORD thy God in vain...*

In how many ways do we do this? Let's look at a few:

We do it continuously, consciously, and unconsciously by merely harbouring and nurturing the replacements of God: the idols, the idolized selves, the ones whom we make into gods.

We do it with wrong prayer, taking God's or Christ's name in vain, by praying that they may remove the consequences of our own evil; be careful how you pray.

We do it by taking His name for granted, overusing and abusing it.

We do it by superstitiously repeating His name and His Son's, degenerating our faith into superstition.

Deuteronomy 5:11: *...for the LORD will not hold him guiltless that taketh his name in vain.*

The mere existence of your idolized selves creates guilt, never mind the fact that you harbour, nurture, and cultivate them. At the same time, the mere existence of your depreciated selves also creates guilt, being an attack on your God-self.

In addition, wrong prayer, abusing God's and Christ's name, degenerating our faith into a superstition, all carry and create guilt.

Commandment IV

Deuteronomy 5:12-15: *[12]Keep the sabbath day to sanctify it, as the LORD thy God hath commanded thee. [13]Six days thou shalt labour, and do all thy work: [14]But the seventh day is the sabbath of the LORD thy God: in it thou shalt not do any work, thou, nor thy son, nor thy daughter, nor thy manservant, nor thy maidservant, nor thine ox, nor thine ass, nor any of thy cattle, nor thy stranger that is within thy gates; that thy manservant and thy maidservant may rest as well as thou.*

We need to rest, to be still, to be, as He is, the *I Am*, thus to receive Him and be in Him, cultivating His presence within.

It confronts our greed, the sloth of overwork.

It compels us to pray, i.e., to invoke, to cultivate receptivity, renewal by being open to the Life Force, the Divine Life Force, God's presence.

Swamis are continuously in the Sabbath. They idolized their own sloth, their deadness. Yuppies are never in the Sabbath, always achieving, even in recreation.

Deuteronomy 5:15: *And remember that thou wast a servant in the land of Egypt, and that the LORD thy God brought thee out thence through a mighty hand and by a stretched out arm: therefore the LORD thy God commanded*

thee to keep the Sabbath day.

The land of Egypt meant the land of plenty, of the easy life. We are servants of our easy life, which we take for granted. We are fat and we sell out to fat. That is how we created terrorists—to wake us up out of our fat.

We have regressed to the automaton level by taking what we have for granted and by not being open to change.

Change for God's sake, for the sake of right. You want freedom? Stop selling out to wealth.

The liberation from Egypt also corresponds to our lifting ourselves up out of the animal state, the state of slavery to the body. We do this by obeying Spiritual Law, *through a mighty hand*. Only through the hand of God can we grow.

By a stretched out arm describes the effort needed for liberation from slavery. Stretch yourself to the limit of your capacity. Stretch all your potentiality on the path to freedom.

Any growth is, therefore, related to this commandment.

Commandment V
Deuteronomy 5:16: ***Honour thy father and thy mother, as the LORD thy God hath commanded thee; that thy days may be prolonged, and that it may go well with thee, in the land which the LORD thy God giveth thee.***

Honouring parents means cleansing the harmful aspects associated with them. It means unifying them in one parent. This is one of our basic exercises done in the beginning of our Path. See The Mother/Father Split exercise my book *Know Thyself.*

We have assimilated our parents, imprinted them on our

souls. Their iniquities have visited us (Deuteronomy 5:9). We have made them our own. They have damaged our lives.

Thus, the contradiction between Deuteronomy 5:9 and 5:16 directs us to the respect of the good side of our parents, not to the harmful.

God is our only parent. We find Him in the cleansing and the unifying of our parents within us.

Respect for our parents means restoring our life to God. It must involve the dissolution of our dependency on our parents, a dependency that still exists, since we have replaced our parents with many substitutes.

This commandment must, therefore, be understood within the context of my writings entitled "Hatred of Parents Explained".

Matthew 10:37-38:
> [37]He that loveth father or mother more than me is not worthy of me: and he that loveth son or daughter more than me is not worthy of me. [38]And he that taketh not his cross, and followeth after me, is not worthy of me.

Gospel of Thomas 60:
> Jesus says: "He who does not hate his father and mother cannot be my disciple; and if he does not hate his brother and sister and does not take up his cross like me, he will not become worthy of me!"

Commandment VI
Deuteronomy 5:17: *Thou shalt not kill.*

Moses comes down with tablets that say this, sees his people worshiping the golden calf, and kills about 3,000 of them!

Exodus 32:27-28:
> ^{27}And he said unto them, Thus saith the LORD God of Israel, Put every man his sword by his side, and go in and out from gate to gate throughout the camp, and slay every man his brother, and every man his companion, and every man his neighbour. ^{28}And the children of Levi did according to the word of Moses: and there fell of the people that day about three thousand men.

So, he grossly contradicted himself. He committed not just murder, but genocide.

This was the first act of ethnic cleansing, committed by the prototype of Jewishness, to repress freedom of religion. This contradicts the purpose of the Exodus itself. So, Moses, the first ethnic cleanser, followed by worse mass murder committed by his successor Joshua, (read the gory details in Joshua) paved the way for Hitler and Stalin. The Jews, who nurture belief in the Bible, create Hitler, Stalin, Saddam Hussein, and the others who persecuted them throughout history. They are not innocent victims.

But, for us, we learn:

1) That justified military intervention is not murder, even if it may involve the killing of civilians, who are also involved, consciously or unconsciously. The founder of international law, Francisco de Vitoria, recommends it. Justified military intervention is different from murder.

2) That on the inmost level, thou shalt not kill the Life Force by numbing or exaggerating, by falsifying and manipulating, or by denying its reality in an ingrate manner. Killing the Life Force by all the means that I have just described has a New Testament antecedent in Christ saying:

Matthew 12:32:

> *And whosoever speaketh a word against the Son of man, it shall be forgiven him: but whosoever speaketh against the Holy Ghost, it shall not be forgiven him, neither in this world, neither in the world to come.*

The Divine Life Force is the Holy Spirit. It flows, enters us, and leaves us, depending on the conditions that we cultivate within us. Denying it and distorting it is, as you can see, a grave offense.

Commandment VII
Deuteronomy 5:18: *Neither shalt thou commit adultery.*

Adultery doesn't just mean betraying marriage vows on the sexual level. Adultery must also be seen:

1) On the emotional level, where betrayal of marriage vows are committed with attractions to others, for evil purposes, such as desiring someone who will better serve our idolized selves and our idols. Extend this also to the mental level—the thoughts going in that direction.

2) Adultery is not merely confined to those who are married. It extends to the betrayal of relationships by lying, pretending commitment, presenting a false self in order to entrap someone into false expectations. Adultery starts when you look at yourself in the mirror when you get dressed, with your intent to seduce, ever so subtly.

3) Adultery covers all the ways that you prostitute the Divine Life Force, the ways you abuse it for all the twisted purposes of your idolized self and your idols.

Commandment VIII
Deuteronomy 5:19: *Neither shalt thou steal.*

Theft must be considered on more than the material:

1) Praise seeking steals others' feelings; so does pretending.

2) Arrogating ideas without crediting their source is theft.

3) Changing the meaning of the truth to suit the specific, conscious or unconscious goals of our distortions is another break of this commandment.

4) Taking teachings for granted is theft.

5) False or half true advertising is theft

6) Any half truth, being worse than an outright lie, is theft.

Consult here *The Yogasutras* of Patanjali for more on this higher type of theft.

Commandment IX
Deuteronomy 5:20: *Neither shalt thou bear false witness against thy neighbour.*

First of all, notice the "against", affirming that any lie, or worse, a half-truth, is a hostility against neighbour and against God, the Life Force.

Bearing false witness is done by gossiping, by the continuous waste of gabbing.

Flattery and seeking praise are also bearing false witness. They too are lies, more vicious than maligning.

Commandment X

Deuteronomy 5:21: *Neither shalt thou desire thy neighbour's wife* [or husband]*, neither shalt thou covet thy neighbour's house, his field, or his manservant, or his maidservant, his ox, or his ass, or any thing that is thy neighbour's.*

Covetousness is theft in the mind and the emotions, the desire to have what belongs to others without earning it.

***

Write your own book on the Commandments, considering your violations and their resolution, restoring you to God.

CHAPTER 41
SOME DEFINITIONS

Atonement. In the Jewish religion, atonement means repenting for one's sins. Yom Kippur is known as the Day of Atonement during which the Jews fast for a period that is a little over 24 hours. This time is supposed to be devoted to repenting for one's sins and restituting for them. In the New Dispensation, we speak in terms of at-onement, which is what happens to us when we have gone through a process of genuine purification and of taking responsibility for our negativities otherwise called sins. In those states we at-one with God and experience grace.

Blasphemy. For us who very rarely use this word, it merely corresponds to the misuse of language. Words have power. When they are misused they create harm. We also talk in terms of dumping when a person abuses his knowledge for the purposes of blame. However, we rarely call this blasphemy.

Celibacy. Since sex is being reinstated, as it were, in the New Age and since it is seen as divine, the idea of reaching God through celibacy becomes absurd. Those who are celibate or who deny their sexuality distort their energies and disconnect themselves from God.

Chastity. According to the dictionary it is not being guilty of unlawful sexual intercourse. However, the word has come to mean antipathy for sexuality. A person who is chaste is "good" and does not have sex. From that point of view and looked at in the context of the New Dispensation it has become an anachronistic term. Somehow, it does not allow for the notion of full sexual enjoyment.

For instance, it would be unchaste to have sex before marriage. However, we recommend sex before marriage. We do not want people to go through the nightmare of finding that they are sexually incompatible for the rest of their lives after they have made a commitment to each other.

For us, therefore, according to the dictionary's definition, sex before marriage is chaste since it conforms to Spiritual Law. However, as you can see, somehow it does not fit; just forget the term and do not use it.

Christmas. For us Christmas and New Year's are represented by the winter solstice. The birth of Christ occurs at the time of the longest night. The greatest hope is to be found in the deepest darkness. Surrendering to the deepest of our darkness will create within us the greatest hope.

Easter. For us, Easter or Passover is the celebration of the renewal of life at spring. It is represented by the spring equinox, the passing over from winter to spring.

Grace. It is a state that can be found when we are able to neutralize our negativities. At that point we are flooded by the love, the beauty, the goodwill and the infinite intelligence of God. It is also known in some other writings as "soul contact." It is also sometimes called "contacting the Higher Self." However, it is more than just a contact, it is an experiential contact, it is allowing those higher spheres to express themselves, penetrate us. It is not to be considered as a neutralizer of negativities. It is available when our negativities are neutralized by us. Actually, it can be an enhancer of negativities. If grace is drawn in before the negativities are worked through, those very negativities will be enhanced by the grace. The grace itself will be polluted by the negativities.

Many have developed the ability to bring in grace by initial good work. The good work is not followed through. However, the ability to bring in grace still remains for a while. In that interim—during which the person still has the capacity to drawn in the grace while his negativities are reemerging—is when the greatest harm is done by an individual.

Most "Golden Ages"—times of great glory and success in a person's life—are unfortunately such states wherein grace has energized negativity. In spite of the fact that people in those times are most popular and seem to be the happiest, this is when the greatest damage is being done by them. This is when the greatest amount of negative karma is being accumulated.

Again, the safest way to call in grace is to first neutralize the negativities, which, by the way, is the way it first becomes available to us. It leaves us if we persist in not cleansing ourselves.

This process of departure of grace is similar to the process of departure of psychic powers when we do not pursue in humility the Path of Purification. Many psychics for a time in their life are able to manifest powers. These powers are later lost to their great disappointment through the same process that we have described above in the case of grace.

INDEX

-A-

Aborigines, 424
Abortion, 13, 34, 179
Abuse
　of power, 108
Accidental death, 337
Adam, 105, 140
Addiction, 162, 265, 267
Adonai, 10
Adultery, 502
Affected conscience, 55
Affirmations, 314
Age of Aquarius, 144, 150
Age of Aries, 144, 147
Age of Pisces, 74, 117, 144, 403
Age of Reason, 373
Age of Taurus, 144
AIDS, 139
Albigensian Crusade, 449
Alchemy, 401
Alexander the Great, 146
Alexandria, 147
Allegory of the dam, 37
American Indians, 423
Animal kingdom, 99
Antahkarana, 208
Anti-God, 46
Antichrist, 203, 205
Apostles, 447
Arab Conquest, 445, 446
Arabs, 147, 221
　General Amr ibn Al-Asth,
　　147
Archangels, 61, 99
Archetypal experiences, 305
Aryan Race, 39
Ascension, 71

Astral level, 108, 362, 370
Astrology, 377
　misuse of, 377
Atheist, 120, 277, 315
Atlantis, 24, 85, 93, 94, 114, 142
Atonement, 505
Attunement, 313
　prayer and meditation, 313
Authority, 194, 235
Automatism, 306

-B-

Babaji, 71, 74, 131
Baghdad, 158
Bailey, Alice A., 14
　the Tibetan, 4
Baptism, 302, 317
　by fire, 114
　definition of, 317
　initiation 2, 270
　magical thinking, 318
　Path of Purification, 317
　self-improvement, 318
　unborn child, 318
Battle with evil, 68
Being of Light, 341, 343, 359
Belial, 93
Belief system creating outer
　　experience, 218
Bible, 7, 11, 49
Birth
　by water, 114
　Initiation 1, 262
　most painful experience, 34
Birth control, 179
Blasphemy, 505
Blavatsky, H.P., 14

Blessings, 321, 325
Born again
   fanaticism, 317
Bruno, Giordano, 7
Buddha, 15, 62, 74, 146
   and women, 476
   early teachings of, 469
   Eightfold Noble Path, 482
   Four Noble Truths, 473
   Middle Path, The, 472, 473
   teachings of, 471
   three stages for each Noble Truth, 491
Burial, 353
Burnout, 118
Byzantine Empire, 148

-C-

Caligastia, 93
Call, The, 27, 287
   a negative religion, 291
   Age of Reason, 290
   and dissatisfactions, 291
   barriers to, 288
   call of nature, 287
   change, 294
   distortion of, 47
   false life, 297
   Higher Self, 291, 292
   is finding God, 196
   is hearing God's voice, 288
   is the plan of salvation, 71
   Jesus, 295
   lower self, 292
   mask, 292
   mimesis, 299
   Mohammed, 295
   Moses, 295
   plan of salvation, 298
   pseudo-call, 298
   purification, 296
   sacrifice, 297, 298
   spiritual development, 294
   spiritual progress, 293
   the Word, 287
   your task, 295
Cancer, 141
Capital punishment, 186
   karmic burden, 187
Capitalism, 29
Carnivores, 100
Catechism, 5
Cathars, 449
Cathedrals, 307
Catherine the Great, 90
Catholic Catechism, 168
Catholic Church, 5, 6, 19, 30, 41, 113, 149, 151, 178, 443
   New Catechism of the, 203
   reincarnation, 347
Catholic hospitals, 318, 368
Celibacy, 34, 505
Cemeteries, 356
Center where the will of God is known, 89
Channeling, 123, 381
Chastity, 505
Children
   raising, 234
   spanking of, 236
China, 411, 427
Choice
   between light and darkness, 462
   to sell out, 125
Christ, 9, 12, 59, 100, 110, 111, 131, 144, 146, 293, 310, 340, 364, 445
   as a brother, 50
   as emissary, 56
   as God, 447
   battle against evil, 65, 68

Christ (continued)
    demonstrated by example, 64
    First Son, 60
    fray a passage, 64, 71
    head of the Hierarchy, 89, 92
    incarnation of, 62
    Jesus versus, 72
    new teachings of, 64
    task of, 46, 64
    teachings, 451
    the loving and accommodating, 452
    the only son of God?, 74
    the rabble rouser, 447, 452
    travels of, 78
    universal teacher, 13, 78
Christ consciousness, 72
Christianity, 11, 74, 178, 443
    paganization of, 448
    true, 451
Christians, 14, 129
    born again, 317
    questions to ask yourself, 451
    real, 451
Christmas, 506
Church of the Path, 45, 53, 81, 131, 150, 271, 318, 456, 459
Civil War, the, 247
Code of Hammurabi, 144
Cold War, 95
Commentary on the Gospel of Thomas, 67, 150, 181
Commitment, 326
Communication with higher spheres, 380
Communism, 29, 40, 441, 443
    a negative religion, 151

Community
    marriage and, 328
Compromise, 157
Confederacy of the American South, 246
Confession, 171
Confirmation, 302
Confusion
    world of, 115
Consciousness
    other kingdoms of nature, 259
    raising of, 206
Constantine, Emperor, 147
Contraception, 179
Conventional religions, 166
Conversion
    death bed, 176
Copernicus, 7
Cordoba, 158
Cosmic evil
    protection from, 66
Count of Saint-Germain, 71, 84, 90
Covetousness
    theft in mind and emotions, 504
Creating the future, 126
Creation, 50, 129
    of the universe, 24
Credo, 17
Cremation, 353
Crisis, 36, 38, 156, 158
    on the mental level, 12
Crucifixion, 282
Crucifixion of the ego, 398
    defined, 1
Cruelty, 107, 157
Crusades, 113
Cultural Revolution, 41
Cupid, 323, 324, 329, 330

Cursillo Movement, 153
Cycles
    of nature, 25

-D-

Dark Ages, 87, 147, 157
Dark night of the soul, 273
Dead Sea Scrolls, 205, 447, 448
Death, 70
    accidental, 337
    ashes, 354
    Being of Light, 341, 343, 359
    burial, 353
    cemeteries, 356
    chakras, 350
    Christ, 340
    colour orange, 352
    confession, 348
    cord, 351
    cremation, 353
    crematoriums, 356
    crisis, 347
    denial of, 352
    disposal of body, 353
    doctors, 364
    dying, the, 347
    embalming, 353, 355
    fear of, 335, 336, 344, 346
    forces of darkness, 358
    Forces of Light, 358
    funeral, 354, 355
    Higher Self, 338
    in war or accident, 337
    Instinct of Self-Preservation, 335
    is it the end?, 345
    karmic death, 346
    last unction, 349
    leaving the body, 351
    liberation, 355
    life after life, 357
    life plan, 342
    life support systems, 352
    living will, 353
    long dark tunnel, 340, 359
    lower self, 337
    mask, 338
    music, 352
    near-death-experience, 340, 341, 344
    of the spirit, 174
    old belief systems, 355
    organ donation, 361
    organ transplant, 361
    out-of-body experiences, 340
    pain, 367
    prayers, 349
    preparation for, 335, 349
    reincarnation, 347
    release of the dying, 350
    risking one's life, 336
    soul, 350
    Spiritual Law, 345
    suicide, 366
    surrender, 346
    terminal illness, 352, 365
    why, 337
    wills and inheritance, 356
    worst crisis, 175
Deceleration, 106
Decision
    Initiation 6, 286
Decision to die, 338
Declaration of Human Rights, 413
    right to education, 434
Democracy, 29, 440, 442
Denial, 6
Descartes, René, 13
Desire, 32, 234
Despotism, enlightened, 429

Destruction, 38, 41
    by water, 94
Determinism, 209
Devas, 101
Devil, 46, 120
    astral home of, 108, 109
Dictatorship, 29
Diderot, Denis, 90
Dignity, 44
Disinformation, 115
Dispensation of the eighteenth
    century, 87, 90
Dispensations, 144, 151
Dissatisfaction, 291
    longing and aspiration, 291
Distortion, 27
    types of, 162
Divine Self
    defined, 2
Divorce, 332
Djwhal Khul, 4, 131
Doctors, 364
Dominant function, 118
Doubt, 6
    cause of, 193
    finding God through, 189
    necessity to look for, 190
    resolution of, 195
Dracula, 27
Dreams
    flying, 340
    out-of-body experiences,
        340
Dualistic state, 182
Duality of evil, 112
Dweller on the Threshold, 276
Dying, support of, 346, 347

-E-

Earth
    future of, 343
    purification sphere, 343
Easter, 506
Eastern philosophy, 128, 305
Ebb and flow of nature, 51, 374
Education
    religious, 434
    systems of, 238
Edward VIII, 39
Egypt, 62, 421
Eightfold Noble Path
    right action, 484
    right effort, 486
    right living, 485
    right meditation, 488
    right memory, 487
    right speech, 484
    right thinking, 483
    right view, 482
Eisenman, Robert, 445
Embalming, 353, 355
Emblem
    Church of the Path, The, 19
Emotional level, 362
Energy
    waste of, 175
Energy forms, 307
Equality of the sexes, 14, 24, 83
Equinox, 374
Escobar, Pablo, 28, 36
Eternal damnation, 203
Eve, 105, 140
Evil, 227
    dissolution of, 27
    distortion of God, 27
    elimination of, 120
    finite, 178
    levels of, 115
    nature of, 112
    of pain, 135
    of the twentieth century, 38
    splits itself, 178

Evil (continued)
    unconscious, 157
    world of confusion, 115
    world of cruelty, 115
    world of darkness, 115
    world of materialism, 115
Evil Empire, 30, 151
Evocation, 314
Evolution, 259
    as a spiritual process, 124
    awareness, 135
    non-human, 258
    universe, 219
Exclusivity, fallacy of, 152
    bigotry and fanaticism, 153
    Messiah, 153
Extraterrestrial life, 101

-F-

Faith
    disconnection from, 191
    doubt and, 190
    Law of Cause and Effect, 278
    unhappiness and, 191
Faithlessness, 34
Fall, The, 99, 106, 107, 121, 128
    as an inner reality, 118
    formation of evil, 64
    of the angels, 26
False life, 35, 230, 297
False teachers, 273
False witness
    bearing, 503
Fanaticism, 87, 113, 151, 196
    defense against initiation, 317
Fascism, 38
Fear
    of death, 335
    of God, 32
    of the unknown, 102
Feelings, 384
Female deity, 81
Female influence, 87
Feminists, 316
Flood, the, 93, 114, 142
Forbidden fruit, 105
Forces of darkness, 59, 93, 120, 185, 358
    defined, 1
    interference by, 59
Forces of Light, 40, 59, 66, 69, 70, 93, 121, 144
    intervention by, 114
Forgiveness, 14, 170
    desire to restitute, 14
    forgetting versus, 183
    God is, 181
    grace of God, 181
    individual choice, 181
    of others, 182
    of self, 182
France, 422
Franco, Francisco, 39, 430
Franco-Prussian War, 39
Frederick II, 39
Free will, 59
    confused as license, 226
    key to, 221
    reconnection with, 220
    versus predestination, 209
Freemasonry, 20
Freeze
    defined, 1
French Revolution, 41, 90, 151, 410
Funeral, 354, 355
Funeral wishes, 355

-G-

Galileo, 7

Gandhi, 283
Genius
    expression of, 173
Genocide, 196
    Moses, 501
Glamour, 109, 110, 264, 382
    creates the lower self, 271
    defined, 2
    world of, 66
Glasnost, 30
Gnosticism, 83, 146, 449
Goal of humanity, 363
God
    affirmation of, 27
    All That Is, 21
    alpha and omega, 19
    and sex, 33
    as adaptability, 23
    as energy, 50
    as love, 23
    as will, 23
    aspects of, 49
    barrier to finding, 55
    capacity to experience, 43
    connection with, 34
    created in His image, 50
    destroyer aspect, 36
    disconnection from, 34
    evil and, 19
    fear of, 32
    feminine aspect, 23, 81
    first seven sons of, 99
    hand of, 29
    immanent, 45
    law of, 42
    Life Force, 50
    longing for, 31, 34
    masculine aspect, 23, 81
    nature of, 22
    perceptions of, 49
    personification of, 46
    personification of three aspects, 81
    presence of, 31
    reconnection with, 35
    return to, 31, 144
    son aspect, 23, 81
    through sex, 57
    transcendent, 45, 49
    will of, 42, 89, 91
    your image of, 55
Gonorrhea, 139
Good
    infinite, 182
Gospel of Thomas, 14, 447
Grace, 176, 281, 506
Great Matriarch, 85
Great Mother, 85
Greater Plan, the, 70
Guidance, 384
Guilt, 169
    by commission, 165
    by omission, 165
    consequences of, 170
    desire to restitute, 170
    false, 56
    fundamental, 169
    punishment, 170
    real, 55

-H-

Hall of Knowledge and Wisdom, 28
Happiness, 57, 230
    experiencing pain yields, 58
    key to, 26
Harmlessness, 15
Healing, 222, 225, 364, 371
    premature, 179, 384
Heaven, 128
Hell, 128, 202
Hercules, 74

Herem, 60, 71, 106, 108, 113, 174
Hierarchy in humanity
   natural, 96
   reality of, 95
Hierarchy, Church, 460
   Board of Examiners, 460
   two levels, 459
Hierarchy, The, 2, 39, 41, 60, 62, 69, 89, 100, 145
   crisis and, 93
   departments of, 89
   energy in 1725, 410
   help from, 357
   intercession on humanity's behalf, 89
   knowledge inspired by, 91
   organization of, 89
   superhuman, 89
Higher Self, 28, 42, 73, 162, 232, 241, 261, 292, 338, 370
   defined, 2
Hinduism, 49, 131
Hirohito, 39
Hitler, Adolf, 28, 39
   Jews created, 501
Holocaust, 214
Holy Ghost, 83
   really the Mother Aspect, 3
Holy Lands, 423
Holy places, 372
Homosexuality, 238
Honesty
   practicing total, 44
Human existence and progress, 27
Hussein, Saddam
   Jews created, 501

-I-

I Ching, 377
Idealized self, 261
   defined, 2
Idolized Self
   defined, 2
Illness and disease, 369
Illusion, 264
Image
   defined, 2
Imam Mahdi, 153
Immaculate conception, 76
   on the emotional level, 77
   on the mental level, 77
   on the Path, 77
   on the physical level, 77
Impregnated by spirituality, 77
Incarnation, 249
   between, 254-256
   of Christ, 62
India, 78
Indulgences, 177
Inferior function, 118, 253
Inheritance, 356
Initiation, 181, 261
   already within us, 284
   before, 264, 265
   Church of the Path, 271
   defense against, 317
   definition of, 261
Initiation 1, 114
   birth, 262
   Instinct of Self-Preservation, 262
Initiation 2, 114
   atheism, 277
   baptism, 270
   dark night of the soul, 273
   false teachers, 273
   forces of darkness, 275
   Instinct of Procreation, 270, 277
   lower self, 272

Initiation (continued)
   negative intent, 272
   Ray VI, 270
   regression and fall, 276
   resistence to pain, 275
   resistence to pleasure, 275
   spirit guides, 274
Initiation 3
   Herd Instinct, 279, 282
   negative intent, 280
   Ray V, 279
   transfiguration, 279
Initiation 4
   Instinct of Self-Assertion, 282
   Ray IV, 282
   renunciation, 282
   surrender, 283
Initiation 5
   Babaji, 285
   Instinct of Inquiry, 285
   Ray I, 285
   Revelation, 285
Initiation 6
   decision, 286
   Ray III, 286
Initiation 7
   Ray II, 286
   resurrection, 286
Initiation 8
   Rays of Attribute, 286
   transition, 286
Initiation 9
   Rays of Aspect, 286
   refusal, 286
Inner experience, 72
Inner life, 60
Innermost self, 42
Instinct
   Herd Instinct, 401
   Instinct of Inquiry, 401
   Instinct of Procreation, 401
   Instinct of Self-Assertion, 401
   Instinct of Self-Preservation, 401
Instinct of Inquiry, 5, 105, 285, 330
Instinct of Procreation, 277
Instinct of Self-Assertion, 282, 284
Instinct of Self-Preservation, 262, 269, 335, 477
Instrumentality, 314
Intent, 489
Intervention, 315
   by Forces of Light, 61, 114
Intimacy, 309, 325, 326
Intolerance, 196
Invocation, 313
Iron Curtain, 30
Islam, 11, 445

-J-

James, 10, 445, 447, 448, 452
Jealousy, 110
Jesus, 10, 68, 82, 445
   and Christ, 73
   despair of, 277
   reincarnated, 73
Jews, 9, 14, 214, 221
   attract persecution, 501
John the Baptist, 73
Joseph, 26
Joshua, 217
Judaism, 11
Judeo-Christian religions, 49
Judgment
   beware of, 47, 165, 239
Judgment Day, 201
Jupiter, 74

-K-

Kaiser Wilhelm, 39
Karma, 218
   of the animal kingdom, 100
Karmic debt, 346
King Herod, 62
Kingdom of God, 14, 60, 71, 80
Kingdom of Heaven, 14
Kingdom of the Devil, 60
Kingdoms below humanity, 99
Knight, J.Z., 383
Koot Hoomi, 132

-L-

Last unction, 302, 349
Law of Adaptability, 393
Law of Attraction, 391
Law of Brotherhood, 29, 40, 392
Law of Cause and Effect, 13, 35, 37, 94, 109, 136, 145, 159, 191, 205, 211, 219, 221, 227, 278, 342, 394
   in Buddhism, 471, 490
Law of Commitment, 403
Law of Conflict, 397
Law of Good Habits, 405
Law of Good versus Evil, 398
Law of Harmony, 394
Law of Inherent Ritual in Creation, 404
Law of Initiation, 390
Law of Inquiry, 401
Law of Magnetism, 392
Law of Release of Energy in Matter, 402
Law of Repulse, 269, 389
Law of Return, 389
Law of Sacrifice, 403
Law of Sharing, 29
Law of the Builder, 392
Law of the Pairs of Opposites, 396
Law of the Perfect Universal Order, 404
Law of the Positive Aspects of Duality, 404
Laws of the Absolute, 403
Life
   risking one's life, 336
Life after life, 357
Life plan, 342
Life support systems, 352
Lincoln, Abraham, 247
Lindbergh, Charles, 39
Line of least resistance, 59, 106, 107, 384
Living will, 353
London, 158
Longing
   dissatisfaction, 291
   existential, 15
   for a better state, 121, 128
   for God, 122, 275
   for greater consciousness, 122
Love, 323, 324, 329
   power of, 321
   versus will and intelligence, 92
Lower self, 60, 110, 111, 261, 272, 292
   created by glamour, 271
   defined, 3
Lucifer, 60, 71, 74, 93, 108, 110
   grip of, 113
   Lesser Son, 60
Luther, Martin, 149, 178

-M-

Magical thinking, 318
Magister Dixit, 5

Male deity, 81
Mantram of Fire, 398
Marriage, 302, 321
    arranged, 323
    blessings, 321, 325
    ceremony, 321
    commitment, 326
    community and, 328
    Cupid, 323, 324, 329, 330
    divorce, 331
    fall in love, 323
    for better or worse, 327
    in the past, 322
    Instinct of Inquiry, 330
    intimacy, 325, 326
    loss of interest in, 333
    love, 323, 324, 329
    of convenience, 322
    power, 321
    promiscuity, 332
    prostitution, 324
    sex, 323, 324, 329
    soulmates, 331
    tender trap, 325
Masada, 445, 449
Mask, 111, 117, 292, 298
    defined, 3
    useful purpose of, 117
Maslow, 269
Mass, the, 302
Master Djwhal Khul, 131
    The Tibetan, 4
Masters
    communication with, 79
Material world, creation of, 122
Matriarchal systems, 87
Maya
    defined, 264
    rampant, 264
Meditation, 315
    prayer and attunement, 313

Mental illness, 371
Mental level, 362
Message of hope, 9
Middle Ages, 148, 307
Military intervention, 69
Mimesis, 299
Mindszenty, Cardinal, 30
Minoan civilization, 144
Mohammed, 71, 74, 147, 445
Monarchy, 439
Montesquieu, 149
Mortal sin, 165
Moses
    first ethnic cleanser, 501
Mosques, 308
Mother, 83
Mother-Father Split
    defined, 3
Motility, 259
Murder, 107
Music, 373
Mussolini, Benito, 39

-N-

Napoleon, 243
Nazis, 39, 143, 221
Near-Death-Experience, 185, 201, 340, 344
Needs, 56
Negative intent, 109, 272, 280, 372
    behind communism, 40
    see Harmful Volition, 165
Negativities
    hidden, 159
New Age, 14, 95, 153, 272, 383, 461
    false practices, 142
    real practices, 142
New Dispensation
    reawakening necessary, 153

Non-violence, 237

-O-

Oaths and commitments
    aspirant, 463
    disciple, 464
    novice, 462
    teacher, 467
Old Testament, 49, 99, 217
One About Whom Naught May Be Said, 56
Organ donation, 361
Organ transplant, 361
Original sin, 119, 124
Other worlds, 127
Out-of-body experience, 340

-P-

Pacifism, 69
Pain, 135, 371
    of death, 367
    of injustice, 62, 184
Pain killers, 359
Palestine, 62, 78
Parent
    honouring, 499
Paris, 158
Passage
    through the astral plane, 64
Past life regression
    misuse of, 378
Past lives, 225, 253
Patanjali, 131
Path of Purification, 120
Path, the, 310, 314, 357
    distinguishing people on, 456
Patriarchal systems, 87
Paul, 10, 74, 83, 445, 447, 448, 450, 452
    the Liar, 205

Pearls to swine, 175
People of God, 455
Peristroika, 30
Personal responsibility for falling, 125
Perversions, 162
Pharaoh, 26
Pharisaic Judaism, 452
Pharisees, 111
Philo the Jew of Alexandria, 146
Physical level, 109
Pirenne, Henri, 446
Plan of Salvation, 28, 31, 71, 100, 133
    becoming, 35, 134
    being with awareness, 35, 134
    being without awareness, 35, 134
    defined, 3
    evil, dissolution of, 133
    evolutionary process, 135
    how organized, 137
    is the call, 298
    return to God, 133
Plato, 146
Pleasure
    function of mutuality, 325
    sensual, 475
    sexual, 475
Plotinus, 146
Point of Relinquishing, 68
Point of tension, 62, 128, 136
Political systems
    coexistence of, 442
    democracy, 440
    monarchy, 439
    socialism, 441
Pope John Paul II, 7, 30, 451
Pope Paul VI, 41
Poseidia, 94, 142

Positive thinking
    fanaticism, 317
Prayer, 310, 313
    and shame, 310
    group, 315
    heard by God, 92
    in school, 237
    meditation and
        attunement, 313
    of Purification, 172
    to God through Christ, 51
Prayers and Code of Conduct on
        the Path , 315
Predestination
    versus free will, 209
Predictions, 226
Premature healing, 306
Pretense, 6, 35
Prince of Darkness, 93
Principle of Discrimination, 403
Privilege, 96
Promiscuity, 332
Prostitution, 324
Protestant Church, 149
Pseudo-altruism, 207
Pseudo-call, 298
Pseudo-goodness, 111
Psychic powers, 141
    primitive, 380
Psychology, 150
Punishment, 228
    fear of, 14
Purgatory, 207
Purification
    before prayer, 311
    surrender, 311
Purification, process of, 55, 62,
        73, 109, 163, 208, 257,
        296, 310, 314, 371,
        374, 383, 456
    avoiding the next step, 359

    baptism, 317
    twelve-step programs, 318

-Q-
Questioning, 6

-R-
Ray I, 36, 74, 82, 100, 145, 285
    and fascism, 40
    Manu, 84
    Spiritual Laws under, 389
    Will and Power, 19
Ray II, 29, 74, 82, 100, 145, 286
    Djwal Khul, 84
    Koot Humi, 84
    Spiritual Laws under, 391
Ray III, 74, 82, 86, 100, 145, 286
    Active Intelligence and
        Adaptability, 19
    and communism, 41
    Mahachohan, The, 84
    Spiritual Laws under, 393
Ray IV
    Harmony through Conflict,
        283
    Spiritual Laws under, 394
Ray V, 279
    Concrete Knowledge, 41
    Spiritual Laws under, 400
Ray VI, 100, 147, 270
    Spiritual Laws under, 402
Ray VII, 262, 266
    Order and Ceremony, 144
    Spiritual Laws under, 404
Rays of Aspect, 19
    Will or Power, 3
Rays of Attribute, 74, 286
Rays, The
    defined, 3
    emblem of The Church of
        the Path, 19

Rays, The (continued)
    initiation and, 261
    personification of, 84
Rebellion
    by the Prince of Darkness, 125
Rebirth, 12
    baptism, 456
    necessity for, 13
    through crisis, 455
Redemption, 174
    wholesale, 184
Reformation, the, 149
Refugees, 423
Regression and fall, 155, 276
Reincarnation, 219, 249, 347, 453
    abortion, 253
    accidental or premature death, 250
    between incarnations, 254, 255
    redemption, 185
    risk, 252
Relationship
    loss of interest in, 333
Religion
    as a way to control the immature, 197
    as a way to liberate the adult, 198
    fundamental core, 11
    origin of, 304
Renaissance, 7, 87, 148, 158, 446
Renunciation
    Initiation 4, 282
Resist not evil, 230
Resistance
    to pain, 275
    to pleasure, 275
Resolution of issues, 44
Responsibility, 96
Restitution, 185
Resurrection
    Initiation 7, 286
Return to God, 25
Revolution of 1989, 41
Right hand of God, 92
Roman Empire, 62, 146, 148, 452
Root races, 137, 138
    Aryan, 5th, 138
    Atlantean, 4th, 138
    Hyperborean, 1st, 138
    Lemurian, 3rd, 138
    Polarean, 2nd, 138
Roquentin, Antoine, 195
Rounds, 137
Russian Orthodox Church, 30

-S-

Sacrament
    Path, the, 310
    work, 310
Sacraments
    ancestral behaviour, 303
    baptism, 302
    building energy forms, 307
    cathedrals, 307
    Christ, 310
    confirmation, 302
    energies, 306
    intimacy, 309
    last unction, 302
    Law of Karma, 304
    marriage, 302
    mosques, 308
    nourish, 312
    patricide, 305
    prayer, 310
    premature healing, 306

Sacraments (continued)
   purification, 310
   religion, origin of, 304
   remembrance day, 302
   sacrifice, 310
   selflessness, 310
   Taj Mahal, 309
   types of, 302
   Universal Life Force, 310
Sacrifice, 33, 297, 298, 310, 403
   of sexuality, 34
Saibaba, 131
Salvation, 66, 68, 117, 204
Sanctity of life, 83
Sartre, Jean Paul, 193
Satan, 40, 60, 93, 106, 174
Saviour, 15, 113, 128, 129
Scriptures, 123
Searching
   and doubt, 6
   doubt and, 6
Seasons, 374
Secular humanism, 373, 409, 443
Seduction
   through meaning well, 114
Self-aggrandizement, 382
Self-destruction, 141
Self-idealization, 382
Self-improvement, 11, 318
Self-realization, 131
Self-worth, 44
Sellout, 119, 120
   recurring, 121
Semites, 85, 143, 145
Sermon on the Mount, 49
Seven Rays
   defined, 3
   personification of, 84
Sexuality, 57, 323, 329
   giving, taking, creativity, 179
   guilt in, 333
   is divinity, 83
Shamballa, 89-91, 97
Sin, 56
   awareness of, 166
   conscious, 165
   consequences of, 167
   emotional, 162
   guilt, 161
   hiding of, 167
   illusion, 161
   Liebnitz's Methodology, 161
   mental, 162
   misconception, 168
   mortal, 163, 207
   physical, 162
   purifying of, 167
   results in inability to pray, 167
   results in loss of dignity, 167
   revelation of, 168
   state of, 168
   taking responsibility for, 167
   unconscious, 166
   venial, 163
   vicious circle, 168
   voluntary, 165
Socialism, 441, 443
Solidarity Movement, 30
Solstice, 374
Sons of Belial, 93
Sons of the Law of One, 93, 94
Sonship, 31
Soul, 180, 319
   contents of, 242, 248
   formation of, 241
Soul substance, 185, 314

Soulmates, 331
Soviet Union, 69
Spirit guides, 101, 128, 256, 274
Spirit, the, 241
Spiritual development, 294
Spiritual laws
    create us, 406
    disconnection from, 388
    pertaining to Ray I, 389
    pertaining to Ray II, 391
    pertaining to Ray III, 393
    pertaining to Ray IV, 394
    pertaining to Ray V, 400
    pertaining to Ray VI, 402
    pertaining to Ray VII, 404
    universality of, 387
Spiritual progress, 293
Spirituality
    is sexuality, 14
    through abstinence, 117
Stages of life
    giving, 461
    taking, 461
Stalin, Joseph, 28
Substance abuse, 105, 106, 157
Suffering
    glamour of, 173
Suicide, 338, 366
Superego, 55
Superhumans
    The Hierarchy, 2
Supreme being, 45
Surrender, 33, 106, 283, 311, 346
Survival Instinct, 335
Sutrama, 208
Swamis, 129
Symbols, 369
    healing, 371
    holy places, 372
    illness and disease, 369
    mental illness, 371
    music, 373
    natural cycles, 374
    pain, meaning of, 371
    purification, process of, 371
    seasons, 374
Syphilis, 139

-T-

Task, your, 295
Temple of Jerusalem, 65
Temptation, 110
Ten Commandments, 60, 144
    approached as adults, 493
Terminal diseases, 365
Terrorist, 337
Theft, 107
    feelings, ideas, truth, 503
Theosophists, 100
Third World, 116
Tibetan, the, 40, 69, 86, 100, 131, 150, 221
    dictated to Alice A. Bailey, 4
    Master Djwhal Khul, 4
Time
    end of, 203
    evil and, 155
    space and, 127
Transfiguration, 282
    Initiation 3, 279
Transition, 349
Tree of Knowledge, 105, 106, 108
Trinity, 20, 81
    balance between its aspects, 82
Triumph of the Forces of Light, 201
Truth
    perceptions of, 15

Tunnel, long dark, 71, 201, 254, 273, 340, 359
Twelve-step programs, 318

-U-

UFOs, 101, 102
Unhappiness, 191
Unitarian Church, 95
United Nations, the, 413
Universal Consciousness, 25, 38, 50, 173, 281, 311
   mind of God, 51
   relationship to cause and effect, 51
Universal Declaration of Human Rights
   accidental, 431
   and the Path, 437
   and the Ten Commandments, 437
   arbitrary arrest, detention or exile, 419
   arbitrary interference, 420
   asylum from persecution, 420
   basis of the authority of government, 429
   discrimination of human rights, 416
   equal protection of the law, 417
   equality before the law, 417
   fair and public hearing, 419
   freedom and equality, 415
   freedom of movement and residence, 420
   importance of, 410
   innocent until proved guilty, 419
   intervention of one nation over another, 411
   motherhood and childhood, 432
   nationality, 426
   penal offence, 419
   preamble, 413
   remedy for acts violating fundamental rights, 418
   right to education, 433
   right to equal pay for equal work, 431
   right to form trade unions, 431
   right to freedom of opinion and expression, 428
   right to freedom of peaceful assembly, 428
   right to freedom of thought, conscience and religion, 428
   right to life, liberty and security, 416
   right to marry and found a family, 426
   right to own property, 427
   right to participate in cultural life, 435
   right to protection of moral and material interests, 435
   right to rest and leisure, 432
   right to take part in government, 429
   right to work, 431
   roots of, 409
   slavery, 416
   social and international order, 436
   social security, 430
   torture, 417

Universal Life Force, 25, 38, 50, 52, 94, 106, 111, 169, 173, 176, 281, 310, 324
    feminine principle, 26
Universal rounds, 137
Universe, 101

-V-
Vegetarianism, 100
Venial sin, 163
Vesuvius, 450
Victims, 212
Virgin birth, 74
Virgin Mary, 74
    cult of, 85
Visualization, 76
Vitamins, 359
Vows, 326

-W-
War, 265
War of liberation, 61
Waste, 175
Welfare, 442
West, the, 164
Will
    bad, 182
    Greater, the, 232
    inner, 232
    of God, 43, 89
    of the lower self, 232
    outer, 232
    versus love and intelligence, 92
Wills, 356
Wojtyla, Cardinal, 30
Word of God, 11, 287
Word, the, 249
Work, 310
Work ethic, 432
World of feelings, 65

World Saviour, 73
World War I, 39, 95
World War II, 29, 68, 70, 95, 342
Writer's block, 289
Wyszynski, Cardinal, 30

-Y-
Yogananda, 131
Yukteswar, Swami Sri, 131

ABOUT THE AUTHOR

For over forty years, Reverend Dr. Albert Gani (1943-2018), through faith and seeking the presence of God, helped people find purpose and meaning in their lives, motivating them towards the pursuit of happiness through ethics and faith.

His work took him from coast to coast in the United States, as well as Europe and Mexico. He authored over thirty books, wrote numerous articles, and lectured extensively. Throughout his life, he motivated people and organizations to effect major changes through the application of spiritual and ethical principles.

A true Renaissance man, he brought to his teachings a keen wit, a versatile knowledge of world history and politics, proficiency in languages, and great knowledge of music and philosophy. In this way, he challenged, entertained, and provoked people to rethink and restructure their lives.

He used his own crises and struggles as examples in his teachings. Perhaps most apparent and inspiring of all of his qualities was his courageous, ethical, and loving stance for the truth, regardless of the outcome.

Books by Reverend Dr. Albert Gani available at:
www.churchofthepath.org

www.ingramcontent.com/pod-product-compliance
Lightning Source LLC
Chambersburg PA
CBHW071934220426
43662CB00009B/906